The Moral Psychology
of Boredom

Moral Psychology of the Emotions

Series editor: Mark Alfano, Associate Professor, Department of Philosophy, Delft University of Technology

How do our emotions influence our other mental states (perceptions, beliefs, motivations, intentions) and our behavior? How are they influenced by our other mental states, our environments, and our cultures? What is the moral value of a particular emotion in a particular context? This series explores the causes, consequences, and value of the emotions from an interdisciplinary perspective. Emotions are diverse, with components at various levels (biological, neural, psychological, social), so each book in this series is devoted to a distinct emotion. This focus allows the author and reader to delve into a specific mental state, rather than trying to sum up emotions en masse. Authors approach a particular emotion from their own disciplinary angle (e.g., conceptual analysis, feminist philosophy, critical race theory, phenomenology, social psychology, personality psychology, neuroscience) while connecting with other fields. In so doing, they build a mosaic for each emotion, evaluating both its nature and its moral properties.

Other titles in this series:

The Moral Psychology of Forgiveness, edited by Kathryn J. Norlock
The Moral Psychology of Pride, edited by Adam J. Carter and Emma C. Gordon
The Moral Psychology of Sadness, edited by Anna Gotlib
The Moral Psychology of Anger, edited by Myisha Cherry and Owen Flanagan
The Moral Psychology of Contempt, edited by Michelle Mason
The Moral Psychology of Compassion, edited by Justin Caouette and Carolyn Price
The Moral Psychology of Disgust, edited by Nina Strohminger and Victor Kumar
The Moral Psychology of Gratitude, edited by Robert Roberts and Daniel Telech
The Moral Psychology of Admiration, edited by Alfred Archer and André Grahle
The Moral Psychology of Regret, edited by Anna Gotlib
The Moral Psychology of Hope, edited by Claudia Blöser and Titus Stahl
The Moral Psychology of Amusement, edited by Brian Robinson
The Moral Psychology of Boredom, edited by Andreas Elpidorou

The Moral Psychology of Boredom

Edited by
Andreas Elpidorou

ROWMAN & LITTLEFIELD
Lanham • Boulder • New York • London

Published by Rowman & Littlefield
An imprint of The Rowman & Littlefield Publishing Group, Inc.
4501 Forbes Boulevard, Suite 200, Lanham, Maryland 20706
www.rowman.com

British Library Cataloguing in Publication Information Available

Library of Congress Cataloging-in-Publication Data

Library of Congress Control Number: 2021945106

ISBN 9781786615381 (cloth)
ISBN 9781538163573 (paper)
ISBN 9781786615398 (ebook)

Contents

Acknowledgments

I would like to thank the contributors of this volume for their excellent chapters and for their patience in the editing of this work during the COVID-19 pandemic. I would also like to express my sincere gratitude to James Danckert, Lauren Freeman, John Gibson, Wendell O'Brien, G. M. Trujillo Jr., and Josefa Ros Velasco for their helpful feedback and for conversations on boredom. The main thesis of my contribution to this volume ("Boredom and Poverty: A Theoretical Model") was first presented in a nascent form in a blog post that I authored for the Blog of the APA ("Boredom and Injustice," September 23, 2020). I thank David V. Johnson for his editorial feedback and the APA for permission to reuse parts of the blog post in my contribution and in the introduction to the edited volume.

The Moral Significance of Boredom

An Introduction

Andreas Elpidorou

"Oh! Ennui! Ennui! What an answer to everything," wrote French author Jules Barbey d'Aurevilly (quoted in Kuhn 1976, 332). In a sense, d'Aurevilly was right. Boredom can be thought to be an answer to everything because it arises in response to almost any situation. Given enough repetition or exposure, nearly everything can strike us as boring—even our dearest possessions, activities, ideas, or relations. But d'Aurevilly was also, in an important sense, wrong: although boredom can be a response to almost any situation, it is not necessarily a solution. In its wake, boredom leaves behind both beneficial and harmful outcomes. On the positive side, new habits, opportunities, and careers often start with the thought "I am bored." The realization that we are bored can move us to form prosocial intentions and to find meaning in our situations. It can even be the spur we need in order to engage in creative acts. "I painted because I was bored," G. W. Bush admitted in an interview (Bush 2017); "Perhaps some of the greatest masterpieces were written while yawning," Marcel Proust (1982, 866) writes in his *Remembrance*. All the same, boredom has a darker side. Unhealthy eating habits, binge drinking, drug use, arson, the theft of a military tank, sadistic behavior, mass killings—all have been attributed to boredom. "I guess I was just bored," Keith Eugene Mann said explaining why he scorched sixteen acres of wild forests in North Carolina (Washburn and David 2016). "Fact is I had no reason to do it, I just thought . . . fuck it, life is boring so why not?", a gunman who killed twelve people posted on social media during the time of his despicable act (Baer 2018).

Is boredom morally significant? It's complicated. To be in a position to answer the question properly, we need to know what boredom is and what it means to say that a psychological phenomenon is morally significant. Yet, for some, the answer was always clear. Decades ago, Bertrand Russell (2006

[1930], 38) declared that "boredom is a vital problem for the moralist since half the sins of mankind are caused by it." Russell's claim is, of course, an exaggeration (but see Fromm 1973). Nonetheless, his hyperbole is instructive. In trying to understand better our own psychology and role in our social context, we cannot afford to ignore boredom's force. Indeed, Russell's claim is a useful reminder of Søren Kierkegaard's astute observation that despite its "calm and sedate nature," boredom has a remarkable "capacity to initiate motion" (1987 [1843], 285). It is perhaps in its capacity to move us in various ways that we can discern most clearly boredom's moral colors.

Indeed, when thinking of boredom's potential role in our moral existence, it is natural to focus on whether boredom can move us to act in moral or immoral ways. Yet there are additional ways of determining whether a psychological state or a personality trait carries moral significance. A psychological state or trait can be morally significant if any of the following theses is true:

ACTION THESIS:
The psychological state/personality trait can motivate prosocial or antisocial behavior.

JUDGMENT THESIS:
The psychological state/personality trait can influence moral judgment.

PERCEPTION THESIS:
The psychological state/personality trait can facilitate (or hinder) moral perception—the state or trait makes it more likely (or less likely) for the agent to perceive morally relevant situations and facts.

FLOURISHING THESIS:
The psychological state/personality trait can promote (or hinder) flourishing or the achievement of the good life.

APPROPRIATENESS THESIS:
The experience of the psychological state or the presence of the personality trait is morally inappropriate (or appropriate) insofar as one is, morally speaking, worse off (or better off) when experiencing the state or possessing the trait.

The aim of this introduction is to discuss the ways in which boredom is morally significant. An additional but equally important aim is to introduce briefly the nature of boredom. This latter aim takes priority. Only once we have familiarized ourselves with the character of boredom, we can properly articulate boredom's moral character.

1. ACEDIA AS A MORAL PRECURSOR

Traces of what we now call "boredom" can be found in ancient Greek and Roman thought (Kuhn 1976; O'Brien 2018; Toohey 1988, 2011). Plutarch,

Lucretius, Horace, and Seneca give voice to this phenomenon, but the history of boredom, because of boredom's relationship to sloth and idleness, can be traced even further back in time and outside of Western civilization (Raposa 1999; Wishnitzer 2021).

All the same, commentators often begin to document the history of boredom with a discussion of acedia, a type of religious boredom experienced, moralized, and, in some cases, literally demonized by the early Christian Fathers (Cassian 2000; Evagrius in Sinkewicz 2003; Jütte 2020; Wenzel 1967). Such a beginning point is, in a sense, a natural one. Within the Western tradition, the religious discourse on acedia is the first sustained discussion of the nature of boredom, including its effects, antecedents, and its relationship to other emotional and physical states. It is sophisticated, develops over centuries, and exposes plainly the moral significance of this type of boredom. For the founders of Christian monasticism and the third- and fourth-century hermits and cenobites of northern Egypt, acedia was a vice (or sin) and a threat to monastic life (Wenzel 1967; Bloomfield 1952). To be sieged by acedia ("the noonday demon" as it was then known) was a felt indication of one's failure to perform one's religious duties (Evagrius in Sinkewicz 2003, 102). When one contemplates and devotes oneself to God, one should not be bored with God; one ought not to be distracted, listless, slothful, never mind wishing for an alternative engagement. Hence, to be bored with, unexcited by, or even indifferent to God can mean only one thing: that one is failing to perform properly one's religious duties. Worse, acedia was thought to be a condition that pervades all of monastic life. This demon was capable of "enveloping the entire soul and strangling the mind" (Evagrius in Sinkewicz 2003, 104). It did not merely distract the monk temporarily; it tempted and tested the monk. Sometimes it was even the reason why the monk gave up the monastic life.

Thus, the discourse on acedia reveals to us the fact that acedia (and thus spiritual or religious boredom) was a morally significant affective state. Although common enough in monastic circles, it was an inappropriate experience, not befitting of one's role as a monk. And it was problematic because of its potential effects on the agent experiencing or besieged by acedia. Both its likening to a demon and its later transformation into a disease or a disorder underline the fact that acedia was conceived of as a threat to one's self.

The moral inappropriateness of the experience of acedia and its harmful or untoward consequences illustrate that this precursor of contemporary boredom is a morally significant phenomenon: both the ACTION THESIS and the APPROPRIATENESS THESIS are true for acedia. Hence, reflecting on the nature of acedia shows that we ought to take boredom seriously as a moral phenomenon. At the very least, the discourse on acedia reveals that the history of boredom involves a moral phenomenon. But the assessment that boredom is a morally significant phenomenon does not rest solely on boredom's history and its presumed relation to acedia. Conceptual and empirical investigations into the nature of boredom also highlight its moral importance.

2. VARIETIES OF BOREDOM

What is boredom? The term "boredom" is polysemic: the same term names and picks out many different phenomena. The polysemic character of "boredom" and the confusion that it may engender have been noted in the literature before. Adams Phillips (1994) wrote that we should not speak of boredom but of "boredoms." Otto Fenichel warned "that the conditions and forms of behavior called 'boredom' are psychologically quite heterogeneous" (Fenichel, 1951, p. 349). And others have distinguished between different types of boredom (see, e.g., Doehlemann 1991; Goetz et al. 2014; Healy 1984; Heidegger 1995; Neu 2000; O'Brien this book; Svendsen 2005). What is more, a look at the history of boredom shows that there exists a family of terms and phenomena that are either loosely or tightly connected to our concept of *boredom*. These include *horror loci, fastidium*, acedia, *tedium vitae*, sloth, mal du siècle, melancholy, ennui, spleen, *noia*, monotony, and listlessness (Elpidorou and Ros Velasco 2021). So, where does one begin with boredom? For present purposes, difficult questions concerning the history of this phenomenon and our linguistic practices about "boredom" and other semantically related terms will be put aside (see instead Goodstein 2005; Kuhn 1976; Petro 1993; Spacks 1995).

This introduction does not address whether "boredom" means different things, nor does it consider the history and historicity of the phenomenon of boredom (see instead Ros Velasco this book). Rather, the introduction sets to explore the moral nature of boredom as it is currently and widely experienced. Consequently, the introduction is tasked with explaining what our (contemporary) boredom is: What does it feel like? How does it affect us? Is it morally significant?

Given the task at hand, it seems proper to start with the boredom with which we are most familiar: the everyday experience of boredom; our "ordinary" or "simple" boredom. This is the sort of experience that we undergo when, in our everyday dealings, we engage with the uninteresting, mundane, meaningless, or repetitive. We experience it, for instance, when we wait in a doctor's office to be seen, when our flight is delayed, when we have to endure the same conversation for the umpteenth time, when we watch the same old rerun, when we scroll through our social media feed without purpose, or when we are forced to complete a mind-numbing task. Not only is this type of boredom readily recognizable by us, it has also been the focus of a wave of recent and historical experimental studies. For the most part, the type of boredom that psychologists induce in experimental settings and study either in such settings or in the wild is this simple or everyday boredom. Following common practice, I call this type of boredom "state boredom," and I understand it to be a temporary affective state that is largely (but neither entirely nor invariably) dependent on external conditions.

Alongside this familiar notion or understanding of boredom, others lurk in the offing. In particular, boredom researchers often talk of a different, more profound, type of boredom. Unfortunately, the label "profound boredom" has come to designate different affective phenomena, and discussions of boredom do not always keep those apart. For that reason, it is important to disambiguate between them (see also O'Brien in this book). Here I note six possible articulations of the notion of profound boredom.

Type A: Profound because of its object. Boredom might turn profound depending on what bores us. We are often bored by events, tasks, or situations that do not hold any moral weight: a song, an outfit, a homework assignment, a work presentation, a bad comedy routine, a terrible book, or an unreadable introductory chapter. Sometimes, however, the object of our boredom can change into something much more important. Indeed, we could become bored with something that we think should not bore us. Imagine, for instance, a judge bored with justice, a doctor bored with caring for patients, a parent bored with the well-being of their children, or a monk bored with prayer. We might be quick to note that such feelings of boredom are not, morally speaking, on par with our ordinary experiences of boredom. What the judge, doctor, or parent are feeling are instead indications that a more serious boredom is present. Depending on their particular circumstances, their boredom might be morally inappropriate or even grounds for the assignment of blame.

Type B: Profound because of its scope. Boredom becomes profound when its scope turns expansive. Whereas we are usually bored with particular things and activities, it is possible to become bored with something much broader: ourselves, life, or the world itself (see Maltsberger, Sakinofsky, and Jha 2000). This notion of boredom might be related to perceived life boredom (see Tam, Van Tilburg, and Chan 2021) and could indicate an inability to find sources of engagement, interest, or meaning in many domains of our life (see also Heidegger 1995).

Type C: Profound because of its frequency. A different type of profound boredom might arise when we experience state boredom often. Regardless of its cause, such an increase in the frequency of the experience of boredom can bring about important changes in the manner in which we experience ourselves and the world (see Elpidorou this book) and can have problematic consequences for our well-being (Elpidorou 2017; Vodanovich and Watt 2016; cf. Williams 1973).

Type D: Profound because of its duration. Whereas frequent boredom is worrisome or potentially problematic because we experience state boredom frequently, there can be a different type of profound boredom which gains its gravity from the fact that it lasts much longer than state boredom. Such type of boredom might be the affective "soundtrack" of our lives—we almost always experience it, or, if it is not constantly present, its experience, whenever it arises, lasts for an extended period of time. Such a chronic affective condition pervades and affects many of our everyday dealings.

Type E: Profound because of its intensity. Boredom may become profound when the intensity of the experience of boredom increases. It might still be the case that we are bored infrequently, and that boredom has not become a chronic condition. Nonetheless, when we experience this type of boredom, we find it, because of its intensity, overwhelming.

Type F: Profound because of its cause. Boredom could become profound because of its cause. If the cause of boredom lies in us or in our social or environmental conditions, boredom has the potential to transform our lives. It is a part of who we are (either personally or socially), and thus escape from this type of boredom becomes exceedingly hard.

Although I presented the above varieties of profound boredom as separate types, they often coexist and interact with each other. For instance, profound boredom caused by environmental conditions that are resistant to change will likely give rise to frequent, and perhaps even chronic, boredom. The same could hold for a type of boredom that is expansive in terms of its scope: if life itself bores us, then we should expect that we will be bored most of the time (see, e.g., Bargdill 2000; Maltsberger, Sakinofsky, and Jha 2000; Moravia 2011 [1960]).

Knowing the various types of boredom is important. It allows us to better understand the history of boredom and the various discourses concerning boredom; it also safeguards us from conceptual errors when discussing boredom. What is more, the aforementioned taxonomy permits us to mark properly the present object of inquiry. When considering whether boredom is morally significant, I shall focus on two kinds of boredom: (1) the simple, everyday boredom (i.e., boredom as a transient affective state that is largely situation dependent, or "state boredom") and (2) the type of boredom that is due to lasting personality characteristics ("trait boredom"). There are two main reasons for this decision. First, these two kinds of boredom, *state* boredom and *trait* boredom, are the focus of many contemporary analyses and empirical studies of boredom. As a result, we are, I believe, in a good position to articulate their moral significance. Second, the other types of boredom that I delineated are, of course, important, yet it is unclear that they are not in some sense reducible to state boredom, trait boredom, or their combination. A straightforward case can be made about Type A, C, and E: all of them appear to be forms of state boredom. Type A is state boredom that is about specific objects or situations, Type B is frequent state boredom, and Type E is intense state boredom. If Type F is due to individual psychological characteristics, then it is trait boredom. If it arises instead because of stable material, social, or environmental conditions, then it could be thought to be a form of state boredom that is due to some inescapable eliciting conditions. Type B and D are harder to reduce to state and trait boredom. Regarding Type B, it is unclear whether one's boredom with life or the world is a form of state boredom. The intelligibility of this proposed identification will depend, among other things, on whether the subject of this type of boredom also experiences a desire to find activities that are stimulating, meaningful, or interesting to the subject—I take this desire to be a necessary component of state boredom (see section 4). Regarding Type D, the duration of this type of profound boredom rules out an identification with state boredom. Nonetheless, it could still be a form of trait boredom, especially if it involves the perception that one's life is boring (see Tam, Van Tilburg, and Chan 2021).

Having said that, I do not insist that all forms of boredom reduce, one way or another, to state boredom or trait boredom. It is possible that there are forms of boredom that are genuine types of boredom (not varieties of depression or apathy) and which cannot be explained in terms of state boredom or trait boredom. This potential concession does not take away from what the rest of the introduction has to offer—it simply entails that there is more to be said about possible varieties of boredom and their moral significance.

Before concluding this section, I would like to raise one last issue. Is state boredom an emotion or not? Several chapters in this book address this question. Contributions by Meagher and Robbins, Bortolotti and Aliffi, and Yucel and Westgate all provide reasons to think that state boredom should be taken to be an emotion. On the contrary, in her chapter, Yao offers an alternative conceptualization of state boredom, arguing that it ought to be understood as a cognitive appetite. Additionally, it has also been suggested that state boredom is (or can be) a mood insofar as it is a psychological state that lacks (or can lack) a specific intentional object (e.g., Feldges and Pieczenko 2020; Heidegger 1995). The question of whether state boredom is an emotion or not is undoubtedly of great theoretical and practical importance. For the purposes of the introduction, I operate under the assumption that state boredom is an emotion. (I defend this view in Elpidorou 2018b and in press.) All the same, the claims that I advance concerning state boredom's relation to morality hold (more or less) regardless of whether state boredom is ultimately an emotion, a mood, a cognitive attitude, or some other kind of psychological state.

3. BOREDOM AS A PERSONALITY TRAIT

What does it mean to say that boredom is a personality trait? Putting aside general skepticism concerning the existence of personality traits, a personality trait, if it exists, must be (i) *enduring*, (ii) *measurable*, and (iii) a *causally relevant* characteristic of an individual's behavior. First, it is enduring both insofar as it is long lasting and insofar as it cannot be induced or alleviated by limited exposure to some endogenous or exogenous condition. In other words, a personality trait can neither be too easily acquired nor too easily dispensed with, and once possessed, it is thought to be a stable characteristic of the individual. Second, a trait must be measurable in some way—otherwise we will not be able to ascertain its existence and the extent to which an individual possesses it. Third, a trait must be causally relevant insofar as observed outcomes can be attributed to the presence (or lack) of the trait. Such a requirement is important for at least two reasons. On the one hand, the requirement suggests that a personality trait is something over and above the set of occurrences of its corresponding state, when such a state exists. In the case of boredom, to possess the trait of boredom it is not sufficient to experience state boredom frequently. The experience of boredom (or our responses to it) must be, at least partly, due to some psychological characteristic that we possess. On the other hand, the requirement allows us to account for observed interpersonal differences. The existence of a trait helps us to explain why different individuals may behave differently when faced with similar situations.

There have been several attempts to operationalize and assess the presence of trait boredom (Vodanovich 2003; Vodanovich and Watt 2016). Among them, the Boredom Proneness Scale (BPS) (Farmer and Sundberg 1986), a multi-item self-report scale, has been the most widely used measure of trait boredom. It was devised with the aim of measuring boredom proneness: an individual's "tendency toward experiencing boredom" (1986, 5). The original format of BPS consisted of twenty-eight items that were marked either as true or false. It was later revised to be scored on a seven-point Likert-type scale (Vodanovich and Kass 1990).

Despite its use in numerous studies, there are known issues with BPS and subsequent attempts to revise this measure (see also Gana, Broc, and Bailly 2019; Mercer-Lynn, Bar, and Eastwood 2014; Struk et al. 2017). Here I mention two. First, there is no consensus regarding the factorial structure of

BPS (Ahmed 1990; Gana and Akremi 1998; Struck et al. 2017; Vodanovich and Kass 1990; Vodanovich, Wallace, and Kass 2005) and some have even reported that the original BPS lacks a replicable factorial structure (Melton and Schulenberg 2009). Second, boredom researchers have voiced concerns regarding the theoretical underpinnings of BPS and its external validity. For one, it has been suggested that, as a measure, BPS fails to distinguish between frequency of the occurrence of boredom and one's inability to cope with the experience of boredom when that arises (Mercer-Lynn, Bar, and Eastwood 2014; Danckert et al. 2018). In addition, work by Tam, Van Tilburg, and Chan (2020) has shown that there are at least three distinct characterizations of boredom proneness (boredom frequency, boredom intensity, and perception of life boredom), each of which represents some aspect of boredom proneness.

There are important psychometric and conceptual issues with existing measures of trait boredom (see Gana, Broc, and Bailly 2019). Such issues emphasize the pressing need for conceptual clarity when it comes to the very notion of trait boredom and for improved instruments to assess its presence. Nonetheless, measures of trait boredom (specifically BPS and shorter forms of BPS) have yielded consistent results. For instance, available research reveals that trait boredom is a reliable indicator of poorer well-being, at-risk behavior and impulsivity, depression, difficulties in sustaining attention, and decreased purpose in life (for reviews, see Elpidorou 2017; Vodanovich 2003; Vodanovich and Watt 2016). These known and robust associations between trait boredom, on the one hand, and mental health issues and problematic behavior, on the other hand, demonstrate both the clinical significance of trait boredom and its relevance in understanding a host of behaviors. In turn, the value of and need for a better understanding of trait boredom are dictated by theoretical positions that take characteristics of individuals to be important determinants of their experience of boredom (Mercer-Lynn, Bar, and Eastwood 2014; see also Fisher 1993; Hamilton 1981; Neu 2000). In sum, trait boredom is an important theoretical construct that demands our attention. As a consequence, the moral significance of trait boredom ought to be considered.

4. BOREDOM AS AN AFFECTIVE STATE

As a transient affective state, state boredom is a major part of human existence. It is experienced often and widely (Chin et al. 2017; Goetz et al. 2014; Larson and Richards 1991; Smith et al. 2015), by individuals of all genders and ages, and by members of different cultures (Gana and Akremi 1998; Musharbash 2007; Ng et al. 2015; Sundberg et al. 1991; Vodanovich, Watt, and Piotrowski 1997). It typically arises in situations that are perceived to be monotonous or lacking in novelty or meaning (Thackray, Bailey, and Touchstone 1977; Van Tilburg and Igou 2012), that cannot grab our attention (Hunter and Eastwood 2018), that fail to engage sufficiently or optimally our cognitive resources (Csikszentmihalyi 1975), or that are low in perceived autonomy (van Hooft and van Hooff 2018; Fisher 1993; cf. Fenichel 1953).

Most of us have little trouble recognizing boredom and distinguishing it from other related affective experiences (Goldberg et al. 2011; Van Tilburg and Igou 2012; but see Svendsen 2005). First and foremost, boredom is a felt psychological state characterized by its aversive phenomenology (Harris 2000; Hartocollis 1972; Mikulas and Vodanovich 1993; Pekrun et al. 2010; Todman 2003; Vogel-Walcutt et al. 2012). Although the felt unpleasantness of boredom is perhaps its most obvious feature, its phenomenology carries a complexity that is often underappreciated. Boredom is reported to be experienced both as an apathetic and as an agitated state and co-occurs with other negative emotions and affective states (Chin et al. 2017; Goetz et al. 2014; Harris 2000; Martin, Sadlo, and Stew 2006; Steinberger, Moeller, and Schroeter 2016). It involves feelings of apathy, weariness, listlessness, but also of aggravation and frustration (Fahlman et al. 2013; Harris, 2000; Martin, Sadlo, and Stew 2006; O'Brien 2014). Moreover, the phenomenological character of the experience of boredom is neither stable over time nor invariable through situations—it appears to change depending on endogenous or exogenous factors (Eastwood et al. 2012; Danckert et al. 2018; Elpidorou 2021; Mills and Christoff 2018; van Hooft and van Hooff, 2018; Westgate 2020; Westgate and Wilson 2018).

Boredom is also characterized by its volitional character. It is crucial to note that boredom is not apathy (Goldberg et al., 2011; Nisbet 1982): only the former involves a desire for alternative engagement (Fahlman et al. 2013). Indeed, boredom can be separated from other negative emotions in terms of its volitional content and action tendencies (Van Tilburg and Igou 2012, 2017a). In particular, the experience of boredom is not exhausted by its associated phenomenology. When one is bored, one also itches to escape from one's situation.

In terms of its cognitive elements or characteristics, boredom has been associated with attentional difficulties, negative appraisals regarding one's situation, the perception of a slower passage of time, and mind wandering (for a review, see Elpidorou 2018a). The first two characteristics deserve further mention. On the one hand, attentional difficulties have long been implicated in the experience of boredom and have been used either to define boredom (i.e., boredom is characterized *essentially* by an inability to pay attention) (Damrad-Frye and Laird 1989; Hamilton 1981; Leary et al. 1986), to explain how and why it arises (attentional difficulties are the necessary or sufficient conditions of the experience of boredom) (Hunter and Eastwood 2018; Tam et al. in press; Westgate and Wilson 2018), or to account for its experiential profile (boredom's different characteristics—e.g., its phenomenology or volitional component—can be explained in terms of attentional mechanisms; see, e.g., Eastwood et al. 2012). On the other hand, researchers have also implicated the presence of negative appraisals in the experience of boredom. Again, similarly to attentional difficulties, the hypothesized role of these negative appraisals varies. Sometimes negative appraisals are thought to be the psychological or cognitive antecedents of boredom. That is, boredom arises because we have appraised our situation to be monotonous, repetitive, lacking in meaning, lacking in novelty, involving no control, or being nonoptimally engaging. Alternatively, negative appraisals have been thought to be a key characteristic of the very experience of boredom. For instance, some accounts of boredom hold that it is a state of perceived meaninglessness and an attempt to reestablish a sense of meaningfulness (Van Tilburg and Igou 2012, 2017a). It is worth noting that the presence of negative appraisals could be a consequence of attentional difficulties: we come to appraise our situation negatively because it cannot sufficiently engage our attention. But negative appraisals regarding one's situation could also cause attentional difficulties: we cannot pay attention to our situation precisely because we deem it to be meaningless, monotonous, repetitive, or uninteresting.

The presence of some kind of negative appraisal about our situation appears to be a necessary part of the experience of boredom. In the same way that it is hard to imagine a state of boredom that is not aversive, it is hard to imagine someone being bored and being satisfied with one's situation. All this is to say that boredom is a state of discontent—indeed, it is one that we readily recognize as such. Furthermore, we typically attribute our felt discontent to our situation and not to our own inability to satisfactorily engage with the situation (Eastwood et al. 2012).

Boredom is also partly characterized by its physiological and neurological correlates, and by its motor and expressive features. Having said that, it is unclear as to whether or not these features are able to distinguish boredom from other affective states. Experimental work has not yet revealed a pattern of physiological activation (or deactivation) that is characteristic of boredom. In fact, a review of the literature yields findings that suggest that boredom is a low arousal state, a high arousal state, or even a state of mixed arousal (for a review, see Elpidorou 2021). This lack of consensus could mean that, even though boredom has a specific pattern of physiological activation (or deactivation) associated with its experience, we have not yet discovered it. Alternatively, the lack of consensus could mean that the experience of boredom does not give rise to any particular pattern of physiological arousal—perhaps, there are many patterns of physiological arousal that accompany the experience of boredom. Some have even argued that boredom should not be characterized in terms of its physiological arousal (Hill and Perkins 1985; Elpidorou 2021). Regardless of how we settle this issue, extant findings regarding boredom's physiological character indicate that during an experience of boredom we are disengaging from the task or situation at hand, preparing for an escape from the boring situation, or both (for more, see Elpidorou 2021).

The neurological correlates of boredom are the subject of an open and active investigation. Research has found boredom to be correlated with lower beta activity in the left dorsolateral prefrontal cortex (Tabatabaie et al., 2014) and with the presence of alpha waves (Oswald 1962). Perone, Anderson, and Weybright (2020) reported that the theta/beta ratio was lower during an easy (and thus boring) condition compared to an optimal condition—an indication that subjects experienced difficulties maintaining their attention in the former condition. Moreover, Perone and colleagues observed frontal alpha asymmetry, a measure of the presence of self-regulatory processes, and found that when the easy condition followed the optimal condition there was an increase in right frontal activity. The researchers interpret this finding as a sign that self-regulatory processes were engaged during the easy/boring condition (when the optimal condition preceded it). Other studies reported activation of parts of the default mode network during boredom (Danckert and Merrifield 2018; Ulrich et al. 2014), a finding that suggests that one's attention is directed toward inner thoughts (Raffaelli, Mills, and Christoff 2018). These and other findings allow us to gain a better understanding of the neurological correlates of boredom. Importantly, they also pave the road for further investigations and permit us to test hypotheses regarding the relationship between, on the one hand, the experience of boredom, and, on the other hand, attention, mental effort, self-regulation, and mind wandering.

Different movements and bodily postures have been associated with the experience of boredom. For instance, it has been reported that during boredom there is an attenuation of movement (Walbott 1998). Furthermore, the upper body of bored subjects tends to collapse, and they raise their chin and lean their head backward (Walbott 1998; see also Bull 1987). Other studies reported that bored individuals tend to fidget (Martin, Sadlo, and Stew 2006), and even though they do not move a lot, they tend to perform sudden movements when they do move (Kroes 2005). Studies of the facial expressions of boredom are currently inconclusive—although some studies have associated boredom with specific action units, others have failed to find any significant and reliable associations (see Craig et al. 2008; Kroes 2005; Scherer and Ellgring 2007; McDaniel et al. 2007). Lastly, investigations into the speech of bored individuals reveal that it tends to be slow and soft, with a low and narrow pitch range (Johnstone and Scherer 2000; Scherer 2013).

In sum, state boredom is a transient, unpleasant experience that involves both an awareness of the presence of a situation that fails to sufficiently cognitively engage us (because it is not interesting, novel, exciting, or meaningful) and a strong desire for alternative and more fulfilling engagement. Due to its affective, volitional, cognitive, and physiological characteristics, boredom is a sign that we are facing a situation that is uninteresting, unengaging, or meaningless to us and a drive to seek escape from such a situation, when escape is possible.

5. THE MORALITY OF BOREDOM

What then can we say about the moral character of boredom—understood either as state or trait boredom? To address this question, we should consider whether the five theses that are meant to capture the moral significance of a psychological state or personality trait (ACTION THESIS, JUDGMENT THESIS, PERCEPTION THESIS, FLOURISHING THESIS, and APPROPRIATENESS THESIS) are true for boredom.

ACTION THESIS: Does boredom promote prosocial or antisocial conduct? The possibility that something like trait boredom can lead to destructive and antisocial behavior has been explored in detail by Eric Fromm (1973) who theorized that the pervasive or frequent experience of boredom can become intolerable, so much so that often times one can only escape it by harming oneself or others (see also Pfattheicher et al. 2020; Danckert this book; Igou and Van Tilburg this book). Fromm's pessimistic outlook regarding the possible outcomes of trait boredom has found some empirical support. Correlational studies investigating individual differences in trait boredom report that trait boredom is related to maladaptive or antisocial tendencies and behaviors (e.g., sadistic tendencies, aggression, narcissism) and to actions indicative of low self-control and impulsiveness (Dahlen et al. 2004; Isacescu and Danckert 2018; Mercer-Lynn et al. 2013; Moynihan, Igou, Van Tilburg 2017; Pfattheicher et al. 2020; Struk, Scholer, and Danckert 2016; Vodanovich and Watt 2016; Watt and Vodanovich 1992; Wink and Donahue 1997). Because of their correlational nature, these findings are incapable of proving the existence of a causal relationship between trait boredom and morally untoward behaviors. However, they suggest the possibility that trait boredom could be a morally significant personality trait insofar as it could lead to antisocial behavior.

The role of trait boredom can be discerned perhaps more clearly when we consider specific examples of how the frequent experience of boredom can affect the behavior of an individual. Consider, for instance, the example of Niels Hoegel, a German nurse who has been convicted for the killing of eighty-five patients, but who might have killed many more (Eddy 2017; Elpidorou 2020). During his career as a nurse in different medical institutions, Hoegel injected patients with drugs that caused them heart failure or circulatory collapse so that he could try to revive them. According to his own account, he was bored and was searching for a thrill to escape his tedious routine and an opportunity to impress his colleagues and supervisors. It is not known whether trait boredom (as this is measured by BPS) is a personality characteristic of Hoegel. Still, his case provides an illustration as to how the frequent experience of boredom could lead to antisocial actions (for other examples, see Yucel and Westgate this book; Danckert this book). Consistent with the suggestion that trait boredom can lead to harmful behaviors, Pfattheicher and colleagues (2020) have reported that sadistic tendencies were more pronounced among boredom-prone individuals compared to those who were less prone to boredom. Indeed, the relationship between boredom proneness and sadistic tendencies was robust and was observed across a variety of contexts (e.g., sadism in the military, online trolling, sadistic fantasies) and across different countries and samples. These findings are once again correlational and thus preclude us from drawing any definitive conclusions regarding boredom's causal role. Nonetheless, the reported association between boredom proneness and sadistic tendencies remained significant even after the researchers controlled for the Big Five and HEXACO personality models. Most importantly, in one of their studies (Study 5), Pfattheicher and colleagues found that experimentally inducing state boredom increased the likelihood that subjects would shred worms for pleasure. Such a finding is preliminary evidence in support of the claim that boredom causes sadistic behavior.

It is crucially important to note that it matters a great deal *why* boredom might lead to these sorts of behavior. If it is because of either a need for excitement or novelty (Bench and Lench 2019) or a desire to secure or reestablish a sense of meaningfulness (Igou and Van Tilburg this book; Yucel and Westgate this book), then boredom's outcomes and action tendencies are neither inherently moral nor immoral. Boredom motivates behaviors that can help us to alleviate its aversive experience, and although it is possible that some reactions to boredom are immoral, they need not be so. This realization is especially important when we turn our attention to state boredom. Our characterization of state boredom revealed that it is a response to a perceived dissatisfaction with one's situation. Understood in that light, boredom appears to be a self-regulatory state: its aim or function is to resolve a perceived dissatisfaction by promoting change or action. As a result, the action that is born out of the experience of boredom might be immoral (Elpidorou 2020; Pfattheicher et al. 2020), but it could also be moral (Van Tilburg and Igou 2017b) or, as it is commonly the case, amoral. Such a result does not render boredom (either as a state of trait) morally insignificant. Rather, it forces us to pay attention to the environmental and psychological factors that might facilitate or promote one type of response to boredom over another. It also underlines the need for emotional literacy when it comes to the experience of boredom and for the development of proper and efficient avoidance, mitigation, and response strategies to boredom (see Todman this book).

JUDGMENT THESIS: The relationship between emotions (or affective states in general) and moral judgments is a topic that has received a great deal of attention both in the history of philosophy (e.g., Hume 1978 [1740]; Kant 1964 [1785]; Smith 1759) and in the interdisciplinary field of moral psychology (e.g., Haidt 2001; Nichols 2002; Prinz 2007). Scholars are actively examining whether emotions or affective states are a source or a consequence of moral judgments, whether it is possible to have moral judgments in the absence of emotions, or whether mature moral responses and judgments require the integration of both emotional and cognitive processes in order to best represent information regarding intentions, beliefs, and consequences. It would take us too far afield to try to summarize current debates concerning the potential role of affectivity in moral judgment. Indeed, the relationship between the two is complicated and multifaceted, and many different versions of it have been advanced and defended in the literature. Here, I follow a categorization presented by Avramova and Inbar (2013) and simply note three theses that explicate the possible relationship between emotions and moral judgments:

Thesis 1: Emotions (or affective states) are the consequences of moral judgments. For instance, moral judgments about the permissibility or impermissibility of an action might give rise to certain emotional states (e.g., anger or disgust).

Thesis 2: Emotions amplify moral judgments. For example, emotions of disgust or anger amplify the wrongness of particular actions, whereas emotions of awe or gratitude amplify the perceived goodness of a person.

Thesis 3: Emotions are necessary for moral judgments. This claim can be split into two:

a. An emotional reaction is the necessary psychological antecedent for the formation of a moral judgment; or

b. Emotions ground moral judgments, that is, emotions *moralize* nonmoral behaviors and situations insofar as it is on the basis of some emotional experience that we come to perceive certain behaviors or situations as moral or immoral.

Only Thesis 2 and Thesis 3 assign a moral role to emotions. Thesis 1 is consistent with the view that moral judgments are the products of "pure" (nonemotional) cognitive processes. Although numerous experimental findings

Andreas Elpidorou

have been reported in support of either the claim that affective states (emotions, gut feelings, or intuitions of emotional nature) amplify moral judgments (Thesis 2) or the claim that such states play a causal or constitutive role in the formation of moral judgments (Thesis 3), the significance and exact interpretation of these findings remains unclear (Avramova and Inbar 2013; Huebner, Dwyer, and Hauser 2008; May 2018).

In the case of boredom, there is no experimental evidence demonstrating that boredom directly affects moral cognition and judgment. Still, models of boredom that understand it to be a regulatory state that motivates individuals to search for meaning are consistent with the possibility that boredom (either as a trait or as a state) can indirectly influence moral judgment. Empirical findings in support of this hypothesis are scarce and, at this point, merely suggestive. Nonetheless, two studies are worth mentioning. First, Van Tilburg and Igou (2016) found that experimentally induced boredom leads to more extreme political orientations and that high boredom-prone individuals tend to adhere to more extreme political views compared to low boredom-prone individuals. Van Tilburg and Igou's (2016) study does not reveal a relationship between boredom and morality. Rather, it suggests the possibility that one's political preferences can be influenced by one's experiences of boredom. Although there are connections between our moral beliefs and our political views, these are neither obvious nor direct. Second, in a different set of studies, Van Tilburg and Igou (2011) reported that the onset of state boredom affected subjects' attitudes concerning social identity. Specifically, state boredom was shown to increase the valuation of their in-groups (as measured by subjects' preference of an in-group name over an out-group name and by their positive evaluations of a symbol associated with their national in-group) and the devaluation of out-groups (as measured by subjects' willingness to dispense harsher punishment to a hypothetical out-group offender compared to a hypothetical in-group offender). Although important, such findings do not demonstrate that boredom causes or grounds moral judgments (Thesis 3). Nonetheless, they might serve as preliminary support for the claim that boredom, through its potential to motivate a search for meaning, amplifies certain preexisting moral opinions (Thesis 2), insofar as a stronger adherence to or focus on those opinions bolsters a sense of meaningfulness. In sum, the relationship between boredom and moral judgment has not been adequately explored in the literature. As such, this is a topic that deserves future attention.

PERCEPTION THESIS: There is no evidence showing that boredom can affect the perception of morally salient facts. Nonetheless, given boredom's intimate connection to attentional mechanisms, the relationship between boredom and moral perception should be explored further. It is well documented in the empirical literature that both trait and state boredom are linked to attentional difficulties (Eastwood et al. 2012; Hunter and Eastwood 2018; Tam et al. in press). Indeed, extant research makes it clear that boredom cognitively disengages us from our situation. As a result, it is likely that during the experience of boredom we might miss morally salient facts. Such a conclusion is consistent with the affect-as-information model of emotions (Schwarz and Clore 1983, 1988, 2003) and with reports that emotional states may affect attention (e.g., Gasper and Clore 2002). If boredom's primary informational function is to convey the message that our current situation is uninteresting or meaningless to us, then we might be led to think that we should not pay attention to our situation. In light of its capacity to cognitively disengage us from a situation, boredom appears to be an affective experience that can hinder moral perception. More work, however, is needed in order to confirm or disconfirm this potential aspect of boredom.

FLOURISHING THESIS: A large body of research has consistently found that measures of trait boredom are correlated, on the one hand, with the presence of maladaptive behaviors and, on the other hand, with states or conditions that are potentially harmful or worrisome (e.g., depression, alexithymia, and hopelessness; reduced life satisfaction; reduced meaning in life and self-determination) (see Vodanovich 2003; Vodanovich and Watt 2016). Furthermore, a review of the available correlational data has shown that the presence of trait boredom is negatively related to several measures of hedonic and eudaimonic well-being: for example, trait boredom is associated with lower levels of subjective well-being, lower reported life satisfaction, lack of meaning in life, and reduction in autonomy (Elpidorou 2017). On the basis of this review, it was concluded that trait boredom is morally significant insofar as it is a serious impediment to living a flourishing life. Bargdill's (2000) phenomenological existential analysis of boredom offers complementary evidence insofar as it shows that life boredom, a construct closely related to trait boredom, might be harmful to individuals because it makes it harder for them to care for their projects and to pursue their goals. As such, trait boredom appears to be morally significant in the sense explicated by the FLOURISHING THESIS. Even though we must be mindful of the fact that there is not just one type of life that qualifies as the *good* life, a person that is often bored is likely to experience difficulties in their attempts to pursue a variety of projects that are constitutive of different notions of the good life.

This result however does not readily apply to state boredom. Given our characterization of state boredom as largely situationally dependent, the frequency and intensity of the experience of state boredom will differ depending on the subjects' circumstances, way of life, and psychological characteristics. In turn, subjects' response to state boredom will also depend on what type of psychological and material resources are available to them. So, even though the experience of boredom might stand as an obstacle to the achievement of the good life for some, it will not be an obstacle for all. In fact, it seems that what is most important in such cases is not the experience of state boredom as such, but the underlying and often systemic conditions that give rise to boredom frequently and persistently and which make it harder for the experiencing subject to respond to it appropriately (Elpidorou this book).

Moreover, boredom may turn out to be a beneficial state if experienced infrequently and responded to correctly. For instance, it has been argued that the experience of state boredom can inform us of the presence of an unfulfilling or meaningless situation and, at the same time, can motivate us to escape from such a situation (Bench and Lench 2013; Elpidorou 2014; Van Tilburg and Igou 2012). On account of that, boredom might contribute to eudaimonic well-being insofar as it propels us into situations that are more in line with our interests and which we find meaningful and important to us (Elpidorou 2018b, 2021, in press). Others have suggested that boredom can lead to creative outcomes (Gasper and Middlewood 2014; Hunter et al. 2016; Mann and Cadman 2014) and provide important epistemic benefits (Bortolotti and Aliffi this book). However, it bears repeating that both the range of available responses to boredom and whether or not those would be beneficial to oneself heavily depend on the type of resources that one possesses (Todman this book). For that reason, our ethical and social theories should consider how distributive and systemic injustices might disproportionally affect certain groups of individuals over others.

APPROPRIATENESS THESIS: Is boredom, either as trait or state, morally appropriate or inappropriate? With regards to trait boredom, high boredom-prone individuals experience impulse control deficits (Dahlen et al. 2004; Isacescu and Danckert 2018; Mercer-Lynn et al. 2013; Moynihan, Igou, Van Tilburg 2017; Watt and Vodanovich 1992; Leong and Schneller 1993), are more likely than low boredom-prone individuals to engage in risk-taking behavior (Dahlen et al. 2005; Kass, Beede, and Vodanovich 2010; Vodanovich and Watt 2016), and are prone to addictive behavior such as drug and alcohol abuse (Biolcati, Mancini, and Trombini 2018; LePera 2011; cf. Paulson, Coombs, and Richardson 1990), hypersexuality (Reid, Garos, and Carpenter 2011), and problem gambling (Blaszczynski, McConaghy, and Frankova 1990; see though Mercer and Eastwood 2010). If morality involves duties to oneself, in addition to duties to others, then one could argue that the APPROPRIATENESS THESIS is true for trait boredom: morally speaking, we are better off not possessing this particular trait. This conclusion rests, however, on the rather contentious moral premise that engaging in risk-taking, impulsive, or potentially addictive behaviors is morally inappropriate.

With regards to state boredom, most experiences of state boredom are morally neutral and thus having the affective experience of boredom is neither appropriate nor inappropriate. Still, our brief discussions of acedia and Type A profound boredom suggest, strongly I believe, that there are cases of state boredom that ought to be considered morally inappropriate. If we are bored by violations of human rights, the pain and suffering of others, or our own moral responsibilities, then we are the subjects of an experience that appears to be morally inappropriate.

There has been little, if any, discussion as to whether there can be instances of state boredom that are morally appropriate. Is it ever the case that it is good or praiseworthy to be bored by something? It is unclear whether such examples exist. Boredom signals a lack of care with our situation; it is a stance of indifference and disengagement. Unless there are cases in which indifference or lack of care is the right reaction to have (viz., it is a moral and not merely appropriate or beneficial attitude), then state boredom is never a morally *desirable* state.[1] But even if that is the case, it does not mean that state boredom has to be morally inappropriate. State boredom can also be—and indeed it is very often—morally neutral.

Summary

Boredom's moral character lies primarily in its ability to drive moral or immoral behavior, to hinder the pursuit of the good life when it is experienced frequently or chronically, and to potentially promote eudaimonic well-being when experienced infrequently and responded to appropriately. In turn, boredom is also morally significant insofar as certain experiences of boredom are indicative of moral shortcomings or failures.

6. SUMMARIES OF CHAPTERS

The present volume is the outcome of an interdisciplinary collaboration. In an attempt to advance our theoretical understanding of boredom and its relationship to morality, it brings together chapters from different perspectives— philosophy; clinical, social, and personality psychology; and animal studies. The chapters that follow this introduction examine the character of boredom, its function and role in our personal and social lives, and its relationship to other emotions and psychological states. By doing so, they explore how the presence of boredom can make a moral difference.

In the volume's opening chapter "From Electric Shocks to the Electoral College: How Boredom Steers Moral Behavior," Meltem Yucel and Erin C. Westgate draw upon the Meaning and Attentional Components model of boredom (Westgate and Wilson 2018) and consider the various causes and outcomes of the experience of boredom. They pay particular attention to how boredom can affect moral decision-making and behavior and to the conditions which are conducive to either prosocial or antisocial behavior. Yucel and Westgate's chapter also provides an informative and helpful overview of the ways in which emotions and affective states may impact moral attention, decision-making, and conduct. As such, the chapter is an appropriate beginning point for readers interested in how an affective state like boredom may relate to morality.

In "The Existential Sting of Boredom: Implications for Moral Judgments and Behavior," Eric R. Igou and Wijnand A. P. van Tilburg evaluate the moral character of boredom in light of a meaning-regulatory view of boredom. Such a view conceives of boredom as the signal of a potential or actual lack of meaning and, at the same time, as an attempt to reestablish or bolster a sense of meaningfulness. In previous work, Igou and Van Tilburg have provided theoretical and experimental support for this understanding of boredom (Van Tilburg and Igou 2011, 2012, 2017a). In their contribution to this volume, they consider what such a view of boredom can tell us about its moral character. By presenting different meaning-regulation processes related to the experience of boredom they articulate the conditions under which such processes can give rise to prosocial or antisocial behaviors. Their contribution makes evident both that situational factors can greatly affect the moral character of the outcomes of the experience of boredom and that the meaning-regulatory view carries great promise in elucidating boredom's complex relationship to morality.

In the next chapter, "Boredom and the Lost Self," Shane W. Bench, Heather C. Lench, Yidou Wan, Kaitlyn Kaiser, and Kenneth A. Perez take up the important question of what happens to us when we are constantly or frequently bored. The authors examine the implications of the presence of trait boredom to the perception and development of our concept of self. They argue that if state boredom is an experiential indication that a goal has lost its value for the experiencing subject, then trait boredom, which is conceptualized as a propensity to experience boredom frequently, is a sign of a poor fit between the person and the environment. Specifically, trait boredom indicates that there are no rewarding or valuable goals in the subject's environment. Bench and colleagues provide empirical support for this understanding of trait boredom and develop the implications of the presence of trait boredom for our personal existence and well-being.

The role of agency in boredom is considered in the next two chapters. In "'Rage Spread Thin': Boredom and Aggression," James Danckert examines the relationship between boredom and aggression (see also Igou and Van Tilburg this book). Specifically, Danckert asks whether there is something inherent in boredom that leads to aggressive acts. Although the two have been linked together, insofar as aggressive acts appear to follow the experience of boredom, Danckert argues that such a link does not demonstrate the immorality of boredom. Instead, the observed association between the two is explained by the fact that during the experience of boredom one's sense of agency is threatened or disrupted. In an attempt to restore their sense of agency, bored individuals might find recourse in acts of aggression: Because of their tangible outcomes, such acts offer the subjects an efficient way of reclaiming their agency and alleviating boredom. However, as Danckert shows, responding to boredom with aggression is not inevitable. Indeed, a functional account of boredom suggests that adaptive and beneficial responses to boredom are also available to us.

John D. Eastwood and Dana Gorelik zoom in on the nature of the crisis of agency that is characteristic, according to them, of boredom. In their chapter, "Losing and Finding Agency: The Crisis of Boredom," they argue that boredom presents the experiencing agent with a conundrum that is almost impossible to solve: Boredom demands from the agent that they do something, yet it also prevents them from desiring anything doable. In this way, Eastwood and Gorelik conceive of boredom as simultaneously both an opportunity and a danger. Depending on how one responds to boredom, one might reclaim (and even promote) one's agency or further degrade one's ability to act. The authors suggest ways in which one could effectively respond to the crisis of agency that lies at the heart of boredom. They underline, however, that structural forces can thwart individual agency and thus the task of reclaiming agency in the face of boredom is not merely personal but also social.

The social character of boredom is further highlighted in the two chapters that follow Eastwood and Gorelik's contribution. In "Boredom Mismanagement and Attributions of Social and Moral Costs," McWelling Todman considers and evaluates the commonly held belief that healthy adults ought to be able to regulate their experience of boredom in ways that promote group cohesion and minimize the possibility of antisocial or dangerous behavior. In his chapter, he presents different types of boredom management strategies that permit effective self-regulation and discusses how individuals who are not able to make proper use of such strategies are blamed and judged as having done something immoral. Todman cautions that moral judgments about individuals whose problematic behavior might be motivated by (or rooted in) boredom are often unfair. Such judgments may fail to consider how structural inequities in our society make it harder (sometimes even impossible) for socially marginalized individuals to acquire and practice effective boredom management skills in various institutional settings.

In my own contribution to the volume, "Boredom and Poverty: A Theoretical Model," I continue the conversation regarding the manner in which social conditions may affect one's experience of and response to boredom. I present and defend a theoretical account that holds that low SES individuals are disproportionately negatively affected by boredom because of their social standing. The account holds that, compared to individuals of

higher SES, individuals of low SES tend to experience boredom more frequently. Furthermore, because of the presence of constraints and of poverty's
effects on their psychology, individuals of low SES are placed in a disadvantageous position when dealing with boredom. Overall, their social standing
renders them susceptible to the experience of boredom and makes it harder
for them to respond to it in adaptive ways.

The question of whether boredom can be a beneficial affective state has
been considered before in the literature. Still, boredom's possible connection
to knowledge and self-knowledge has received far less attention. In their
contribution, "The Epistemic Benefits of Irrational Boredom," Lisa Bortolotti
and Matilde Aliffi argue that state boredom can be both epistemically irrational and epistemically beneficial. They usefully explicate the notion of *being
epistemically rationally assessable* and argue that boredom is a state that can
be epistemically rationally assessable. In fact, they convincingly show that
some cases of state boredom may turn to be epistemically irrational insofar
as they provide the agent with information that conflicts with available evidence. All the same, the authors argue that even though state boredom may be
epistemically irrational it can still offer important epistemic benefits.

The most common conceptualization of state boredom in the relevant
literature places it in the category of emotion. Indeed, many of the chapters in this book make explicit use of this conceptualization. In "Boredom
as Cognitive Appetite," Vida Yao offers an alternative understanding of
boredom. In her contribution, Yao introduces and characterizes the notion
of cognitive appetite, distinguishes it from that of emotion, and argues that
boredom should be considered to be a cognitive appetite. Importantly, Yao
draws out the benefits of this way of understanding boredom and illustrates
how the proposed understanding can make sense of our ethical assessments
of boredom and interest.

In "Boredom, Interest, and Meaning of Life," Wendell O'Brien takes a
close look at the relationship between boredom and interest. He argues that
lack of interest is a necessary condition for boredom (understood either as
a temporary affective experience, personality trait, or a chronic, existential
condition). In addition, he argues that interest is a necessary component of
subjective meaning of life, insofar as a life that is experienced as meaningful
has to be also experienced as interesting to the subject. These two conclusions
allow O'Brien to clarify the sense of interest that is of relevance to subjective
meaning and to explicate boredom's connection to the meaningful.

In "Parallels to Boredom in Nonhuman Animals," Rebecca K. Meagher
and Jesse Robbins take up the question of animal boredom. Do nonhuman animals experience boredom? If so, how can we tell? And what is the
relationship between human and animal boredom? In their contribution, the
authors provide a helpful review of evidence that shows that animals exhibit

signs of boredom in situations that appear to be analogous to ones that induce boredom in humans. They also compare conceptualizations of the human experience of boredom to operational definitions of boredom that are used in the study of animal boredom. The authors argue for the need of a comparative approach to the study of boredom and conclude their chapter by discussing the practical and moral implications of animal boredom as these relate to animal welfare and ethics.

The edited volume concludes with Josefa Ros Velasco's contribution, "The Long Hard Road Out of Boredom." In her chapter, Ros Velasco traces the moral history of boredom and explores the ways in which our attitudes concerning the experience of boredom have been transformed through the centuries and shaped by various cultural forces. One of Ros Velasco's aims is to make clear that boredom's relationship to morality has been a topic that received considerable attention in the history of Western tradition. After canvasing the rich history of boredom, Ros Velasco highlights boredom's adaptive function and potential benefits and underscores the dangers of pathologizing it.

It is my hope that the present book will not only allow readers to become more familiar with boredom and its moral significance but that it will also inspire and inform future research. As the chapters clearly demonstrate, the study of boredom has a storied past and a lively present. It also has a bright future.[2]

NOTES

1. I suppose one could argue that an appropriate dosage of boredom (with our own skills and abilities or with our social relationships and competencies) might be necessary in order to better oneself. And if bettering oneself is a moral duty, then boredom turns out to be a morally desirable state.

2. I am grateful to G. M. Trujillo Jr. and Wendell O'Brien for detailed and incredibly helpful comments on a previous version of this introduction.

REFERENCES

Ahmed, S. M. S. 1990. "Psychometric Properties of the Boredom Proneness Scale." *Perceptual and Motor Skills* 71, no. 3: 963–66. https://doi.org/10.2466/pms.1990 .71.3.963.

Avramova, Yana R., and Yoel Inbar. 2013. "Emotion and Moral Judgment." *Wiley Interdisciplinary Reviews: Cognitive Science* 4, no. 2: 169–78. https://doi.org/10 .1002/wcs.1216.

Baer, K. Stephanie. 2018. "'I Hope People Call Me Insane': Thousand Oaks Shooter Posted to Instagram During the Massacre." *BuzzFeed News,* November 9, 2018.

https://www.buzzfeednews.com/article/skbaer/thousand-oaks-shooter-social-media-instagram.

Bargdill, Richard. 2000. "The Study of Life Boredom." *Journal of Phenomenological Psychology* 31, no. 2: 188–219. https://doi.org/10.1163/15691620051090979.

Bench, Shane W., and Heather C. Lench. 2013. "On the Function of Boredom." *Behavioral Sciences* 3, no. 3: 459–72. https://doi.org/10.3390/bs3030459.

Bench, Shane W., and Heather C. Lench. 2019. "Boredom as a Seeking State: Boredom Prompts the Pursuit of Novel (Even Negative) Experiences." *Emotion* 19, no. 2: 242–54. https://doi.org/10.1037/emo0000433.

Biolcati, Roberta, Giacomo Mancini, and Elena Trombini. 2018. "Proneness to Boredom and Risk Behaviors During Adolescents' Free Time." *Psychological Reports* 121, no. 2: 303–23. https://doi.org/10.1177/0033294117724447.

Blaszczynski, Alex, Neil McConaghy, and Anna Frankova. 1990. "Boredom Proneness in Pathological Gambling." *Psychological Reports* 67, no. 1: 35–42. https://doi.org/10.2466/pr0.1990.67.1.35.

Bloomfield, Morton W. 1952. *The Seven Deadly Sins: An Introduction to the History of a Religious Concept, with Special Reference to Medieval English Literature.* East Lansing, MI: Michigan State College Press.

Bull, Peter E. 1987. *Posture and Gesture* (International Series in Experimental Social Psychology, Volume 16). Oxford: Pergamon Press.

Bush, George W. 2017. "George W. Bush, Bill Clinton Conversation on Leadership from the George W. Bush Presidential Center." July 13, 2017, Presidential Center in Dallas, TX. Available at: https://www.youtube.com/watch?v=rrMBoI6co2c.

Cassian, John. 2000. *John Cassian, the Institutes.* Vol. 58. Translated by Boniface Ramsey. New York, NY: Newman Press.

Chin, Alycia, Amanda Markey, Saurabh Bhargava, Karim S. Kassam, and George Loewenstein. 2017. "Bored in the USA: Experience Sampling and Boredom in Everyday Life." *Emotion* 17, no. 2: 359–68. https://doi.org/10.1037/emo0000232.

Craig, Scotty D., Sidney D'Mello, Amy Witherspoon, and Art Graesser. 2008. "Emote Aloud During Learning With AutoTutor: Applying the Facial Action Coding System to Cognitive–Affective States During Learning." *Cognition and Emotion* 22, no. 5: 777–88. https://doi.org/10.1080/02699930701516759.

Csikszentmihalyi, Mihaly. 1975. *Beyond Boredom and Anxiety.* San Francisco, CA: Jossey-Bass.

Dahlen, Eric R., Ryan C. Martin, Katie Ragan, and Myndi M. Kuhlman. 2004. "Boredom Proneness in Anger and Aggression: Effects of Impulsiveness and Sensation Seeking." *Personality and Individual Differences* 37, no. 8: 1615–27. https://doi.org/10.1016/j.paid.2004.02.016.

Dahlen, Eric R., Ryan C. Martin, Katie Ragan, and Myndi M. Kuhlman. 2005. "Driving Anger, Sensation Seeking, Impulsiveness, and Boredom Proneness in the Prediction of Unsafe Driving." *Accident Analysis and Prevention* 37, no. 2: 341–48. https://doi.org/10.1016/j.aap.2004.10.006.

Damrad-Frye, Robin, and James D. Laird. 1989. "The Experience of Boredom: The Role of the Self-Perception of Attention." *Journal of Personality and Social Psychology* 57, no. 2: 315–20.

Danckert, James, and Colleen Merrifield. 2018. "Boredom, Sustained Attention and the Default Mode Network." *Experimental Brain Research* 236, no. 9: 2507–18. https://doi.org/10.1007/s00221-016-4617-5.

Danckert, James, Jhotisha Mugon, Andriy Struk, and John Eastwood. 2018. "Boredom: What Is It Good For?." In *The Function of Emotions*, edited by Heather C. Lench, 93–119. Cham: Springer.

Doehlemann, Martin. 1991. *Langeweile? Deutung eines verbreiteten Phänomens*. Suhrkamp: Frankfurt am Main.

Eastwood, John D., Alexandra Frischen, Mark J. Fenske, and Daniel Smilek. 2012. "The Unengaged Mind. Defining Boredom in Terms of Attention." *Perspectives on Psychological Science* 7, no. 5: 482–95. https://doi.org/10.1177/1745691612456044.

Eddy, Melissa. 2017. "German Nurse Is Thought to Have Killed at Least 86, Officials Say." *New York Times,* August 28, 2017. https://www.nytimes.com/2017/08/28/world/europe/niels-hogel-german-nurse-killed-at-least-86-patients-officials-say.html.

Elpidorou, Andreas. 2014. "The Bright Side of Boredom." *Frontiers in Psychology* 5:1245. https://doi.org/10.3389/fpsyg.2014.01245.

Elpidorou, Andreas. 2017. "The Moral Dimensions of Boredom: A Call for Research." *Review of General Psychology* 21, no. 1: 30–48.

Elpidorou, Andreas. 2018a. "The Bored Mind is a Guiding Mind: Toward a Regulatory Theory of Boredom." *Phenomenology and the Cognitive Sciences* 17, no. 3: 455–84. https://doi.org/10.1007/s11097-017-9515-1.

Elpidorou, Andreas. 2018b. "The Good of Boredom." *Philosophical Psychology* 31, no. 3: 323–51. https://doi.org/10.1080/09515089.2017.1346240.

Elpidorou, Andreas. 2020. *Propelled: How Boredom, Frustration, and Anticipation Lead Us to the Good Life*. New York: Oxford University Press. https://doi.org/10.1093/oso/9780190912963.001.0001.

Elpidorou, Andreas. 2021. "Is Boredom One or Many? A Functional Solution to the Problem of Heterogeneity." *Mind & Language* 36, no. 3: 491–511. https://doi.org/10.1111/mila.12282.

Elpidorou, Andreas. In press. "Précis. Propelled: How Boredom, Frustration, and Anticipation Lead Us to the Good Life." *Journal of Philosophy of Emotion*.

Elpidorou, Andreas, and Josefa Ros Velasco. 2021. "Philosophy of Boredom." In Oxford Bibliographies in Philosophy, edited by Duncan Pritchard. New York: Oxford University Press.

Fahlman, Shelley A., Kimberley B. Mercer-Lynn, David B. Flora, and John D. Eastwood. 2013. "Development and Validation of the Multidimensional State Boredom Scale." *Assessment* 20, no. 1: 68–85. https://doi.org/10.1177/1073191111421303.

Farmer, Richard, and Norman D. Sundberg. 1986. "Boredom Proneness--the Development and Correlates of a New Scale." *Journal of Personality Assessment* 50, no. 1: 4–17. https://doi.org/10.1207/s15327752jpa5001_2.

Feldges, Tom, and Sonia Pieczenko. 2020. "Boredom in Educational Contexts: A Critical Review." *Encyclopaideia* 24, no. 57: 1–15. https://doi.org/10.6092/issn.1825-8670/11035.

Fenichel, Otto. 1951. "On the Psychology of Boredom." In *Organization and Pathology of Thought: Selected Sources*, edited by David Rapaport, 349–61. New York, NY: Columbia University Press.

Fisher, C. D. 1993. "Boredom at Work: A Neglected Concept." *Human Relations*, 46: 395–417. https://doi.org/10.1177/001872679304600305.

Fromm, Erich. 1973. *The Anatomy of Human Destructiveness*. New York, NY: Holt, Rinehart, & Winston.

Gana, Kamel, and Malek Akremi. 1998. "L'échelle de Disposition à l'Ennui (EDE): Adaptation française et validation du Boredom Proneness Scale (BP)." *L'année Psychologique* 98, no. 3: 429–50. https://doi.org/10.3406/psy.1998.28576.

Gana, Kamel, Guillaume Broc, and Nathalie Bailly. 2019. "Does the Boredom Proneness Scale Capture Traitness of Boredom? Results from a Six-Year Longitudinal Trait-State-Occasion Model." *Personality and Individual Differences* 139: 247–53. https://doi.org/10.1016/j.paid.2018.11.030.

Gasper, Karen and Gerald L. Clore. 2002. "Attending to the Big Picture: Mood and Global Versus Local Processing of Visual Information." *Psychological Science, 13,* no. 1: 34–40. https://doi.org/10.1111/1467-9280.00406.

Gasper, Karen, and Brianna L. Middlewood. 2014. "Approaching Novel Thoughts: Understanding Why Elation and Boredom Promote Associative Thought More than Distress and Relaxation." *Journal of Experimental Social Psychology* 52: 50–7. https://doi.org/10.1016/j.jesp.2013.12.007.

Goetz, Thomas, Anne C. Frenzel, Nathan C. Hall, Ulrike E. Nett, Reinhard Pekrun, and Anastasiya A. Lipnevich. 2014. "Types of Boredom: An Experience Sampling Approach." *Motivation and Emotion* 38, no. 3: 401–19. https://doi.org/10.1007/s 11031-013-9385-y.

Goldberg, Yael K., John D. Eastwood, Jennifer LaGuardia, and James Danckert.2011. "Boredom: An Emotional Experience Distinct from Apathy, Anhedonia, or Depression." *Journal of Social and Clinical Psychology* 30, no. 6: 647–66. https://doi.org/10.1521/jscp.2011.30.6.647.

Goldstein, Elizabeth. 2005. *Experience Without Qualities: Boredom and Modernity.* Palo Alto, CA: Stanford University Press.

Haidt, Jonathan. 2001. "The Emotional Dog and its Rational Tail: A Social Intuitionist Approach to Moral Judgment." *Psychological Review* 108, no. 4: 814–34. https://doi.org/10.1037/0033-295X.108.4.814.

Hamilton, Jean A. 1981. "Attention, Personality, and the Self-Regulation of Mood: Absorbing Interest and Boredom." *Progress in Experimental Personality Research, 10,* 281–315.

Harris, Mary B. 2000. "Correlates and Characteristics of Boredom Proneness and Boredom." *Journal of Applied Social Psychology* 30, no. 3: 576–98. https://doi.org /10.1111/j.1559-1816.2000.tb02497.x.

Hartocollis, Peter. 1972. "Time as a Dimension of Affects." *Journal of the American Psychoanalytic Association* 20, no. 1: 92–108. https://doi.org/10.1177/000306 517202000104.

Healy, Seán Desmond. 1984. *Boredom, Self, and Culture*. Rutherford, NJ: Fairleigh Dickinson University Press.

Heidegger, Martin. 1995. *Basic Concepts of Metaphysics: World—Finitude. Solitude.* Translated by William McNeil and Nicholas Walker. Bloomington, IN: Indiana University Press. (Originally published as *Die Grundbegriffe der Metaphysik. Welt, Endlichkeit, Einsamkeit* (GA 29/30). Frankfurt am Main: Vittorio Klostermann, 1983.)

Hill, Austin Bradford, and Rachel E. Perkins. 1985. "Towards a Model of Boredom." *British Journal of Psychology* 76, no. 2: 235–40. https://doi.org/10.1111/j.2044 -8295.1985.tb01947.x.

Huebner, Bryce, Susan Dwyer, and Marc Hauser. 2009. "The Role of Emotion in Moral Psychology." *Trends in Cognitive Sciences* 13, no. 1: 1–6. https://doi.org/10 .1016/j.tics.2008.09.006.

Hume, David. 1978. *A Treatise of Human Nature.* Oxford, UK: Oxford University Press. (Original publication date: 1740)

Hunter, Andrew, and John D. Eastwood. 2018. "Does state boredom cause failures of attention? Examining the Relations Between Trait Boredom, State Boredom, and Sustained Attention." *Experimental Brain Research* 236, no. 9: 2483–92. https:// doi.org/10.1007/s00221-016-4749-7.

Hunter, Jennifer A., Eleenor H. Abraham, Andrew G. Hunter, Lauren C. Goldberg, and John D. Eastwood. 2016. "Personality and Boredom Proneness in the Prediction of Creativity and Curiosity." *Thinking Skills and Creativity* 22: 48–57. https://doi.org/10.1016/j.tsc.2016.08.002.

Isacescu, Julia, and James Danckert. 2018. "Exploring the Relationship between Boredom Proneness and Self-Control in Traumatic Brain Injury (TBI)." *Experimental Brain Research* 236, no. 9: 2493–505. https://doi.org/10.1007/s 00221-016-4674-9.

Johnstone, Tom, and Klaus R. Scherer. 2000. "Vocal Communication of Emotion." In *Handbook of Emotions* (Second Edition), edited by Michael Lewis and Jeannette M. Haviland-Jones, 220–235. New York: Guilford.

Jütte, Daniel. 2020. "Sleeping in Church: Preaching, Boredom, and the Struggle for Attention in Medieval and Early Modern Europe." *American Historical Review* 125, no. 4: 1146–74.

Kant, Immanuel. 1964. *Groundwork of the Metaphysics of Morals.* New York: Harper and Row. (Original publication date: 1785)

Kass, Steven J., Kristen E. Beede, and Stephen J. Vodanovich. 2010. "Self-Report Measures of Distractibility as Correlates of Simulated Driving Performance." *Accident Analysis and Prevention* 42, no. 3: 874–80. https://doi.org/10.1016/j.aap. 2009.04.012.

Kierkegaard, Søren. 1987. *Either/Or*, Part I. Translated by Howard V. Hong and Edna H. Hong, Princeton: Princeton University Press. (Originally published in 1843)

Kroes, Stefan. "Detecting Boredom in Meetings." University of Twente, Enschede.

Kuhn, Reinhard C. 1976. *The Demon of Noontide: Ennui in Western Literature.* Princeton, NJ: Princeton University Press.

Larson, Reed W., and Maryse H. Richards. 1991. "Boredom in the Middle School Years: Blaming Schools Versus Blaming Students." *American Journal of Education* 99, no. 4, 418–443. https://doi.org/10.1086/443992.

Leary, Mark R., Patricia A. Rogers, Robert W. Canfield, and Celine Coe. 1986. "Boredom in Interpersonal Encounters: Antecedents and Social Implications." *Journal of Personality and Social Psychology* 51, no. 5: 968–75. https://doi.org/10.1037/0022-3514.51.5.968.

Leong, Frederick T.L., and Gregory R. Schneller. 1993. "Boredom Proneness: Temperamental and Cognitive Components." *Personality and Individual Differences* 14, no. 1: 233–39. http://dx.doi.org/10.1016/0191-8869(93)90193-7.

LePera, Nicole. 2011. "Relationships Between Boredom Proneness, Mindfulness, Anxiety, Depression, and Substance Use." *The New School Psychology Bulletin* 8, no. 2: 15–25.

Maltsberger, John T., Issac Sakinofsky, and Aruna Jha. 2000. "Case Consultation: Mansur Zaskar: A Man Almost Bored to Death/Comments." *Suicide and Life-Threatening Behavior* 30, no. 1: 83–90.

Mann, Sandi, and Rebekah Cadman. 2014. "Does Being Bored Make Us More Creative?." *Creativity Research Journal* 26, no. 2: 165–73. https://doi.org/10.1080/10400419.2014.901073.

Martin, Marion, Gaynor Sadlo, and Graham Stew. 2006. "The Phenomenon of Boredom." *Qualitative Research in Psychology* 3, no. 3: 193–211. https://doi.org/10.1191/1478088706qrp066oa.

May, Joshua. 2018. "The Limits of Emotion in Moral Judgment." In *The Many Moral Rationalisms,* edited Karen Jones and François Schroeter, 286–306. Oxford: Oxford University Press.

Melton, Amanda M.A., and Stefan E. Schulenberg. 2009. "A Confirmatory Factor Analysis of the Boredom Proneness Scale." *The Journal of Psychology* 143, no. 5: 493–508. https://doi.org/10.3200/JRL.143.5.493-508.

Mercer-Lynn, Kimberley B., David B. Flora, Shelley A. Fahlman, and John D. Eastwood. 2013. "The Measurement of Boredom: Differences Between Existing Self-Report Scales." *Assessment* 20, no. 5: 585–96. https://doi.org/10.1177/1073191111408229.

Mercer-Lynn, Kimberley B., Rachel J. Bar, and John D. Eastwood. 2014. "Causes of Boredom: The Person, the Situation, or Both?." *Personality and Individual Differences* 56: 122–26. https://doi.org/10.1016/j.paid.2013.08.034.

Mercer, Kimberley B., and John D. Eastwood. 2010. "Is Boredom Associated With Problem Gambling Behaviour? It Depends on What You Mean By 'Boredom'." *International Gambling Studies* 10, no. 1: 91–104. https://doi.org/10.1080/14459791003754414.

Mikulas, William L., and Stephen J. Vodanovich. 1993. "The Essence of Boredom." *The Psychological Record* 43, no. 1: 3–12.

Mills, Caitlin, and Kalina Christoff. 2018. "Finding Consistency in Boredom by Appreciating Its Instability." *Trends in Cognitive Sciences* 22, no. 9: 744–47. https://doi.org/10.1016/j.tics.2018.07.001.

Moravia, Alberto. 2011. *Boredom.* Translated by William Weaver. New York, NY: New York Review Books. (Originally published as *La Noia.* Milan: Valentino Bompiani & Co, 1960.)

Moynihan, Andrew B., Eric R. Igou, and Wijnand A.P. van Tilburg. 2017. "Boredom Increases Impulsiveness: A Meaning-Regulation Perspective." *Social Psychology* 48: 293–309. https://doi.org/10.1027/1864-9335/a000317.

Musharbash, Yasmine. 2007. "Boredom, Time, and Modernity: An Example from Aboriginal Australia." *American Anthropologist* 109, no. 2: 307–17. https://doi.org /10.1525/aa.2007.109.2.307.

Neu, Jerome. 2000. *A Tear Is an Intellectual Thing: The Meanings of Emotion.* Oxford: Oxford University Press.

Ng, Andy H., Yong Liu, Jian-zhi Chen, and John D. Eastwood. 2015. "Culture and State Boredom: A Comparison Between European Canadians and Chinese." *Personality and Individual Differences* 75: 13–18. https://doi.org/10.1016/j.paid.2014.10.052.

Nichols, Shaun. 2002. "Norms With Feeling: Towards a Psychological Account of Moral Judgment." *Cognition* 84, no. 2: 221–236.

Nisbet, Robert. 1982. *"Boredom."* In *Prejudices: A Philosophical Dictionary.* Cambridge, MA: Harvard University Press.

O'Brien, Wendell. 2014. "Boredom." *Analysis* 74, no. 2: 234–44. https://doi.org/10 .1093/analys/anu041.

O'Brien, Wendell. 2018. Boredom: A History of Western Philosophical Perspectives. In *Internet Encyclopedia of Philosophy.* https://iep.utm.edu/boredom/.

Oswald, Ian. 1962. "The EEG of Sleep." In *Sleeping and Waking: Physiology and Psychology,* 35–41. Amsterdam: Elsevier.

Paulson, Morris J., Robert H. Coombs, and Mark A. Richardson. 1990. "School Performance, Academic Aspirations, and Drug Use Among Children and Adolescents." *Journal of Drug Education* 20, no. 4: 289–303. https://doi.org/10.2 190/8J0X-LY6D-PL7W-42FA.

Pekrun, Reinhard, Thomas Goetz, Lia M. Daniels, Robert H. Stupnisky, and Raymond P. Perry. 2010. "Boredom in Achievement Settings: Exploring Control–Value Antecedents and Performance Outcomes of a Neglected Emotion." *Journal of Educational Psychology* 102, no. 3: 531–49.

Perone, Sammy, Alana J. Anderson, and Elizabeth H. Weybright. 2021. "It Is All Relative: Contextual Influences on Boredom and Neural Correlates of Regulatory Processes." *Psychophysiology* 58, no. 3: e13746. https://doi.org/10.1111/psyp.13746.

Petro, Patrice. 1993. "After Shock/Between Boredom and History." *Discourse* 16, no. 2: 77–99. https://www.jstor.org/stable/41389315.

Pfattheicher, Stefan, Ljiljana B. Lazarević, Erin C. Westgate, and Simon Schindler. 2020. "On the Relation of Boredom and Sadistic Aggression." *Journal of Personality and Social Psychology.* Advance online publication. https://doi.org/10 .1037/pspi0000335.

Phillips, Adam. 1994. *On Kissing, Tickling, and Being Bored: Psychoanalytic Essays on the Unexamined Life.* Cambridge, MA: Harvard University Press.

Prinz, Jesse. 2007. *The Emotional Construction of Morals.* Oxford: Oxford University Press.

Proust, Marcel. 1982. *Remembrance of Things Past, Volume 1, Swann's Way. Within a budding grove.* Translated by C. K. Scott Moncrieff and Terence Kilmartin. New

York. Random House, Inc., and Chatto & Windus. (Originally published as *À la Recherce du Temps Perdu* by Edtions Gallimard, Paris in 1954).

Raffaelli, Quentin, Caitlin Mills, and Kalina Christoff. 2018. "The Knowns and Unknowns of Boredom: A Review of the Literature." *Experimental Brain Research* 236, no. 9: 2451–62. https://doi.org/10.1007/s00221-017-4922-7.

Raposa, Michael L. 1999. *Boredom and the Religious Imagination.* Charlottesville, VA: University of Virginia Press.

Reid, Rory C., Sheila Garos, and Bruce N. Carpenter. 2011. "Reliability, Validity, and Psychometric Development of the Hypersexual Behavior Inventory in an Outpatient Sample of Men." *Sexual Addiction & Compulsivity* 18, no. 1: 30–51. https://doi.org/10.1080/10720162.2011.555709.

Russell, Bertrand. 2006. *Conquest of Happiness.* Abingdon, Oxon, UK: Routledge Classics. (Originally published in 1930)

Scherer, Klaus R. 2013. "Nonlinguistic Vocal Indicators of Emotion and Psychopathology." In *Emotions in Personality and Psychopathology,* edited by Carroll Izard, 495–529. New York and London: Plenum Press.

Scherer, Klaus R., and Heiner Ellgring. 2007. "Multimodal Expression of Emotion: Affect Programs or Componential Appraisal Patterns?." *Emotion* 7, no. 1: 158–71.

Schwarz, Norbert, and Gerald L. Clore. 1983. "Mood, Misattribution, and Judgments of Well-Being: Informative and Directive Functions of Affective States." *Journal of Personality and Social Psychology* 45, no. 3: 513–23. https://doi.org/10.1037/0 022-3514.45.3.513.

Schwarz, Norbert, and Gerald L. Clore. 1988. "How Do I Feel About It? The Informative Function of Affective States." In *Affect, Cognition and Social Behavior: New Evidence and Integrative Attempts*, edited by In Klaus Fiedler and Joseph Forgas, 44–62. Toronto, Ontario, Canada: C.J. Hogrefe

Schwarz, Norbert, and Gerald L. Clore. 2003. "Mood As Information: 20 years Later." *Psychological Inquiry* 14, no. 3–4: 296–303. https://doi.org/10.1080/1 047840X.2003.9682896.

Sinkewicz, Robert E. 2003. *Evagrius of Pontus: the Greek Ascetic Corpus.* New York; Oxford: Oxford University Press.

Smith, Aaron, Kyley McGeeney, Maeve Duggan, Lee Rainie, and Scott Keeter. 2015. "U.S. Smartphone Use in 2015." PewResearch Internet Project. Retrieved July 03, 2020. https://www.pewresearch.org/internet/2015/04/01/us-smartphone-use-in-2015/.

Smith, Adam. 1759. *The Theory of Moral Sentiments.* Reprinted in *The Glasgow Edition of the Works and Correspondence of Adam Smith, vol. I,* edited by David D. Raphael and Alec L. Macfie. Oxford: Oxford University Press.

Spacks, Patricia Meyer. 1995. *Boredom: The Literary history of a State of Mind.* Chicago: The University of Chicago Press.

Steinberger, Fabius, April Moeller, and Ronald Schroeter. 2016. "The Antecedents, Experience, and Coping Strategies of Driver Boredom in Young Adult Males." *Journal of Safety Research* 59: 69–82. https://doi.org/10.1016/j.jsr.2016.10.007.

Struk, Andriy A., Abigail A. Scholer, and James Danckert. 2016. "A Self-Regulatory Approach to Understanding Boredom Proneness." *Cognition and Emotion* 30, no. 8: 1388–1401. https://doi.org/10.1080/02699931.2015.1064363.

Struk, Andriy A., Jonathan S. A. Carriere, J. Allan Cheyne, and James Danckert. 2017. "A Short Boredom Proneness Scale: Development and Psychometric Properties." *Assessment* 24, no. 3: 346–59. https://doi.org/10.1177/1073191115609996.

Sundberg, Norman D., Carl A. Latkin, Richard F. Farmer, and Jihad Saoud. 1991. "Boredom in Young Adults: Gender and Cultural Comparisons." *Journal of Cross-Cultural Psychology* 22, no. 2: 209–23. https://doi.org/10.1177/0022022191222003.

Svendsen, Lars. 2005. *A Philosophy of Boredom*. Translated by John Irons. London: Reaktion Books.

Tabatabaie, Ashkan F., Mohammad Reza Azadehfar, Negin Mirian, Maryam Noroozian, Ahmad Yoonessi, Mohammad Reza Saebipour, and Ali Yoonessi. 2014. "Neural Correlates of Boredom in Music Perception." *Basic and Clinical Neuroscience* 5, no. 4: 259–66.

Tam, Katy Y. Y., Wijnand A.P. Van Tilburg, and Christian S. Chan. 2021. "What Is Boredom Proneness? A Comparison of Three Characterizations." *Journal of Personality* (Early View). https://doi.org/10.1111/jopy.12618.

Tam, Katy, Wijnand A. P. Van Tilburg, Christian Chan, Eric Igou, and Hakwan Lau. In press. "Attention Drifting In and Out: The Boredom Feedback Model." *Personality and Social Psychology Review*. Advance Online Publication. https://doi.org/10.1177/10888683211010297.

Thackray, Richard I., J. Powell Bailey, and R. Mark Touchstone. 1977. "Physiological, Subjective, and Performance Correlates of Reported Boredom and Monotony While Performing a Simulated Radar Control Task." In *Vigilance: Theory, Operational Performance and Physiological Correlates*, edited by Robert Mackie, 203–16. New York: Plenum.

Todman, McWelling. 2003. "Boredom and Psychotic Disorders: Cognitive and Motivational Issues." *Psychiatry: Interpersonal and Biological Processes* 66, no. 2: 146–67. https://doi.org/10.1521/psyc.66.2.146.20623.

Toohey, Peter. 1988. "Some Ancient Notions of Boredom." *Illinois Classical Studies* 13, no. 1: 151–164.

Toohey, Peter. 2011. *Boredom. A Lively History*. New Haven: Yale University Press.

Ulrich, Martin, Johannes Keller, Klaus Hoenig, Christiane Waller, and Georg Grön. 2014. "Neural Correlates of Experimentally Induced Flow Experiences." *Neuroimage* 86: 194–202. https://doi.org/10.1016/j.neuroimage.2013.08.019.

van Hooft, Edwin A. J., and Madelon L. M. van Hooff. 2018. "The State of Boredom: Frustrating or Depressing?" *Motivation and Emotion* 42, no. 6: 931–46. https://doi.org/10.1007/s11031-018-9710-6.

Van Tilburg, Wijnand A. P, and Eric R. Igou. 2016. "Going to Political Extremes in Response to Boredom." *European Journal of Social Psychology* 46, no. 6: 687–99. https://doi.org/10.1002/ejsp.2205.

Van Tilburg, Wijnand A.P., and Eric R. Igou. 2012. "On Boredom: Lack of Challenge and Meaning as Distinct Boredom Experiences." *Motivation and Emotion* 36, no. 2: 181–94. https://doi.org/10.1007/s11031-011-9234-9.

Van Tilburg, Wijnand A.P., and Eric R. Igou. 2017a. "Boredom Begs to Differ: Differentiation from Other Negative Emotions." *Emotion* 17, no. 2: 309–322. https://doi.org/10.1037/emo0000233.

Van Tilburg, Wijnand A.P., and Eric R. Igou. 2017b. "Can Boredom Help? Increased Prosocial Intentions in Response to Boredom." *Self and Identity* 16, no. 1: 82–96. https://doi.org/10.1080/15298868.2016.1218925.

Van Tilburg, Wijnand AP, and Eric R. Igou. 2011. "On Boredom and Social Identity: A Pragmatic Meaning-Regulation Approach." *Personality and Social Psychology Bulletin* 37, no. 12: 1679–91. https://doi.org/10.1177/0146167211418530.

Vodanovich, Stephen J. 2003. "Psychometric Measures of Boredom: A Review of the Literature." *The Journal of Psychology* 137, no. 6: 569–95. https://doi.org/10.1080/00223980309600636.

Vodanovich, Stephen J., and John D. Watt. 2016. "Self-Report Measures of Boredom: An Updated Review of the Literature." *The Journal of Psychology* 150, no. 2: 196–228. https://doi.org/10.1080/00223980.2015.1074531.

Vodanovich, Stephen J., and Steven J. Kass. 1990. "A Factor Analytic Study of the Boredom Proneness Scale." *Journal of Personality Assessment* 55, no. 1–2: 115–23. https://doi.org/10.1080/00223891.1990.9674051.

Vodanovich, Stephen J., J. Craig Wallace, and Steven J. Kass. 2005. "A Confirmatory Approach to the Factor Structure of the Boredom Proneness Scale: Evidence for a Two-Factor Short Form." *Journal of Personality Assessment* 85, no. 3: 295–303. https://doi.org/10.1207/s15327752jpa8503_05.

Vodanovich, Stephen J., John D. Watt, and Chris Piotrowski. 1997. "Boredom Proneness in African-American College Students: A Factor Analytic Perspective." *Education* 118, no. 2: 229–37.

Vogel-Walcutt, Jennifer J., Logan Fiorella, Teresa Carper, and Sae Schatz. 2012. "The Definition, Assessment, and Mitigation of State Boredom Within Educational Settings: A Comprehensive Review." *Educational Psychology Review* 24, no. 1: 89–111. https://doi.org/10.1007/s10648-011-9182-7.

Wallbott, Harald G. 1998. "Bodily Expression of Emotion." *European Journal of Social Psychology* 28, no. 6: 879–96. https://doi.org/10.1002/(SICI)1099-0992(1998110)28:6<879::AID-EJSP901>3.0.CO;2-W.

Washburn, Mark and Maria David. 2016. "Aaron Suspect Said He Lit Wildfires Out of Boredom." *The Herald,* December 01, 2016. https://www.heraldonline.com/news/local/crime/article118292693.html.

Watt, John D., and Stephen J. Vodanovich. 1992. "Relationship between Boredom Proneness and Impulsivity." *Psychological Reports* 70, no. 3 (Pt 1): 688–90. https://doi.org/10.2466%2Fpr0.1992.70.3.688.

Wenzel, Siegfried. 2017. *The Sin of Sloth: Acedia in Medieval Thought and Literature.* Chapel Hill: University of North Carolina Press.

Westgate, Erin C., and Timothy D. Wilson. 2018. "Boring Thoughts and Bored Minds: The MAC Model of Boredom and Cognitive Engagement." *Psychological Review* 125, no. 5: 689–713. https://doi.org/10.1037/rev0000097.

Westgate, Erin C. 2020. "Why Boredom is Interesting." *Current Directions in Psychological Science* 29, no. 1: 33–40. https://doi.org/10.1177/0963721419884309.

Williams, Bernard. 1973. "The Makropulos Case: Reflections on the Tedium of Immortality." In *Problems of the Self,* 82–100. Cambridge: Cambridge University Press.

Wink, Paul, and Karen Donahue. 1997. "The Relation Between Two Types of Narcissism and Boredom." *Journal of Research in Personality* 31, no. 1: 136–40. https://doi.org/10.1006/jrpe.1997.2176.

Wishnitzer, Avner. 2021. "Yawn: Boredom and Powerlessness in the Late Ottoman Empire." *Journal of Social History*. Advance Online Publication. https://doi.org/10.1093/jsh/shab013.

Chapter 1

From Electric Shocks to the Electoral College

How Boredom Steers Moral Behavior

Meltem Yucel and Erin C. Westgate

Among charming tales of quirky haircuts conjured up out of boredom, lurk more chilling stories. On June 2017, motorists in Ireland were disturbed by an odd sight: a man on a bridge aiming a gun. When police arrived, they found a teenager, perched above an Irish highway overpass, centering passing cars in the sights of his 6-mm air rifle. When asked later in court, he explained simply: he was "bored" (Ferguson and McLean 2019). Although boredom has been associated with prosocial behavior (e.g., Van Tilburg and Igou 2017), it has also been associated with a wide array of morally questionable and disturbing outcomes, including self-harm (Nederkoorn et al. 2016), reckless driving (Steinberger et al. 2017), and sadism (Pfattheicher et al. 2020).

We all experience boredom, from being stuck in airport security lines to reading poorly written book chapters. But what is boredom, why do we experience it, and what happens when we do? We suggest a new take on this everyday emotion as an important and useful cue that we are not cognitively engaged in meaningful experiences. According to the Meaning and Attentional Components (MAC) model of boredom, people feel bored when they cannot successfully engage their attention in meaningful activities. Boredom can be painful, but it provides important feedback about our lives, by signaling a lack of meaningful attentional engagement. In short, boredom tells us whether we *want to* and are *able to* focus on what we are doing (or thinking), and then directs us toward behaviors that are more challenging or meaningful.

In doing so, boredom plays an important role in regulating moral thoughts and behaviors. Following recent calls urging researchers to consider boredom as a moral emotion (Elpidorou 2017), we explore how boredom influences our *moral* actions and perceptions. We start by reviewing how emotions (broadly) impact morality, and when and how positive and negative affects lead to moral behavior. We then zoom in on one specific form of negative affect—boredom—and explore how feeling bored leads us to behave in more pro- or antisocial ways, depending on the environment.

1. HOW EMOTIONS STEER MORALITY

Moral philosophers and psychologists have long been interested in the role of emotions in morality (Blair 1995; Haidt 2001; Hume 1896; Smith 1976; Yucel, Hepach, and Vaish 2020). One question, in particular, has centered many debates: do emotions precede our moral judgments, or do they follow afterward, once moral judgments have been formed? Some have emphasized the causal role of reasoning in moral behavior (e.g., Kohlberg 1976), while others have stressed the causal role of emotions (e.g., Smith 1976).

Early developmental researchers such as Piaget and Kohlberg argued for a cognitive approach, where logic and reasoning give rise to our moral evaluations and acts. They proposed a stage-like progression of moral development, where each moral stage that children achieve corresponds to cognitive skills gained (Kohlberg 1976; Piaget 1960). Although their primary focus was on cognition, even Kohlberg (1964) does not dismiss the possibility that emotions are involved in morality.

Emotivists, on the contrary, place a strong emphasis on the importance of emotions (or "affect," more generally) as the source of morality. While *emotions* refer to discrete states, tied to a specific eliciting situation (e.g., "anger," "awe"; Clore and Ortony 2013), *affect* refers to general feelings of goodness or badness, tied to interoceptive perceptions of physiological change (e.g., racing pulse; Barrett 2017). More specifically, emotivists have argued for the centrality of emotions in drawing a distinction between the moral and nonmoral (Hume 1896; Nichols 2002, 2004; Prinz 2006, 2007; Smith 1976). For example, Hume (1896) and Smith (1976) argued that emotions serve as an internal compass from which moral reasons are derived. If we feel bad when others physically hurt us, these negative feelings will coalesce as moral judgments and make us perceive hitting as immoral.

Similarly, Haidt (2001) claimed that adults form moral judgments based primarily on affective intuitions. Consider, for instance, the decision of whether to have sex with your sibling. Rather than relying on reasoned moral judgment, people instead rely on their quick intuitive feelings of repulsion to reject the idea of two siblings having sex. Haidt argues that people come up with post hoc reasons only after reacting to moral situations, or what he terms "the emotional dog and its rational tail" (814). For instance, in moral dumbfounding experiments, adult participants typically respond to moral scenarios (such as consensual incest) with condemnation, even when they do not have rational reason for doing so (Haidt, Björklund, and Murphy 2000). Although theorists may disagree on the *degree* to which emotions are involved in what we perceive as moral or how we act in righteous ways, most agree that emotions do play an important role in morality. Emotions influence our perceptions of what is moral, direct our attention toward actions that are (im)moral, and motivate us to behave in (im)moral ways (Prinz and Nichols 2010). Below we briefly consider how emotions influence perception, motivation, and behavior, before turning to the case of one emotion in particular: boredom.

Emotions Steer Moral Attention

How do we know an action is immoral? As the previous section highlights, emotions and affect play an important role in how we construe morality. But before we can categorize an act as moral or immoral, we first need to attend to it. Affective arousal, together with situational factors, directs our attention—much like a spotlight—to affect-inducing events in our environment. For instance, feeling fearful upon seeing a snake may lead us to consciously notice the snake and direct our attention toward possible escape routes (or rocks with which to defend ourselves). These embodied experiences of affect then influence our judgments and even memory (Peters et al. 2006; Storbeck and Clore 2008).

Little work has investigated whether affect is present in our perceptions of (and responses to) immoral acts. In a recent study we investigated the role of affect in developing this moral/nonmoral distinction (Yucel, Hepach, and Vaish 2020). If emotions are integral to morality, we reasoned, then violating a moral norm (e.g., against nonviolence) should elicit more emotion than violating a nonmoral or conventional norm (e.g., wearing shoes at work). Therefore, we randomly assigned young children and adults to watch a video of either a moral norm violation (e.g., a person destroying someone else's artwork) or a nonmoral norm violation (e.g., a person playing a game incorrectly; Yucel, Hepach, and Vaish 2020). We recorded participants' physiological responses by measuring how much their pupils dilated as they watched these videos. Physiological arousal, in the form of pupil dilation, is an important marker of emotionality, and a sign that participants were experiencing more intense affect (Bradley, Miccoli, Escrig, and Lang 2008). Across all age groups, witnessing moral violations resulted in greater physiological arousal (i.e., pupil dilation) than witnessing a nonmoral violation. We concluded that affective arousal is not only present to a greater degree when it comes to moral actions but that even young children draw such emotional distinctions between moral and nonmoral rules. Research with older children corroborates this relationship between emotions and morality; children rate moral violations to be more affectively negative than nonmoral (conventional) violations (Arsenio and Ford 1985).

Just as moral violations evoke more powerful emotions, so too do affective reactions indicate that a moral violation has occurred. According to an enormously influential theory in emotion, affect acts as "information" about its perceived object (affect-as-information; Clore, Gasper, and Garvin 2001; Clore and Tamir 2002). We assume that what feels good *is* good, and that what feels bad *is* bad. Feeling distress upon seeing a person rip up someone else's artwork thus lends moral judgment to the event: destroying other people's property must be a "bad" thing to do. Furthermore, discrete emotions provide more fine-grained information than core affect (e.g., valence and arousal). Anger, for instance, is elicited when someone intentionally does something blameworthy; thus, feeling anger is a sign that morally suspect behavior has occurred (Ortony, Clore, and Collins 1988). Thus, all emotions that include approval or disapproval of one's own behavior (or the behavior of others), as one of their eliciting components, are likely to be *moral* emotions. This includes emotions in response to both positive praiseworthy (e.g., pride, admiration, gratitude) as well as negative blameworthy (e.g., anger, shame, guilt) behavior. Taken together, affect directs our attention to moral events and helps us distinguish moral from nonmoral (conventional) concerns.

Emotions Motivate (Im)moral Behavior

Emotions not only direct attention and interpretation of moral events but also motivate us to behave in (im)moral ways. For example, anger can motivate us to act in both morally good (e.g., to protect those who have been hurt) and bad ways (e.g., to hurt those who have engaged in wrongdoing). Affect influences our reactions by motivating us to act on our feelings. Upon witnessing a moral transgression, for instance, we might feel more compassion toward the victim (e.g., experience affective arousal) and offer to help, to decrease our own arousal. For instance, people who paid more attention to the news after the 2016 presidential election of Donald Trump felt more anger, but were also more likely to take political action due to that anger (Ford et al. 2018).

Contrary to popular wisdom, emotions do not "trigger" behaviors directly, but rather do so via an indirect push-and-pull reminiscent of operant conditioning. People are generally motivated to maintain positive affective states (and reduce negative ones) in an effort to feel good. Just as rats will press a lever in anticipation of the food pellet they expect to receive, so too do people select actions in anticipation of the emotions they expect to experience as a consequence. Consider anger. Despite popular conceptions, feeling angry does not inherently make people violent. But if, upon being insulted, a person (1) feels great anger *and* (2) believes that violence will reduce that anger *and* (3) that violence constitutes a socially acceptable response, they are likely to lash out aggressively at the perpetrator (e.g., Cohen and Nisbett 1994; Cohen et al. 1996). Because of this, there is no one-to-one mapping between emotion and behavior; rather, people's behavior depends on what they feel at the moment, the options available, and the perceived affective consequences of each option. What people do depends on what they *want* to feel (Tamir and Ford 2012).

This is also true in the moral domain. For instance, prosocial behavior has been linked to both positive *and* negative affect (e.g., boredom). In other words, feeling good and feeling bad can *both* make people behave prosocially (Lyubomirsky, King, and Diener 2005; Cialdini and Fulz 1990; Van Doorn, Zeelenberg, and Breugelmans 2014). People are more likely to help others after being surprised with a cookie or finding a dime in a phone booth, because surprises make us feel good (Isen and Levin 1972; Cunningham, Steinberg, and Grev 1980). Likewise, recalling happy events increases blood donation (O'Malley and Andrews, 1983); reading mood-boosting messages increases volunteering, charitable donations, and helping behavior (Aderman 1972; Cunningham, Steinberg, and Grev 1980); and feeling grateful increases willingness to help even at personal expense (Bartlett and DeSteno 2006). Finally, environmental features that induce positive moods, such as attractive fragrances and lighting, prolong how long people are willing to help (Baron and Bronfen 1994; Baron, Rea, and Daniels 1992). If *positive* moods increase helping by making it more pleasant, *negative* moods may also make us more likely to help, because helping others makes us feel better (i.e., negative-state relief hypothesis; Cialdini, Darby, and Vincent 1973). For instance, thinking about sad experiences makes teenagers (though not younger children) more likely to help (Cialdini and Kenrick 1976), and experiencing failure leads adults to help if doing so is especially easy or valuable (Benson 1978; Weyant 1978).

Beyond core affect, specific discrete emotions can also directly motivate moral behavior (or the lack thereof). People help others when they feel an emotional response to their distress, and refrain from harm when the thought of others' suffering pains them. Even young children are motivated to behave prosocially in response to such feelings. For instance, two-year-olds exhibit physiological arousal (measured via changes in pupil dilation) upon seeing someone in need (Hepach, Vaish, and Tomasello 2012). This arousal quickly decreases if the child (or another person) is able to help the adult in need. However, if children are held back from helping, their arousal remains elevated (Hepach, Vaish, and Tomasello 2012). Furthermore, two-year-olds with higher arousal are faster to help an adult in need (Hepach et al. 2016). In contrast, in the absence of such emotional distress, people behave prosocially only if they expect rationally to benefit from doing so (i.e., *empathy-altruism hypothesis*; Batson and Shaw 1991).

Other specific emotions that convey moral information (and motivate strategies to remedy moral wrongs) include anger, guilt, and shame (Čehajić-Clancy et al. 2016). For instance, anger in response to specific incidents increases prosocial behavior to address perceived wrongs—people who experience more anger and outrage in response to moral violations are more likely to support, spend time with, and compensate perceived victims (Montada and Schneider, 1989; Iyer, Schmadel, and Liker 2007) and more likely to punish wrongdoers (Lotz et al. 2011; Vitaglione and Barnett 2003; van Doorn, Zeelenberg, and Breugelmans, 2014). Likewise collective guilt and shame predict endorsement of reparations to indigenous groups among Chileans (Brown et al. 2008) and to Bosnian Muslims among Bosnian Serbs (Brown and Čehajić 2008).

In sum, affect and emotion steer our attention toward morally relevant actions, inform us whether actions are moral, and motivate us to behave in both moral and immoral ways. They do this by providing a self-reinforcing system for morality, incentivizing "good" behavior with positive emotions (e.g., pride, gratitude) and "punishing" bad behavior with negative ones (e.g., shame, guilt, anger). Below we turn to the question of how one specific negative emotion in particular—boredom—affects our moral perceptions and behaviors.

2. HOW BOREDOM STEERS MORAL DECISION-MAKING

As "situated affective appraisals," all emotions share an affective core—emotions are inherently positive *or* negative (Clore and Ortony 2013). That boredom is aversive may seem obvious, but it is strong evidence for boredom's status as an emotion. Earlier theorizing held boredom to be a neutral state, neither positive nor negative (Gasper 2018; Gasper, Spencer, and Hu 2019). However, people routinely report boredom to be affectively negative (Van Tilburg and Igou 2016; Goetz et al. 2006, 2014); they will pay to avoid it (Dal Mas and Wittmann 2017), and prefer even unpleasant experiences, including electric shocks and disturbing images, over feeling bored (Bench and Lench 2019; Haverman et al.,2015; Nederkoorn et al. 2016; Wilson et al. 2014).

Boredom is not only *affective*, but it also shares other core features of emotions. Classical views posit the existence of a discrete set of core emotions, each triggering certain behaviors, and reliably mapping onto unique facial expressions, physiological features, and neural activity. However, recent data provide strong evidence against this approach (e.g., Barrett 2006). Rather than the one-to-one mapping suggested by classical theories, researchers find that specific emotions cannot be reliably identified by their facial expressions (Gendron et al. 2014a, 2014b; Barrett et al. 2019), physiological features (e.g., heart rate; Siegel et al. 2018), or neural activity in the brain (Lindquist et al. 2012). Instead, what does reliably distinguish specific emotions are the situational construals (or appraisals) that elicit them (e.g., Schachter and Singer 1962; Barrett 2006).

The Origins of Boredom: Meaning and Attention

If emotions are defined by the construals that elicit them, what reliably elicits boredom? Early theories of boredom focused on environmental elicitors; boredom was thought to be caused by lack of stimulation (e.g., Berlyne 1960; Cox 1980). However, it is unclear *why* understimulating environments would be boring. One explanation is that such environments make it hard to pay attention (e.g., Danckert and Merrifield 2016; Eastwood et al. 2012). However, understimulation is not the only situation that gives rise to inattention; overstimulation can also make it difficult to pay attention. Nor is lack of attention the only reason why something might be boring. Another set of theories focus on boredom's existential origins (e.g., Barbalet 1999; Locke and Latham 1990; Van Tilburg and Igou 2012). To the extent that attention leads to boredom, such existential theories suggest, it is because the situation was meaningless to begin with.

There is good evidence that each of these—understimulation, overstimulation, attention deficits, meaning deficits—plays an important role in boredom, and each of these theories has made important contributions to understanding what boredom is and why we experience it. The MAC model of boredom and cognitive engagement brings these individual theories together to reconcile competing predictions for the causal role of meaning and attention in producing boredom (Westgate and Wilson 2018). For instance, attentional theories predict that people should not be bored if they are successfully paying attention, even if what they are doing feels meaningless. Conversely, existential theories predict that people would feel bored under those circumstances, but should *not* feel bored if they have trouble paying attention during an otherwise meaningful task.

The MAC model tests these predictions empirically by experimentally manipulating both attention and meaning at the same time. By doing so, we can isolate the relative contributions of meaning and attention, and test whether the effects of attention on boredom are dependent on meaning (or vice versa) using the gold standard test of causality: randomized control experiments. When meaning and attention are manipulated in this way, we find strong evidence for *both* the attentional and existential accounts of boredom (Westgate and Wilson 2018). In other words, attention deficits and meaning deficits both produce boredom, and do so equally. Nor do they interact; the effect of attention on boredom does not depend on meaning, and the effect of meaning does not depend on attention. Instead, people are bored if they are unable to pay attention, and they are bored if meaning is lacking; these effects stack. In other words, both attentional and existential theories get it (partially) right. People *will* feel bored if they are successfully paying attention, if what they are doing feels meaningless. But people will *also* feel bored if they have trouble paying attention during an otherwise meaningful task.

Further evidence that both attention and meaning play equal and independent roles in boredom comes from correlational data. Aggregating across fourteen studies, we compared how well attention (vs. meaning) deficits predict self-rated boredom across a variety of tasks (Westgate and Wilson 2018). After each task, people were asked to retrospectively rate how boring and meaningful the task was, and how hard it was to concentrate. By pitting attention and meaning against each other in this way, we were able to examine the relative contributions of each component, while statistically controlling for each other's presence. Once again, we found strong independent effects of meaning and attention. Greater difficulty paying attention predicted increased boredom (meta-analytic $r = 0.34$), even after controlling for how meaningful the task was. Likewise, the less meaningful the task felt, the more boredom people experienced (meta-analytic $r = 0.35$), even after controlling for attention. Again, there was no interaction, meta-analytic $r = 0.00$: people were *least* bored when meaning and attention were high, and *most* bored when attention and meaning were low. Nor were attention and meaning highly related, meta-analytic $r = -0.12$ $[-0.21, -0.04]$.

In other words, empirical evidence supports the MAC model's claim that boredom is an affective signal of unsuccessful attentional engagement in valued goal-congruent activity. Deficits in *either* attention (e.g., unsuccessful attentional engagement) *or* meaning (e.g., valued goal-congruent activity) are thus sufficient to induce boredom. Across a broad range of situations, both attention and meaning independently predict boredom, are not highly correlated, and do not interact. Furthermore, boredom results when something is too easy or too hard, because both make it hard to pay attention. Like other emotions, boredom conveys information, in this case that one's current activity is not meaningful, or is too hard (or too easy), making it difficult to pay attention. Because of this, when manipulated experimentally, attention and meaning deficits result in different profiles of boredom with different downstream consequences for how people behave (Westgate and Wilson 2018).

For instance, being bored because what you are doing lacks meaning feels different and has different consequences than being bored because you cannot pay attention, as they signal different problems.

Reducing Boredom: Restoring Meaning and Attention

Why we are bored shapes what we want to do next and helps explain why bored people make often puzzling decisions, such as choosing to self-administer painful electric shocks or turning to political extremism. In short, like pain, boredom may be unpleasant but it plays an important role in alerting us when we do not want to (or are unable to) pay attention to what we're doing and motivating us to change our behavior to restore attention and meaning to our lives. This may be especially powerful when it comes to moral decision-making due to boredom's aversive nature; people are highly motivated to escape boredom, even at their own cost (e.g., Dal Mas and Wittmann 2017; Wilson et al. 2014) and perhaps at the cost of others.

If boredom is caused by deficits in meaning and attention, then effective means of reducing boredom will restore those deficits. As such, there are three ways that people can effectively reduce boredom: regulating attention, regulating meaning, or switching activities altogether. Regulating attention restores the balance between cognitive resources and cognitive demands such that both are high (e.g., resulting in feelings of interest) or both low (e.g., resulting in feelings of enjoyment). This can be done by altering either side of the person-situation interaction. For instance, we can alter the situation to be more (or less) challenging, such as when people add time limits to otherwise overly easy tasks (Sansone et al. 1992). However, we can also alter the person side of the equation, by increasing (or decreasing) our own available cognitive resources, through long-term (e.g., skill-building) or short-term (e.g., caffeine) means. For instance, work by Silvia (2005) suggests that abstract art is boring unless you have the capacity to make sense of it, presumably an art degree would remedy this issue.

Likewise, regulating meaning involves restoring the connection between what you are currently doing and your own valued goals. For instance, helping students draw connections between their coursework and their own personal goals increases interest and achievement (Hulleman et al. 2010). The final option, rather than tinkering with the current task to make it more appropriately challenging or meaningful, is to switch tasks altogether. Activity-switching is the most commonly studied response to boredom, in part because switching activities carries with it the potential to remedy deficits of both attention and meaning simultaneously. In the next section, we discuss the implications of this strategy for moral decision-making.

Boredom as a Moral Emotion

Thus far, we have explained how emotions matter for both moral decision-making and behavior. We have also situated boredom as one such emotion and shown that boredom is an important signal indicating a lack of meaningful attentional engagement. In this section, we posit that depending on the context, boredom can be a *moral* emotion and lead us to behave in both moral (and immoral) ways.

Boredom motivates (im)moral behavior. Much research has focused on moral emotions such as anger, guilt, and disgust. Indeed, these emotions have been implicated in how morality is perceived and enforced. Prinz, in his seminal book, *The Emotional Construction of Morals*, argues that "different emotions have different motivational consequences, and a token of the concept *wrong* will motivate us differently depending on which emotion it happens to manifest on a particular occasion" (Prinz 2007, 103). We suggest that boredom is one such emotion.

Moral benefits of boredom. In uplifting news, several studies have found associations between boredom and prosocial behavior. For instance, among thirty-one students asked to estimate how much money they would donate to a hypothetical educational charity in Zambia, participants who first completed a repetitive odds-estimation task said they would donate an average of €12.94 (vs. €5.73 among participants who did not complete the task first). Likewise, among eighty-eight students who completed a long (vs. short) estimation task and were then asked to read about a charity that was very effective (or not very effective), participants in the longer task said they felt more bored and claimed they would donate more. However, these sample sizes are small and fall below recommendations calling for a minimum of fifty participants per cell to ensure adequate statistical power in experimental designs (Simmons, Nelson, and Simonsohn 2013).

It is also unclear whether behavioral *intentions*, as measured in hypothetical scenarios, translate into actual behavior; such links are notoriously weak (Ajzen and Fishbein 1977; La Piere 1934). For instance, another study finds that religious people, who typically contribute more to charity, actually appear to experience less boredom than nonreligious people (Van Tilburg et al. 2019). The link between actual and intended behavior may be particularly weak when it comes to behavior with moral implications. For instance, a recent intervention to increase sustainable food purchases in a café (Piester et al. 2020) found that almost half of customers ended up ordering a different menu item than they had told researchers they planned to purchase only moments earlier, while in line!

We examined actual prosocial behavior while simultaneously inducing boredom (Pfattheicher et al. 2020) by randomly assigning 634 participants to watch either a 5-minute video of magic tricks (control) or a 5-minute video of a rock (boredom condition). During the video participants could press up to ten available buttons: five buttons boosted the pay of another yoked participant in 10-cent increments and the other five buttons docked their pay in 10-cent increments. People could press pay-boosting buttons or pay-docking buttons, but not both; there was no personal gain or cost to the participant of pressing any of the buttons. Participants who watched the rock video felt more bored, but were not more likely to press the pay-boosting button than participants in the control condition. In fact, rates of prosocial behavior across both conditions were very high (89 percent overall). In contrast, in another large study we found that inducing boredom experimentally did increase the extent to which people punished a wrongdoer in a third-party punishment paradigm ($n = 983$), raising punishment rates from 66 percent (control condition) to 76 percent (boredom condition). If boredom does increase prosocial behavior, the relationship may depend both on the behavior in question and people's existing motivations.

Irresponsible behavior. Boredom has long been associated with irresponsible behavior at school, at work, and in the polling booth. Boredom is common in schools and the workplace, and bored students and workers perform more poorly than their more engaged classmates and colleagues (Pekrun et al. 2006; Fisher 1993, 1998). For instance, cops report that they are more likely to make traffic stops when bored (Phillips 2016). Boredom has also been an inadvertent side effect of increasing automation (Cummings et al. 2015), including in anesthesiology and air traffic control, where lapses of attention have potentially life-altering consequences. A well-publicized series of collisions between U.S. naval vessels occupied headlines in summer 2019 (Faturechi, Rose, and Miller 2019); official reports attributed the mishaps to sailor fatigue while standing long watches on deck—an anonymous sailor wrote to one of the authors of this chapter stating they believed boredom played a central role in such incidents.

Boredom can also drive irresponsible or impulsive behavior in more mundane settings. People are more likely to speed when bored, and interventions that reduce roadway boredom also improve responsible driving (Steinberger et al. 2017). Likewise, bored people snack more (Moynihan et al. 2015; Havermans et al. 2015) and may gossip more (Yucel, Buttrick, and Westgate 2020). If boredom leads people to seek out sources of meaning, it may also inadvertently lead to political extremism. For instance, in a study of ninety-seven visitors (seventy-one liberal, twenty-six conservative) to a college campus in Ireland, liberals reported being *more* liberal after a boredom induction (Van Tilburg and Igou 2016). There was no corresponding effect of boredom among conservatives.

Prejudice and discrimination. Boredom has also been associated with in-group bias. In several small samples, Irish participants, after completing a boring task, favored the name Eion over Owen ($n = 39$), liked shamrock symbols more ($n = 60$), and recommended longer prison sentences for an English criminal defendant but shorter sentences for an Irish defendant ($n = 90$; Van Tilburg and Igou 2011). Taken together, the above work suggests that boredom can (at least sometimes) lead people to engage in irresponsible, impulsive, and immoral behaviors.

Substance use and self-harm. These effects also extend to behaviors that, while not necessarily moral, do cause harm to the self, including disturbing associations with substance use and self-injury. Boredom has been consistently linked to alcohol and drug use in correlational research (e.g., Weybright et al. 2015). For instance, state-level differences in boredom predict drug-related deaths across all fifty U.S. states, even after controlling for background demographics (Baldwin and Westgate 2020). Alcohol and drug use constitute suppression strategies, a method of coping with emotion by making the emotion simply "go away" (Gross 2014). Alcohol effectively reduces boredom short term; in experimental lab studies, people feel less bored after drinking vodka cranberry (vs. plain cranberry juice; Westgate and Fairbairn 2020) cocktails. Suppression does not, ultimately, work well as an effective long-term emotion regulation strategy, however, because it does not resolve the underlying issues that produced. For instance, smoking marijuana (Block et al. 1998) actually *increases* boredom over time in experimental lab administration.

Both experimental and correlational research have also linked boredom explicitly to forms of self-injury and self-harm (e.g., Wilson et al. 2014). For instance, in one study, 67% of men and 25% of women asked to sit and entertain themselves with their own thoughts chose to shock themselves during this period. These effects appear specific to boredom. For instance, in an experimental follow-up, boredom increased self-administered electric shocks, particularly among those with a history of nonsuicidal self-injury, but sadness did not (Nederkoorn et al. 2016). In another experiment, 93% of participants shocked themselves while watching a boring excerpt (on repeat for an hour) from a documentary on neuroscientist Erik Kandel, whereas only 37% shocked themselves while watching the full documentary; this effect was not moderated by boredom proneness (Havermans et al. 2015).

Interpersonal cruelty and sadism. Perhaps the clearest evidence for the moral implications of boredom stems from work on interpersonal cruelty, aggression, and sadism. Alarmingly, boredom in life is correlated with higher sadistic tendencies ($r = 0.37$; Pfattheicher et al. 2020). Internet trolls report higher boredom proneness, soldiers who experience more boredom during military service report behaving more sadistically toward their colleagues, and parents who experience more boredom during childcare report behaving more sadistically toward their own children. In experimental studies, inducing boredom increases the percentage of people willing to kill helpless worms for fun (i.e., by grinding them up in a coffee grinder) from 2% (control condition) to almost 18% (experimental boredom condition). And inducing boredom significantly increases the number of people willing to dock other participants' pay for their own amusement.

(Im)moral behavior as emotion regulation. People may make immoral decisions out of a genuine but misguided desire to reduce boredom. According to the MAC model of boredom, when we are bored, we seek out challenging and/or meaningful activities (Westgate 2020; Westgate and Wilson 2018). Hence, we argue that lack of meaning and attention motivates us by (1) increasing our desire for activities that happen to be (im)moral and (2) by shaping what we construe to be moral while we are bored.

People may pursue (im)moral activities as challenging and/or meaningful alternatives to boredom. For instance, attentional deficits in boredom tell us to seek ways to change stimulation in our environment; our willingness to hurt ourselves or others when bored may stem from the desire to remedy under-stimulation. In the above studies, for instance, excitement-seeking (but not need for meaning) mediated sadistic behavior in response to experimentally induced boredom (Pfattheicer et al. 2020). Likewise, boredom tells us to seek meaning in our actions; in-group biases and political extremism in response to boredom may reflect such motives, as may the increased tendency to sanc-tion moral offenders. Because meaning is inherently subjective, such attempts to remedy meaning deficits need not necessarily be prosocial or positive, from society's standpoint. Together, these deficits in meaning and attention draw us to engage with our environment: combined, they increase novelty-seeking (Kapoor et al. 2015; Bench and Lench 2019) and reward-sensitivity (Milyavsakaya et al. 2019). Whether these impulses are morally good or bad depends in part on whether available options are good ones.

Deficits in meaning and attention can also shape whether we *perceive* an action as more or less moral, thus changing how we construe morality. Just as feeling angry or disgusted may lead us to perceive certain actions as moral, feeling bored may make certain immoral actions more acceptable. For instance, we may relax norms against deviant or antisocial behaviors when bored; such tendencies may account for why bored people are more willing to kill worms, dock other participants' pay, and engage in third-party punishment. By relaxing our definitions of what constitutes moral behavior, boredom may also affect our desire to act on our construals. In a situation where our only way out of feeling bored is by doing something wrong, we may come to rationalize immoral behavior. For instance, in classic work on cognitive dissonance, participants induced to lie to others about their enjoy-ment of a boring task subsequently came to believe their own lies (Festinger and Carlsmith 1959). Thus, we predict that boredom will lead people to rationalize potentially immoral behavior to the extent that they believe such actions will make them feel better.

Situations limit moral behavior. Whether boredom leads to anti- or prosocial behavior depends on the situation: when environments allow us to intervene and help others, we can do so. However, in situations where we are unable to help others, we may settle on inaction or worse, harm, if we believe it will reduce boredom. In such cases, boredom itself may incentivize immoral behavior. Below we consider factors that affect our abilities to act morally.

Good choices require good options. We predict boredom will only increase antisocial behavior when prosocial options are unavailable. For instance, Pfattheicher et al. (2020) find that boredom increases antisocial behavior. However, when given a choice between pressing a button to *dock* other participants' pay and pressing a button to *boost* their pay by the same amount, people are overwhelmingly prosocial (Pfattheicher et al. 2020). When people have a prosocial option available, the effect of boredom on antisocial behavior largely disappears (except for individuals already high in dispositional sadism). In contrast, when only an antisocial option is available, boredom significantly increases the number of people who choose to take it. In cases where the environment limits our ability to behave morally, doing nothing may result in continued boredom.

Overall, people prefer action over inaction (Albarracín et al. 2019); this tendency may be exaggerated when bored. Thus, we predict that in situations with limited options, boredom will increase *prosocial* behavior when taking action is positive (i.e., when only prosocial actions available), and increase *antisocial* behavior when taking action is negative (i.e., when only antisocial options available). For instance, classic work by Cialdini, Darby, and Vincent (1973) found that sad moods increased helping *only* if other positive events did not intervene. That is, if helping others was the only way to feel better, people did so, but not otherwise.

The same phenomenon plays out societally as well. In a large national study using Google searches to index feelings of boredom, we found that U.S. states that were psychologically diverse (e.g., California, Texas) experienced less boredom than states that were less diverse (e.g., Ohio, Utah). And, in turn, these states experienced fewer drug-related deaths (Baldwin and Westgate 2020). Importantly, however, this link between drug-related deaths and national boredom rates was contingent upon social ecology; in places rich in meaning and psychological diversity, people not only experienced boredom less frequently but may have better alternatives available to them to reduce boredom when it occurs. In sum, doing good when bored is influenced by the opportunity to do good in the first place.

The perils and promise of deliberation. Situations may affect moral behavior in a second way, by imposing cognitive loads that influence whether we behave pro- or antisocially. The Social Heuristic Hypothesis dictates that people intuitively behave in cooperative/prosocial ways (Rand et al. 2014). Despite our intuitive prosociality, when asked to deliberate before deciding to act, people are often less cooperative. Cognitive load may differentially affect our ability to act morally depending on the type of boredom we are experiencing. When boredom is induced by high cognitive load (i.e., when we are overstimulated), we may act in line with intuitions and behave prosocially, because we do not have the cognitive space to think through what is most beneficial to us. But in low cognitive load boredom (i.e., when we are understimulated), we may deliberate more and act less cooperatively or more antisocially, because we do have the cognitive space to think through what is most beneficial to us. Thus, we predict that attentional boredom due to overload is more likely to result in prosocial behavior, while attentional boredom due to underload is more likely to result in antisocial behavior.

Thus, boredom interacts with the environment; while boredom provides motivation to act, environments limit and facilitate our ability to behave in pro- or antisocial ways. Whether boredom results in moral or immoral behavior is therefore a function of how people's motivation to reduce it interacts with the options available to do so.

3. CHARTING A BETTER COURSE

In this chapter we have reviewed what boredom is, why it occurs, how it influences our moral decision-making process, and how we can redirect ourselves when this occurs. We want to close by considering ways we can shape our environments—at work, at school, and at home—to reduce boredom and encourage moral behavior at those times when boredom is unavoidable. People cannot do good if they do not have the opportunity to do so. Boredom motivates action, which is a good thing, but environments channel the direction that action can take. By providing psychologically rich and diverse environments, we not only prevent boredom but expand the range of moral options available to people when they are bored. Societal change to improve accessibility and equality of health care, employment, education, and the humanities (including literature and the arts) is thus an important factor not only in psychological well-being but also in moral decision-making. By expanding citizens' ability to lead psychologically rich, interesting lives, we expand their ability to live morally consistent ones as well.

REFERENCES

Aderman, David. 1972. "Elation, Depression, and Helping Behavior." *Journal of Personality and Social Psychology* 24, no.1: 91–101.

Albarracín, Dolores, Aashna Sunderrajan, Wenhao Dai, and Benjamin X. White. 2019. "The Social Creation of Action and Inaction: From Concepts to Goals to Behaviors." In *Advances in Experimental Social Psychology* Vol. 60, edited by James M. Olson, 223–271. Cambridge: Academic Press.

Arsenio, William F., and Martin E. Ford. 1985. "The Role of Affective Information in Social-Cognitive Development: Children's Differentiation of Moral and Conventional Events." *Merrill-Palmer Quarterly* 31, no. 1: 1–17.

Baldwin, Matthew., and Erin C. Westgate. 2020. "States of Boredom: Downsides to Being Bored in the USA." Unpublished manuscript.

Baron, Robert A., and Marna I. Bronfen. 1994. "A Whiff of Reality: Empirical Evidence Concerning the Effects of Pleasant Fragrances on Work-Related Behavior 1." *Journal of Applied Social Psychology* 24, no. 13: 1179–1203.

Baron, Robert A., Mark S. Rea, and Susan G. Daniels. 1992. "Effects of Indoor Lighting (Illuminance and Spectral Distribution) on the Performance of Cognitive Tasks and Interpersonal Behaviors: The Potential Mediating Role of Positive Affect." *Motivation and Emotion* 16, no. 1: 1–33.

Barrett, Lisa Feldman. 2006. "Are Emotions Natural Kinds?." *Perspectives on Psychological Science* 1, no. 1: 28–58.

Barrett, Lisa Feldman. 2017. *How Emotions are Made: The Secret Life of the Brain.* Boston: Houghton Mifflin Harcourt.

Barrett, Lisa Feldman, Ralph Adolphs, Stacy Marsella, Aleix M. Martinez, and Seth D. Pollak. 2019. "Emotional Expressions Reconsidered: Challenges to Inferring Emotion from Human Facial Movements." *Psychological Science in the Public Interest* 20, no. 1: 1–68.

Bartlett, Monica Y., and David DeSteno. 2006. "Gratitude and Prosocial Behavior: Helping When it Costs You." *Psychological Science* 17, no. 4: 319–325.

Barbalet, Jack M. 1999. "Boredom and Social Meaning." *British Journal of Sociology* 50: 631–646.

Batson, C. Daniel, and Laura L. Shaw. 1991. "Evidence for Altruism: Toward a Pluralism of Prosocial Motives." *Psychological Inquiry* 2, no. 2: 107–122.

Bench, Shane W., and Heather C. Lench. 2019. "Boredom as a Seeking State: Boredom Prompts the Pursuit of Novel (Even Negative) Experiences." *Emotion* 19, no. 2: 242–254.

Benson, Peter L. 1978. "Social Feedback, Self-Esteem State, and Prosocial Behavior." *Representative Research in Social Psychology* 9: 43–56.

Berlyne, Daniel E. 1960. *Conflict, Arousal and Curiosity.* New York, NY: McGraw-Hill.

Blair, Robert James Richard. 1995. "A Cognitive Developmental Approach to Morality: Investigating the Psychopath." *Cognition* 57, no. 1: 1–29.

Block, Robert I., Wesley J. Erwin, Roxanna Farinpour, and Kathleen Braverman. 1998. "Sedative, Stimulant, and Other Subjective Effects of Marijuana: Relationships to Smoking Techniques." *Pharmacology Biochemistry and Behavior* 59, no. 2: 405–412.

Bradley, Margaret M., Laura Miccoli, Miguel A. Escrig, and Peter J. Lang. 2008. "The Pupil as a Measure of Emotional Arousal and Autonomic Activation." *Psychophysiology* 45, no. 4: 602–607.

Brown, Rupert, and Sabina Cehajic. 2008. "Dealing with the Past and Facing the Future: Mediators of the Effects of Collective Guilt and Shame in Bosnia and Herzegovina." *European Journal of Social Psychology* 38, no. 4: 669–684.

Brown, Rupert, Roberto González, Hanna Zagefka, Jorge Manzi, and Sabina Čehajić. 2008. "Nuestra Culpa: Collective Guilt and Shame as Predictors of Reparation for Historical Wrongdoing." *Journal of Personality and Social Psychology* 94, no. 1: 75–90.

Čehajić-Clancy, Sabina, Amit Goldenberg, James J. Gross, and Eran Halperin. 2016. "Social-Psychological Interventions for Intergroup Reconciliation: An Emotion Regulation Perspective." *Psychological Inquiry* 27, no. 2: 73–88.

Cialdini, Robert B., Donald J. Baumann, and Douglas T. Kenrick. 1981. "Insights from Sadness: A Three-Step Model of the Development of Altrism as Hedonism." *Developmental Review* 1: 207–223.

Cialdini, Robert B., Betty Lee Darby, and Joyce E. Vincent. 1973. "Transgression and Altruism: A Case for Hedonism." *Journal of Experimental Social Psychology* 9, no. 6: 502–516.

Cialdini, Robert B., and Jim Fultz. 1990. "Interpreting the Negative Mood-Helping Literature via 'Mega'-Analysis: A Contrary View." *Psychological Bulletin* 107, no. 2: 210–214.

Cialdini, Robert B., and Douglas T. Kenrick. 1976. "Altruism as Hedonism: A Social Development Perspective on the Relationship of Negative Mood State and Helping." *Journal of Personality and Social Psychology* 34, no. 5: 907–914.

Clore, G. L., Gasper, K., & Garvin, E. (2001). Affect as information. In *Handbook of Affect and Social Cognition*, edited by J. P. Forgas, 121–144. Mahwah, NJ.: Lawrence Erlbaum Associates.

Clore, Gerald L., and Andrew Ortony. 2013. "Psychological Construction in the OCC Model of Emotion." *Emotion Review* 5: 335–343.

Clore, Gerald L., and Maya Tamir. 2002. "Affect as Embodied Information." *Psychological Inquiry* 13, no. 1: 37–45.

Cohen, Dov, Richard E. Nisbett, Brian F. Bowdle, and Norbert Schwarz. 1996. "Insult, Aggression, and the Southern Culture of Honor: An 'Experimental Ethnography.'" *Journal of Personality and Social Psychology* 70, no. 5: 945–960.

Cohen, Dov, Richard E. Nisbett, Brian. 1994. "Self-Protection and the Culture of Honor: Explaining Southern Violence." *Personality and Social Psychology Bulletin* 20, no. 5: 551–567.

Cox, T. 1980. "Repetitive Work." In *Current Concerns in Occupational Stress,* edited by Cary L. Cooper and Roy Payne. London, UK: Wiley.

Cummings, Mary L., Fei Gao, and Kris M. Thornburg. 2016. "Boredom in the Workplace: A New Look at an Old Problem." *Human Factors* 58, no. 2: 279–300.

Cunningham, Michael R., Jeff Steinberg, and Rita Grev. 1980. "Wanting to and Having to Help: Separate Motivations for Positive Mood and Guilt-Induced Helping." *Journal of Personality and Social Psychology* 38, no. 2: 181–192.

Dal Mas, Dennis E., and Bianca C. Wittmann. 2017. "Avoiding Boredom: Caudate and Insula Activity Reflects Boredom-Elicited Purchase Bias." *Cortex* 92: 57–69.

Danckert, James, and Colleen Merrifield. 2018. "Boredom, Sustained Attention and the Default Mode Network." *Experimental Brain Research* 236, no. 9: 2507–2518.

Eastwood, John D., Alexandra Frischen, Mark J. Fenske, and Daniel Smilek. 2012. "The Unengaged Mind: Defining Boredom in Terms of Attention." *Perspectives on Psychological Science* 7, no. 5: 482–495.

Elpidorou, Andreas. 2017. "The Moral Dimensions of Boredom: A Call for Research." *Review of General Psychology* 21, no. 1: 30–48.

Faturechi, Robert, Megan Rose and T. Christian Miller. 2019. "Years of Warnings, then Death and Disaster. How the Navy Failed its Sailors." *ProPublica.* Accessed November 30, 2020: https://features.propublica.org/navy-accidents/us-navy-crash es-japan-cause-mccain/

Ferguson, Fiona, and Sonya McLean. 2019. "Teen Pointed Gun at Passing Cars from M50 Bridge 'Was Bored and Messing.'" *Echo.* Accessed November 30, 2020: http://www.echo.ie/tallaght/article/teen-pointed-gun-at-passing-cars-from-m50-br idge-was-bored-and-messing

Festinger, Leon, and James M. Carlsmith. 1959. "Cognitive Consequences of Forced Compliance." *The Journal of Abnormal and Social Psychology* 58, no. 2: 203–210.

Fisher, Cynthia D. 1993. "Boredom at Work: A Neglected Concept." *Human Relations* 46: 395–417.

Fisher, Cynthia D. 1998. "Effects of External and Internal Interruptions on Boredom at Work: Two Studies." *Journal of Organizational Behavior* 19: 503–522.

Ford, Brett Q., Matthew Feinberg, Phoebe Lam, Iris B. Mauss, and Oliver P. John. 2018. "Using Reappraisal to Regulate Negative Emotion After the 2016 US Presidential Election: Does Emotion Regulation Trump Political Action?." *Journal of Personality and Social Psychology* 117, no. 5: 998.

Gasper, Karen. 2018. "Utilizing Neutral Affective States in Research: Theory, Assessment, and Recommendations." *Emotion Review* 10, no. 3: 255–266.

Gasper, Karen, Lauren A. Spencer, and Danfei Hu. 2019. "Does Neutral Affect Exist? How Challenging Three Beliefs About Neutral Affect Can Advance Affective Research." *Frontiers in Psychology* 10: 2476.

Gendron, Maria, Debi Roberson, Jacoba Marieta van der Vyver, and Lisa Feldman Barrett. 2014a. "Cultural Relativity in Perceiving Emotion from Vocalizations." *Psychological Science,* no. 25: 911–920.

Gendron, Maria, Debi Roberson, Jacoba Marietta van der Vyver, and Lisa Feldman Barrett. 2014b. "Perceptions of Emotion from Facial Expressions are not Culturally Universal: Evidence From a Remote Culture." *Emotion* 14, no.2: 251–264.

Gross, James J. 2014. "Emotion Regulation: Conceptual and Empirical Foundations." In *Handbook of Emotion Regulation*, edited by James J. Gross, 3–20. New York: The Guilford Press.

Goetz, Thomas, Anne C. Frenzel, Nathan C. Hall, Ulrike E. Nett, Reinhard Pekrun, and Anastasiya A. Lipnevich. 2014. "Types of Boredom: An Experience Sampling Approach." *Motivation and Emotion* 38, no. 3: 401–419.

Goetz, Thomas, Anne C. Frenzel, Reinhard Pekrun, and Nathan C. Hall. 2006. "The Domain Specificity of Academic Emotional Experiences." *The Journal of Experimental Education* 75, no. 1: 5–29.

Haidt, Jonathan. 2001. "The Emotional Dog and its Rational Tail: A Social Intuitionist Approach to Moral Judgment." *Psychological Review* 108, no. 4: 814–834.

Haidt, Jonathan, Fredrik Bjorklund, and Scott Murphy. 2000. "Moral Dumbfounding: When Intuition Finds no Reason." Unpublished manuscript, University of Virginia: 191–221.

Havermans, Remco C., Linda Vancleef, Antonis Kalamatianos, and Chantal Nederkoorn. 2015. "Eating and Inflicting Pain out of Boredom." *Appetite 85*: 52–57.

Hepach, Robert, Amrisha Vaish, Tobias Grossmann, and Michael Tomasello. 2016. "Young Children Want to See Others Get the Help They Ned." *Child Development* 87, no. 6: 1703–1714.

Hepach, Robert, Amrisha Vaish, and Michael Tomasello. 2012. "Young Children are Intrinsically Motivated to See Others Helped." *Psychological Science* 23, no. 9: 967–972. https://doi.org/10.1177/0956797612440571

Hulleman, Chris S., Olga Godes, Bryan L. Hendricks, and Judith M. Harackiewicz. 2010. "Enhancing Interest and Performance With a Utility Value Intervention." *Journal of Educational Psychology* 102, no. 4: 880.

Hume, David. 1896. *A Treatise of Human Nature.* Oxford: Clarendon Press.

Isen, Alice M., and Paula F. Levin. 1972. "Effect of Feeling Good on Helping: Cookies and Kindness." *Journal of Personality and Social Psychology* 21, no. 3: 384–388.

Iyer, Aarti, Toni Schmader, and Brian Lickel. 2007. "Why Individuals Protest the Perceived Transgressions of Their Country: The Role of Anger, Shame, and Guilt." *Personality and Social Psychology Bulletin* 33, no.4: 572–587.

Kapoor, Komal, Karthik Subbian, Jaideep Srivastava, and Paul Schrater. 2015. "Just in Time Recommendations: Modeling the Dynamics of Boredom in Activity Streams." In *Proceedings of the Eighth ACM International Conference on Web Search and Data Mining*, 233–242. New York, NY: ACM.

Kohlberg, Lawrence. 1964. "Development of Moral Character and Moral Ideology." *Review of Child Development Research* 1: 383–431.

Kohlberg, Lawrence. 1976. "Moral Stages and Moralization: The Cognitive-Developmental." In *Moral Development and Behavior: Theory, Research and Social Issues*, edited by Thomas Lickona, 31–53. New York: Holt, Rinehart & Winston.

Lindquist, Kristen A., Tor D. Wager, Hedy Kober, Eliza Bliss-Moreau, and Lisa Feldman Barrett. 2012. "The Brain Basis of Emotion: A Meta-Analytic Review." *The Behavioral and Brain Sciences 35*, no. 3: 121–143.

Locke, Edwin A., and Gary P. Latham. 1990. *A Theory of Goal Setting and Task Performance.* Englewood Cliffs, NJ: Prentice.

Lotz, Sebastian, Tyler G. Okimoto, Thomas Schlösser, and Detlef Fetchenhauer. 2011. "Punitive Versus Compensatory Reactions to Injustice: Emotional Antecedents to Third-Party Interventions." *Journal of Experimental Social Psychology* 47: 477–480.

Lyubomirsky, Sonja, Laura King, and Ed Diener. 2005. "The Benefits of Frequent Positive Affect: Does Happiness Lead to Success?." *Psychological Bulletin* 131, no.6: 803–855.

Milyavskaya, Marina, Michael Inzlicht, Travis Johnson, and Michael J. Larson. 2019. "Reward Sensitivity Following Boredom and Cognitive Effort: A High-Powered Neurophysiological Investigation." *Neuropsychologia* 123: 159–168.

Montada, Leo, and Angela Schneider. 1989. "Justice and Emotional Reactions to the Disadvantaged." *Social Justice Research* 3: 313–344.

Moynihan, Andrew B., Wijnand A.P. van Tilburg, Eric R. Igou, Arnaud Wisman, Alan E. Donnelly, and Jessie B. Mulcaire. 2015. "Eaten Up by Boredom: Consuming Food to Escape Awareness of the Bored Self." *Frontiers in Psychology* 6: 369.

Nederkoorn, Chantal, Linda Vancleef, Alexandra Wilkenhöner, Laurence Claes, and Remco C. Havermans. 2016. "Self-Inflicted Pain Out of Boredom." *Psychiatry Research* 237: 127–132.

Nichols, Shaun. 2002. "Norms With Feeling: Towards a Psychological Account of Moral Judgment." *Cognition* 84, no. 2: 221–236.

Nichols, Shaun. 2004. *Sentimental Rules.* Oxford: Oxford University Press.

O'Malley, Michael N., and Lester Andrews. 1983. "The Effect of Mood and Incentives on Helping: Are There Some Things Money Can't Buy?" *Motivation and Emotion* 7: 179–189.

Ortony, Andrew, Gerald L. Clore, and Allan Collins. 1988. *The Cognitive Structure of Emotions.* New York: Cambridge University Press.

Pekrun, Reinhard, Andrew J. Elliot, and Markus A. Maier. 2006. "Achievement Goals and Discrete Achievement Emotions: A Theoretical Model and Prospective Test." *Journal of Educational Psychology* 98, no. 3: 583–597.

Peters, Ellen, Daniel Västfjäll, Tommy Gärling, and Paul Slovic. 2006. "Affect and Decision Making: A "Hot" Topic." *Journal of Behavioral Decision Making* 19, no. 2: 79–85.

Pfattheicher, Stefan, Ljiljana B. Lazarević, Erin C. Westgate, and Simon Schindler. 2020. "On the Relation of Boredom and Sadistic Aggression." *Journal of Personality and Social Psychology.* Advance online publication. https://doi.org/10 .1037/pspi0000335.

Piaget, Jean. 1960. "Problems of the Social Psychology of Childhood." In *Sociological Studies*, edited by Leslie Smith, translated by Terence Brown, 287–318. London: Routledge.

Piester, Hannah E., Christine M. DeRieux, Jane Tucker, Nicholas R. Buttrick, James N. Galloway, and Timothy D. Wilson. 2020. "'I'll Try the Veggie Burger': Increasing Purchases of Sustainable Foods with Information about Sustainability and Taste." *Appetite* 155: 104842.

Prinz, Jesse. 2006. "The Emotional Basis of Moral Judgments." *Philosophical Explorations* 9, no. 1: 29–43.

Prinz, Jesse. 2007. *The Emotional Construction of Morals.* Oxford: Oxford University Press.

Prinz, Jesse, and Shaun Nichols. 2010. "Moral Emotions". In *The Moral Psychology Handbook,* edited by John M. Doris, 111–146. Oxford: Oxford University Press.

Rand, David G., Alexander Peysakhovich, Gordon T. Kraft-Todd, George E. Newman, Owen Wurzbacher, Martin A. Nowak, and Joshua D. Greene. 2014. "Social Heuristics Shape Intuitive Cooperation." *Nature Communications* 5, no. 1: 1–12.

Sansone, Carol, Charlene Weir, Lora Harpster, and Carolyn Morgan. 1992. "Once a Boring Task Always a Boring Task? Interest as a Self-Regulatory Mechanism." *Journal of Personality and Social Psychology* 63: 379–390.

Siegel, Erika H., Molly K. Sands, Wim Van den Noortgate, Paul Condon, Yale Chang, Jennifer Dy, Karen S. Quigley, and Lisa Feldman Barrett. 2018. "Emotion Fingerprints or Emotion Populations? A Meta-Analytic Investigation of Autonomic Features of Emotion Categories." *Psychological Bulletin* 144, no. 4: 343–393.

Silvia, Paul J. 2005. "What Is Interesting? Exploring the Appraisal Structure of Interest." *Emotion* 5, no. 1: 89–102.

Simmons, Joseph P., Leif D. Nelson, and Uri Simonsohn. 2013. "Life After P-Hacking." Paper Presented at the Society for Personality and Social Psychology, New Orleans, LA. Retrieved from http://ssrn.com/abstract=2205186

Smith, Adam. 1976. *The Glasgow Edition of the Works and Correspondence of Adam Smith: I: The Theory of Moral Sentiments,* edited by David D. Raphael and Alec L. Macfie. Oxford: Oxford University Press.

Steinberger, Fabius, Ronald Schroeter, and Christopher N. Watling. 2017. "From Road Distraction to Safe Driving: Evaluating the Effects of Boredom and Gamification on Driving Behaviour, Physiological Arousal, and Subjective Experience." *Computers in Human Behavior* 75: 714–726.

Storbeck, Justin, and Gerald L. Clore. 2008. "Affective Arousal as Information: How Affective Arousal Influences Judgments, Learning, and Memory." *Social and Personality Psychology Compass* 2, no. 5: 1824–1843.

Tamir, Maya, and Brett Q. Ford. 2012. "When Feeling Bad is Expected to Be Good: Emotion Regulation and Outcome Expectancies in Social Conflicts." *Emotion* 12, no. 4: 807–816.

Van Doorn, Janne, Marcel Zeelenberg, and Seger M. Breugelmans. 2014. "Anger and Prosocial Behavior." *Emotion Review* 6, no. 3: 261–268.

Van Tilburg, Wijnand AP, and Eric R. Igou. 2011. "On Boredom and Social Identity: A Pragmatic Meaning-Regulation Approach." *Personality and Social Psychology Bulletin* 37, no. 12: 1679–1691.

Van Tilburg, Wijnand AP, and Eric R. Igou. 2012. "On Boredom: Lack of Challenge and Meaning as Distinct Boredom Experiences." *Motivation and Emotion* 36, no. 2: 181–194.

Van Tilburg, Wijnand AP, and Eric R. Igou. 2017. "Boredom Begs to Differ: Differentiation From Other Negative Emotions." *Emotion* 17, no. 2: 309–322.

Van Tilburg, Wijnand AP, and Eric R. Igou. 2016. "Going to Political Extremes in Response to Boreom." *European Journal of Social Psychology* 46, no. 6: 687–699.

Van Tilburg, Wijnand AP, and Eric R. Igou. 2017. "Can Boredom Help? Increased Prosocial Intentions in Response to Boredom." *Self and Identity* 16, no. 1: 82–96.

Van Tilburg, Wijnand AP, Eric R. Igou, Paul J. Maher, Andrew B. Moynihan, and Dwn G. Martin. 2019. "Bored like Hell: Religiosity Reduces Boredom and Tempers the Quest for Meaning." *Emotion* 19, no. 2: 255–269.

Vitaglione, Guy D., and Mark A. Barnett. 2003. "Assessing a New Dimension of Empathy: Empathic Anger as a Predictor of Helping and Punishing Desires." *Motivation and Emotion* 27, no. 4: 301–325.

Westgate, Erin C. 2020. "Why Boredom is Interesting." *Current Directions in Psychological Science* 29, no. 1: 33–40.

Westgate, Erin C., and Catherine Fairbairn. 2020. "Buzzed, But Not Bored: How Boredom Leads to "Bad" Behavior." Unpublished manuscript.

Westgate, E. C., & Steidle, B. (2020). Lost by definition: Why boredom matters for psychology and society. *Social and Personality Psychology Compass* 14, no. 11: e12562.

Westgate, Erin C., and Timothy D. Wilson. 2018. "Boring Thoughts and Bored Minds: The MAC Model of Boredom and Cognitive Engagement." *Psychological Review* 125, no. 5: 689–713.

Weyant, James M. 1978. "Effects of Mood States, Costs, and Benefits on Helping." *Journal of Personality and Social Psychology* 36, no. 10: 1169–1176.

Weybright, Elizabeth H., Linda L. Caldwell, Nilam Ram, Edward A. Smith, and Lisa Wegner. 2015. "Boredom Prone or Nothing to Do? Distinguishing Between State and Trait Leisure Boredom and Its Association with Substance Use in South African Adolescents." *Leisure Sciences* 37, no. 4: 311–331.

Wilson, Timothy D., David A. Reinhard, Erin C. Westgate, Daniel T. Gilbert, Nicole Ellerbeck, Cheryl Hahn, Casey L. Brown, and Adi Shaked. 2014. "Just Think: The Challenges of the Disengaged Mind." *Science* 345 (6192): 75–77.

Yucel, Meltem, Robert Hepach, and Amrisha Vaish. 2020. "Young Children and Adults Show Differential Arousal to Moral and Conventional Transgressions." *Frontiers in Psychology* 11: 548.

Yucel, Meltem, Nicholas Buttrick, and Erin C. Westgate. Unpublished data. "Gossip-as-entertainment: Bored People Gossip More."

Chapter 2

The Existential Sting of Boredom

Implications for Moral Judgments and Behavior

Eric R. Igou and Wijnand A. P. van Tilburg

Kevin was ten years old. He was in his room, not knowing what to do, and his friends were busy. It was raining. His dad was far away, his mother was out shopping, and the TV offered only a rerun of a cheesy soap opera, a cartoon from the 1960s, and part 13 of a mathematics seminar for long-distance learners. There was also nothing exciting on the radio; too many love songs and something about Camp David. Boredom crept up inside of him. It was a taunting experience, and he did not know how to address this pain. Then, he saw the family's pet, a cat, on the sofa, peacefully licking its fur. Kevin approached the cat. Complete the story yourself. What would Kevin do? Would Kevin pet the cat? Would he pick on the cat? Would he get the small ball and encourage the cat to play with him? Any form of engagement, positive or negative, is possible, while some form of engagement might be more likely than another, depending on the specific situation, Kevin's personality, and his relationship with the pet. That is, the particular behavior depends on a set of variables. Yet, any of these behaviors would be directed at reducing the taunting experience of boredom and the meaninglessness it produces. Boredom can be understood as an experience that motivates change via self-regulatory processes within particular contexts.

1. INTRODUCTION

The Existential Sting

Boredom is an unpleasant affective state characterized by a negative valence and low, or perhaps mixed, arousal (e.g., Leary et al. 1986; Harris 2000;

57

Merrifield and Danckert 2014; Van Tilburg and Igou 2017a). The experience of boredom is common (Chin et al. 2017; Larson and Richards 1991) and typically arises in situations that fail to yield challenge (Csikszentmihalyi 2000; Van Tilburg and Igou 2012), stimulation (Blaszczynski et al. 1990), or interest (Sansone et al. 1992; Silvia 2006). Boredom is a state of meaninglessness (Chan et al. 2018; Van Tilburg and Igou 2012) and low levels of attention (e.g., Eastwood et al. 2012; Hunter and Eastwood 2018), motivating either withdrawal from the situation (for a review, see Moynihan, Igou, and Van Tilburg 2021) or a search process (e.g., Bench and Lench 2013, 2019) to once again perceive the situation or life in general as more meaningful (e.g., Van Tilburg and Igou 2017a).

From an existential perspective, boredom can be described as an experience inherent to human existence but not an experience humans endorse. It is an essential part of life but signals a way of living that is not desirable. It is a common experience that people either try to avoid or try to escape. It is an element of existence that motivates people to engage in behaviors that change the situation, the state of mind, or life in general (Elpidorou 2014, 2018a, 2018b, 2020; Van Tilburg and Igou 2017a, 2019).

Understanding boredom as an existential threat is not new. This perspective is prominent in boredom theorizing old and new, as it can be attested by the entry on the history of Western approaches to boredom in *Internet Encyclopedia of Philosophy* (O'Brien 2018). Schopenhauer (1970 [1851], 53), to take one case, linked boredom to the pains that come with human intelligence and human needs:

> That human life must be some kind of mistake is sufficiently proved by the simple observation that man is a compound of needs which are hard to satisfy; that their satisfaction achieves nothing but a painless condition in which he is only given over to boredom; and that boredom is a direct proof that existence is in itself valueless, for boredom is nothing other than the sensation of the emptiness of existence.

Kierkegaard (1852) attributed human reproduction and culture to attempts to escape boredom. In the *Anti-Christ*, Nietzsche went one step further and attributed human and animal existence to a bored god (1895; from O'Brien 2018).

The Boredom-Aggression Link

Impacted by the profoundness of boredom in these philosophical reflections, Fromm (1955, 1968, 1973) drew links between boredom in modern societies to consumerism, drug use, and forms of aggression at individual and societal levels. Fromm (1973) argued that some people respond "productively" to a stimulus, countering boredom. He argued that people might be able to turn to stimuli and engage in meaningful activities that prevent or resolve boredom in such cases. In some cases, potential boredom or boredom experiences pose a challenge people can master. This resolution of the challenge that boredom poses is, however, limited. There are instances where people have a permanent need to expose themselves to stimuli that distract from boredom but that do not offer lasting changes, such as alcohol consumption, drug use, sexual excesses, hours-long TV watching. Perhaps an updated list of instances would include hours-long Internet browsing and relentless social media engagement via smartphones. Some people are chronically bored but manage to compensate for this experience via these mechanisms; accordingly, Fromm refers to this type as "chronic, compensated boredom." Others may be unable to compensate for these boredom experiences, which Fromm refers to as "depressed boredom."

Fromm (1973) linked boredom to aggression, arguing that people try to resolve their boredom by turning to aggressive stimuli or engaging in aggressive, sadistic, or destructive acts. One mild form of this self-regulation attempt is to focus on aggressive content in the media to increase arousal via stimulation, which he thought was achieved by TV and newspaper reports in particular. Nowadays, we might add Internet searches with aggressive content and aggressive video games to the list. More serious forms of aggression are destructive behaviors toward others or the self. In each case, from Fromm's perspective, such acts of destruction might provide stimulation, as desperate attempts to escape boredom. As for destructive behavior affecting the self, Fromm described an adolescent who threw large rocks on a roof. These would roll down, and the adolescent would try to catch them with their head, just to feel anything. These behaviors are conceptualized as attempts to escape a boring life, even to the degree that the death of others or oneself becomes acceptable to the bored individual. The literature on boredom has since provided a more detailed understanding of the association with aggression and the conditions that increase and reduce this association. Crucially, the idea that links between boredom and aggression largely reflects self-regulatory attempts, both those that succeed and those that fail, stood the test of time.

Some of the most well-documented boredom correlates are found in behaviors and sentiments related to aggression (Boyle, Richards, and Baglioni 1993; Rupp and Vodanovich 1997; Vodanovich 2003). For example, Vodanovich, Verner, and Gilbride (1991) observed a positive correlation between boredom proneness and hostility. Dahlen and colleagues (2004) consistently observed increased anger, hostility, physical and verbal aggression among people prone to feeling bored. Similarly, Van Tilburg and colleagues (2019; Study 2) found that boredom proneness predicted aggressive tendencies as measured by Buss and Perry's (1992) aggression questionnaire. Looking into more extreme forms of aggression, Pfattheicher and colleagues (2020) recently found in a series of correlational and experimental studies that boredom predicted sadistic impulses and behavior.

Why does boredom predict aggressive tendencies? Researchers suggest that aggression can result from the lack of impulse control and the need for stimulation prevalent among people who are easily bored (Leong and Schneller 1993; Rupp and Vodanovich 1997; Watt and Vodanovich 1992). Essentially, bored people may fail to control their immediate, undesirable responses and pursue possibilities for stimulation (Moynihan, Igou, and Van Tilburg 2017). Aggression thus may result from failing to restrain oneself and may also provide a source of stimulation. In a large correlational study, Dahlen and colleagues (2004) found that the well-documented association between boredom proneness and aggression can, in part, be attributed to a lack of impulse control and increased sensation-seeking among people who are prone to boredom, as evident from hierarchical regression models. Importantly, however, these authors emphasize that these two factors do not fully explain the boredom-aggression link. A substantial part of the relation between boredom proneness and aggression does *not* seem to be explained by sensation-seeking and the lack of impulse control alone. Pfattheicher et al. (2020) found that sadism increased with boredom, including for those low in dispositional sadism, and that this was partly explained by excitement *and* novelty-seeking.

2. MEANING-REGULATION HYPOTHESES OF BOREDOM

Our work on boredom was inspired by the early research on its links to aggression and the relevance of self-regulatory processes, not unlike those that Fromm (1973) outlined in explaining the link between boredom, aggression, and destructiveness. We will detail our approach (e.g., Van Tilburg and Igou 2011a, 2012, 2017a, 2019) and its potential to explain further the links between boredom and moral judgment and behavior. Specifically, we will present three types of meaning-regulation processes: *meaning enhancement* via a search for meaning, *meaning protection* via existential escape, and *meaning as a resource* via infusions of meaning that serve as a buffer. The first type, *meaning enhancement*, is characterized by a search for meaning in order to reestablish a sense of meaning in life. In searching for sources of meaning in life, this regulatory process compensates (e.g., Heine et al. 2006) for the meaning-threatening potential of boredom (e.g., Van Tilburg and Igou 2011a, 2012, 2016, 2017b; Van Tilburg, Igou, and Sedikides 2013). The second type, *meaning protection*, is characterized by a withdrawal from the existential conflict, that is, the threat to the meaning system posed by boredom. This regressive tendency is referred to as "existential escape" (Moynihan et al. 2015; Moynihan et al. 2017, 2021a, 2021b). The third type, *meaning as a resource*, is characterized by meaning sources' capacity to buffer against boredom and its inherent meaninglessness (Igou et al. 2021; Van Tilburg et al. 2019). We argue that boredom's relationships to morality and immorality largely run through these processes and can be identified by acts of pro- and antisocial behaviors.

3. ENHANCEMENT VIA SEARCH FOR MEANING: AGGRESSION AND HELPING

Boredom has been shown to spur attempts aimed at *overcoming* the void of meaninglessness. As expressed by Barbalet (1999), "boredom emotionally registers an absence of meaning and leads the actor in question towards meaning" (631). This assessment is broadly consistent with Schubert's (1977, 1978) notion that boredom can steer people toward creative engagement. Similarly, Vodanovich and Kass (1990) contended that boredom sparks the "search for change and variety, thereby exposing themselves to new ideas and environments" (121). Thus, boredom is not only a chore but also a resource as it triggers self-regulatory processes (e.g., Elpidorou 2018b) that potentially restore meaning. Consistently, self-regulatory processes instigated by boredom that serve meaning enhancement have been documented for various judgments and behaviors, including social identity, political polarization, and nostalgia (Van Tilburg and Igou 2011a, 2012, 2016; Van Tilburg et al. 2013).

Aggression as a Meaning Source

Aggression is in part related to the pursuit or defense of a sense of meaningfulness in one's life and activities in the face of factors that challenge life's meaningfulness (McGregor et al. 1998), for example, in forms of hostility, anger, or derogation directed at members of out-groups that challenge one's worldviews (Greenberg, Pyszczynski, and Solomon 1997; Van Tilburg and Igou 2011b). Essentially, the behaviors that contribute to people's perceived meaning in life and those that can be deemed aggressive partly overlap, for example, in the case of out-group derogation and racism. Thus, aggressive behaviors may partly reflect the outcome of a self-regulatory process to attain a sense of meaning in life. Consistent with these findings, we examined whether aggression would be partly based on boredom due to people's central need to perceive life as meaningful (Van Tilburg et al. 2019). Two hundred and fifty-two participants filled in a paper-and-pencil questionnaire. We measured boredom proneness (Farmer and Sundberg 1986; see also Vodanovich and Kass 1990). We assessed meaning in life using the Meaning in Life Questionnaire (Steger et al. 2006), which contains five items assessing the search for meaning in life. Finally, we measured aggression using Buss and Perry's (1992) aggression questionnaire. We found a significant indirect association between boredom and aggressive tendencies via search for meaning in life. Consistent with our findings, the recent study on boredom and sadism (Pfattheicher et al. 2020) found that novelty-seeking, arguably a psychologically close cousin of meaning search (Steger et al. 2008), partly explained the effects of boredom and this form of aggression.

Further supporting the notion that boredom is linked to aggressive behavior through an existential route, we found that boredom bolsters intergroup bias and, in particular, the positive assessments of one's in-group at the cost of an out-group and its members (Van Tilburg and Igou 2012). Specifically, we found that boredom caused Irish participants to recommend harsher sentences to an Englishman prosecuted for a violent attack on a fellow Irish person. Swapping the perpetrator and the victor's roles, we found that boredom instead *reduced* sentencing when the aggressor, but not the victim, belonged to one's group. Furthermore, we found that this social identity process was mediated by the elevated search for meaning under boredom.

Helping as a Meaning Source

Strikingly, boredom's relationship to social behavior is more complicated and interesting than some might think. In particular, it can also facilitate aggression's seeming opposite: helping others. Helping others is arguably one of the most potent and universal sources of meaning (e.g., Furrow, King, and White 2004; Shek, Ma, and Cheung 1994). Consistent with our reasoning that bored people strive for meaning in life, we found that boredom can increase the readiness to help other people, especially if helping seems useful and meaningful in the eyes of the bored person (Van Tilburg and Igou 2017b). Specifically, in two studies, we examined whether boredom increases intentions to help others if the corresponding prosocial behavior is seen as purposeful. As predicted, boredom promoted intentions to help. Further, we found that this boredom effect was more substantial when the helping behavior was functional and thus meaningful. Therefore, we concluded that boredom would promote helping if the helping behavior was instrumental in helping to succeed.

Further, on the link of boredom to helping, we investigated whether boredom was positively associated with evaluations of people very well known for helping others, namely, heroes. Essentially, heroes are actors that help others in a self-sacrificing way (Kinsella, Ritchie, and Igou 2015). Through these rather unconventional and extreme forms of helping, heroes are sources of meaning to others (Kinsella, Igou, and Ritchie 2019). Consistent with this reasoning, we found that boredom proneness predicted positive evaluations of heroes (e.g., Dr. Martin Luther King) through searching for meaning in life (Coughlan et al. 2019). Additionally, we found that these evaluations of positive heroes increased meaning in life, which, in turn, predicted lower levels of boredom.

How can boredom be associated with both pro- *and* antisocial behaviors? What might integrate these two seemingly contradictory findings on aggression and helping? Despite their superficial differences, both behaviors potentially enhance a sense of meaning. So it seems that boredom does not promote anti- or prosocial behaviors merely for its own sake but rather encourages these responses when they promise a path toward meaningful engagement— for better or worse. Although pro-social behavior is generally more desirable for society than antisocial behavior, boredom may thus promote either activity on account of its perceived instrumentality for reviving meaning (e.g., Van Tilburg and Igou 2011a, 2013).

Implications for Morality

Judgments and behaviors that reflect pro-social engagement and those that reflect antisocial engagement may both follow from boredom. Bored people seek sources of meaning, and these can either facilitate anti- or pro-social engagement, depending on the behavioral function within the contextual constraints. Extending this to morality in general, we can thus anticipate that boredom, an unpleasant emotion, might commit people to moral judgments and behaviors, if, within a particular context, these actions are perceived as meaningful. For moral judgments and behaviors to increase under boredom, it is thus important that people perceive moral engagement not as an end but as a means to overcome the meaning threat posed by boredom.

Further, if immoral judgments and behavior did not serve meaning in life and more meaningful moral alternatives were present, boredom would unlikely promote immorality. Finally, if moral behavior were seen as more feasible in achieving meaning in life than immoral behavior, it would also increase moral over immoral engagement. In essence, boredom increases the need for meaning. Thus, it can be seen as a catalyst of either moral or immoral engagement, depending on how much any judgments or behaviors represent sources of meaning and how easily they can be pursued. This process characterizes bored people as a more or less pragmatic or even rational being, weighing self-regulatory options such that those chosen have the most significant potential of serving as sources of meaning (e.g., Van Tilburg and Igou 2013). However, this is not the only way to conceptualize bored individuals. Rather than weighing sources of meaning for pursuing those that are most promising, bored individuals might regulate meaning by escaping the threats to the meaning system—rather quickly, yet still effective in the short term.

4. PROTECTION VIA EXISTENTIAL ESCAPES: FOOD, SEX, AND IMPULSIVITY

Meaning enhancement is limited to the availability of meaning sources in particular contexts and the capacity to engage in such a self-regulatory process (e.g., Moynihan et al. 2021a; Van Tilburg and Igou 2019). An alternative, rudimentary, regressive process, one referred to as "pre-symbolic"—implying the absence of any cultural or social context—describes how people disengage from the situation they experience as threatening (e.g., Moynihan et al. 2021a). This process resembles basic coping strategies of withdrawal and distraction (e.g., Carver, Scheier, and Weintraub 1989) and escapes from the self (Baumeister 1991). Wisman (2006) reasons that turning to sources that reduce attention to the existential conflict protects the self. These regressive self-regulatory strategies are functional response options that typically involve basic, biological processes, such as consuming foods, alcohol, and sex (e.g., Heatherton and Baumeister 1991; Hull 1981; for an overview, see Wisman 2006 but also Fromm 1973). Building on this notion, we investigated and found that boredom increased the consumption of tempting, unhealthy (vs. healthy) foods (Moynihan et al. 2015; see also Crockett, Myhre, and Rokke 2015). Specifically, we observed this relationship in a weeklong diary study and used two experiments to manipulate boredom. Interestingly, we found an attraction to healthy foods if they were exciting in taste and appearance. Consistent with the notion that these distractive preferences indicate an escape from the self and, consequently, from the existential threat of meaninglessness under boredom, we found that these effects of boredom on food consumption were more pronounced for people with high than low objective self-awareness (Duval and Wicklund 1972; Heatherton and Baumeister 1991).

We further investigated the relationship between boredom and impulsiveness (Moynihan, Igou, and Van Tilburg 2017; see also Dahlen et al. 2004, 2005; Fahlman et al. 2011). Consistent with the notion that boredom can facilitate fast and sometimes unreasonable action to escape the unpleasant situation quickly, we found—using the Barrett Impulsiveness Scale-11 (BIS-11; Patton, Stanford, and Barratt, 1995)—that boredom was associated with impulsiveness. High impulsiveness scores using this measure have been linked to risk-taking, aggression, alcohol consumption, drug-taking, driving under the influence of alcohol, sensation-seeking, disinhibition, difficulty with executive functioning, and problems sustaining attention (e.g., Stanford et al. 1996; Stanford et al. 2009). We also found that boredom predicted impulsiveness on a behavioral task in which waiting time on several trials of the study could be cut short in exchange for reductions of additional financial rewards we offered (Moynihan, Igou, and Van Tilburg 2017). In line with our reasoning, these effects of boredom on impulsiveness were mediated by perceptions of meaninglessness. Further, we found that these patterns of results were more pronounced for people with high (vs. low) levels of self-awareness, who might suffer existential conflicts particularly intensely (Arndt et al. 1998; Kesebir and Pyszczynski 2012).

Although the literature postulates a link between boredom and risk-taking (e.g., Mercer and Eastwood 2010), another critical marker of impulsiveness, little work has examined this link at the behavioral level. We thus recently sought to investigate this relationship more closely (Kılıç, Van Tilburg, and Igou 2020). We predicted and found that state boredom was indeed associated with greater risk-taking. We found this pattern on responses to a risk inventory across financial, ethical, recreational, and health and safety domains (Blais and Weber 2006) and for preferences of risky gambles. This was mostly the case among people high in self-control, suggesting that boredom erodes their otherwise potent ability to resist temptation.

Sexual desires and behavior can be romantic, reflect caring, love for another person, and symbolically celebrate one's relationship (e.g., Muise et al. 2013). That said, this is indeed not always the case and not for everyone. Sexual experiences can also function as a quick relief of distress, especially among men (e.g., Shackelford, Schmitt, and Buss 2005). In line with the existential escape hypothesis (Wisman 2006), we thus reasoned that (heterosexual and bisexual) men would show greater interest in sex with increased boredom because this engagement could distract from the existential threat and instead provide pleasant experiences (Gana et al. 2001; Reid, Harper, and Anderson 2009). Our study's focus was on sensational and uncommitted sexual behavior (Gaither and Sellbom 2003; Simpson and Gangestad 1991). Supporting our reasoning, we found that boredom susceptibility predicted this type of sexual behavior. Moreover, we observed that this sexual behavior functioned as a coping strategy (Reid, Garos, and Carpenter, 2011).

In sum, these studies highlight the options for those who are bored to retreat or withdraw from sources of meaning. This behavior might still be useful at a general level, especially if the bored people have no sources of meaning available to which they can turn. We understand these escapes as regressive, short-term fixes that might swiftly protect the self and associated meaning systems. If, however, this type of self-regulatory process or coping is habitualized, the bored individual might become a person "on the run," rather than one dealing with the existential conflict as an opportunity to find an attachment to sources of meaning.

Implications for Morality

Given that moral judgments and behavior serve principles and values that—often—involve reflection, commitment, and perseverance (e.g., Gino et al. 2011), it is unlikely that existential escapes under boredom promote morality. The strong relationship to hedonic and risky behaviors that undermine reflection may tilt this type of self-regulation to immoral rather than moral judgments and behavior, particularly when others are objectified to serve one's needs, and even when such behaviors are detrimental to one's psychological and physical health. Thus, appealing to gut responses when facing boredom might not always be socially desirable. Only if these engagements serve their goals to reduce meaning threats and are channeled through harmless behavior for the self and others should they improve the situation for the bored self and others. For example, engaging in some form of a video game might be just fine. If these behaviors are addictive and harmful to others, they will pose a problem for the person and society.

5. MEANING AS A RESOURCE: PREVENTING BOREDOM

When and for whom is boredom and the associated meaninglessness more or less likely? We argue that a range of experiences, mindsets, and traits *buffer* against boredom experiences, their associated meaninglessness, and the consequences that normally arise from boredom. Our understanding of this process builds on the notion that strengthening perceived meaning reduces the overall severity of potential psychological threats. In agreement with such a proposal, research on cognitive dissonance demonstrated that self-affirmations lessen the threat to self-integrity that can arise from inconsistent cognitions and behavior (Steele 1988). This principle has also been demonstrated concerning an openness to potentially threatening information about one's health (e.g., Reed and Aspinwall 1998; see also Aspinwall and Taylor 1993, 1997). The self is an inherent part of one's meaning system (e.g., Heine et al. 2006). Thus, from a meaning-regulation perspective, the meaning system's boosts should reduce boredom and the associated meaninglessness.

We tested this idea by assessing and inducing gratitude (Igou et al. 2021). As predicted, we found that boredom was negatively associated with gratitude. This association was explained by the meaning in life gleaned from gratitude, and that gratitude not only boosted meaning in life and reduced boredom but also reduced search for meaning in life, a likely response to boredom. The reduction in the search process shows that it is rendered unnecessary, given the resource function that gratitude has concerning boredom. Note that these patterns of results were observed for both boredom proneness and state boredom. We conclude that gratitude as chronic character strength is likely to reduce the likelihood of boredom. Further, the same seems to be the case for gratitude as a state experience.

In other work, we found comparable results for religiosity (Van Tilburg et al. 2019), for some, a source of meaning in life (Batson and Stocks 2004; Steger and Frazier 2005). We measured whether or not people identified as religious persons. For example, in an online study, we measured participants' religiosity (vs. atheism and agnosticism) and used it to predict boredom proneness and state boredom. Independent of state or individual differences in boredom, religiosity predicted lower levels of boredom, higher levels of meaning in life, and lower levels of search for meaning in life. The regulatory process described here is consistent with the finding on boredom and assessments of heroes. Here, we found that positive evaluations of heroes predicted higher levels of meaning in life, which in turn predicted reduced boredom (Coughlan et al. 2019). This process's validity is further supported by our findings that images of nature buffer against boredom (see Igou & Van Tilburg 2019).

These studies suggest that momentary and habitual experiences that boost meaning in life are effective in reducing the chances that boredom arises. Ironically, by operating in this way, meaning sources hinder change, whether positive or negative. In that sense, gratitude and religiosity are "conservative" in preventing further change or growth for the individual. Not only do these results suggest that the likelihood of individual change is prevented, but they also suggest that individualized strategies—via boosting meaning—might prevent societal changes or conditions that breed boredom and meaninglessness for others.

Implications for Morality

The results of these studies, especially those on the effects of religiosity (Van Tilburg et al. 2019), suggest that sources of meaning, closely related to some people's moral beliefs, can reduce boredom experiences. Moral principles and values are meaningful and might thus serve as "input" to temper boredom and its less desirable consequences. However, it is also important to highlight that these processes reduce the search for meaning in life resulting from boredom. In this sense, meaning as a resource that buffers against boredom resembles a conservative process that can undermine a search-and-find process of new meaning. It is certainly a stretch to argue that meaning search fosters morality. That said, at least search for meaning can lead to personal growth (e.g., Steger et al. 2008) and increase social connectedness, which can be beneficial for others (e.g., Van Tilburg and Igou 2017).

6. CONCLUSIONS: BOREDOM, MEANING-REGULATION, AND MORALITY

Boredom is a common unpleasant experience. It occurs in unchallenging situations, when purpose appears to be lacking or where repetition prevails. The paths to and from boredom differ, and so do the relationships to judgments and behavior that we might classify as moral or immoral. Yet, we argue that nothing inherent to boredom makes it conclusively moral or immoral. Indeed, lay perceptions of boredom are not strongly associated with moral judgment and behavior (e.g., Van Tilburg and Igou 2017a). Inherent to boredom is a challenge to people's meaning system, which elicits compensatory self-regulatory efforts to this challenge. These efforts can promote, inhibit, or counteract morality.

There is little reason to believe that any of these meaning-regulatory subtypes directly and unequivocally serve moral or immoral judgments and behavior. However, the processes underlying meaning-regulation can be linked to judgments and behaviors that are more or less moral. The question is whether the particular processes differ in their typicality in serving morality.

Theoretically, *meaning enhancement* processes can be linked to both moral and immoral judgments and behavior. It depends on whether the sources of meaning serve morality or not in a particular context. For example, belongingness is a powerful source of meaning (Baumeister and Leary 1995; Heine et al. 2016). Striving for belongingness to reestablish meaning when bored might promote helping behavior in one context (e.g., Van Tilburg and Igou 2017b); however, it might promote in-group favoritism and thus unfair treatment of out-group members in another context (Van Tilburg and Igou 2011a). Practically, though, the meaning search processes could be exploited to promote morality by reinforcing meaning associated with morality and making these links salient in particular contexts. One could expect that people who are bored or who are likely to be bored engage in more of these behaviors than most other people in such situations.

Theoretically, *meaning protection* processes do not naturally and directly promote either morality or immorality. These retreat or withdrawal processes can, in principle, reduce engagement in meaning that serves immorality. Yet, we argue that prototypically meaning-regulatory processes are linked to self-distractions that are often hedonic, impulsive, and risky, which may be unrelated to (other-regarding) morality but more likely serve temptation than self-control, perhaps due to a lack of self-regulatory resources (Baumeister et al. 1998). On average, we might expect a stronger association of this meaning-regulatory process with immoral judgments and behavior than moral ones. More research is needed to examine the conditions under which this assumed link is strengthened or weakened.

Theoretically, *meaning as resource* processes can play out in different ways concerning moral judgments and behavior. At the heart of such processes is the reduction or prevention of boredom via the infusion of meaning-fulness. As per the regulatory processes highlighted in our model of boredom, meaning as resource processes likely render meaning enhancement and meaning protection unnecessary. Thus, by reducing boredom, they decrease its potential positive *and* negative consequences that follow the meaning-regulatory processes.

Infusions of meaning in life might enhance morality, in line with claims of humanistic and positive psychology (e.g., Haidt 2003). This impact might be direct, and it might be mediated via the reduction of boredom. Plausibly, by reducing the regressive existential escape processes, the typical immoral behaviors (e.g., objectifying sex, unhealthy, and risky behavior) would become less likely. However, we want to stress that reducing meaning search processes might hinder progress and long-term change. Perhaps, when life seems meaningful, this is not needed for the self. However, speculatively, its impact on questioning and reflections on meaninglessness and potential improvement for the self and perhaps others then stagnates. In that sense, this regulatory process can be characterized as conservative.

Before Good and Evil

We conceptualize boredom as a challenge. It is a relatively mild negative experience that challenges perceptions of meaning in life. Research has highlighted that boredom can have self-regulatory benefits (Elpidorou 2018a, 2018b). Our existential model of boredom is based on the assumption that human beings strive for meaning in life in the face of challenges to this super-ordinate need (e.g., Heine et al. 2006). The experience of boredom is one of these challenges.

Given that humans are essentially social, sources of meaning often relate to others and their needs. Crucially, then the question is whether boredom enhances or reduces engagement with others that serve their needs. Our answer to this question is that boredom has the potential of increasing immoral judgment and behavior. Some immorality might, in part, be under-stood as particular attempts to reduce boredom and the meaninglessness that is inherent in this experience (e.g., Fromm 1973). Boredom also has the potential of increasing morality via various meaning-regulatory processes in contexts that allow for and foster such engagements. For example, the latter is the case if, as a consequence of boredom, meaning is searched and found in engagement that serves others' needs. We would not necessarily subscribe to a generally positive view of boredom, especially concerning moral judgments and behavior. Ample evidence suggests the existence of negative, antisocial effects of boredom, which could arise through meaning search processes. Although speculative, existential escape processes predicted by boredom might facilitate rather basic processes that conflict with moral principles and values. Future research would have to examine these specific relationships more closely. Finally, we find it reasonable to suggest that moral principles, values, and behavior, which themselves operate as sources of meaning, reduce the likelihood of boredom. This hypothesis also warrants further investigation.

In 2014, Frédéric Desnard claimed that his company tried to make him resign by deliberately making him bored. Mr. Desnard sued his company because of the experienced hardship, which he referred to as a "nightmare," and an intentional "bore-out" by the company (Lichfield 2016). This event highlights how boredom can be linked to immorality when the meaningless-ness of social situations causes boredom. It also highlights the importance of contextual features contributing to the link between boredom and morality. The same is true for Kevin, to whom we referred at the beginning. Had he not been alone with profoundly dissatisfying options on TV, boredom might not have arisen in him. And we are still wondering what happened to the pet after it licked its fur.

We conclude that more research on the causes and consequences of bore-dom concerning morality and immorality is necessary and promising. We suggest and hope that our meaning-regulatory approach proves useful for such examinations.

REFERENCES

Arndt, Jamie, Jeff Greenberg, Linda Simon, Tom Pyszczynski, and Sheldon Solomon. 1998. "Terror Management and Self-Awareness: Evidence that Mortality Salience Provokes Avoidance of the Self-Focused State." *Personality and Social Psychological Bulletin* 24, no. 11: 1216–27. https://doi.org/10.1177/01461672982 411008

Aspinwall, Lisa G., and Shelley E. Taylor. 1993. "Effects of Social Comparison Direction, Threat, and Self-Esteem on Affect, Self-Evaluation, and Expected Success." *Journal of Personality and Social Psychology* 64, no. 5: 708–22. https://doi.org/10.1037/0022-3514.64.5.708

Aspinwall, Lisa G., and Shelley E. Taylor. 1997. "A Stitch in Time: Self-Regulation and Proactive Coping." *Psychological Bulletin* 121, no. 3: 417–36. https://doi.org/10.1037/0033-2909.121.3.417

Barbalet, Jack M. 1999. "Boredom and Social Meaning." *British Journal of Sociology* 50, no. 4: 631–46. https://doi.org/10.1111/j.1468-4446.1999.00631.x

Batson, C. Daniel, and Eric L. Stocks. 2004. "Religion: Its Core Psychological Functions." In *Handbook of Experimental Existential Psychology*, edited by Jeff Greenberg, Sander Leon Koole, and Thomas A. Pyszczynski, 141–55. New York, NY: Guilford Press.

Baumeister, Roy F. 1991. *Escaping the Self: Alcoholism, Spirituality, Masochism, and Other Flights from the Burden of Selfhood.* New York, NY: Basic Books.

Baumeister, Roy F., Ellen Bratslavsky, Mark Muraven, and Dianne M. Tice. 1998. "Ego Depletion: Is the Active Self a Limited Resource?" *Journal of Personality and Social Psychology* 74, no. 5: 1252–65. https://doi.org/10.1037/0022-3514.74.5.1252

Baumeister, Roy F., and Mark R. Leary. 1995. "The Need to Belong: Desire for Interpersonal Attachments as a Fundamental Human Motivation." *Psychological Bulletin* 117, no. 3: 497–529.

Bench, Shane W., and Heather C. Lench. 2013. "On the Function of Boredom." *Behavioral Sciences* 3, no. 3: 459–72. https://doi.org/10.3390/bs3030459

Bench, Shane W., and Heather C. Lench. 2019. "Boredom as a Seeking State: Boredom Prompts the Pursuit of Novel (even Negative) Experiences." *Emotion* 19, no. 2: 242–52. https://doi.org/10.1037/emo0000433

Blais, Ann-Renée, and Elke U. Weber. 2006. "A Domain-Specific Risk-Taking (DOSPERT) Scale for Adult Populations." *Judgment and Decision making* 1, no. 1: 33–47. https://ssrn.com/abstract=1301089

Buss, Arnold H., and Mark Perry. 1992. "The Aggression Questionnaire." *Journal of Personality and Social Psychology* 63, no. 3: 452–59. https://doi.org/10.1037/t00691-000

Carver, Charles S., Michael F. Scheier, and Jagdish K. Weintraub. 1989. "Assessing Coping Strategies: A Theoretically Based Approach." *Journal of Personality and Social Psychology* 56, no. 2: 267–83. https://doi.org/10.1037/0022-3514.56.2.267

Chan, Christian S., Wijnand A.P. van Tilburg, Eric R. Igou, Cyanea YS Poon, Katy Y.Y. Tam, Venus U.T. Wong, and S.K. Cheung. 2018. "Situational Meaninglessness and State Boredom: Cross-Sectional and Experience Sampling Findings." *Motivation and Emotion* 42, no. 4: 555–65. https://doi.org/10.1007/s11031-018-9693-3

Chin, Alycia, Amanda Markey, Saurabh Bhargava, Karim S. Kassam, and George Loewenstein. 2017. "Bored in the USA: Experience Sampling and Boredom in Everyday Life." *Emotion* 17, no. 2: 359–68. https://doi.org/10.1037/emo0000232

Coughlan, Gillian, Eric R. Igou, Wijnand A.P. van Tilburg, Elaine L. Kinsella, and Timothy D. Ritchie. 2019. "On Boredom and Perceptions of Heroes: A Meaning-Regulation Approach to Heroism." *Journal of Humanistic Psychology* 59, no. 4: 455–73. https://doi.org/10.1177/0022167817705281

Crockett, Amanda C., Samantha K. Myhre, and Paul D. Rokke. 2015. "Boredom Proneness and Emotion Regulation Predict Emotional Eating." *Journal of Health Psychology* 20, no. 5: 570–680. https://doi.org/10.1177/1359105315573439

Csikszentmihalyi, Mihaly. 2000. *Beyond Boredom and Anxiety: Experiencing Flow in Work and Play*. San Francisco: Jossey-Bass.

Dahlen, Eric R., Ryan C. Martin, Katie Ragan, and Myndi M. Kuhlman. 2004. "Boredom Proneness in Anger and Aggression: Effects of Impulsiveness and Sensation Seeking." *Personality and Individual Differences* 37, no. 8: 1615–27. https://doi.org/10.1016/j.paid.2004.02.016.

Dahlen, Eric R., Ryan C. Martin, Katie Ragan, and Myndi M. Kuhlman. 2005. "Driving Anger, Sensation Seeking, Impulsiveness, and Boredom Proneness in the Prediction of Unsafe Driving." *Accident Analysis and Prevention* 37, no. 2: 341–48. https://doi.org/10.1016/j.aap.2004.10.006

Danckert, James, and Colleen Merrifield. 2016. "Boredom, Sustained Attention, and the Default Mode Network." *Experimental Brain Research* 236, no. 9: 2507–18. https://doi.org/10.1007/s00221-016-4617-5

Duval, Shelley, and Robert A. Wicklund. 1972. *A Theory of Objective Self-Awareness*. New York, NY: Academic Press.

Eastwood, John D., Alexandra Frischen, Mark J. Fenske, and Daniel Smilek. 2012. "The Unengaged Mind: Defining Boredom in Terms of Attention." *Perspectives on Psychological Science* 7, no. 5: 482–95. https://doi.org/10.1177/1745691612456044

Elpidorou, Andreas. 2014. "The Bright Side of Boredom." *Frontiers in Psychology* 5: 1245. https://doi.org/10.3389/fpsyg.2014.01245

Elpidorou, Andreas. 2018a. "The Good of Boredom." *Philosophical Psychology* 31, no. 3: 323–51. https://doi.org/10.1080/09515089.2017.1346240

Elpidorou, Andreas. 2018b. "The Bored Mind Is a Guiding Mind: Toward a Regulatory Theory of Boredom." *Phenomenology and the Cognitive Sciences* 17, no. 3: 455–84. https://doi.org/10.1007/s11097-017-9515-1

Elpidorou, Andreas. 2020. "Is Boredom One or Many? A Functional Solution to the Problem of Heterogeneity." *Mind and Language*. Advance online publication. https://doi.org/10.1111/mila.12282

Fahlman, Shelley A., Kimberley B. Mercer, Peter Gaskovski, Adrienne E. Eastwood, and John D. Eastwood. 2009. "Does a Lack of Life Meaning Cause Boredom? Results from Psychometric, Longitudinal, and Experimental Analyses." *Journal of Social and Clinical Psychology* 28, no. 3: 307–40. https://doi.org/10.1521/jscp.2009.28.3.307

Farmer, Richard, and Norman D. Sundberg. 1986. "Boredom Proneness——The Development and Correlates of a New Scale." *Journal of Personality Assessment* 50, no. 1: 4–17. https://doi.org/10.1207/s15327752jpa5001_2

Fromm, Erich. 1955. *The Sane Society*. New York, NY: Rinehart.

Fromm, Erich. 1968. *The Revolution of Hope. Toward a Humanized Technology*. New York, NY: Harper & Row.

Fromm, Erich. 1973. *The Anatomy of Human Destructiveness*. New York, NY: Holt, Rinehart, & Winston.

Furrow, James L., Pamela Ebstyne King, and Krystal White. 2004. "Religion and Positive Youth Development: Identity, Meaning, and Pro-Social Concerns." *Applied Developmental Science* 8, no. 1: 17–26. https://doi.org/10.1207/S15324 80XADS0801_3

Gana, Kamel, Raphael Trouillet, Bettina Martin, and Leatitia Toffart. 2001. "The Relationship Between Boredom Proneness and Solitary Sexual Behaviors in Adults." *Social Behavior & Personality: An International Journal* 29, no. 4: 385–89. https://doi.org/10.2224/sbp.2001.29.4.385

Gaither, George A., and Martin Sellbom. 2003. "The Sexual Sensation Seeking Scale: Reliability and Validity Within a Heterosexual College Student Sample." *Journal of Personality Assessment* 81, no. 2: 157–67. https://doi.org/10.1207/S15327752JP A8102_07

Gino, Francesca, Maurice E. Schweitzer, Nicole L. Mead, and Dan Ariely. 2011. "Unable to Resist Temptation: How Self-Control Depletion Promotes Unethical Behavior." *Organizational Behavior and Human Decision Processes* 115, no. 2: 191–203. https://doi.org/10.1016/j.obhdp.2011.03.001

Greenberg, Jeff, Sheldon Solomon, and Tom Pyszczynski. 1997. "Terror Management Theory of Self-Esteem and Cultural Worldviews: Empirical Assessments and Conceptual Refinements." *Advances in Experimental Social Psychology* 29: 61–141. https://doi.org/10.1016/S0065-2601(08)60016-7

Haidt, Jonathan. 2003. "Elevation and the positive psychology of morality." In *Flourishing: Positive Psychology and the Life Well-Lived*, edited by Corey L.M. Keyes and Jonathan Haidt, 275–89. Washington, DC: American Psychological Association. https://doi.org/10.1037/10594-012

Harris, Mary B. 2000. "Correlates and Characteristics of Boredom Proneness and Boredom." *Journal of Applied Social Psychology* 30, no. 3: 576–98. https://doi.org /10.1111/j.1559-1816.2000.tb02497.x

Heatherton, Todd F., and Roy F. Baumeister. 1991. "Binge Eating as Escape from Self-Awareness." *Psychological Bulletin* 110, no. 1: 86–108. https://doi.org/10.1 037/0033-2909.110.1.86

Heine, Steven J., Travis Proulx, and Kathleen D. Vohs. 2006. "The Meaning Maintenance Model: On the Coherence of Social Motivations." *Personality and Social Psychology Review* 10, no. 2: 88–110. https://doi.org/10.1207/s15327957pspr1002_1

Hull, Jay G. 1981. "A Self-Awareness Model of the Causes and Effects of Alcohol Consumption." *Journal of Abnormal Psychology* 90, no. 6: 586–600. https://doi .org/10.1037/0021-843X.90.6.586

Hunter, Andrew, and John D. Eastwood. 2018. "Does State Boredom Cause Failures of Attention? Examining the Relations Between Trait Boredom, State Boredom, and Sustained Attention." *Experimental Brain Research* 236, no. 9: 2483–92. https://doi.org/10.1007/s00221-016-4749-7

Igou, Eric R., Muireann O'Dea, and Wijnand A.P. van Tilburg. 2021. "Preventing Boredom With Gratitude: The Role of Meaning in Life." *Manuscript under review*.

Igou, Eric R., and Wijnand A.P. van Tilburg. 2019. "A Remedy for Boredom: Natural Environments as a Psychological Resource." In *Physical Activity in*

Natural Settings: Green and Blue Exercise, edited by Aoife A. Donnelly and Tadhg E. Mac Intyre, 152–161. New York: Routledge. https://doi.org/10.4324 /9781315180144

Kesebir, Pelin, and Tom Pyszczynski. 2012. "The Role of Death in Life: Existential Aspects of Human motivation." In *The Oxford Handbook of Human Motivation,* edited by Richard M. Ryan, 43–64. Oxford: Oxford University Press. https://doi .org/10.1093/oxfordhb/9780195399820.013.0004

Kierkegaard, Søren. 1852. "The Rotation of Crops: A Venture in a Theory of Social Prudence." *Søren Kierkegaard.* https://www.sorenkierkegaard.nl/. Accessed 26 Feb 2019.

Kılıç, Ayşenur, Wijnand A.P. van Tilburg, and Eric R. Igou. 2020. "Risk-Taking Increases Under Boredom." *Journal of Behavioral Decision-Making* 33, no. 3: 257–69. https://doi.org/10.1002/bdm.2160

Kinsella, Elaine L., Eric R. Igou, and Timothy D. Ritchie. 2019. "Heroism and the Pursuit of a Meaningful Life." *Journal of Humanistic Psychology* 59, no. 4: 474–98. https://doi.org/10.1177/0022167817701002

Kinsella, Elaine L., Timothy D. Ritchie, and Eric R. Igou. 2015. "Zeroing in on Heroes: A Prototype Analysis of Hero Features." *Journal of Personality and Social Psychology* 108, no. 1: 114–27. https://doi.org/10.1037/a0038463

Larson, Reed W., and Maryse H. Richards. 1991. "Boredom in the Middle School Years: Blaming Schools Versus Blaming Students." *American Journal of Education* 99, no. 4: 418–43. https://doi.org/10.1086/443992

Leary, Mark R., Patricia A. Rogers, Robert W. Canfield, and Celine Coe. 1986. "Boredom in Interpersonal Encounters: Antecedents and Social Implications." *Journal of Personality and Social Psychology* 51, no. 5: 968–75. https://doi.org/10 .1037/0022-3514.51.5.968

Leong, Frederick T.L., and Gregory R. Schneller. 1993. "Boredom Proneness: Temperamental and Cognitive Components." *Personality and Individual Differences* 14, no. 1: 233–39. https://doi.org/10.1016/0191-8869(93)90193-7

Lichfield, John. 2016. "Frenchman Seeks £280,000 Payout After Claiming He Was 'Bored Out' of His Job." *The Independent.* https://www.independent.co.uk/news/ world/europe/frenchman-seeks-ps280-000-payout-after-claiming-he-was-bored-o ut-his-job-a7010506.html

McGregor, Holly A., Joel D. Lieberman, Jeff Greenberg, Sheldon Solomon, Jamie Arndt, Linda Simon, and Tom Pyszczynski. 1998. "Terror Management and Aggression: Evidence that Mortality Salience Motivates Aggression Against Worldview-Threatening Others." *Journal of Personality and Social Psychology* 74, no. 3: 590–605. https://doi.org/10.1037//0022-3514.74.3.590

Mercer, Kimberley B., and John D. Eastwood. 2010. "Is Boredom Associated With Problem Gambling Behaviour? It Depends on What You Mean by Boredom." *International Gambling Studies* 10, no. 1: 91–104. https://doi.org/10.1080/144597 91003754414

Merrifield, Colleen, and James Danckert. 2014. "Characterizing the Psychophysiological Signature of Boredom." *Experimental Brain Research* 232, no. 2: 481–91. https:// doi.org/10.1007/s00221-013-3755-2

Moynihan, Andrew B., Eric R. Igou, and Wijnand A.P. van Tilburg. 2021a. "Existential Escape of the Bored: A Review of Meaning-Regulation Processes Under Boredom." *European Review of Social Psychology* 32, no. 1: 161–200. https ://doi.org/10.1080/10463283.2020.1829347

Moynihan, Andrew B., Eric R. Igou, and Wijnand A.P. van Tilburg. 2021b. "Bored Stiff: The Relationship Between Meaninglessness, Sexual Sensation Seeking, and Promiscuous Attitudes via Boredom Susceptibility." *Personality and Individual Differences* 168: 110295. https://doi.org/10.1016/j.paid.2020.110295

Moynihan, Andrew B., Eric R. Igou, and Wijnand A.P. van Tilburg. 2017. "Boredom Increases Impulsiveness: A Meaning-Regulation Perspective." *Social Psychology* 48: 293–309. https://doi.org/10.1027/1864-9335/a000317

Moynihan, Andrew B., Wijnand A.P. van Tilburg, Eric R. Igou, Arnaud Wisman, Alan E. Donnelly, and Jessie B. Mulcaire. 2015. "Eaten Up by Boredom: Consuming Food to Escape Awareness of the Bored Self." *Frontiers in Psychology* 6: 369. https://doi.org/10.3389/fpsyg.2015.00369

Muise, Amy, Emily A. Impett, Aleksandr Kogan, and Serge Desmarais. 2013. "Keeping the Spark Alive: Being Motivated to Meet a Partner's Sexual Needs Sustains Sexual Desire in Long-Term Romantic Relationships." *Social Psychological and Personality Science* 4, no. 3: 267–73. https://doi.org/10.1177 /1948550612457185

O'Brien, Wendell. 2018. Boredom: A History of Western Philosophical Perspectives. In *Internet Encyclopedia of Philosophy.* https://iep.utm.edu/boredom/.

Patton, Jim H., Matthew S. Stanford, and Ernest S. Barratt. 1995. "Factor Structure of the Barrett Impulsiveness Scale." *Journal of Clinical Psychology* 51, no. 6: 768–74. https://doi.org/10.1002/1097-4679(199511)51:6<768::AID-JCLP2270 510607>3.0.CO;2-1

Pfattheicher, Stefan, Ljiljana B. Lazarević, Erin C. Westgate, and Simon Schindler. 2020. "On the Relation of Boredom and Sadistic Aggression." *Journal of Personality and Social Psychology.* Advance online publication. https://doi.org/10 .1037/pspi0000335

Reed, Mark B., and Lisa G. Aspinwall. 1998. "Self-Affirmation Reduces Biased Processing of Health-Risk Information." *Motivation and Emotion* 22, no. 2: 99–132. https://doi.org/10.1023/A:1021463221281

Reid, Rory C., Sheila Garos, and Bruce N. Carpenter. 2011. "Reliability, Validity, and Psychometric Development of the Hypersexual Behavior Inventory in an Outpatient Sample of Men." *Sexual Addiction & Compulsivity* 18, no. 1: 30–51. https://doi.org/10.1080/10720162.2011.555709

Reid, Rory C., James M. Harper, and Emily H. Anderson. 2009. "Coping Strategies Used by Hypersexual Patients to Defend Against the Painful Effects of Shame." *Clinical Psychology & Psychotherapy* 16, no. 2: 125–38. https://doi.org/10.1002/ cpp.609

Rupp, Deborah E., and Stephen J. Vodanovich. 1997. "The Role of Boredom Proneness in Self-Reported Anger and Aggression." *Journal of Social Behavior and Personality* 12, no. 4: 925–36.

Sansone, Carol, Charlene Weir, Lora Harpster, and Carolyn Morgan. 1992. "Once a Boring Task Always a Boring Task? Interest as a Self-Regulatory Strategy." *Journal of Personality and Social Psychology* 63, no. 3: 379–90. https://doi.org/10 .1037//0022-3514.63.3.379

Schopenhauer, Arthur. 1970 [1851]. *Essays and Aphorisms.* Translated by R. J. Hollingdale. London: Penguin Books.

Schubert, Daniel S. 1978. "Creativity and Dealing with Boredom." *Psychiatric Annals* 8, no. 3: 46–54. https://psycnet.apa.org/record/1980-12380-001

Schubert, Daniel S. 1977. "Boredom as an Antagonist of Creativity." *Journal of Creative Behavior* 11, no. 4: 233–40. https://doi.org/10.1002/j.2162-6057.1977 .tb00631.x

Shackelford, Todd K., David P. Schmitt, and David M. Buss. 2005. "Universal Dimensions of Human Mate Preferences." *Personality and Individual Differences* 39, no. 2: 447–58. https://doi.org/10.1016/j.paid.2005.01.023

Shek, Daniel T.L., H.K. Ma, and P.C. Cheung. 1994. "Meaning in Life and Adolescent Anti-Social and Pro-Social Behaviour in a Chinese Context." *Psychologia* 37, no. 4: 211–19.

Silvia, Paul J. 2006. *Exploring the Psychology of Interest.* New York: Oxford University Press.

Simpson, Jeffry A., and Steven W. Gangestad. 1991. "Individual Differences in Sociosexuality: Evidence for Convergent and Discriminant Validity." *Journal of Personality and Social Psychology* 60, no. 6: 870–83. https://doi.org/10.1037/0022 -3514.60.6.870.

Stanford, Matthew S., Kevin W. Greve, Jill K. Boudreaux, Charles W. Mathias, and Jennifer L. Brumbelow. 1996. "Impulsiveness and Risk-Taking Behavior: Comparison of High-School and College Students Using the Barrett Impulsiveness Scale." *Personality and Individual Differences* 21, no. 6: 1073–75. https://doi.org /10.1016/S0191-8869(96)00151-1

Stanford, Matthew S., Charles W. Mathias, Donald M. Dougherty, Sarah L. Lake, Nathaniel E. Anderson, and Jim H. Patton. 2009. "Fifty Years of the Barrett Impulsiveness Scale: An Update and Review." *Personality and Individual Differences* 47, no. 5: 385–95. https://doi.org/10.1016/j.paid.2009.04.008

Steele, Claude M. 1988. "The Psychology of Self-Affirmations: Sustaining the Integrity of the Self." In *Advances in Experimental Social Psychology, Volume 21*, edited by Leonard Berkowitz, 261–302. San Diego: Academic Press. https://doi .org/10.1016/S0065-2601(08)60229-4

Steger, Michael F., and Patricia Frazier. 2005. "Meaning in Life: One Link in the Chain From Religiousness to Well-Being." *Journal of Counseling Psychology* 52, no. 4: 574–82. https://doi.org/10.1037/0022-0167.52.4.574

Steger, Michael F., Patricia Frazier, Shigehiro Oishi, and Matthew Kaler. 2006. "The Meaning in Life Questionnaire: Assessing the Presence of and Search for Meaning in Life." *Journal of Counseling Psychology* 53, no.1: 80–93. https://doi.org/10.1 037/0022-0167.53.1.80

Steger, Michael F., Todd B. Kashdan, Brandon A. Sullivan, and Danielle Lorentz. 2008. "Understanding the Search for Meaning in Life: Personality, Cognitive

Style, and the Dynamic Between Seeking and Experiencing Meaning." *Journal of Personality* 76, no. 2: 199–228. https://doi.org/10.1111/j.1467-6494.2007.0048 4.x

Van Tilburg, Wijnand A.P., and Eric R. Igou. 2011a. "On Boredom and Scial Identity: A Pragmatic Meaning-Regulation Approach." *Personality and Social Psychology Bulletin* 37, no. 12: 1679–91. https://doi.org/10.1177/0146167211418530

Van Tilburg, Wijnand A.P., and Eric R. Igou. 2011b. "On the Meaningfulness of Existence: When Life Salience Boosts Adherence to Worldviews." *European Journal of Social Psychology* 41, no. 6: 740–50. https://doi.org/10.1002/ejsp.819

Van Tilburg, Wijnand A.P., and Eric R. Igou. 2012. "On Boredom: Lack of Challenge and Meaning as Distinct Boredom Experiences." *Motivation and Emotion* 36, no. 2: 181–94. https://doi.org/10.1007/s11031-011-9234-9

Van Tilburg, Wijnand A.P., and Eric R. Igou. 2013. "On the Meaningfulness of Behavior: An Expectancy X Value Approach." *Motivation and Emotion* 37, no. 3: 373–88. https://doi.org/10.1007/s11031-012-9316-3

Van Tilburg, Wijnand A.P., and Eric R. Igou. 2016. "Going to Political Extremes in Response to Boredom." *European Journal of Social Psychology* 46, no. 6: 687–99. https://doi.org/10.1002/ejsp.2205

Van Tilburg, Wijnand A.P., and Eric R. Igou. 2017a. "Boredom Begs to Differ: Differentiation From Other Negative Emotions." *Emotion* 17, no. 2: 309–22. https://doi.org/10.1037/emo0000233

Van Tilburg, Wijnand A.P., and Eric R. Igou. 2017b. "Can Boredom Help? Increased Pro-Social Intentions in Response to Boredom." *Self and Identity* 16, no. 1: 82–96. https://doi.org/10.1080/15298868.2016.1218925

Van Tilburg, Wijnand A.P., and Eric R. Igou. 2019. "The Unbearable Lightness of Bboredom: A Pragmatic Meaning-Regulation Hypothesis." In *Boredom Is in Your Mind: A Shared Psychological-Philosophical Approach*, edited by J. Ros Velasco, 11–35. Cham: Springer. https://doi.org/10.1007/978-3-030-26395-9

Van Tilburg, Wijnand A.P., Eric R. Igou, Paul J. Maher, and Joseph Lennon. 2019. "Various Forms of Existential Distress are Associated With Aggressive Tendencies." *Personality and Individual Differences* 144: 111–19. https://doi.org/10.1016/j.paid.2019.02.032

Van Tilburg, Wijnand A.P., Eric R. Igou, Paul J. Maher, Andrew B. Moynihan, and Dawn G. Martin. 2019. "Bored Like Hell: Religiosity Reduces Boredom and Tempers the Quest for Meaning." *Emotion* 19, no. 2: 255–69. https://doi.org/10.1037/emo0000439

Van Tilburg, Wijnand A.P., Eric R. Igou, and Constantine Sedikides. 2013. "In Search of Meaningfulness: Using Nostalgia as an Antidote to Boredom." *Emotion* 13, no. 3: 450–61. https://doi.org/10.1037/a0030442

Vodanovich, Stephen J. 2003. "Psychometric Properties of Boredom: A Review of the Literature." *Journal of Psychology* 137: 569–95. https://doi.org/10.1080/0 0223980309600636

Vodanovich, Stephen J., and Steven J. Kass. 1990. "A Factor Analytic Study of the Boredom Proneness Scale." *Journal of Personality Assessment* 55, no. 1–2: 115–23. https://doi.org/10.1080/00223891.1990.9674051

Vodanovich, Stephen J., Kathryn M. Verner, and Thomas V. Gilbride. 1991. "Boredom Proneness: Its Relationship to Positive and Negative Affect." *Psychological Reports* 69, no. 3 suppl: 1139–46. https://doi.org/10.2466/pr0.1991.69.3f.1139

Watt, John D., and Stephen J. Vodanovich. 1992. "Relationship Between Boredom Proneness and Impulsivity." *Psychological Reports* 70, no. 3: 688–690. https://doi.org/10.2466/pr0.1992.70.3.688

Wisman, Arnaud. 2006. "Digging in Terror Management Theory: To 'Use' or 'Lose' the Symbolic Self?" *Psychological Inquiry* 17, no. 4: 319–27. https://doi.org/10.1080/10478400701369468

Wisman, Arnaud, and Sander L. Koole. 2003. "Hiding in the Crowd: Can Mortality Salience Promote Affiliation With Others Who Oppose One's Worldviews?" *Journal of Personality and Social Psychology* 84, no. 3: 511–26. https://doi.org/10.1037/0022-3514.84.3.511

Chapter 3

Boredom and the Lost Self

Shane W. Bench, Heather C. Lench, Yidou Wan, Kaitlyn Kaiser, and Kenneth A. Perez

I wish I knew what to do with my life, what to do with my heart. . . . I do nothing all day, *boredom* settles in, I look at the sky so I get to feel even smaller than I already feel and my mind keeps poisoning itself uselessly—Quote often attributed to Sylvia Plath

I'm considered wise, and sometimes I see myself as knowing. Most of the time, I see myself as wanting to know. And I see myself as a very interested person. I've never been *bored* in my life.—Maya Angelou (quoted in Bloom 2009, 110)

Boredom is a negative emotion that people want to avoid feeling (Danckert et al. 2018; Damrad-Fyre and Laird 1989; Eastwood et al. 2012; Izard 1977). However, boredom is also a common experience (Chin et al. 2017), with research suggesting that the frequency with which people experience boredom may be increasing (Weybright, Schulenberg, and Caldwell 2020). Boredom appears to be distinct from other negative emotions like anger and sadness (Goldberg et al. 2011; Van Tilburg and Igou 2017) and is important for people—it can result in costly or harmful choices (e.g., Bench and Lench 2019; Havermans et al. 2015). People vary in their experiences with boredom (Bench and Lench 2013): some people are more likely to experience boredom, and others are less likely to experience boredom. In our opening quotes, Plath calls attention to the agony of long periods of boredom, and Angelou reflects on how a person who is intellectually engaged rarely experiences boredom. According to emotion theory, the emotion of boredom serves as a signal to us about our environment, motivating us and directing us to take action. Under normal circumstances, this means that boredom helps us respond appropriately to our environment (Bench and Lench 2013). But what about people who are frequently or even constantly bored? In this chapter, we explore the question: What does it mean for us, as human beings, if we are constantly and frequently bored?

1. HOW DO WE LEARN ABOUT OURSELVES?

People develop their sense of self, or self-concept, through their surroundings, experiences, and perceptions (Sebastian, Burnett, and Blakemore 2008). Carl Rogers (1959) defines self-concept as "the organized, consistent conceptual gestalt composed of characteristics of the 'I' or 'me' and the perceptions of the relationships of the 'I' or 'me' to others and to various aspects of life, together with the value attached to these perceptions" (quoted in Meador and Rogers 1984, 158). Essentially, our self-concept is an overall perception of the self, including how you see yourself (your self-image), how much value you feel you have (your self-esteem), and (controversially) who you believe you truly are (your true self; Rogers 1959).

People are not born with a self-concept, and infants must learn to differentiate themselves and others (Burns and Dobson 1984; Rochat 2004). The self-concept is constructed over time and from two primary sources: direct and reflected appraisals (Sebastian et al. 2008). Direct appraisals are our perceptions of "who we are" based on our own experiences and past life events. Reflected appraisals are the result of our beliefs about how other people perceive us. Thus, people's self-concept changes with experiences and events over the life span (McAdams and Olson 2010).

The self-concept is not developed haphazardly. The goals that people set are one of the frameworks that people reference for their self-concept, and progress toward goals is important for self-concept development (e.g., Sheldon 2014). Abstractly, a goal is a cognitive representation of a desirable target or focus. Goals can be approaching something desirable or avoiding something undesirable, and can be fluid (e.g., making progress toward earning a bachelor's degree) or static (e.g., having completed the requirements and earned a bachelor's degree). While our simplified examples may conjure images of people moving sequentially from one goal to the next, people can, and do, hold multiple goals simultaneously, with the priority of goals shifting over time and situations (Bargh 1997; Carver and Scheier 2002; Simon 1967). Goals, whether conscious or nonconscious, motivate human behavior (Aarts, Custers, and Holland 2007). People commit a great deal of time and effort into keeping their behavior aligned with their goals (Carver and Scheier 2002), and report more well-being when their daily lives are in accordance with their goals (Sheldon and Elliot 1999; Sheldon and Kasser 1995).

Goals drive the development of ourselves (Deci and Ryan 2000), shape our perceptions of ourselves (Sheldon 2014), and may themselves be integrated into our selves—research, for example, shows that people invest more effort into goals that they consider to be core to their self-concept (Burkley et al. 2015). Many theories focus on the idea that we are what we do—our actions provide feedback to us about what we value, what we want, and, as a result, who we are. Those actions are guided by our goals in the world. Indeed, some theories structure the self around goal pursuit, with goals arranged in hierarchies (Carver and Scheier 1998). As an example of a hierarchy, a person might have the goal to "succeed in life"—that would be at the top of the hierarchy—under that might be subgoals of "sustain strong family connection" and "be recognized in career." Each of those subgoals, in turn, would consist of multiple lower-level goals that contribute to attaining that subgoal, and so on, until the goals are represented in a daily form (e.g., "call my daughter today"). According to this framework, people are not actively pursuing all their goals at one point in time. Instead, they switch between goals constantly depending on their context and the opportunities they have at the moment. The goals at the top of the hierarchy are those that are more integral to the person's sense of self. In the example, sustaining strong family connections is a higher-level goal that would be integral to the sense of self, but whether or not the person calls their daughter in a given day is not as integral to the sense of self or whether or not they see themselves as succeeding at the higher-level goal. This view of the self, as oriented in action and founded in the goals that we hold, has interesting implications when we think about people who are bored.

2. WHAT DOES BOREDOM TELL US ABOUT OUR GOALS?

Goals provide a powerful connection between emotions and self-concept. Functional theories of emotion argue that emotions are adaptations that serve specific purposes (e.g., Barrett 2012; Lench et al. 2015). Emotions are reactions to specific events and are focused on said events (Eich et al. 2000; Lench, Tibbett, and Bench 2016; Verduyn, Van Mechelen, and Tuerlinckx 2011). Specifically, emotions act as indicators of the progress (or lack thereof) between the current situation and goals (e.g., Carver 2004; Carver and Scheier 1990, 2013; Frijda 1987; Lench et al. 2015). Successfully achieving goals, for example, results in happiness (Lench et al. 2011). Additionally, emotions coordinate systems (cognition, behavior, and physiology) to enable an optimal response to the specific situation that elicited the emotion (Arnold 1960; Frijda 1987; Lench, Flores, and Bench 2011). That is, emotions indicate the progress of goal pursuit, and, through coordinating responses across systems, enable individuals to progress toward the successful attainment of goals. Happiness, for example, indicates that a goal has been achieved and that the environment is conducive to more goal pursuits.

Most emotions enable people to adjust their effort toward goals, giving more effort when goals are about to fail and less effort when goals are progressing well (Carver 2004). What is not clear in these models, however, is how and why people disengage from prior goals and shift to new goals. Extreme sadness has been proposed as a reason for goal disengagement, but this would only account for instances of disengagement when a goal is irrevocably lost (e.g., Carver 2004; Lench et al. 2016). Theorists have also suggested that goal disengagement could result from goal-relevant negative affective reactions diminishing the desirability of a goal—effectively making a once desired goal undesirable (Aarts et al. 2007). For example, if a person wants to be a physician but fails an organic chemistry exam, the negative affective experience of the failed test could result in the person viewing a career as a physician as less desirable, making it less likely they will continue their pursuit. These theories are limited by only accounting for goal disengagement when there is some form of loss or goal-relevant negative affective experience, yet many goals are abandoned without loss or goal-relevant negative experience. For instance, when a person successfully attains a goal, such as earning a graduate degree, they experience a great deal of happiness. However, to continue to progress in life, they must disengage from the goal of earning a graduate degree and begin to pursue a new goal (like finding employment). Boredom provides an explanation for goal disengagement that does not require negative affective experiences related to the goal or loss.

As a functional emotion, boredom may enable goal disengagement by indicating that the emotional value of the current goal is fading, and enabling (through the coordination of systems) the pursuit of a new, different goal (Bench and Lench 2013, 2019; Elpidorou 2014). For instance, a romantic relationship may start out as highly satisfying and emotionally intensive but become less so over time. The emotion of boredom would permit other goal pursuits, such as returning to work after the honeymoon. However, boredom that is frequent or long-lasting and perceived to be boredom with the relationship itself may motivate change either by pursuing new goals with their current partner (e.g., engaging in novel activities such as going sky diving) or seeking out a new partner (e.g., checking a Tinder account). Importantly, boredom differs from a state of apathy, which is characterized by a lack of motivation for change (Marin 1990).

We hypothesized that boredom fulfills the function of goal disengagement as the intensity of other emotions decreases. The intensity of emotional reactions to events decreases over time (e.g., Frederick and Loewenstein 1999;

Gilbert et al. 2004), and the intensity of an emotional response to an emotional stimulus decreases with repeated exposures to that stimulus (Wilson and Gilbert 2008). The fading of emotional intensity with time and repetition results in boredom, which we hypothesize motivates disengaging from the no-longer-satisfying goal to pursue an alternative goal that affords greater emotional potential (Bench and Lench 2013). Boredom could motivate novel goals (i.e., completely new experiences and pursuits), or it could motivate the pursuit of affectively novel experiences (i.e., experiences that differ in affective valence from the boredom eliciting state; Bench and Lench 2019). A series of experiments found that state boredom resulted in a heightened desire for novelty and increased the likelihood that participants would choose a novel experience—even if that novel experience was more affectively negative than the boredom-inducing experience (Bench and Lench 2019).

There is also evidence that boredom, as with other emotions, coordinates systems to enable the disengagement from current goals and the pursuit of alternative goals (Bench and Lench 2013). For instance, boredom has been found to result in difficulty sustaining attention on a given task (Eastwood et al. 2012), to produce a sense of a lack of meaning (Van Tilburg and Igou 2012), and to increase a desire for novelty (Bench and Lench 2019). These outcomes enable the disengagement from a current goal and encourage the pursuit of an alternative goal. More broadly, state boredom has been found to motivate the pursuit of a variety of experiences that differ from the experience that elicited boredom, including those that are painful (Havermans et al. 2015; Wilson et al. 2014), interesting (Bryant and Zillmann 1984), meaningful (Van Tilburg and Igou 2011, 2016), and enjoyable (Havermans et al. 2015; Moynihan et al. 2015).

We view boredom—like other emotions—as an evolutionary adaptation that provides a solution to a specific problem (Lench et al. 2015). For example, if a goal is to find shelter, it would be adaptive to pursue the goal until shelter is found then pursue a new goal (e.g., food), instead of perseverating on the value of the (now found) shelter. Typically goal disengagement is an important component of successful goal pursuit—meaning that boredom is beneficial. It is important to disengage from goals and pursue alternative goals as this encourages growth, innovation, and accomplishment. As one example, state boredom has been found to result in increased creativity during problem solving (e.g., Mann and Cadman 2014). When stuck and trying to develop a solution, boredom may promote disengagement from a specific approach to the problem, making it more likely that people will attempt a novel method of problem resolution (i.e., divergent thinking; but see Haager et al. 2016 for some of the ways that task-related boredom may hinder creativity. For example, task-related boredom may decrease the number of solutions generated for a problem).

3. WHAT DOES IT MEAN WHEN WE
ARE CONSTANTLY BORED?

Boredom, then, is a functional emotion that helps people determine when to disengage from the pursuit of a particular goal and dedicate their efforts elsewhere. While we argue that boredom as a fleeting emotional state is functional and can encourage growth, this does not mean that boredom results in optimal outcomes (Lench et al. 2015). Especially if boredom is experienced constantly (or too frequently), it can be dysfunctional. Trait boredom proneness is associated with a host of negative outcomes. Behaviorally it is correlated with risk-taking (e.g., Vodanovich and Watt 2016), impulsivity (Watt and Vodanovich 1992), substance use (Gordon and Caltabiano 1996; Iso-Ahola and Crowley 1991; Wasson 1981), juvenile delinquency (Newberry and Duncan 2011), and procrastination (Blunt and Pychyl 1998). Emotionally it is correlated with deficits in emotion regulation and self-control (Isacescu and Danckert 2018), and negative affective experiences such as depression (Goldberg et al. 2011; Malkovsky et al. 2012; Mercer-Lynn, Flora, Fahlman, and Eastwood 2013; Vodanovich, Verner, and Gilbride 1991), anxiety (Fahlman et al. 2009, 2013), and anger (Dahlen et al. 2004; Fahlman et al. 2013; Rupp and Vodanovich 1997). Psychologically it is correlated with paranoia (Brotherton and Eser 2015; von Gemmingren, Sullivan, and Pomerantz 2003), conspiracist ideation (Brotherton and Eser 2015), hopelessness (Farmer and Sundberg 1986), loneliness (Farmer and Sundberg 1986), feelings of a loss of autonomy (Farmer and Sundberg 1986), valuing external over internal rewards (Vodanovich, Weddle, and Piotrowski 1997), discomfort in being present with one's self (i.e., self-actualization; McLeod and Vodanovich 1991), and with the perception of more negative possible versions of the self (Newberry and Duncan 2001).

Even more fundamentally, being constantly and frequently bored sends us a strong signal about our fit with the environment. If state boredom is a cue that a goal is no longer eliciting emotions and that we ought to disengage and pursue alternative goals, then recurrent boredom is a sign that a person is unable to find motivating or rewarding goals to pursue within their current environment. In other words, chronic or frequent boredom would signal that there is nothing in a person's world worth doing. Person-environment fit (hereafter "P-E fit") theory asserts that an environment is a good match when the requirements and opportunities available are perceived to match the person's needs, skills, and goals (van Vianen 2018). Much of the research on P-E fit centers around workplace environments, and within this context, work is perceived to be meaningful when the job offers rewards that align with the person's values and requires effort commensurate with their skills (Schnell, Hoge, and Pollet 2013). Person-job fit is associated with both satisfaction and job performance (van Vianen 2018), demonstrating how a "fitting" environment promotes meaningful and productive goal pursuit.

Conversely, P-E fit theory asserts that a perceived mismatch between a person and their environment creates stress, which must be coped with or defended against in order to avoid negative psychological, physical, or behavioral consequences (Edwards, Caplan, and Harrison 1998). Returning to the context of the workplace, people evaluate their work as having less meaning when they perceive that their aspirations, values, and skills are incompatible with their workplace's values and offerings (Zhang et al. 2013). In this way, the pursuit of meaningful goals is disrupted by person-environment incongruence, much as it is by recurring and chronic boredom. There is significant overlap between the negative correlates of trait boredom and P-E misfit: both are strongly associated with job dissatisfaction (Kass, Vodanovich, and Callender 2001; van Vianen 2018), depression (Goldberg et al. 2011; Caplan 1987), and absenteeism (Kass et al. 2001).

A perpetually bored person may wonder what it means if they cannot engage with the world. We are not claiming that the bored person necessarily reflects on their inability to engage with the world, although they might (e.g., "What's wrong with me? Everyone else seems excited about these things, and I'm just not."). Instead, we propose that the frequent experience of boredom, over time, signals there is a fundamental misfit between the values and the desires of the individual—what would cause them to feel motivated and emotional—and the environment in which they function. In other words, they constantly want something that they cannot find. In response, they may fall into a state of apathy or begin taking extreme risks to try to find something that is in line with their desires.

4. TRAIT BOREDOM AS EXISTENTIAL CRISIS AND MORAL CONUNDRUM

Ultimately, the results of long-term or frequent boredom from the disconnect between the values and the desires of the individual and their environment resemble an existential crisis. Existential crisis is an umbrella term that can be used to describe issues related to the meaning of life, authenticity, or death and illness (Center for Substance Abuse Treatment 1999; Kim et al. 2014; Yang, Staps, and Hijmans 2010). Here, we focus on the aspect of an existential crisis where a person experiences a loss of goals (Butenaite, Sondaite, and Mockus 2016) and is unable to find meaning, value, or purpose in their life (Kim et al. 2014). Wolman (1975) described people in this type of existential crisis as follows: "Most of them failed to find meaning in life. They felt they had nothing to live for, nothing to struggle for, nothing to hope for" (157). He also added that such individuals were

> unable to find any goal or direction in life. Some of them look for escape in drugs, others in alcohol, and still others in aimlessly cruising through life, wasting their best years with no accomplishments because nothing seems to be worthwhile to them. (Ibid.)

We have termed this component of an existential crisis the "lost self"—as, due to a misfit between the self (goals, values, meaning, and purpose) and the environment, a person no longer has goal pursuits essential to their self-concept and loses their self from their own life.

The loss of goals is central to the lost self as goal pursuits provide feedback to the development of the self-concept (Carver and Scheier 1998; Deci and Ryan 2000; Sheldon 2014), and people hold a goal to know their "true selves" (Sheldon 2014). The true self is the commonly held belief that the self is an innate construct that individuals must discover within themselves (Rogers 1959; Schlegel and Hicks 2011). Classically, it was considered that there is an innate set of traits and characteristics that a person must act in accord with to behave authentically, or a person's "true" self (e.g., Rogers 1959). The idea of an innate true self is appealing, and something many laypeople report believing, yet it is unlikely to be the case given both that the environment impacts the self (Schlegel and Hicks 2011) and that people change over the life span (McAdams and Olson 2010). More recent theories of the true self consider it to be an essentialist construct (Christy, Schlegel, and Cimpian 2019; Schlegel and Hicks 2011), supported by the folk belief that the true self is discovered within an individual (Bench et al. 2015; Schlegel and Hicks 2011). Paradoxically, people recognize that they change over time (Bench et al. 2015), yet report being more authentic and more like their true selves across the life span (Seto and Schlegel 2018). While it is unlikely that people have a core set of innate traits defining who they are, the true self remains an important component of the self-concept. People use their belief in their true self (i.e., their subjective feeling of who they truly are) as a guide for their values, goals, and decisions (Rivera et al. 2019).

A state of lost self could prevent people from feeling like they know their true selves, or, due to an inability to "find" the true self in the environment, a sense that the self does not have value. The lost self could indicate that the self is "bad" in a moral sense—that the self should not be considered when determining behavior and consequences. This introduces the opportunity for immoral behavior or behavior that demonstrates an inability to be responsible for one's own existence (Elpidorou 2017). We have reviewed a great deal of evidence supporting a link between the frequent experience of boredom and maladaptive behaviors (e.g., Vodanovich and Watt 2016), but there is also independent evidence that the lost self may be related to maladaptive functioning.

A state of lost self would prevent people from living their life in subjective accordance with their true self. This would result in living a life that is (subjectively) inauthentic. Research shows that living an authentic life in (subjective) accordance with your perception of your true self is correlated with a host of benefits to well-being (see Rivera et al. 2019), including self-esteem (Heppner et al. 2008), happiness (Saricam 2015), lower levels of anxiety and depression (Sheldon et al. 1997), and more satisfaction with personal relationships (Baker et al. 2017). In addition, people who subjectively live their life in accordance with their true self report being more satisfied with their lives (Reich, Kessel, and Bernieri 2013), perceive more meaning in their lives (Schlegel et al. 2011), and report more well-being (e.g., Sheldon, 2014). Additionally, people who subjectively feel like they know their true selves report better well-being (Davis et al. 2015). There is also evidence that a state of lost self is correlated with decreased motivation to pursue goals (Kim et al. 2017). These findings support the value of the self in seeking and motivating meaningful goals.

5. CONCLUSION

Boredom is a functional emotion that serves the disengagement of goals (Bench and Lench 2013). Goal disengagement is paramount for success in life, meaning that boredom in theory promotes successful goal pursuits. However, the frequent experience of boredom signals a disconnect between a person's values and desires and their surrounding environment—causing a lost self, or a state where one loses their goals, values, purpose, and direction in their own life. This state is associated with a host of negative outcomes that relate to immorality through a loss of responsibility for one's own existence (Elpidorou 2017). Importantly, we do not intend to suggest that people who are bored frequently are "bad," rather that their emotional system is signaling (through boredom) that their environment does not afford opportunities for goals that they value, and this influences behavior that can perpetuate a state of person-environment misfit.

REFERENCES

Aarts, Henk, Ruud Custers, and Rob W. Holland. 2007. "The Nonconscious Cessation of Goal Pursuit: When Goals and Negative Affect Are Coactivated."

Journal of Personality and Social Psychology 92, no. 2: 165–78. https://doi.apa
.org/doi/10.1037/0022-3514.92.2.165.

Arnold, Magda B. *Emotion and Personality.* New York, NY: Columbia University
Press, 1960.

Baker, Zachary G., Reese Y.W. Tou, Jennifer L. Bryan, and C. Raymond Knee. 2017.
"Authenticity and Well-Being: Exploring Positivity and Negativity in Interactions
as a Mediator." *Personality and Individual Differences* 113 (July): 235–39. http://
doi.org/10.1016/j.paid.2017.03.018.

Bargh, John A. 1997. "The Automaticity of Everyday Life." In *The Automaticity
of Everyday Life: Advances in Social Cognition, Vol. 10* (Advances in Social
Cognition, Vol. 10), edited by Robert S. Wyer Jr., 1–61. Mahwah, NJ: Lawrence
Erlbaum Associates Publishers.

Barrett, Lisa Feldman. 2012. "Emotions Are Real." *Emotion* 12, no. 3: 413–29. http://
doi.org/10.1037/a0027555.

Bench, Shane W., and Heather C. Lench. 2013. "On the Function of Boredom."
Behavioral Sciences 3, no. 3: 459–72. http://doi.org/10.3390/bs3030459.

Bench, Shane W., and Heather C. Lench. 2019. "Boredom as a Seeking State:
Boredom Prompts the Pursuit of Novel (Even Negative) Experiences." *Emotion* 19,
no. 2: 242–54. https://doi.apa.org/doi/10.1037/emo0000433.

Bench, Shane W., Rebecca J. Schlegel, William E. Davis, and Matthew Vess. 2015.
"Thinking about Change in the Self and Others: The Role of Self-Discovery
Metaphors and the True Self." *Social Cognition* 33, no. 3: 169–85. http://doi.org
/10.1521/soco.2015.33.3.2.

Bloom, Harrold, ed. 2009. Maya Angelou's *I Know Why the Caged Bird Sings*—New
Edition. New York: Infobase Publishing.

Blunt, Allan, and Timothy A. Pychyl. 1998. "Volitional Action and Inaction in the
Lives of Undergraduate Students: State Orientation, Procrastination and Proneness
to Boredom." *Personality and Individual Differences* 24, no. 6: 837–46. https://doi
.org/10.1016/S0191-8869(98)00018-X.

Brotherton, Robert, and Silan Eser. 2015. "Bored to Fears: Boredom Proneness,
Paranoia, and Conspiracy Theories." *Personality and Individual Differences* 80
(July): 1–5. https://doi.org/10.1016/j.paid.2015.02.011.

Bryant, Jennings, and Dolf Zillmann. 1984. "Using Television to Alleviate
Boredom and Stress: Selective Exposure as a Function of Induced Excitational
States." *Journal of Broadcasting* 28, no. 1: 1–20. http://doi.org/10.1080
/08838158409386511.

Burkley, Edward, Jessica Curtis, Melissa Burkley, and Thomas Hatvany. 2015. "Goal
Fusion: The Integration of Goals Within the Self-Concept." *Self and Identity* 14,
no. 3: 348–68. http://doi.org/10.1080/15298868.2014.1000959.

Burns, Robert B., Clifford B. Dobson, Robert B. Burns, and Clifford B. Dobson.
1984. "The Self-Concept." In *Introductory Psychology,* 473–505. Lancaster: MTP
Press Limited. https://doi.org/10.1007/978-94-011-6279-1_13.

Butenaitė, Joana, Jolanta Sondaitė, and Antanas Mockus. 2016. "Components of
Existential Crisis: A Theoretical Analysis." *International Journal of Psychology :
A Biopsychosocial Approach* 18: 9–27. http://doi.org/10.7220/2345-024X.18.1.

Caplan, Robert D. 1987. "Person-Environment Fit Theory and Organizations: Commensurate Dimensions, Time Perspectives, and Mechanisms." *Journal of Vocational Behavior* 31, no. 3: 248–67. https://doi.org/10.1016/0001 -8791(87)90042-X.

Carver, Charles S. 2004. "Negative Affects Deriving from the Behavioral Approach System." *Emotion* 4, no. 1: 3–22. https://doi.org/10.1037/1528-3542.4.1.3.

Carver, Charles S., and Michael F. Scheier. 1998. *On the Self-Regulation of Behavior. On the Self-Regulation of Behavior.* Cambridge: Cambridge University Press. https://doi.org/10.1017/CBO9781139174794.

Carver, Charles S., and Michael F. Scheier. 1990. "Origins and Functions of Positive and Negative Affect: A Control-Process View." *Psychological Review* 97, no. 1: 19–35. https://psycnet.apa.org/doi/10.1037/0033-295X.97.1.19.

Carver, Charles S., and Michael F. Scheier. 2002. "Control Processes and Self-Organization as Complementary Principles Underlying Behavior." *Personality and Social Psychology Review* 6, no. 4: 304–15. https://doi.org/10.1207%2FS153 27957PSPR0604_05.

Carver, Charles S, and Michael F Scheier. 2013. "Goals and Emotion." In *Handbook of Cognition and Emotion*, edited by Michael D. Robinson, Edward R. Watkins, and Eddie Harmon-Jones, 176–94. New York: The Guilford Press.

Center for Substance Abuse Treatment. 1999. *Brief Intervention and Brief Therapies for Substance Abuse.* Treatment Improvement Protocol (TIP) Series, Number 34. DHHS Publication No. (SMA) 99-3353. Rockville, MD: U.S. Department of Health and Human Services.

Chin, Alycia, Amanda Markey, Saurabh Bhargava, Karim S. Kassam, and George Loewenstein. 2017. "Bored in the USA: Experience Sampling and Boredom in Everyday Life." *Emotion* 17, no. 2: 359–68. http://doi.org/10.1037/emo 0000232.

Christy, Andrew G., Rebecca J. Schlegel, and Andrei Cimpian. 2019. "Why Do People Believe in a 'True Self'? The Role of Essentialist Reasoning about Personal Identity and the Self." *Journal of Personality and Social Psychology* 117, no. 2: 386–416. http://doi.org/10.1037/pspp0000254.

Dahlen, Eric R., Ryan C. Martin, Katie Ragan, and Myndi M. Kuhlman. 2004. "Boredom Proneness in Anger and Aggression: Effects of Impulsiveness and Sensation Seeking." *Personality and Individual Differences* 37, no. 8: 1615–27. https://doi.org/10.1016/j.paid.2004.02.016.

Danckert, James, Tina Hammerschmidt, Jeremy Marty-Dugas, and Daniel Smilek. 2018. "Boredom: Under-Aroused and Restless." *Consciousness and Cognition* 61 (May): 24–37. https://doi.org/10.1016/j.concog.2018.03.014.

Damrad-Frye, Robin, and James D. Laird. 1989. "The Experience of Boredom: The Role of the Self-Perception of Attention." *Journal of Personality and Social Psychology* 57, no. 2: 315–20. http://doi.org/10.1037/0022-3514.57.2.315.

Davis, William E., Joshua A. Hicks, Rebecca J. Schlegel, Christina M. Smith, and Matthew Vess. 2015. "Authenticity and Self-Esteem across Temporal Horizons." *Journal of Positive Psychology* 10, no. 2: 116–26. http://doi.org/10.1080/1743976 0.2014.910830.

Deci, Edward L., and Richard M. Ryan. 2000. "The 'What' and 'Why' of Goal Pursuits: Human Needs and the Self-Determination of Behavior." *Psychological Inquiry* 11, no. 4: 227–68. https://doi.org/10.1207/S15327965PLI1104_01.

Eastwood, John D., Alexandra Frischen, Mark J. Fenske, and Daniel Smilek. 2012. "The Unengaged Mind: Defining Boredom in Terms of Attention." *Perspectives on Psychological Science : A Journal of the Association for Psychological Science* 7, no. 5: 482–95. http://doi.org/10.1177/1745691612456044" http://doi.org/10.1177/1745691612456044.

Edwards, Jeffrey R., Robert Caplan, and R. Van Harrison. 1998. "Person-Environment Fit Theory: Conceptual Foundations, Empirical Evidence, and Directions for Future Research." In *Theories of Organizational Stress*, edited by Cary L. Cooper, 28–67. Oxford: Oxford University Press.

Eich, Eric, John F. Kihlstrom, Gordon H. Bower, Joseph P. Forgas, and Paula M. Niedenthal, eds. 2000. *Cognition and Emotion.* New York. Oxford University Press.

Elpidorou, Andreas. 2014. "The Bright Side of Boredom." *Frontiers in Psychology* 5 (NOV): 1245. http://doi.org/10.3389/fpsyg.2014.01245" http://doi.org/10.3389/fpsyg.2014.01245.

Elpidorou, Andreas. 2017. "The Moral Dimensions of Boredom: A Call for Research." *Review of General Psychology* 21, no. 1: 30–48. http://doi.org/10.1037/gpr0000098" http://doi.org/10.1037/gpr0000098.

Elpidorou, Andreas. 2020. "Is Boredom One or Many? A Functional Solution to the Problem of Heterogeneity." *Mind & Language.* Advance Online Publication. https://doi.org/10.1111/mila.12282.

Fahlman, Shelley A., Kimberley B. Mercer, Peter Gaskovski, Adrienne E. Eastwood, and John D. Eastwood. 2009. "Does a Lack of Life Meaning Cause Boredom? Results from Psychometric, Longitudinal, and Experimental Analyses." *Journal of Social and Clinical Psychology* 28, no. 3: 307–40. https://doi.org/10.1521/jscp.2009.28.3.307.

Fahlman, Shelley A., Kimberley B. Mercer-Lynn, David B. Flora, and John D. Eastwood. 2013. "Development and Validation of the Multidimensional State Boredom Scale." *Assessment* 20, no. 1: 68–85. https://doi.org/10.1177%2F1073191111421303.

Farmer, Richard, and Norman D. Sundberg. 1986. "Boredom Proneness-The Development and Correlates of a New Scale." *Journal of Personality Assessment* 50, no. 1: 4–17. https://doi.org/10.1207/s15327752jpa5001_2.

Frederick, Shane, and George Loewenstein. 1999. "Hedonic Adaptation." In *Well-Being: The Foundations of Hedonic Psychology*, edited by Daniel Kahneman, Ed Diener, and Norbert Schwarz, 302–29. New York, NY: Russell Sage Foundation Press.

Frijda, Nico H. 1987. "Emotion, Cognitive Structure, and Action Tendency." *Cognition and Emotion* 1, no. 2: 115–43. http://doi.org/10.1080/02699938708408043" http://doi.org/10.1080/02699938708408043.

Gilbert, Daniel T., Matthew D. Lieberman, Carey K. Morewedge, and Timothy D. Wilson. 2004. "The Peculiar Longevity of Things Not So Bad." *Psychological Science* 15, no. 1: 14–19. https://doi.org/10.1111/j.0963-7214.2004.01501003.x.

Goldberg, Yael K., John D. Eastwood, Jennifer Laguardia, and James Danckert. 2011. "Boredom: An Emotional Experience Distinct from Apathy, Anhedonia, or Depression." *Journal of Social and Clinical Psychology* 30, no. 6: 647–66. https://doi.org/10.1521/jscp.2011.30.6.647.

Gordon, Winsome R., and Marie L. Caltabiano. 1996. "Urban-Rural Differences in Adolescent Self-Esteem, Leisure Boredom, and Sensation-Seeking as Predictors of Leisure-Time Usage and Satisfaction." *Adolescence* 31, no. 124: 883–902.

Haager, Julia S., Christof Kuhbandner, and Reinhard Pekrun. 2016. "To be bored or not to be bored—How task-related boredom influences creative performance." *The Journal of Creative Behavior 52*, no. 4: 297–304. https://doi.org/10.1002/jocb.154.

Havermans, Remco C., Linda Vancleef, Antonis Kalamatianos, and Chantal Nederkoorn. 2015. "Eating and Inflicting Pain out of Boredom." *Appetite* 85: 52–57. http://doi.org/10.1016/j.appet.2014.11.007" http://doi.org/10.1016/j.appet.2014.11.007.

Heppner, Whitney L., Michael H. Kernis, John B. Nezlek, Joshua Foster, Chad E. Lakey, and Brian M. Goldman. 2008. "Within-Person Relationships among Daily Self-Esteem, Need Satisfaction, and Authenticity." *Psychological Science* 19, no. 11: 1140–45. http://doi.org/10.1111/j.1467-9280.2008.02215.x" http://doi.org/10.1111/j.1467-9280.2008.02215.x.

Isacescu, Julia, and James Danckert. 2018. "Exploring the Relationship between Boredom Proneness and Self-Control in Traumatic Brain Injury (TBI)." *Experimental Brain Research* 236, no. 9: 2493–505. https://doi.org/10.1007/s00221-016-4674-9.

Iso-Ahola, Seppo E., and Edward D. Crowley. 1991. "Adolescent Substance Abuse and Leisure Boredom." *Journal of Leisure Research* 23, no. 3: 260–71.

Izard, Carroll E. 1977. *Human Emotions*. Boston, MA: Springer US. http://doi.org/10.1007/978-1-4899-2209-0" http://doi.org/10.1007/978-1-4899-2209-0.

Kass, Steven J., Stephen J. Vodanovich, and Anne Callender. 2001. "State-Trait Boredom: Relationship to Absenteeism, Tenure, and Job Satisfaction." *Journal of Business and Psychology* 16, no. 2: 317–27. https://doi.org/10.1023/A:1011121503118.

Kim, Jinhyung, Andrew G. Christy, Rebecca J. Schlegel, M. Brent Donnellan, and Joshua A. Hicks. 2018. "Existential Ennui: Examining the Reciprocal Relationship Between Self-Alienation and Academic Amotivation." *Social Psychological and Personality Science* 9, no. 7: 853–62. https://doi.org/10.1177%2F1948550617727587.

Kim, Jinhyung, Elizabeth Seto, William E. Davis, and Joshua A. Hicks. 2014. "Positive and Existential Psychological Approaches to the Experience of Meaning in Life." In *Meaning in Positive and Existential Psychology*, edited by Alexander Batthyany and Pninit Russo-Netzer, 221–38. New York, NY: Springer University Press. https://doi.org/10.1007/978-1-4939-0308-5_13.

Lench, Heather C., Shane W. Bench, Kathleen E. Darbor, and Melody Moore. 2015. "A Functionalist Manifesto: Goal-Related Emotions from an Evolutionary Perspective." *Emotion Review* 7, no. 1: 90–98. http://doi.org/10.1177/1754073914553001" http://doi.org/10.1177/1754073914553001.

Lench, Heather C., Thomas P. Tibbett, and Shane W. Bench. 2016. "Exploring the Toolkit of Emotion: What Do Sadness and Anger Do for Us?" *Social and Personality Psychology Compass* 10, no. 1: 11–25. http://doi.org/10.1111/spc3 .12229" http://doi.org/10.1111/spc3.12229.

Lench, Heather C., Sarah A. Flores, and Shane W. Bench. 2011. "Discrete Emotions Predict Changes in Cognition, Judgment, Experience, Behavior, and Physiology: A Meta-Analysis of Experimental Emotion Elicitations." *Psychological Bulletin* 137, no. 5: 834–55. http://dx.doi.org/10.1037/a0024244.

Malkovsky, Ela, Colleen Merrifield, Yael Goldberg, and James Danckert. 2012. "Exploring the Relationship between Boredom and Sustained Attention." *Experimental Brain Research* 221, no. 1: 59–67. https://doi.org/10.1007/s00221 -012-3147-z.

Mann, Sandi, and Rebekah Cadman. 2014. "Does Being Bored Make Us More Creative?" *Creativity Research Journal* 26, no. 2: 165–73. https://doi.org/10.1080 /10400419.2014.901073.

Marin, Robert S. 1990. "Differential Diagnosis and Classification of Apathy." *American Journal of Psychiatry* 147, no. 1: 22–30. https://doi.org/10.1176/ajp.147.1.22.

McAdams, Dan P., and Bradley D. Olson. 2010. "Personality Development: Continuity and Change Over the Life Course." *Annual Review of Psychology* 61, no. 1: 517–42. https://doi.org/10.1146/annurev.psych.093008.100507.

McLeod, Carol R., and Stephen J. Vodanovich. 1991. "The Relationship between Self-Actualization and Boredom Proneness." *Journal of Social Behavior & Personality* 6, no. 5: 137–46.

Meador, Betty D., and Carl R. Rogers. 1984. "Person-Centered Therapy." In *Current Psychotherapies*, edited by Raymond J. Corsini, 3rd ed., 142–95. Itasca, IL: Peacock.

Mercer-Lynn, Kimberley B., David B. Flora, Shelley A. Fahlman, and John D. Eastwood. 2013. "The Measurement of Boredom: Differences between Existing Self-Report Scales." *Assessment* 20, no. 5: 585–96. https://doi.org/10.1177%2 F1073191111408229.

Moynihan, Andrew B., Wijnand A. P. van Tilburg, Eric R. Igou, Arnaud Wisman, Alan E. Donnelly, and Jessie B. Mulcaire. 2015. "Eaten up by Boredom: Consuming Food to Escape Awareness of the Bored Self." *Frontiers in Psychology* 6 (APR): 369. http://doi.org/10.3389/fpsyg.2015.00369" http://doi.org/10.3389/ fpsyg.2015.00369.

Newberry, Angela L., and Renae D. Duncan. 2001. "Roles of Boredom and Life Goals in Juvenile Delinquency1." *Journal of Applied Social Psychology* 31, no. 3: 527–41. https://doi.org/10.1111/j.1559-1816.2001.tb02054.x.

Reich, Warren A., Ellen M. Kessel, and Frank J. Bernieri. 2013. "Life Satisfaction and the Self: Structure, Content, and Function." *Journal of Happiness Studies* 14, no. 1: 293–308. https://doi.org/10.1007/s10902-012-9332-8.

Rivera, Grace N., Andrew G. Christy, Jinhyung Kim, Matthew Vess, Joshua A. Hicks, and Rebecca J. Schlegel. 2019. "Understanding the Relationship Between Perceived Authenticity and Well-Being." *Review of General Psychology* 23, no. 1: 113–26. https://doi.org/10.1037/gpr0000161.

Rochat, Phillipe. 2004. "Origins of Self-Concept." In *Blackwell Handbook of Infant Development*, edited by Gavin Bremner and Alan Fogel, 192–212. Oxford, UK: Blackwell Publishing Ltd. https://doi.org/10.1002/9780470996348.

Rogers, Carl R. 1959. "A Theory of Therapy and Personality Change: As Developed in the Client-Centered Framework." In *Psychology: A Study of a Science*, edited by Sigmund Koch, 184–256. New York, NY: Elsevier. https://doi.org/10.1016/b978-0-08-017738-0.50039-9.

Rupp, Deborah E., and Stephen J. Vodanovich. 1997. "The Role of Boredom Proneness in Self-Reported Anger and Aggression." *Journal of Social Behavior and Personality* 12, no. 4: 925–36.

Sariçam, Hakan. 2015. "Life Satisfaction: Testing a Structural Equation Model Based on Authenticity and Subjective Happiness." *Polish Psychological Bulletin* 46, no. 2: 278–84. http://doi.org/10.1515/ppb-2015-0034" http://doi.org/10.1515/ppb-2015-0034.

Schlegel, Rebecca J., and Joshua A. Hicks. 2011. "The True Self and Psychological Health: Emerging Evidence and Future Directions." *Social and Personality Psychology Compass* 5, no. 12: 989–1003. http://doi.org/10.1111/j.1751-9004.2011.00401.x" http://doi.org/10.1111/j.1751-9004.2011.00401.x.

Schlegel, Rebecca J., Joshua A. Hicks, Laura A. King, and Jamie Arndt. 2011. "Feeling like You Know Who You Are: Perceived True Self-Knowledge and Meaning in Life." *Personality & Social Psychology Bulletin* 37, no. 6: 745–56. https://doi.org/10.1177/0146167211400424.

Schnell, Tatjana, Thomas Höge, and Edith Pollet. 2013. "Predicting Meaning in Work: Theory, Data, Implications." *Journal of Positive Psychology* 8, no. 6: 543–54. https://doi.org/10.1080/17439760.2013.830763.

Sebastian, Catherine, Stephanie Burnett, and Sarah Jayne Blakemore. 2008. "Development of the Self-Concept during Adolescence." *Trends in Cognitive Sciences* 12, no. 11: 441–46. https://psycnet.apa.org/doi/10.1016/j.tics.2008.07.008.

Seto, Elizabeth, and Rebecca J. Schlegel. 2018. "Becoming Your True Self: Perceptions of Authenticity across the Lifespan." *Self and Identity* 17, no. 3: 310–26. https://doi.org/10.1080/15298868.2017.1322530.

Sheldon, Kennon M. 2014. "Becoming Oneself: The Central Role of Self-Concordant Goal Selection." *Personality and Social Psychology Review* 18, no. 4: 349–65. https://doi.org/10.1177/1088868314538549.

Sheldon, Kennon M., and Andrew J. Elliot. 1999. "Goal Striving, Need Satisfaction, and Longitudinal Well-Being: The Self-Concordance Model." *Journal of Personality and Social Psychology* 76, no. 3: 482–97. https://psycnet.apa.org/doi/10.1037/0022-3514.76.3.482.

Sheldon, Kennon M., and Tim Kasser. 1995. "Coherence and Congruence: Two Aspects of Personality Integration." *Journal of Personality and Social Psychology* 68, no. 3: 531–43. https://psycnet.apa.org/doi/10.1037/0022-3514.68.3.531.

Sheldon, Kennon M., Richard M. Ryan, Laird J. Rawsthorne, and Barbara Ilardi. 1997. "Trait Self and True Self: Cross-Role Variation in the Big-Five Personality Traits and Its Relations with Psychological Authenticity and Subjective Well-Being."

Journal of Personality and Social Psychology 73, no. 6: 1380–93. http://doi.org/10 .1037/0022-3514.73.6.1380.

Simon, Herbert A. 1967. "Motivational and Emotional Controls of Cognition." *Psychological Review* 74, no. 1: 29–39. https://psycnet.apa.org/doi/10.1037/h002 4127.

Van Tilburg, Wijnand A.P., and Eric R. Igou. 2012. "On Boredom: Lack of Challenge and Meaning as Distinct Boredom Experiences." *Motivation and Emotion* 36, no. 2: 181–94. https://doi.org/10.1007/s11031-011-9234-9.

Van Tilburg, Wijnand A.P., and Eric R. Igou. 2017. "Boredom Begs to Differ: Differentiation from Other Negative Emotions." *Emotion* 17, no. 2: 309–22. http:// doi.org/10.1037/emo0000233.

Van Vianen, Annelies E.M. 2018. "Person–Environment Fit: A Review of Its Basic Tenets." *Annual Review of Organizational Psychology and Organizational Behavior* 5, no. 1: 75–101. https://doi.org/10.1146/annurev-orgpsych-032117-104702.

Verduyn, Philippe, Iven Van Mechelen, and Francis Tuerlinckx. 2011. "The Relation Between Event Processing and the Duration of Emotional Experience." *Emotion* 11, no. 1: 20–28. http://doi.org/10.1037/a0021239.

Vodanovich, Stephen J., Kathryn M. Verner, and Thomas V. Gilbride. 1991. "Boredom Proneness: Its Relationship to Positive and Negative Affect." *Psychological Reports* 69, no. 3 (Pt 2): 1139–46. https://doi.org/10.2466%2Fpr0.1991.69.3f.1139.

Vodanovich, Stephen J., and John D. Watt. 2016. "Self-Report Measures of Boredom: An Updated Review of the Literature." *Journal of Psychology: Interdisciplinary and Applied* 150, no. 2: 196–228. https://doi.org/10.1080/00223980.2015.1074531.

Vodanovich, Stephen J., Chris Weddle, and Chris Piotrowski. 1997. "The Relationship between Boredom Proneness and Internal and External Work Values." *Social Behavior and Personality* 25, no. 3: 259–64. https://doi.org/10.2224/sbp.1997.25 .3.259.

Von Gemmingen, Mitchell J., Bryce F. Sullivan, and Andrew M. Pomerantz. 2003. "Investigating the Relationships between Boredom Proneness, Paranoia, and Self-Consciousness." *Personality and Individual Differences* 34, no. 6: 907–19. https:// doi.org/10.1016/S0191-8869(01)00219-7.

Wasson, Avtar S. 1981. "Susceptibility to Boredom and Deviant Behavior at School." *Psychological Reports* 48, no. 3: 901–2. https://doi.org/10.2466%2Fpr0.1981.48 .3.901.

Watt, John D., and Stephen J. Vodanovich. 1992. "Relationship between Boredom Proneness and Impulsivity." *Psychological Reports* 70, no. 3 (Pt 1): 688–90. https ://doi.org/10.2466%2Fpr0.1992.70.3.688.

Westgate, Erin C., and Timothy D. Wilson. 2018. "Boring Thoughts and Bored Minds: The MAC Model of Boredom and Cognitive Engagement." *Psychological Review* 125, no. 5: 689–713. http://doi.org/10.1037/rev0000097" http://doi.org/10 .1037/rev0000097.

Weybright, Elizabeth H., John Schulenberg, and Linda L. Caldwell. 2020. "More Bored Today Than Yesterday? National Trends in Adolescent Boredom From 2008 to 2017." *Journal of Adolescent Health* 66, no. 3: 360–65. https://doi.org/10.1016 /j.jadohealth.2019.09.021.

Wilson, Timothy D., and Daniel T. Gilbert. 2008. "Explaining Away: A Model of Affective Adaptation." *Perspectives on Psychological Science : A Journal of the Association for Psychological Science* 3, no. 5: 370–86. https://doi.org/10.1111/j .1745-6924.2008.00085.x.

Wilson, Timothy D., David A. Reinhard, Erin C. Westgate, Daniel T. Gilbert, Nicole Ellerbeck, Cheryl Hahn, Casey L. Brown, and Adi Shaked. 2014. "Just Think: The Challenges of the Disengaged Mind." *Science* 345, no: 6192: 75–77. https://doi.org /10.1126/science.1250830.

Wolff, Wanja, and Corinna S. Martarelli. 2020. "Bored Into Depletion? Toward a Tentative Integration of Perceived Self-Control Exertion and Boredom as Guiding Signals for Goal-Directed Behavior." *Perspectives on Psychological Science.* Advance online publication. https://doi.org/10.1177/1745691620921394.

Wolman, Benjamin B. 1975. "Principles of Interactional Psychotherapy." *Psychotherapy* 12, no. 2: 149–59. https://doi.org/10.1037/h0086419.

Yang, William, Ton Staps, and Ellen Hijmans. 2010. "Existential Crisis and the Awareness of Dying: The Role of Meaning and Spirituality." *Omega* 61, no. 1: 53–69. https://doi.org/10.2190/OM.61.1.c,

Zhang, Hong, Kaiyuan Chen, Changkai Chen, and Rebecca Schlegel. 2019. "Personal Aspirations, Person-Environment Fit, Meaning in Work, and Meaning in Life: A Moderated Mediation Model." *Journal of Happiness Studies* 20, no. 5: 1481–97. https://doi.org/10.1007/s10902-018-0005-0.

Chapter 4

"Rage Spread Thin"

Boredom and Aggression

James Danckert

Paul Tillich, a German American philosopher, is often cited as the author of the quote that leads this chapter—"boredom is rage spread thin."[1] Regardless of the true author of the phrase, it has intuitive appeal. Boredom is not something we take lying down. We are distressed by it, hostile toward the world that is failing to satisfy us. At least, it feels as though it has that intuitive appeal until you try to break down what is intended by it. Is it suggesting that boredom is indeed merely subthreshold rage? Anger not quite intense enough to galvanize us into aggressive acts? Or does the "spread" of bored rage hint that boredom pervades all aspects of our lives? Or is it both? A sense of disaffection with everything felt as an aggressively dissatisfying[2] experience? That's the problem with cool quotes—they give the illusion of understanding, the fragility of which is exposed on the merest interrogation.

But there is something to it. Boredom is uncomfortable (Danckert et al. 2018; Eastwood et al. 2012). It is quite distinct from other negative emotions, in particular apathy, the absence of any desire to act, and anhedonia, the inability to experience pleasure (Goldberg et al. 2011; Van Tilburg and Igou 2011, 2017). Boredom, as with rage, speaks to a discontent with our current circumstances. This casts boredom in a functional light. The experience of state boredom is a signal telling us that what we are doing now is failing to satisfy an important need—the need to act and to have those actions matter in some demonstrable way (Danckert 2019; Danckert et al. 2018).[3] In other words, not *simply* to act, but to act with observable outcomes that feel purposeful and consequential to us in some obvious way. Here, rage can be quite useful, if not entirely morally defensible.

Our in-the-moment feelings of boredom are neither morally good nor bad. It is our response to the signal that makes it so. When people claim that "only boring people get bored," they are really saying that when the boredom signal descends on them, they are easily able to rapidly and effectively respond. Only those who struggle to swiftly and adaptively respond to boredom will continually get bored.[4] What this also highlights is that there are more ways than one to skin a cat.[5] That is, there are a multitude of ways one can respond to boredom.

The feeling of the state of boredom poses a conundrum. It signals that we want something to occupy our minds, to give an outlet to our mental energy (Eastwood et al. 2012; Danckert et al. 2018). But despite recognizing that desire for what it is, we can't bring ourselves to want any of the options currently on offer. The conundrum is quintessentially evident in the bored child, pleading with their parent to remedy their situation. The dutiful forebears trot out a list of potential options for the child, each of which is summarily dismissed. What this anecdote highlights is that the child has no trouble identifying available options for actions, but does not feel like any of those options will satisfy their needs in the moment.[6] Adult boredom is no different.

So boredom is a call to action (Elpidorou 2014, 2018), one the boredom-prone individuals experience more often and more intensely. The boredom conundrum signals a kind of uncertainty as to what might possibly satisfy the desire to be engaged. This in turn brings on a kind of restlessness as we cast about for potential solutions to boredom (Danckert et al. 2018). This is not such a problematic search for some. Those who adhere to a strong religious or ideological framework tend to experience boredom less (Van Tilburg et al. 2019; Van Tilburg and Igou 2011, 2016). These relations hint at the possibility that a strong external framework that guides individual actions (and in so doing relieves the actor of the burden of choosing) and provides the scaffolding for a robust identity can keep boredom at bay.

Any such framework is no guarantee of ethical action choices. In one study, when people were more bored they doubled down on in-group ties (Van Tilburg and Igou 2011). That is, people were presented with scenarios in which a crime had been committed and they must choose the punishment. When bored, people tended to hand out harsher punishments to out-group (fictional) criminals and more lenient punishments to in-group criminals (Van Tilburg and Igou 2011). One interpretation of this finding is that boredom signals the need to find or make meaning. In trying to fulfill that need, we turn to those frameworks that provide a strong sense of belonging (see also Van Tilburg and Igou 2016). While such a retreat into our own identity may provide some sense of certainty and meaning, which in turn eradicates our boredom, it clearly does not guarantee an ethical action choice.

It is also a truism of boredom research to say that highly boredom-prone individuals tend to choose maladaptive responses to being bored (Danckert et al. 2018). They struggle with drug and alcohol abuse (Biolcati, Passini, and Mancini 2016; Iso-Ahola and Crowley 1991; Orcutt 1984; Patterson, Pegg, and Dobson-Patterson 2000), problem gambling (Blaszczynski, McConaghy, and Frankova 1990; but see Mercer and Eastwood 2010), and demonstrate problematic relations with technology (Elhai et al. 2018; Lin and Chiang 2017). Indeed, high boredom proneness has also been associated with elevated watching of pornography and increased solitary sexual acts, particularly in men (Watt and Ewing 1996). Each of these responses represents not just short-term fixes to the discomfort of boredom, but potentially also long-term failures in addressing the underlying cause. While alcohol, drugs, gambling, and porn might occupy our minds in the moment, they consistently fail to stand in for the real need signaled by boredom—a need to exercise our own sense of agency, to act in ways that provide opportunities to display our own skills and talents.[7] Such maladaptive responding to boredom forces us to ask why boredom arises in the first place?

To address that question, we need a slightly more nuanced take on the self-regulatory role of the feeling state of boredom. Boredom signals that we are currently disengaged and need to explore options for reengaging with the world. But any old action won't do. We need something to occupy *more purposefully* our mental energy to enable us to showcase our skills and talents (Danckert 2019). This builds from Robert White's (1959) theory of effectance motivation. White suggested that mammals have a drive to demonstrate their own efficacy, that is, to highlight our capacity to engage actions that lead directly to change in our environs.

Casting boredom within the framework of satisfaction of effectance motivation suggests that boredom threatens our sense of agency (Danckert and Eastwood 2020). In other words, the boredom conundrum starkly reminds us that we are responsible for choosing our next goal or action and that in this moment, we are failing to do so. We are being ineffective agents. Again, rage, or at least aggressive acts that have tangible outcomes, seems like a viable option to expunge the discomfort brought on by the boredom conundrum.

There are many anecdotal examples of aggressive acts purportedly executed in response to boredom. One of the teenagers convicted of shooting a man in the back while he was out jogging claimed he did so because he was "bored" and so "decided to kill somebody."[8] Teens who joined in the looting and rioting in London in 2011 also reported that they did so out of boredom.[9] A German nurse accused of killing ninety-seven people said he did so out of boredom. He would give his patients a deadly drug and then attempt to revive them, and claimed he did so first out of boredom and second, to experience the thrill of bringing his patients back to life (when he succeeded).[10] Taking control of the life of another is perhaps the ultimate way to demonstrate one's own agency.[11]

More prosaically, vandalism has been related to feelings of boredom (Fisher and Baron 1982; see also Shachaf and Hara 2010 for a case of Internet vandalism—trolling—and boredom). Destruction of property becomes a way to demonstrate one's agency and the thrill of transgression eliminates boredom. In addition, incarcerated teens report boredom not only as a fact of their every-day lives while in prison, but importantly as a prime driver prompting them to engage in the acts that landed them in prison in the first instance (Bengtsson 2012). At least in these latter studies there seems to be some evidence that boredom can prompt a kind of lashing out at the world. Alternatively, when bored we may be pushed to seek out ever more stimulating experiences. Certainly, there is data to suggest that highly boredom-prone individuals also report higher levels of sensation-seeking (e.g., Dahlen et al. 2004).

There has been a long association between boredom proneness and self-reported feelings of aggression (Dahlen et al. 2004; Isacescu, Struk, and Danckert 2017; Rupp and Vodanovich 1997). In our own work, the scale we used (the Buss-Perry Aggression Questionnaire; Buss and Perry 1992) can be broken down into four subscales that measure physical and verbal aggression separately, anger, and, finally, hostility. It is this latter scale that most strongly correlates with boredom proneness (Isacescu et al. 2017). Whether feelings of hostility are directed more externally—a feeling that the world is not enough, or internally as a response to one's own sense of failure, is an open question. Whether increased hostility in response to being bored in turn leads to aggressive acts also requires more research.

It is also true that the highly boredom-prone individuals tend to exhibit lower levels of self-control (Isacescu et al. 2017). While this conception of self-control is less about impulse control and more akin to marshaling one's thoughts, emotions, and behaviors in the pursuit of goals, it is plausible that the highly boredom-prone struggle with elements of both aspects of self-regulatory behavior. Indeed, research has shown that boredom proneness is associated with impulsivity and overeating (Moynihan, Igou, and Van Tilburg 2017).[12] In addition, we have shown that people who have suffered traumatic brain injury (TBI) also report higher levels of boredom proneness (Isacescu and Danckert 2018; see also Goldberg and Danckert 2013 for results showing a stronger relation between boredom and depression in TBI patients). The sine qua non of TBI is the dysexecutive syndrome (Arcinieages and Wortzel 2014; Studd and Alexander 2007) which prominently involves poor impulse control, inappropriate social behaviors, poor decision-making, and elevated levels of aggression (e.g., Rao et al. 2009 estimate rates of post-TBI aggression range from 11 to 34 percent; see also Greve et al. 2001; Kim 2002; Wortzel and Arciniegas 2013). Any causal link between TBI, boredom, and elevated aggression has yet to be definitively demonstrated, but the relations are striking.

The suggestion from all of this is that boredom may open the door to aggressive acts becoming permissible. When bored we feel both a lack of meaning and purpose and an acute awareness that we are being ineffective agents, failing to demonstrate that we are capable of effecting change in our world. Eric Fromm (1955), writing in the middle of the twentieth century, suggested that people felt alienated from the fruits of their labors. In this sense, we can be engaged in actions that have tangible outcomes but little meaning—a kind of *meaningless agency* (Kustermans and Ringmar 2011). Kustermans and Ringmar (2011) go so far as to suggest that such conditions of alienation and meaningless agency are fertile grounds for enthusiasm for war.

This is not the same as suggesting that boredom *leads to war*. Instead, the suggestion is that boredom leads to a fascination with and glorification of war (Kustermans and Ringmar 2011). Their framework begins with the Enlightenment notion that a rational society will reject war as each man (it's always men) is granted the freedom to pursue his own destiny. But when the reality of this fails to live up to the promise, that is, when people feel that their work is disconnected from their own life goals, boredom will ensue. Put another way, Kustermans and Ringmar suggest that attention is not captured, especially among "energetic young" (2011, 1776), by the goals touted by society as important for them to pursue. Put yet another way, when (bourgeois) life has too little of challenge to it, youth become disenfranchised, disengaged, frustrated, and bored. This casts boredom not merely as a prompt to aggression, but as a prompt to rebellion (Ferrell, 2004), an extreme version of the logic that boredom breeds vandalism (Horowitz and Tobaly 2003; Iso-Ahola and Weissinger 1990; Scitovsky 1999). In Kustermans and Ringmar's (2011) words, "the *anticipation* of war harbours the dream of the restoration of meaningful agency" (1777, emphasis added).

If aggression and the glorification of war are a response to meaningless agency, then the aggressive acts pursued must contain some sense of meaning. It is the boredom conundrum that makes this so. Boredom is the stymied desire for something to engage with. It is objectless and in being so, represents a gaping hole that we are desperate to fill. Violence in the name of some well-defined framework—fighting for the glory of King and country, or in the name of God—fits the bill. Even the sense that one is waiting for something important to happen could be a gateway to aggression and ultimately war.[13]

The case put by Kustermans and Ringmar (2011) is a sociological argument framed largely in the context of circumstances preceding World War I. But we are likely not immune from similar circumstances today. Our lives are increasingly lived online with vast opportunities for meaningless agency (endless games of Candy Crush or hours spent down the rabbit hole of Instagram). Consumerism—the desire to own things beyond one's basic needs—seems rampant,[14] turning us into passive recipients rather than active creators. Indeed, boredom is associated with problematic smartphone use

(Elhai et al. 2018; Lin and Chiang 2017) and increased consumptive (if not consumerist) behaviors (Abramson and Stinson 1977; Crockett, Myhre, Rokke 2015; Kim and Brendl 2012; Moynihan et al. 2015).

According to Kustermans and Ringmar (2011) this is a tinderbox for seeing war or other forms of aggression as at least permissible. This casts boredom in the context of not only our need to demonstrate our own agency but also of a desire to seek meaning in what we do (Coughlan et al. 2019; Van Tilburg and Igou 2011). This blend can be seen in popular culture in circumstances where aggression and meaning are blended together in narrative. At least in the West, we are constantly sold the myth of the individual triumphing against all odds to save the day. Whether it be facing invading aliens (*Independence Day*, 1996) or nefarious gangsters (*John Wick*, 2014), through violence our heroes not only triumph, they establish a framework for a strong sense of identity and purpose. Indeed, Coughlan and colleagues (2019) recently showed that boredom can be kept at bay by positive affirmations of heroes, presumably because the act of doing so provides meaning in our lives.

All this myth-making provides a strong framework to reach for when we are feeling alienated, bored, or both. Never mind that the reality does not match the expectations. Soldiers hoping to gain a sense of purpose and meaningful agency are required to strictly follow orders and as Kustermans and Ringmar (2011) point out, often reflect on their lived experience as having been meaningless.[15] The myth of individual triumph over insurmountable odds in movies is clearly fictitious. But the images of these things are appealing as they show us others clearly demonstrating a strong sense of agency and doing it all for a moral fairytale we can align with, even if only temporarily. This is all an excellent way to channel aggression toward the destruction of boredom.

Perhaps the last word on boredom and aggression should go to self-harm. Is our need to be engaged so powerful that we would even act against our own self-interests? Certainly, all the negative associations with boredom proneness already mentioned suggest that people make poor choices in order to alleviate their boredom, turning to drugs, alcohol, gambling, and excessive smartphone use (Biolcati, Passini, and Mancini 2016; Blaszczynski et al. 1990; Elhai et al. 2018; Iso-Ahola and Crowley 1991; Lin and Chiang 2017; Orcutt 1984; Patterson, Pegg, and Dobson-Patterson 2000). There is also more direct evidence that when bored we will even resort to self-harm just to alleviate the tedium. Wilson and colleagues (2014) conducted a series of experiments in which they had people sit in an empty room for fifteen minutes with nothing to entertain themselves but their own thoughts. Many people—around one-third of their samples—found the experience to be pleasant. But about the same number reported this to be unpleasant in part because it was boring. In their final version of this experiment they gave people an option—sit with only your thoughts to entertain you or self-administer an electric shock. People were exposed to the shock before beginning their fifteen minutes of nothing and were asked whether (and how much) money they would pay to avoid the shock. So they knew what it felt like and had reported that they would indeed pay to avoid it. And yet, when placed in the room with nothing to do many people chose to shock themselves (men did this more than women and one bright spark shocked himself more than 190 times—clearly, this was not engaged in to merely satisfy curiosity; see also Struk et al. 2020 in which boredom was higher when people were placed in a room with options for engagement that they were precluded from engaging with).

In the Wilson and colleagues (2014) study boredom was not explicitly induced. Follow-up work showed that when people were induced to feel bored (by watching boring movies) they self-administered electric shocks more than when they had watched either interesting (Havermans et al. 2015) or sad movies (Nederkoorn et al. 2016). So it seems clear that when bored, we would rather poke our eyes out—so to speak—than do nothing. These findings can hardly be construed as attempts to establish meaning in our lives. Instead, the aggression directed at the self suggests that when bored we want to establish, or at least reestablish, our sense of agency. It might seem stupid to self-administer an electric shock but in this context it likely serves at least two purposes: first, one pain alleviates another, the shock distracting us from the pain of boredom; and second, we get to demonstrate that we are in control of the circumstance—we can choose when and how often we'll shock ourselves.

It seems incontrovertible that boredom and aggression are linked. What this link suggests is that aggressive acts serve to demonstrate one's agency when boredom has raised the alarm that agency is diminished. This is certainly not an inevitability. We can choose to respond to boredom in all kinds of adaptive ways. Many want to suggest that boredom can *make* us creative (e.g., Mann and Cadman 2014). This claim is, in my view, absurd. If one has cultivated creative outlets—and creativity requires cultivation—then those outlets will prove useful when boredom strikes. But just as boredom is itself not the culprit for war or murder or other acts of aggression, it also can't be credited with being the genesis of creativity. Instead, boredom signals that we are disengaged, a state that we find deeply uncomfortable. Whether we pursue adaptive (e.g., creative acts being one such class) or maladaptive (e.g., vandalism, acts of personal aggression, etc.) avenues to alleviate our boredom is up to us. Boredom may indeed be rage spread thin in its initial phenomenological sense—we feel agitated, restless, and dissatisfied. To make things worse, we do not see viable avenues to alleviate those unpleasant feelings. But boredom need not be rage spread thin. We could instead choose to use the signal of boredom as a prompt to personal reflection directed toward at least two purposes: first, to determine why it is this particular circumstance feels boring, and second, to reflect on what a purposeful, adaptive response to that circumstance might look like. In other words, boredom may only prompt aggression when we fail to fully hear what the signal is telling us.

NOTES

1. Despite repeated attempts from myself, my colleague John Eastwood, and many librarians at both York University and the University of Waterloo, we have been unable to definitively ascertain the provenance of this quote. I would welcome any input on its true origins.

2. Ralph Greenson (1953) was the first to describe two types of boredom, one of which he labeled "agitated boredom" and the other "apathetic boredom." The literature is rife with associations between boredom and restlessness, so while there is a debate as to whether boredom should be considered a high or low arousal state, there is no debate about it being an unpleasant experience. I originally published work that sprang from Greenson's distinction. I now believe there is really only one boredom—Greenson's apathetic boredom is quite simply, apathy.

3. I am choosing my words carefully here. Meaning, in particular life meaning, has been shown to be related to boredom (Barbalet 1999; Fahlman et al. 2009; Melton and Schulenberg 2007), but what I want to convey here is that the state signal that is boredom can be independent of our need to seek and make meaning in our lives.

4. Certainly, in our lab we find that boredom proneness is characterized by an increase in both frequency and intensity of experiencing boredom. When participants were asked how frequently and intensely they experienced boredom, both questions were positively correlated with the shortened boredom proneness scale (SBPS; Struk et al. 2017). The association was consistently stronger for frequency. (Across the three terms of Fall 2017 and 2018 and Winter 2018, with an average $n=2,161$, intensity correlations with the SBPS ranged from 0.45 to 0.49, while for frequency the range was 0.63–0.64.)

5. For a humorous and insightful dive into the origins of this unseemly phrase visit: https://www.bnd.com/living/liv-columns-blogs/answer-man/article181298616.html.

6. Why this conundrum exists is an open matter for further research—do we devalue the available options? Do we see the options as too effortful and so are less willing to engage? Are we afraid that attempting any of the available options will lead to failure? My current reading of the literature would suggest that these are very much open questions. The focus of this chapter is instead on the maladaptive responses to being bored.

7. Elpidorou (2017) outlines a compelling case for the moral dimension of boredom and calls for more work on the issue. Essentially, in his framework, boredom signals the fact that we are failing to live an "authentic" life. Each of the maladaptive

responses outlined here relieves boredom temporarily, but in failing to align with our personal goals and beliefs, they do nothing to propel us toward an authentic life.

8. For a full report of this case, see https://bleacherreport.com/articles/1744262-a ustralian-baseball-player-christopher-lane-killed-by-teenagers-in-oklahoma.

9. This claim is made in the following article: https://www.npr.org/2011/08/13 /139598062/boredom-and-alienation-may-factor-into-uk-riots.

10. For an account of this story, see https://www.cnn.com/2018/01/23/europe/ge rman-nurse-charged-97-murders-intl/index.html.

11. The abuses at Abu Ghraib prison in Afghanistan can also be cast in this light. There's no evidence that soldiers were bored, but torturing another human being will certainly establish a strong sense, however repugnant, of agency. This event had the added component of reinforcing identity (us vs. them) and meaning (i.e., rooting out future terrorists), however disconnected from reality those functions may have been.

12. This is true in animals too (Meagher and Mason 2012; Meagher, Campbell, and Mason 2017). These authors looked at mink housed in bland or interesting cages to show that the former experienced boredom. One of their metrics was how many treats the animals in bland cages ate, despite being well fed. The animals in the bland cages consistently overate the treats provided.

13. Kustermans and Ringmar (2011) quote two French authors, Henri Massis and Alfred de Tarde in 1913 who surveyed young men one of whom said, "Better a war than this perpetual wait" (1784).

14. This is of course a big claim—what counts as evidence to back it up? The rise in online sales of goods through sites like Amazon? Deaths at Black Friday sale events in the United States? Rising plastic levels in our oceans?

15. They refer to memoirs written a decade after the end of World War I such as *All Quiet on the Western Front* by Erich Maria Remarque and *Goodbye to All That* by Robert Graves.

REFERENCES

Abramson, Edward E., and Shawn G. Stinson. 1977. "Boredom and Eating in Obese and Non-obese Individuals." *Addictive Behaviors* 2, no. 4: 181–85.

Arciniegas, David B., and Hal S. Wortzel. 2014. "Emotional and Behavioral Dyscontrol After Traumatic Brain Injury." *Psychiatric Clinics* 37, no. 1: 31–53.

Barbalet, Jack M. 1999. "Boredom and Social Meaning." *The British Journal of Sociology* 50, no. 4: 631–46.

Bengtsson, Tea Torbenfeldt. 2012. "Boredom and Action—Experiences from Youth Confinement." *Journal of Contemporary Ethnography* 41, no. 5: 526–53.

Biolcati, Roberta, Stefano Passini, and Giacomo Mancini. 2016. "'I Cannot Stand the Boredom.' Binge Drinking Expectancies in Adolescence." *Addictive Behaviors Reports* 3: 70–76.

Blaszczynski, Alex, Neil McConaghy, and Anna Frankova. 1990. "Boredom Proneness in Pathological Gambling." *Psychological Reports* 67, no. 1: 35–42.

Buss, Arnold H., and Mark Perry. 1992. "The Aggression Questionnaire." *Journal of Personality and Social Psychology* 63, no. 3: 452–59.

Coughlan, Gillian, Eric R. Igou, Wijnand AP van Tilburg, Elaine L. Kinsella, and Timothy D. Ritchie. 2019. "On Boredom and Perceptions of Heroes: A Meaning-Regulation Approach to Heroism." *Journal of Humanistic Psychology* 59, no. 4: 455–73.

Crockett, Amanda C., Samantha K. Myhre, and Paul D. Rokke. 2015. "Boredom Proneness and Emotion Regulation Predict Emotional Eating." *Journal of Health Psychology* 20, no. 5: 670–80.

Dahlen, Eric R., Ryan C. Martin, Katie Ragan, and Myndi M. Kuhlman. 2004. "Boredom Proneness in Anger and Aggression: Effects of Impulsiveness and Sensation Seeking." *Personality and Individual Differences* 37, no. 8: 1615–27.

Danckert, James, and John D. Eastwood. 2020. *Out of My Skull: The Psychology of Boredom*. Cambridge: Harvard University Press.

Danckert, James. 2019. "Boredom: Managing the Delicate Balance Between Exploration and Exploitation." In *Boredom Is in Your Mind: A Shared Psychological-Philosophical Approach*, edited by Josefa Ros Velasco, 37–53. Cham: Springer.

Danckert, James, Jhotisha Mugon, Andriy Struk, and John Eastwood. 2018. "Boredom: What Is It Good For?" In *The Function of Emotions*, edited by Heather C. Lench, 93–119. Cham: Springer.

Eastwood, John D., Alexandra Frischen, Mark J. Fenske, and Daniel Smilek. 2012. "The Unengaged Mind: Defining Boredom in Terms of Attention." *Perspectives on Psychological Science* 7, no. 5: 482–95.

Elhai, Jon D., Juanita K. Vasquez, Samuel D. Lustgarten, Jason C. Levine, and Brian J. Hall. 2018. "Proneness to Boredom Mediates Relationships Between Problematic Smartphone Use with Depression and Anxiety Severity." *Social Science Computer Review* 36, no. 6: 707–20.

Elpidorou, Andreas. 2018. "The Good of Boredom." *Philosophical Psychology* 31, no. 3: 323–51.

Elpidorou, Andreas. 2017. "The Moral Dimensions of Boredom: A call for research." *Review of General Psychology* 21, no. 1: 30–48.

Elpidorou, Andreas. 2014. "The Bright Side of Boredom." *Frontiers in Psychology* 5: 1245.

Fahlman, Shelley A., Kimberley B. Mercer, Peter Gaskovski, Adrienne E. Eastwood, and John D. Eastwood. 2009. "Does a Lack of Life Meaning Cause Boredom? Results from Psychometric, Longitudinal, and Experimental Analyses." *Journal of Social and Clinical Psychology* 28, no. 3: 307–40.

Ferrell, Jeff. 2004. "Boredom, Crime and Criminology." *Theoretical Criminology* 8, no. 3: 287–302.

Fisher, Jeffrey D., and Reuben M. Baron. 1982. "An Equity-Based Model of Vandalism." *Population and Environment* 5, no. 3: 182–200.

Fromm, Erich. 1955. *The Sane Society*. New York, NY: Rinehart and Winston.

Goldberg, Yael, and James Danckert. 2013. "Traumatic Brain Injury, Boredom and Depression." *Behavioral Sciences* 3, no. 3: 434–44.

Goldberg, Yael K., John D. Eastwood, Jennifer LaGuardia, and James Danckert. 2011. "Boredom: An Emotional Experience Distinct from Apathy, Anhedonia, or Depression." *Journal of Social and Clinical Psychology* 30, no. 6: 647–66.

Greenson, Ralph R. 1953. "On Boredom." *Journal of the American Psychoanalytic Association* 1, no. 1: 7–21.

Greve, Kevin W., Elisabeth Sherwin, Matthew S. Stanford, Charles Mathias, Jeff Love, and Paul Ramzinski. 2001. "Personality and Neurocognitive Correlates of Impulsive Aggression in Long-Term Survivors of Severe Traumatic Brain Injury." *Brain Injury* 15, no. 3: 255–62.

Havermans, Remco C., Linda Vancleef, Antonis Kalamatianos, and Chantal Nederkoorn. 2015. "Eating and Inflicting Pain Out of Boredom." *Appetite* 85: 52–57.

Horowitz, Tamar, and David Tobaly. 2003. "School Vandalism: Individual and Social Context." *Adolescence* 38, no. 149 131–40.

Isacescu, Julia, and James Danckert. 2018. "Exploring the Relationship Between Boredom Proneness and Self-Control in Traumatic Brain Injury TBI." *Experimental Brain Research* 236, no. 9: 2493–505.

Isacescu, Julia, Andriy Anatolievich Struk, and James Danckert. 2017. "Cognitive and Affective Predictors of Boredom Proneness." *Cognition and emotion* 31, no. 8: 1741–48.

Iso-Ahola, Seppo E., and Edward D. Crowley. 1991. "Adolescent Substance Abuse and Leisure Boredom." *Journal of Leisure Research* 23, no. 3: 260–71.

Iso-Ahola, Seppo E., and Ellen Weissinger. 1990. "Perceptions of Boredom in Leisure: Conceptualization, Reliability and Validity of the Leisure Boredom Scale." *Journal of Leisure Research* 22, no. 1: 1–17.

Kim, Edward. 2002. "Agitation, Aggression, and Disinhibition Syndromes After Traumatic Brain Injury." *NeuroRehabilitation* 17, no. 4: 297–310.

Kim, Soo, and C. Miguel Brendl. 2012. "Two Paths From Boredom to Consumption." *ACR North American Advances*. https://www.acrwebsite.org/volumes/v40/acr_v40_12030.pdf

Kustermans, Jorg, and Erik Ringmar. 2011. "Modernity, Boredom, and War: A Suggestive Essay." *Review of International Studies* 37, no. 4: 1775–92.

Lin, Trisha T. C., and Yi-Hsuan Chiang. 2017. "Investigating Predictors of Smartphone Dependency Symptoms and Effects on Academic Performance, Improper Phone Use and Perceived Sociability." *International Journal of Mobile Communications* 15, no. 6: 655–76.

Mann, Sandi, and Rebekah Cadman. 2014. "Does Being Bored Make Us More Creative?." *Creativity Research Journal* 26, no. 2: 165–73.

Meagher, Rebecca K., and Georgia J. Mason. 2012. "Environmental Enrichment Reduces Signs of Boredom in Caged Mink." *PLoS One* 7, no. 11: e49180.

Meagher, Rebecca K., Dana L. M. Campbell, and Georgia J. Mason. 2017. "Boredom-like States in Mink and their Behavioural Correlates: A Replicate Study." *Applied Animal Behaviour Science* 197: 112–19.

Melton, Amanda M. A., and Stefan E. Schulenberg. 2007. "On the Relationship Between Meaning in Life and Boredom Proneness: Examining a Logotherapy Postulate." *Psychological Reports* 101, no. 3 suppl: 1016–22.

Mercer, Kimberley B., and John D. Eastwood. 2010. "Is Boredom Associated with Problem Gambling Behaviour? It Depends on What You Mean by 'Boredom'." *International Gambling Studies* 10, no. 1: 91–104.

Moynihan, Andrew B., Eric R. Igou, and Wijnand A.P. van Tilburg, W. A. 2017. "Boredom Increases Impulsiveness." *Social Psychology*, 48, 293–309.

Moynihan, Andrew B., Wijnand A. P. van Tilburg, Eric R. Igou, Arnaud Wisman, Alan E. Donnelly, and Jessie B. Mulcaire. 2015. "Eaten Up by Boredom: Consuming Food to Escape Awareness of the Bored Self." *Frontiers in Psychology* 6: 369.

Mugon, Jhotisha, Andriy Struk, and James Danckert. 2018. "A Failure to Launch: Regulatory Modes and Boredom Proneness." *Frontiers in Psychology* 9: 1126.

Nederkoorn, Chantal, Linda Vancleef, Alexandra Wilkenhöner, Laurence Claes, and Remco C. Havermans. 2016. "Self-Inflicted Pain Out of Boredom." *Psychiatry Research* 237: 127–32.

Orcutt, James D. 1984. "Contrasting Effects of Two Kinds of Boredom on Alcohol Use." *Journal of Drug Issues* 14, no. 1: 161–73.

Patterson, Ian, Shane Pegg, and Roberta Dobson-Patterson. 2000. "Exploring the Links Between Leisure Boredom and Alcohol Use Among Youth in Rural and Urban Areas of Australia." *Journal of Park & Recreation Administration* 18, no. 3: 53–75.

Rao, Vani, Paul Rosenberg, Melaine Bertrand, Saeed Salehinia, Jennifer Spiro, Sandeep Vaishnavi, Pramit Rastogi, Kathy Noll, David J. Schretlen, Jason Brandt, Edward Cornwell, Michael Makley, and Quincy Samus Miles. 2009. "Aggression After Traumatic Brain Injury: Prevalence and Correlates." *The Journal of Neuropsychiatry and Clinical Neurosciences* 21, no. 4: 420–29.

Rupp, Deborah E., and Stephen J. Vodanovich. 1997. "The Role of Boredom Proneness in Self-Reported Anger and Aggression." *Journal of Social Behavior and Personality* 12, no. 4: 925–36.

Scitovsky, Tibor. 1999. "Boredom-An Overlooked Disease?." *Challenge* 42, no. 5: 5–15.

Shachaf, Pnina, and Noriko Hara. 2010. "Beyond Vandalism: Wikipedia trolls." *Journal of Information Science* 36, no. 3: 357–70.

Struk, Andriy A., Jonathan S.A. Carriere, J. Allan Cheyne, and James Danckert. 2017. "A Short Boredom Proneness Scale: Development and Psychometric Properties." *Assessment* 24, no. 3: 346–59.

Stuss, Donald T., and Michael P. Alexander. 2007. "Is There a Dysexecutive Syndrome?." *Philosophical Transactions of the Royal Society B: Biological Sciences* 362, no. 1481: 901–15.

Van Tilburg, Wijnand A.P., Eric R. Igou, Paul J. Maher, Andrew B. Moynihan, and Dawn G. Martin. 2019. "Bored like Hell: Religiosity Reduces Boredom and Tempers the Quest for Meaning." *Emotion* 19, no. 2: 255–69.

Van Tilburg, Wijnand A.P., and Eric R. Igou. 2017. "Boredom Begs to Differ: Differentiation from Other Negative Emotions." *Emotion* 17, no. 2: 309–22.

Van Tilburg, Wijnand A.P., and Eric R. Igou. 2016. "Going to Political Extremes in Response to Boredom." *European Journal of Social Psychology* 46, no. 6: 687–99.

Van Tilburg, Wijnand A.P., and Eric R. Igou. 2011. "On Boredom and Social Identity: A Pragmatic Meaning-Regulation Approach." *Personality and Social Psychology Bulletin* 37, no. 12: 1679–91.

Watt, John D., and Jackie E. Ewing. 1996. "Toward the Development and Validation of a Measure of Sexual Boredom." *Journal of Sex Research* 33, no. 1: 57–66.

White, Robert W. 1959. "Motivation Reconsidered: The Concept of Competence." *Psychological Review* 66, no. 5: 297–333.

Wilson, Timothy D., David A. Reinhard, Erin C. Westgate, Daniel T. Gilbert, Nicole Ellerbeck, Cheryl Hahn, Casey L. Brown, and Adi Shaked. 2014. "Just Think: The Challenges of the Disengaged Mind." *Science* 345, no. 6192: 75–77.

Wortzel, Hal S., and David B. Arciniegas. 2013. "A Forensic Neuropsychiatric Approach to Traumatic Brain Injury, Aggression, and Suicide." *Journal of the American Academy of Psychiatry and the Law Online* 41, no. 2: 274–86.

Zandstra, E. H., M. F. Weegels, A. A. Van Spronsen, and M. Klerk. 2004. "Scoring or Boring? Predicting Boredom Through Repeated In-Home Consumption." *Food Quality and Preference* 15, no. 6: 549–57.

Chapter 5

Losing and Finding Agency

The Crisis of Boredom

John D. Eastwood and Dana Gorelik

Boredom—the experience of an unfulfilled desire to be engaged in satisfying activity—can be a very uncomfortable feeling. It's associated with the slow passage of time, difficulty concentrating, the sense that what's at hand is pointless, and a mixture of lethargy and restlessness (Danckert and Eastwood 2020). Functional accounts (e.g., Bench and Lench 2013; Danckert et al. 2018; Elpidorou 2014; Barbalet 1999) suggest boredom is adaptive because it pushes us out of stagnation and into meaningful engagement. The idea is that the discomfort of boredom won't let us squander our resources and it won't let us persist in dead-end activities.

However, any parent who has dealt with a restless child pleading for a solution to their boredom knows the ability of boredom to motivate change is not so straightforward. In fact, telling a bored person to take up this or that possible action can feel a bit like telling a drowning person to swim to shore. Trying to solve our own boredom can be perilous, too, as we cast about this way and that, unsuccessfully "trying on" possible activities. When bored, we feel powerless as we search for a solution that refuses to materialize. As we'll see, boredom signals a deeper problem than the simple need for an alternative activity.

Leo Tolstoy, the Russian writer, summed up boredom in four words: *a desire for desires*. Boredom is a strong desire to do something, thwarted by a lack of desire to do anything in particular. The bored person wants to, but can't, muster up an actionable desire. That is, the bored person can't want to do anything that's currently doable. In the novel *Humboldt's Gift*, Saul Bellow puts his finger on the second key component to boredom: *the pain of unused powers*. Boredom is also a state of disuse. Our mental abilities lay fallow, and we are itching to engage our minds.

Tolstoy and Bellow cut to the heart of the matter. To respond well to boredom's call, we need to exercise our *agency*. Agency is the ability to make choices, effectively execute our intentions, and be self-determined. In short, having agency is to be the author of your life. To be bored is to lack agency. To overcome boredom, then, we must reclaim our agency.

But being bored is like being forced to solve an impossible problem. Boredom demands that we do something, yet it simultaneously prevents us from desiring anything doable. We're torn, pulled in opposite directions by irreconcilable forces. The immobilization of boredom is anything but sedate. And until we've wrestled with this Gordian Knot, we have not come to terms with a boredom worthy of the name. At its core, boredom is a crisis of agency.

Frankfurt's (1971) distinction between first- and second-order desires, and analysis of what it means to exhibit freedom of will, helps illuminate boredom's crisis of agency. For Frankfurt a first-order desire is the simple desire to do something or other, whereas a second-order desire is a desire to have certain first-order desires. For example, we may want to eat ice cream (first order). But we may also wish we did not want to eat ice cream (second order). Second-order desires require self-reflection and evaluation. Applying Frankfurt's framework to boredom we suggest the bored person has conflicting first-order desires. They both *want to do something* and also *do not want to do anything*. Critically, however, they are not neutral about the conflict between these first-order desires. They care about which desire effectively moves them. Because the bored person cares about the efficacy of their conflicting first-order desires they exhibit what Frankfurt calls second-order volition. Second-order volition occurs when we want a certain first-order desire to determine our behavior. In the case of boredom, the bored person *wants* wanting to do something to be the desire which ultimately wins out. In so doing the bored person identifies with one of their first-order desires and by identifying with it is experienced as *their* desire. However, because the bored person does not manage to want to do something, because their behavior is not in line with their second-order volition, they lack what Frankfurt called freedom of will.[1] Thus, according to Frankfurt the bored person "is estranged from himself" and "a helpless or passive bystander to the forces that move him" (1971, 17)—such a person lacks agency.

Bernstein (1975; see also Fenichel 1951; Todman 2003), for example, highlights the centrality of agency in boredom when he observed that chronically bored people feel like "phonies" because they are "always observers of the passing scene, watching it all happen as though from some distant vantage point" (517). Qualitative studies have corroborated Bernstein's notion, showing that bored individuals suffer from diminished agency (Bargdill 2000; Fahlman et al. 2013; Kanevsky and Keighley 2003; Martin et al. 2006). Bargdill put it as follows: "In becoming, people have goals and then attempt to actualize those possible goals . . . [boredom is] the blocking of the process of becoming" (2000, 191). Correlational studies have found a robust relationship between self-report trait boredom and constructs related to agency such as locus of control (Hunter and Csikszentmihalyi 2003), assertiveness (Tolor 1989), psychosocial development (Watt and Vodanovich 1999), self-actualization (McLeod and Vodanovich 1991), self-control (Mugon et al. 2018), and procrastination (Blunt and Pychyl 1998).

It is not obvious how to reconcile the "desire for desires" of Tolstoy with the notion that boredom is a functional goad to meaningful action. If being bored is to lack agency, then how can it also be a push to engage with the world? Desperately desiring meaningful engagement does not simply make it so; in fact, to be bored is to hold this desire in abeyance. What, then, is the function of boredom? If boredom is underpinned by a desire bind—a strong desire to do something but a lack of desire to do anything on offer—it is difficult to see how boredom can also be a call to action or an effective motivation to change. These are the questions we seek to explore in the present chapter. We argue that properly understood *boredom is a crisis of agency*. Although a difficult moment, *boredom is a critical turning point, possessing both danger and opportunity, leading to either a protracted degradation or an enhancement of our agency*. In other words, the way we react to boredom when it happens is critically important. While some approaches strengthen boredom's grip, others can help us move through boredom effectively. Moreover, we argue *structural forces can thwart individual agency, which makes it more difficult to successfully work through boredom*. A failure to identify structural injustices can result in unfairly blaming marginalized people for their boredom. Thus, a complete and effective analysis of the morality of boredom will need to move beyond the psychology of the individual to a consideration of social, political, and economic factors.

1. THE BEST WAY OUT IS ALWAYS THROUGH

A comparison to physical pain helps elucidate functional accounts of boredom.[2] Pain protects our body. If we did not feel pain, then our well-being would be seriously compromised because we would persist in dangerous activities unaware that we were doing harm to our body. Similarly, the aversive feeling of boredom motivates us to rectify a problem, namely, we are failing to be agentic. However, we have to dig a little deeper here to appreciate some important nuance. For example, we would not say that bodily damage is a good thing. It is not a good thing to be in pain because this means our body is being damaged, but it is clearly good that pain feels bad because this motivates us to rectify the problem. So, it could be said that it is adaptive that boredom feels aversive, but that it is not good to be bored per se.

However, if, as we suggest, boredom is underpinned by a desire bind (Eastwood and Gorelik 2019), then it is difficult to also say that the discomfort of boredom can effectively motivate action because to be bored is to be unable to engage in agentic action. This is where the analogy to pain breaks down. Tissue damage does not directly block resolution of the problem signaled by the feeling of pain, whereas a desire bind directly thwarts the problem of engagement signaled by the feeling of boredom. On the face of it, it would seem impossible to hold both that boredom is underpinned by a desire bind and that boredom can be an effective goad to engagement. When bored, you cannot find anything you want to do. So, how can boredom push you toward meaningful engagement?

We believe there is a way to wriggle out of the trap of boredom—and as we'll see, even emerge the better for it—but, like Alexander's approach to the Gordian Knot, we have to come at it obliquely. The obvious strategy is not the correct strategy. In fact, the uncomfortable feeling of boredom often conspires against us finding the right strategy. On first blush, boredom appears to highlight a need for a new compelling experience or activity, coupled with an urge to find something to do in order to assuage the discomfort. This could be called the "empty bucket" framing of boredom.

However, as Susan Sontag (2011) pointed out, approaching boredom as if we are bereft of compelling experience only strengthens boredom's grip. What she called "aesthetic consumerism" and "captured experience" is a mugs game. "Boredom [as Sontag notes] is just the reverse side of fascination: Both depend on being outside rather than inside a situation, and one leads to the other" (2011, 38). Seeking compelling experience and activity is like thrashing in quicksand—it draws us further down into the muck. Perhaps it numbs the feeling of boredom while the entertainment lasts, but ultimately it leaves us more vulnerable. Grabbing our phones and spending two hours scrolling through Facebook whenever we are bored objectifies us and makes it more difficult to understand and effectively act on our intentions. As long as we continue to treat ourselves like a passive object to be filled, we will struggle to become agentic.

The best way out of boredom, to quote Robert Frost, is through boredom. When bored, we have to refrain from the impulse to make the disagreeable feeling go away by lurching into new activities or seeking new experiences. Instead, we need to lean into boredom, circle back and rediscover our agency, and then move forward again. Lack of agency must be addressed before the distress of boredom can be resolved in a lasting manner.

To be clear, we are firmly committed to the notions that being bored is maladaptive and that we should not seek to cultivate or persist in a state of boredom. What we are claiming is that when bored, we can only effectively extricate ourselves from the bind if our initial response is to stay calm and allow ourselves to become temporarily bored.[3] In doing so, we will resurface more quickly and with strengthened agency. Getting out of boredom is like getting out of the proverbial Chinese finger trap: We have to stop fighting.

Switching from an adversarial relationship to a curious exploration is the best way to stop boredom in its tracks. Simply being in the mode of trying to maximize gains makes a task less boring (Smith, Wagaman and Handley 2009). This same principle is borne out in the classroom where all too often students stagger under crippling boredom. Students who adopt what is called a "cognitive approach" strategy experience less boredom and better outcomes in the classroom. Adopting a cognitive approach strategy means moving toward, not away from, the boring situation and changing how one thinks about the situation. This might include reminding oneself of the reasons for doing the activity and its ultimate value. On the other hand, students that try to evade boredom by distracting themselves or literally get up and leave the boring situation are more often bored (Nett et al. 2010, 2011; Tze et al. 2013). Our own research has also demonstrated that people who chronically try to avoid negative feelings actually find boring situations more boring (Mercer-Lynn et al. 2014). Other research shows that individuals low in trait boredom exhibit brain activity reflecting approach motivation. This suggests individuals low in trait boredom are better able to approach the situation to find engaging activities compared to individuals high in trait boredom who tend to avoid or escape the situation (Perone, Weybright, and Anderson 2019). Bottom line, trying to avoid boredom is counterproductive; conversely moving toward boring situations takes the sting out and allows us to find a resolution.

2. A BORING EXPERIMENT

Tim Lomas put himself in a boring situation for science and discovered that—if you don't run from the initial discomfort—the feeling of boredom can morph into something valuable (Lomas 2017). Midway through a flight from Singapore to London he did nothing for one hour but allow himself to become immersed in boredom. He carefully recorded his experience each and every minute using a modified version of Csikszentmihalyi and Larson's (1987) Experience Sampling Method to see what would happen. After analyzing his observations, he made several discoveries. The first was that his experience shifted as he gave himself over to boredom. He writes: "As I began to engage with the exercise (i.e., at the beginning of the hour), I was in the midst of an ongoing state that I would have no hesitation in describing as 'boredom'" (11). But, as Lomas explored the feeling of boredom it started to change. He notes: "I might still have plausibly and legitimately described the hour as 'boring.' Yet at the same time it began to become vibrant and interesting, full of mystery and depth" (11). Lomas goes on to wonder if the experience still counted as boredom. We suggest at that point he was no longer bored. If we anchor our definition of boredom as the aversive state of wanting but being unable to engage in satisfying activity, then clearly, he had shifted from boredom to some other state. So, Lomas discovered that potentially boring situations are not boring if we can move into, instead of away from, our experience.

On the other side of boredom—not being bored—is where the treasure can be found. Boredom can be thought of as a "liminal space" (Kets de Vries 2015, 170), "passageway" (Stern 1988, 11) that "precedes" (Nietzsche 1974, 126) the reward. Lomas found that, by passing through boredom, his relationship with *time, the external world, and himself* was altered for the better. In each case, we argue, his agency was enhanced for having passed through boredom. As we've seen, our agency is thwarted when bored, but our agency is strengthened by working through boredom. Boredom throws down the gauntlet and asks: Will you or won't you step up and make good on your potential to be an agent?

Lomas first describes how leaning into boredom altered his relation with time. Doing nothing rendered time "strange" (11) as he observed it "up close" (14). Time was foregrounded and experienced directly, at times crawling and at other moments passing with surprising rapidity. At first, he experienced a bittersweet "melancholic awareness of time as a precious resource" and "nostalgia for time gone by"[4] but later, an optimistic resolve to "make the most of time" settled in (14). As Lomas's study showed, direct experience of time, which were it not for boredom would remain subtext, impresses upon us the responsibility to create meaning and act in line with our values. Boredom, by orienting us to time, hammers home an important existential fact.

In addressing the Dartmouth graduating class of 1989, Joseph Brodsky put it this way: "You are finite, time tells you in the voice of boredom . . . which puts your existence into its perspective. . . . Yet, the more finite a thing is, the more it is charged with life, emotions, joy, fears, compassion" (109–110). Although humbling, and perhaps uncomfortable, our boredom-revealed-finiteness is at the foundation of what it means to be human. We are finite, temporally bound creatures, and an awareness of this fact motivates us to make the most of time. We can care and be filled with passion precisely because, for us, time is short. In embracing passion, our agency is vivified and we are able to move from boredom to engagement.

The second discovery Lomas made on the other side of boredom was an altered relation with the external environment. As the hour of self-imposed boredom passed, he experienced a shift from disinterest to an enhanced curiosity in his surroundings. When the option to do something else was removed, the "same old" became somehow surprising as he devoted more attention to it. Patterns on the uniforms of the cabin crew became enchanting. Giving the familiar a second look "defamiliarized" it and made the mundane fresh and exciting (2017, 14). But—and here is the key—the environment became captivating not because the qualities of the external stimuli changed, but because Lomas chose to pay close attention to his environment. This finding accords with research showing that paying close attention to something can make it more positively valanced and less boring (Danckert and Eastwood 2020; see trait boredom as an exception that proves the rule: Bornstein, Kale and Cornell 1990). Perhaps contrary to common sense, it appears that attention precedes initial interest (Mugon et al. 2019) and that by paying close attention we discover value in the familiar and mundane.

In terms of agency, we could say that Lomas switched from an exogenous to an endogenous control of attention (e.g., Yantis 2000). In a boring situation, salient environmental cues, such as novelty, are minimal, which forces us to draw on deliberate, endogenous attention systems. Boredom is the state of being attentionally unengaged, and it can quickly occur when exogenous cues abate. But, in such moments, if we can successfully shift to endogenously controlled attention, then we essentially take back control and can become engaged based on our intentions; and in so doing, we enhance our agency.

William James's (1913) classic work on attention and will proposes that endogenous control of attention is "the essential phenomenon of will" (562) and that "the essential achievement of the will, in short, when it is most 'voluntary' is to attend to a difficult object and hold it fast before the mind" (561). When James says, "difficult object," he means an object that does not attract and hold attention of its own accord. So, according to James, Lomas was manifesting agency in shifting from boredom to endogenously controlled attention. Critical to our argument about the agency boosting opportunities of working through boredom, it could be said that Lomas's boredom created a clearing for endogenous attention control, and in so doing called forth his agency.

Based on his experience sampling research, Csikszentmihalyi (1978) explored the psychological benefits of being able to voluntarily focus attention. He reports:

> In such a state a person feels fully alive and in control, because he or she can direct the flow of reciprocal information that unites person and environment in an interactive system. I know that I am alive, that I am somebody, that I matter, when I can choose to interact with a system of stimuli that I can modify and from which I can get meaningful feedback, whether the system is made up of other people, musical notes, ideas, or tools. The ability to focus attention is

the most basic way of reducing ontological anxiety, the fear of impotence, of nonexistence. (1978, 344)

Csikszentmihalyi's work also demonstrated the negative consequences of what he called "flow disruption," which is the inability to achieve and maintain voluntary focus of attention on limited stimulus field. When participants' "freedom of attention" was thwarted, they experienced a host of negative feelings including a depressed mood (Csikszentmihalyi, 1978). Drawing on the work of James (1913) and Csikszentmihalyi (1978), Eastwood et al. (2012) unpacked the link between attention, agency, and boredom, concluding that "the ability to successfully exert control to utilize attention provides the foundation for our elaborated sense of agency and, conversely, the inability to engage attention results in a self that is blocked" (489). These notions draw into sharp relief the value of being able to wrest control of our attention from external forces and instead direct attention based on our intentions,[5] which is precisely what boredom affords and requires of us. Boredom does not guarantee that we will step up and control our attention, but it clears away exogenous forces so that self-determination is possible.

Finally, by passing through boredom, Lomas transformed his relationship with himself. As Lomas discovered, boredom is associated with enhanced self-focused attention (Danckert and Eastwood 2020). When bored we are unengaged and thrown back onto ourselves. In contrast, in a flow state, for example, the self disappears into the doing; the self becomes a transparent medium we fail to notice when engaged. Critically, as Lomas worked through boredom, he noticed an increasing awareness of not just what he thought and felt but how his mind operated. His mind, usually a tool to think about other things, became turned to self-examination. In addition to increased insight into the functioning of his mind, Lomas noted an increased awareness of his bodily sensations. He became more grounded within his bodily existence.

Critically, the self-focused attention of boredom has the potential to enhance or further impoverish our agency, and once again, we see the liminal nature of boredom. When in the throes of boredom, we focus on our self as an object, and we lose our self as a self-determining agent. If we are not careful, then we can get stuck here and therefore stuck in boredom. Clearly self-focused attention is often maladaptive (e.g., Csikszentmihalyi 2014; 1982; Trapnell and Campbell 1999). However, self-focused attention is also associated with flourishing, enhanced mental health and increased agency (Katz et al. 2017). The key is to shift from rumination and objectification to reflexivity. For example, Rennie (2006, 2007) argued that becoming aware of our awareness, exploring our thoughts and feelings (not just becoming aware of our thoughts and feelings)—what he referred to as "radical reflexivity"—is inextricably linked to agency and effective action. When we become radically reflexive, "self-awareness flows into action" as we are able to form intentions rooted in an understanding of ourself (Rennie 2001, 183). So, boredom brings us face to face with ourselves as we are thrown out of engagement. In the moment of being bored we experience our self as an object, but handled carefully, this can be a starting point to becoming radically reflexive and thereby enhance our agency. Agency forged in the crucible of boredom—by no means an insignificant reward of risking potentially boring situations. But to be clear, the point is not to engender boredom. On the contrary, the goal is to become the kind of person that rarely feels bored.

3. RESOLVING BOREDOM IS NO EASY FEAT

The transition from an objectifying self-focused awareness of boredom to an agency-affirming radically reflexive examination of our boredom may be aided by the skills of mindfulness and decentering. These skills involve observing mental events, coupled with a nonevaluative attitude. Previous work has shown that boredom and mindfulness are incompatible—the more bored the less mindful we are (Koval and McWelling 2015). Further, people with strong mindfulness skills experience less boredom (LePera 2011) and are able to tolerate potentially boring situations with less distress (Hallard 2014; Petranker 2018). The salubrious effect of mindfulness and decentering may arise from enhanced approach motivation in the face of negative affect (Davidson et al. 2003; Eftekhari, Tran and McGregor 2017; Keune et al. 2013). In fact, Eftekhari et al. (2017) showed that decentering enhanced approach motivation without altering affect. Once again, consistent with the work of Nett et al. (2010, 2011), we see that overriding the urge to resist, flee from or, so to speak, get into a fight with our boredom, makes a boring situation less boring and so much easier to resolve.

Although using boredom as a chance to regroup and then move back into engagement armed with more clarity and awareness of our intentions holds great promise, it is by no means an easy thing to do. When asserting the general principle that self-focused attention is uncomfortable and maladaptive, Csikszentmihalyi (2014) notes there are "important exceptions" to his generalization (222). He goes on to say that the exceptions would apply to people who are trained to "use reflection in a systematic and constructive way" (ibid.). It is worth noting in this regard that Lomas is an experienced meditator and that he brought that meditation skill to his experiment in boredom immersion.

In a theoretical article, Immordino-Yang and colleagues (2012) highlight the importance of what they call "constructive internal reflection" for our well-being as individuals and as a society. They argue that constructive internal reflection is a skill that needs to be fostered, and that when the external environment makes excessive demands on us it may be difficult to develop and maintain facility with internal reflection. They propose:

> (a) that time and skills for constructive internal reflection are beneficial for emotional learning and well-being; and (b) that inordinately biasing children's and adolescents' attention to the external world may undermine the development of abilities to think about the abstract, moral, and social-emotional aspects of situations, information, memories, and self. Put another way, we hypothesize that consistently imposing high attention demands on children, either in school, through entertainment, or through living conditions, may rob them of opportunities to advance from thinking about "what happened" or "how to do this" to constructing knowledge about "what this means for the world and for the way I live my life." (357)

For many of us, being in a potentially boring situation is scary. Immordino-Yang and colleagues might say that this is because we are lopsided in our development. Sure, we are good in the external world, but when the press of the external world recedes, it is like we are lost, anxious, and unsure of what to do. We don't see the value in reduced external stimulation, and we lack the confidence and skill needed to engage in constructive internal reflection. So, we panic.[6]

But this may not be just our individual problem. Kets de Vries (2015) argues that this tendency is due to a broader culture where being constantly busy is admired, while engaging in internal activities or reflecting is not seen as useful or productive. Being busy with external stimulation is valued. So, we keep at it, leaving very little time for exploring our inner worlds. However, it is only possible to discover what it is that we most desire by stepping back from external stimulation long enough to allow our desires to crystalize—otherwise we aimlessly lurch from one captivating external activity to another. Immordino-Yang et al. (2012) speculate that "down time" is necessary to develop our ability to engage in constructive internal reflection and they worry that too little "down time" might be depriving us of exactly what we need to construct a clear sense of who we are, what matters to us, and how we ought to live our lives. However, it's not only that we are afraid of down time but also a lot of very clever people are spending huge sums of money figuring out how to grab and hold our attention.

In the stirring call to arms, *Stand Out of Our Light*, James Williams (2018) lays bare how the attention economy conspires against constructive internal reflection and thwarts our agency. Williams unpacks how technology is actually making it harder to do things we want to do. The problem is not simply that technology distracts us from goal pursuit or uses up our limited attention bandwidth; rather, according to Williams, we are losing control of our attention to "attentional adversaries" (xii). The rug is being pulled out from under us and we don't even notice the insidious loss of control. The key for Williams is that technology is "not on our side" in that it is designed to hold our attention rather than support our intention (89). Using a striking analogy Williams states: "The competition to monopolize our attention is like a DDoS attack against the human will" (88). Assaults of the attention economy ultimately compromise our capacity for reflection and self-regulation. "Seen in this light, [Williams argues] these new attentional adversaries threaten not only the success but even the integrity of the human will, at both individual and collective levels" (xi). Thus, Williams boldly asserts: "The liberation of human attention may be the defining moral and political struggle of our time" (xii).

4. BOREDOM AT THE MARGINS

Williams's analysis highlights that structural forces can thwart individual agency, making it more difficult to successfully work through boredom. Not just boring people—or people who have failed to develop the skill of constructive internal reflection—get bored. Rather, bored people may be bored because they are disproportionately subject to oppressive forces. For example, Portwood-Stacer (2012) points out that refusal to participate with social media and other technological "attention adversaries" identified by Williams (2018) is not equally possible for all members of society. Those who lack social and economic advantage may not be able to afford the cost of unplugging. An entrepreneur who is not yet well established and connected, for example, might not risk unplugging from social networking sites which are critical to developing a flourishing career. This highlights the possibility that social and economic disadvantage may increase the risk of diminished agency and therefore increased boredom. Indeed, research has shown that, just like other forms of human suffering, boredom is not equally distributed across all segments of society. The marginalized are hit harder.

Initially, it may appear as if boredom in socially disadvantaged communities is a trivial—even a nonexistent—problem. After all, individuals living in underprivileged circumstances have much bigger problems to deal with. From struggling to make ends meet, to unemployment, family issues, and physical and mental health problems, it seems that they cannot possibly have time to be bored (Pampel, Krueger and Denney 2010). We argue that many of these problems and their associated social disadvantages are precisely what give rise to chronic boredom in these communities. In turn, boredom and attempts to escape it contribute to poor well-being and risky behaviors resulting in vicious cycles. These dynamics maintain inequalities by keeping people at the margins of society—unable to break free from boredom's hold.

In a study of a nationally representative sample of American adolescents, youth who lived in rural, compared to urban, areas were more likely to experience high boredom (Martz, Schulenberg, Patrick and Kloska 2018). Willging, Quintero, and Lilliott (2014) examined the experiences of boredom among youth in rural New Mexico—a state that is characterized by significantly lower personal income and more people living below the poverty line than most U.S. states (Willging, Quintero and Lilliott 2014). They found that many young people in these rural communities experienced boredom and that the youth attributed this feeling to lacking socially valued activities. They often resorted to alcohol and drugs to relieve their boredom and were labeled by others as "troublemakers," further pushing them to the margins of society (Willging et al. 2014).

Other studies found links between one's education (or parent education) and higher levels of boredom. Martz and colleagues (2018) showed parent education predicted boredom, such that adolescents whose parents had a high school degree or less were more likely to experience high boredom compared to those whose parents had completed at least some college. Chin et al. (2017) asked a large sample of U.S. adults to report what emotions they were experiencing at every waking half-hour period for seven to ten days and found that higher education (high school compared to dropping out) was associated with lower boredom, and that income was inversely related to boredom.

Several studies found boredom to be a pervasive experience in homeless communities (e.g., O'Neill 2014, 2015; Marshall et al. 2019). O'Neill (2015) examined the experience of boredom in the homeless population of Romania, following the 2008 financial crisis. In the time of communism, occupation and residence were guaranteed such that even individuals who lacked skill or were poor could get by. However, with the fall of communism and after the financial crisis many were rendered superfluous or "human debris, eliminated permanently from producing society" (Arendt 1966, 150; quoted in O'Neill 2015, 391–92). Many Romanians ended up unemployed, or worse, homeless. Their boredom was characterized by disconnection and social isolation (O'Neill 2015). In another recent study, Marshall and colleagues (2019) found that boredom in the homeless community in a North American context was a pervasive experience. Most of the homeless people studied endorsed boredom as a central feature of their homelessness, along with meaninglessness, disconnection, and a lower sense of belonging to one's community.

5. OPPRESSED AGENCY

There are a number of structural forces faced by those on the margins of society that frustrate agency and thus increase boredom, and only by examining these forces can we come to a full understanding of the morality of boredom as a crisis of agency (Ohlmeier, Finkielsztein and Pfaff 2020; van den Berg and O'Neill 2017).

The increase in boredom among marginalized individuals has been attributed to changes in the global economy. While it was primarily the upper class that had free time in the past, world events/changes like global financial crises and globalization lead to great unemployment and poverty. In this case, excess time is not a privilege but rather a symbol of exclusion—being left at the margins of society. Rising globalization and increased opportunities and resources for some have contributed to rising boredom in those who do not have access to such resources or to meaningful ways to spend their time. According to Jervis, Spicer, and Manson (2003), boredom is a result of one's social position, political economic realities, and one's assessment of possible futures—to be bored means to be unsatisfied with current circumstances and to want something better. O'Neil's (2017) study of homelessness shows how "deepening immiseration [can be] understood and embodied through boredom" (6). Living in circumstances of economic deprivation poses a great deal of challenges and constraints that exclude disadvantaged individuals from meaningful participation in society. Lack of employment, educational opportunities, and a shortage of recreational activities provide a breeding ground for boredom through unoccupied time and a lack of opportunities to engage in meaningful activity. Taken together, boredom is being increasingly recognized as an issue of social and occupational injustice (Marshall et al. 2020).

Knowing about, but being blocked from participating in, desired activities can increase boredom levels. For example, in a recent study, Struk, Scholer, Danckert, and Seli (2020) assigned participants into one of two groups: (1) an empty room with only a chair, an empty bookshelf, a chalkboard with no chalk, a filing cabinet, and a desk (control group), or (2) a room containing engaging objects, including chalk at the chalkboard, a laptop computer, partially completed puzzles, blank paper, and crayons. They instructed participants to refrain from engaging in their environment and to stay seated, awake, and to entertain themselves with only their thoughts for fifteen minutes (Struck et al. 2020). Participants assigned to the room with engaging objects reported higher levels of boredom than those in the control condition. The authors argued that environments characterized by high opportunity costs (i.e., presence of alternative more engaging activities) contribute to more boredom because we are more likely to be dissatisfied with our current activity and to seek an alternative (which is not available). Living in underprivileged circumstances with a lack of meaningful activity—while witnessing the kind of opportunities available to others with higher socioeconomic status (SES)—can lead to boredom because under such circumstances it is harder to want to do what is doable. The desire bind of boredom is more likely to set in when we are constrained.

However, to simply say that socially and financially marginalized people are bored because they face limited opportunities to engage in meaningful activity is to miss deeper injustices afoot. It is important to note that marginalization can lead to a chronic and generalized paralysis of agency and a damaging shift in self-perception, which may result in increased trait boredom beyond any given instance of diminished opportunity for satisfying activity. Ohlmeier et al. (2020), for example, highlight how "inhibition of action . . . lack of freedom and control" due to social inequality can lead to "a sense of powerlessness . . . and thus the lack of agency" to effectively engage (9). They go on to state: "Exclusion makes people feel useless, emptied of legitimate purpose and meaning in life, and a sense of belongingness" (11). Indeed, research suggests that social class/SES shapes psychological processes in specific ways (Kraus, Piff, Mendoza-Denton, Rheinschmidt and Keltner 2012). This is not surprising given that SES shapes many aspects of everyday life, including one's neighborhood, school, and employment (Kraus et al. 2012; Lareau 2003; Argyle 1994). Individuals of low SES are vulnerable to external influences on their lives (e.g., neighborhoods are less safe, threats of job instability, resource fluctuations in schools). Their lives are increasingly characterized by a lack of resources, uncertainty, and unpredictability. These circumstances contribute to a focus on managing external constraints and less focus on internal desires, goals, or emotions (Kraus et al. 2012). This might make it more difficult to explore interests, develop the ability to engage in constructive internal reflection, and contribute to a reduced sense of personal agency/control (i.e., the extent to which they feel freedom and influence over their own lives; Kraus et al. 2012; Johnson and Krueger 2005; Lachman and Weaver 1998; Gallo, Bogart, Vranceanu, and Matthews 2005; Kraus et al. 2009).[7]

Those on the margins of society also experience what Fricker (2007) termed epistemic injustice, that is, a systematic inequality in their capacity to be a knower. On the one hand, those facing epistemic injustice are ignored or not believed, and on the other hand, they may struggle to understand themselves because their lived experience cannot be captured within existing conceptual and social frameworks. For example, a homeless person may not be viewed as a credible witness to a crime, and prior to the creation of the term "sexual harassment" a woman may not have been able to articulate and understand what happened to her at work. Roessler (2015) unpacks how epistemic injustice "damages and unsettles a person's relation to herself" (68) sowing seeds of uncertainty and self-doubt that ultimately result in an "impaired ability to make autonomous decisions and follow autonomous projects in her life" (68). More specifically, Roessler notes how epistemic injustice diminishes self-worth and self-knowledge, both of which are necessary for agency. Without self-worth, it is not possible to pursue valued personal projects and without self-knowledge, it is not possible to know what one wants and desires. For Roessler, a key threat of epistemic injustice is how it challenges the belief that one is "legitimized to make up one's mind and determine what one believes" (79). Epistemic deprivation can lead to an impoverished sense of self and thus, more frequent boredom and increased difficulty responding adaptively when boredom strikes.

In sum, those oppressed by social and political structures might experience a chronic paralysis of agency and they may lack the resources that would normally help people move through boredom. Therefore, they are more likely to get "stuck" in boredom and experience it more frequently.

However, Ohlmeier and colleagues (2020) and O'Neill (2015) highlight it is not just that marginalized people are disadvantaged in particular ways that lead to increased struggles with agency and therefore boredom; social and political forces also devalue certain activities, rendering them boring and thus dooming a segment of society to be bored. Living in a cultural milieu that tells you what you are doing is of little value will lead you to construe your life as boring. Ohlmeier and colleagues (2020) suggest that "the interesting question here, is not what was first, marginalized groups performing a certain task or the cultural devaluation of those tasks, but how those developments go hand in hand" (13). The key point here is that social forces play a complex role in boredom. When we shift focus away from the individual and on to social and structural factors, new and important insights as to how social injustice leads to boredom among marginalized people emerge.

Boredom is often blamed on the individual experiencing it (Ohlmeier, Finkielsztein and Pfaff 2020). When someone complains of boredom, we tend to see them as flawed for their inability to entertain themselves in a world full of opportunities (thinking, "only boring people get bored"; Ohlmeier, Finkielsztein and Pfaff 2020). Although to date the scholarship is limited, there is growing recognition that boredom is caused and maintained by social conditions (e.g., Ohlmeier, Finkielsztein and Pfaff 2020), which frustrate personal agency (e.g., Roessler 2015). An individual's sense of personal agency has important implications for their overall health and more specifically their experience with boredom. The way out of boredom is through it. As we suggested earlier, we can only extricate ourselves from the bind if our initial response is to stay calm and reaffirm our agency, a difficult task when facing systemic barriers. Being unable to effectively deal with boredom can lead to more boredom and consequently a further impoverishment of agency—keeping disadvantaged individuals at the margins of society.

6. CONCLUSION

Boredom is not simply a push for change. Because to be bored *is* to be *unable* to find anything one wants to do. It is to feel adrift, watching the world passing by. It is to lack a sense of control and authorship of one's life. However, if addressed carefully, boredom can be a passageway to understanding what matters to us and to reclaiming our agency. To effectively address boredom, we need to slow down, stop and listen to what it is telling us. Boredom requires us to exercise agency. But that is by no means an easy feat. Structural forces (e.g., social, political, and economic factors) can make this very task extremely challenging, leaving disadvantaged people vulnerable to chronic boredom and keeping them at the margins.

NOTES

1. It is worth noting that Frankfurt's analysis is separate from the question of determinism, that is, he is not claiming that freedom of will is the absence of determination but rather that freedom of will is about an internal relation or the conformity of will to second-order volitions.

2. Elpidorou made this comparison at a Boredom conference in 2015.

3. Phillips (1993) makes a similar claim from a psychoanalytic framework. He argues for the developmental importance of boredom as a precondition for allowing a child to develop a conscious representation of their desires.

4. See also Van Tilburg et al. (2013) for nostalgia as a response to boredom.

5. As we discuss in the second half of the chapter, structural, systematic, historical, and political forces shape situational and psychological factors that make it more or less possible to work through boredom effectively and reclaim agency.

6. Boredom can also occur in moments of overstimulation, and in such cases different skills may be needed to calm oneself and to find a cognitive "foothold" within the situation at hand.

7. However, when agency and meaning is retained, social inequality does not necessarily contribute to more boredom. For example, Jervis and colleagues (2003) found that Indigenous Americans who engaged in meaningful activities like religion and community activism did not experience persistent boredom.

REFERENCES

Arendt, Hannah. 1996. *The Origins of Totalitarianism*. Cleveland: World Publishing Company.

Argyle, Michael. 1994. *The Psychology of Social Class.* New York: Routledge.

Barbalet, Jack M. 1999. "Boredom and Social Meaning." *The British journal of sociology* 50, no. 4: 631–646.

Bargdill, Richard. 2000. "The Study of Life Boredom." *Journal of Phenomenological Psychology* 31, no. 2: 188–219.

Bench, Shane W., and Heather C. Lench. 2013. "On the Function of Boredom." *Behavioral Sciences* 3, no. 3: 459–472.

Bernstein, Haskell E. 1975. "Boredom and the Ready-Made Life." *Social Research* 42, no. 3: 512–537.

Blunt, Allan, and Timothy A. Pychyl. 1998. "Volitional Action and Inaction in the Lives of Undergraduate Students: State Orientation, Procrastination and Proneness to Boredom." *Personality and Individual Differences* 24, no. 6: 837–846.

Bornstein, Robert F., Amy R. Kale, and Karen R. Cornell. 1990. "Boredom as a Limiting Condition on the Mere Exposure Effect." *Journal of Personality and Social Psychology* 58, no. 5: 791–800.

Brodsky, Joseph. 1995. *On Grief and Reason: Essays.* New York, NY: Farrar, Straus and Giroux.

Chin, Alycia, Amanda Markey, Saurabh Bhargava, Karim S. Kassam, and George Loewenstein. 2017. "Bored in the USA: Experience Sampling and Boredom in Everyday Life." *Emotion* 17, no. 2: 359–368.

Csikszentmihalyi, Mihaly. 1978. "Attention and the Holistic Approach to Behavior." In *The Stream of Consciousness*, edited by Kenneth S. Pope and Jerome L. Singer, 335–358. Boston, MA: Springer.

Csikszentmihalyi, Mihaly. 2014. "Toward a Psychology of Optimal Experience." In *Flow and the Foundations of Positive Psychology: The Collected Works of Mihaly Csikszentmihalyi*, edited by Mihaly Csikszentmihalyi, 209–226. Dordrecht: Springer.

Csikszentmihalyi, Mihaly, and Thomas J. Figurski. 1982. "Self-Awareness and Aversive Experience in Everyday Life." *Journal of Personality* 50, no. 1: 15–19.

Csikszenimihalyi, M., and Reed Larson. 1987. "Validity and Reliability of the Experience Sampling Method." *The Journal of Nervous and Mental Disease* 175, no. 9: 526–536.

Danckert, James, and John D. Eastwood. 2020. *Out of My Skull: The Psychology of Boredom.* Cambridge, MA: Harvard University Press.

Danckert, James, Jhotisha Mugon, Andriy Struk, and John Eastwood. 2018. "Boredom: What Is It Good For?." In *The Function of Emotions: When and Why Emotions Help Us*, edited by Heather C. Lench, 93–119. Cham: Springer.

Davidson, Richard J., Jon Kabat-Zinn, Jessica Schumacher, Melissa Rosenkranz, Daniel Muller, Saki F. Santorelli, Ferris Urbanowski, Anne Harrington, Katherine Bonus, and John F. Sheridan. 2003. "Alterations in Brain and Immune Function Produced by Mindfulness Meditation." *Psychosomatic Medicine* 65, no. 4: 564–570.

Eastwood, John D., Alexandra Frischen, Mark J. Fenske, and Daniel Smilek. 2012. "The Unengaged Mind: Defining Boredom in Terms of Attention." *Perspectives on Psychological Science* 7, no. 5: 482–495.

Eastwood, John D., and Dana Gorelik. 2019. "Boredom Is a Feeling of Thinking and a Double-Edged Sword." In *Boredom Is In Your Mind*, edited by Josefa Ros Velasco, 55–70. Cham: Springer.

Eftekhari, Eldar, Alex Tran, and Ian McGregor. 2017. "Decentering Increases Approach Motivation Among Distressed Individuals." *Personality and Individual Differences* 119: 236–241.

Elpidorou, Andreas. 2014. "The Bright Side of Boredom." *Frontiers in Psychology* 5: 1245.

Fahlman, Shelley A., Kimberley B. Mercer-Lynn, David B. Flora, and John D. Eastwood. 2013. "Development and Validation of the Multidimensional State Boredom Scale." *Assessment* 20, no. 1: 68–85.

Frankfurt, Harry G. 1971. "Freedom of the Will and the Concept of a Person." *The Journal of Philosophy* 68, no. 1: 5–20.

Fricker, Miranda. 2007. *Epistemic Injustice: Power and the Ethics of Knowing*. Oxford: Oxford University Press.

Fenichel, Otto. "On the Psychology of Boredom." In *Organization and Pathology of Thought: Selected sources*, edited by David Rapaport, 349–361. New York: Columbia University Press.

Gallo, Linda C., Laura M. Bogart, Ana-Maria Vranceanu, and Karen A. Matthews. 2005. "Socioeconomic Status, Resources, Psychological Experiences, and Emotional Responses: A Test of the Reserve Capacity Model." *Journal of Personality and Social Psychology* 88, no. 2: 386–399.

Hallard, Robert Ian. 2014. "Mindfulness Meditation Practice Can Make Concentration Feel a Little Easier." *Cumbria Partnership Journal of Research Practice and Learning* 4: 17–22.

Hunter, Jeremy P., and Mihaly Csikszentmihalyi. 2003. "The positive Psychology of Interested Adolescents." *Journal of Youth and Adolescence* 32, no. 1: 27–35.

Immordino-Yang, Mary Helen, Joanna A. Christodoulou, and Vanessa Singh. 2012. "Rest Is Not Idleness: Implications of the Brain's Default Mode for Human Development and Education." *Perspectives on Psychological Science* 7, no. 4: 352–364.

James, William. 1913. *The Principles of Psychology*. New York: Henry Holt and Co.

Jervis, Lori L., Paul Spicer, and Spero M. Manson. 2003. "Boredom, 'Trouble,' and the realities of Postcolonial Reservation Life." *Ethos* 3, no. 1: 38–58.

Johnson, Wendy, and Robert F. Krueger. 2005. "Higher Perceived Life Control Decreases Genetic Variance in Physical Health: Evidence from a National Twin Study." *Journal of Personality and Social Psychology* 88, no. 1: 165–173.

Kanevsky, Lannie, and Tacey Keighley. 2003. "To Produce or Not to Produce? Understanding Boredom and the Honor in Underachievement." *Roeper Review* 26, no. 1: 20–28.

Katz, Danielle, Georges Monette, Peter Gaskovski, and John Eastwood. 2017. "The Creation of the Client Reflexivity Scale: A Measure of Minute Fluctuations in Self-Awareness and Exploration." *Psychotherapy Research* 27, no. 6: 724–736.

Keune, Philipp M., Vladimir Bostanov, Martin Hautzinger, and Boris Kotchoubey. 2013. "Approaching Dysphoric Mod: State-Effects of Mindfulness Meditation on Frontal Brain Asymmetry." *Biological Psychology* 93, no. 1: 105–113.

Koval, Samuel R., and Todman McW. 2015. "Induced Boredom Constrains Mindfulness: An Online Demonstration." *Psychology Cognitive Sciences Open Journal* 1, no. 1: 1–9.

Kraus, Michael W., Paul K. Piff, and Dacher Keltner. 2009. "Social Class, Sense of Control, and Social Explanation." *Journal of Personality and Social Psychology* 97, no. 6: 992–1004.

Kraus, Michael W., Paul K. Piff, Rodolfo Mendoza-Denton, Michelle L. Rheinschmidt, and Dacher Keltner. 2012. "Social Class, Solipsism, and Contextualism: How the Rich Are Different From the Poor." *Psychological Review* 119, no. 3: 546–572.

Lachman, Margie E., and Suzanne L. Weaver. 1998. "The Sense of Control as a Moderator of Social Class Differences in Health and Well-Being." *Journal of Personality and Social Psychology* 74, no. 3: 763–773.

Lareau, Annette. 2003. *Unequal Childhoods: Class, Race, and Family Life.* Berkeley: University of California Press.

LePera, Nicole. 2011. "Relationships Between Boredom Proneness, Mindfulness, Anxiety, Depression, and Substance Use." *The New School Psychology Bulletin* 8, no. 2: 15–25.

Lomas, Tim. 2017. "A Meditation on Boredom: Re-Appraising its Value Through Introspective Phenomenology." *Qualitative Research in Psychology* 14, no. 1: 1–22.

Marshall, Carrie Anne, Lisa Davidson, Andrea Li, Rebecca Gewurtz, Laurence Roy, Skye Barbic, Bonnie Kirsh, and Rosemary Lysaght. 2019. "Boredom and Meaningful Activity in Adults Experiencing Homelessness: A Mixed-Methods Study." *Canadian Journal of Occupational Therapy* 86, no. 5: 357–370.

Marshall, Carrie Anne, Laurence Roy, Alyssa Becker, Melanie Nguyen, Skye Barbic, Carina Tjörnstrand, Rebecca Gewurtz, and Sarah Wickett. 2020. "Boredom and Homelessness: A Scoping Review." *Journal of Occupational Science* 27, no. 1: 107–124.

Martin, Marion, Gaynor Sadlo, and Graham Stew. 2006. "The Phenomenon of Boredom." *Qualitative Research in Psychology* 3, no. 3: 193–211.

Martz, Meghan E., John E. Schulenberg, Megan E. Patrick, and Deborah D. Kloska. 2018. "'I Am So Bored!': Prevalence Rates and Sociodemographic and Contextual Correlates of High Boredom Among American Adolescents." *Youth & Society* 50, no. 5: 688–710.

McLeod, Carol R., and Stephen J. Vodanovich. 1991. "The Relationship Between Self-Actualization and Boredom Proneness." *Journal of Social Behavior and Personality* 6, no. 5: 137–146.

Mercer-Lynn, Kimberley B., Rachel J. Bar, and John D. Eastwood. 2014. "Causes of Boredom: The Person, the Situation, or Both?." *Personality and Individual Differences* 56: 122–126.

Mugon, Jhotisha, Andriy Struk, and James Danckert. 2018. "A Failure to Launch: Regulatory Modes and Boredom Proneness." *Frontiers in Psychology* 9: 1126.

Mugon, Jhotisha, James Danckert, and John Eastwood. 2019. "The Costs and Benefits of Boredom in the Classroom." In *The Cambridge Handbook on Motivation and Learning,* edited by K. Ann Renninger and Suzanne E. Hidi, 490–514. Cambridge: Cambridge University Press.

Nett, Ulrike E., Thomas Goetz, and Lia M. Daniels. 2010. "What to Do When Feeling bored?: Students' Strategies for Coping with Boredom." *Learning and Individual Differences* 20, no. 6: 626–638.

Nett, Ulrike E., Thomas Goetz, and Nathan C. Hall. 2011. "Coping with Boredom in School: An Experience Sampling Perspective." *Contemporary Educational Psychology* 36, no. 1: 49–59.

Nietzsche, Friedrich. 1974. *The Gay Science: With a Prelude in Rhymes and an Appendix of Songs.* Translated and edited by Walter Kaufmann. New York: Random House.

Ohlmeier, Silke, Mariusz Finkielsztein, and Holger Pfaff. 2020. "Why We Are Bored: Towards a Sociological Approach to Boredom." *Sociological Spectrum* 40, no. 3: 208–225.

O'Neill, Bruce. 2017. *The Space of Boredom: Homelessness in the Slowing Global Order.* Durham: Duke University Press.

O'Neill, Bruce. 2015. "Bored Stiff: Sex and Superfluity in a Time of Crisis." *Public Culture* 27, no. 2 (76): 387–405.

O'Neill, Bruce. 2014. "Cast Aside: Boredom, Downward Mobility, and Homelessness in Post-Communist Bucharest." *Cultural Anthropology* 29, no. 1: 8–31.

Pampel, Fred C., Patrick M. Krueger, and Justin T. Denney. "Socioeconomic Disparities in Health Behaviors." *Annual Review of Sociology* 36: 349–370.

Perone, Sammy, Elizabeth H. Weybright, and Alana J. Anderson. 2019. "Over and Over Again: Changes in Frontal EEG Asymmetry Across a Boring Task." *Psychophysiology* 56, no. 10: e13427.

Petranker, Rotem. 2018. "Sitting With It: Examining the Relationship Between Mindfulness, Sustained attention, and Boredom." https://yorkspace.library.yorku.ca/xmlui/handle/10315/35545

Phillips, Adam. 1993. *On Kissing, Tickling and Being Bored.* Cambridge: Harvard University Press.

Portwood-Stacer, Laura. 2012. "Media Refusal and Conspicuous Non-Consumption: The Performative and Political Dimensions of Facebook Abstention." *New Media & Society* 15, no. 7: 1041–1057.

Rennie, David L. 2006. "Radical Reflexivity: Rationale for an Experiential Person-Centered Approach to Counseling and Psychotherapy." *Person-Centered & Experiential Psychotherapies* 5, no. 2: 114–126.

Rennie, David L. 2007. "Reflexivity and Its Radical Form: Implications for the Practice of Humanistic Psychotherapies." *Journal of Contemporary Psychotherapy* 37, no. 1: 53–58.

Rennie, David L. 2001. "The Client as a Self-Aware Agent in Counselling and Psychotherapy." *Counselling and Psychotherapy Research* 1, no. 2: 82–89.

Roessler, Beate. 2015. "Autonomy, Self-Knowledge, and Oppression." In *Personal Autonomy and Social Oppression: Philosophical Perspectives,* edited by Marina Oshana, 68–84. New York: Routledge.

Smith, Jessi L., Jill Wagaman, and Ian M. Handley. 2009. "Keeping It Dull or Making It Fun: Task Variation as a Function of Promotion Versus Prevention Focus." *Motivation and Emotion* 33, no. 2: 150–160.

Sontag, Susan. 2011. *On Photography.* New York: Farrar, Straus, & Giroux.

Stern, E. Mark. 1988. "An Awakening and Complexity." *The Psychotherapy Patient* 3, no. 3–4: 5–16.

Struk, Andriy A., Abigail A. Scholer, James Danckert, and Paul Seli. 2020. "Rich Environments, Dull Experiences: How Environment Can Exacerbate the Effect of Constraint on the Experience of Boredom." *Cognition and Emotion* 34, no. 7: 1517–1523.

Todman, McWelling. 2003. "Boredom and Psychotic Disorders: Cognitive and Motivational Issues." *Psychiatry: Interpersonal and Biological Processes* 66, no. 2: 146–167.

Tolor, Alexander. 1989. "Boredom as Related to Alienation, Assertiveness, Internal-External Expectancy, and Sleep Patterns." *Journal of Clinical Psychology* 45, no. 2: 260–265.

Trapnell, Paul D., and Jennifer D. Campbell. 1999. "Private Self-Consciousness and the Five-Factor Model of Personality: Distinguishing Rumination from Reflection." *Journal of Personality and Social Psychology* 76, no. 2: 284–304.

Tze, Virginia M. C., Lia M. Daniels, Robert M. Klassen, and Johnson C-H. Li.2013. "Canadian and Chinese University Students' Approaches to Coping With Academic Boredom." *Learning and Individual Differences* 23: 32–43.

Van den Berg, Marguerite, and Bruce O'Neill. 2017. "Introduction: Rethinking the Class Politics of Boredom." *Focaal* 78: 1–8.

Van Tilburg, Wijnand A. P., Eric R. Igou, and Constantine Sedikides. 2013. "In Search of Meaningfulness: Nostalgia as an Antidote to Boredom." *Emotion* 13, no. 3: 450–461.

de Vries, Manfred F. R. Kets. 2015. "Doing Nothing and Nothing to do: The Hidden Value of Empty Time and Boredom." *Organizational Dynamics* 44, no. 3: 169–175.

Watt, John D., and Stephen J. Vodanovich. 1999. "Boredom Proneness and Psychosocial Development." *The Journal of Psychology* 133, no. 3: 303–314.

Willging, Cathleen E., Gilbert A. Quintero, and Elizabeth A. Lilliott. 2014. "Hitting the Wall: Youth Perspectives on Boredom, Trouble, and Drug Use Dynamics in Rural New Mexico." *Youth & Society* 46, no. 1: 3–29.

Williams, James. 2018. *Stand Out of Our Light: Freedom and Resistance in the Attention Economy.* Cambridge: Cambridge University Press.

Yantis, Steven. 2000. "Goal-Directed and Stimulus-Driven Determinants of Attentional Control." In *Control of Cognitive Processes: Attention and Performance* XVIII, edited by Stephen Monsell and Jon Driver, 73–103. Cambridge: MA: MIT Press.

Chapter 6

Boredom Mismanagement and Attributions of Social and Moral Costs

McWelling Todman

Human communities are built on the shared conviction that the capacity for self-regulation is not only a sign of psychological health and maturity but also necessary for the maintenance of effective social regulation in the form of compliance with social norms and expectations. The management of emotions, both positive and negative, is central to most theories of self-regulation and its disruption is often the earliest and clearest evidence of dysregulation. Boredom, a particularly ubiquitous feeling state, appears to play an important role in the self-regulation of reward-seeking and exploratory behavior by providing a signal to self and others that the current environment (internal or external) is failing in its capacity to yield new sources of potential reinforcement (e.g., Elpidorou 2014; Todman 2003). Most of us respond almost reflexively to such a signal with often subtle changes to the environment and to the strategies being used to interact with it.

In this chapter, I introduce the Integrated Attentional Investment Theory of boredom (IAIT; Weiss et al. 2020) as a framework for describing four types of boredom management strategies that I believe are critical for effective self-regulation. I contend that the skill with which these management strategies are deployed largely determines an individual's perceived regulatory success. I further argue that the success or failure to effectively manage one's boredom is invariably attributed to voluntary, intentional behavior, thus subject to judgments about both competence and moral intent. In this context, I try to illustrate how certain structural inequities in societies are likely to be linked to class differences in the opportunities to acquire and practice normative boredom management skills in various institutional settings (e.g., schools). These inequities in skill acquisition, I also argue, may give rise to the erroneous contention that boredom management deficits are the consequences of fundamental deficits in terms of competencies, potentialities, and moral values. In other words, how we are perceived to choose to manage our boredom necessarily influences assessments by others of both our self-regulatory competencies and our moral standing within our shared community. I will be drawing on examples involving substance misuse, antisocial and schizoid traits, and the problems that arise from the intersection of class and school environments to illustrate the conditions that are likely to give rise to this type of dynamic. But first, we need to establish what is meant by the term "boredom."

1. WHAT IS BOREDOM?

I begin this chapter by openly admitting that there is not yet a universally accepted definition of boredom, a situation that partly reflects the fact that boredom has only recently become an object of rigorous scientific scrutiny. This definitional uncertainty has been further compounded by the still common tendency to conflate the subjective experience of boredom (state boredom) and its frequency of occurrence with the predisposition to be easily bored (commonly referred to as "trait" boredom) (Todman 2003, 2007). While it is by definition true that individuals with high levels of trait boredom would be expected to report more frequent episodes of boredom, it does not follow that all individuals who report high levels of state boredom should also have high levels of trait boredom. Nor is it axiomatic that all individuals who describe themselves as having high levels of trait boredom are destined to lives marked by higher rates of state boredom—especially if we accept the proposition that individuals can learn to avoid or manage situations that are likely to make them bored, just as it is possible to avoid many situations that make us anxious. Consequently, we do not yet know how many of the ever-growing list of untoward correlates of trait boredom (e.g., Harris 2000; Iso-Ahola and Crowley 1991; Wegner and Flisher 2009) are due to higher than normal rates of state boredom rather than the latent and underlying dispositional factors that are presumed to give rise to putative trait differences (Todman 2003, 2007). Indeed, because it is likely that a variety of factors, some inborn and others not, contribute to an atypically high (or low) propensity to become bored, the comments that I will be making about boredom and its putative relationships to moral behavior and decision-making should be viewed with some caution, as many of my arguments must necessarily rely on research where the distinction between trait and state boredom is not always clearly drawn (Todman 2003, 2013).

Boredom and Function: Constraints, Expectations, and Beliefs

To avoid some of the definitional confusion described above, I have chosen to organize my arguments around a functional definition of boredom, which embraces the view that boredom is an emotion. Like other emotions, it is presumed to have a function or evolutionary purpose concerning adaptation (e.g., Bench and Lench 2013; Fisher 1993; Todman 2013). Hence, in the barest of terms, boredom is conceived to be a dysphoric feeling state that signals that the current mode and focus of attentional engagement (e.g., waiting on hold during a phone call to a tech helpline) have failed to yield a satisfactory level of reward or reinforcement, and, critically, there are perceived constraints on one's ability to seek engagement elsewhere (e.g., Todman 2013). I would also suggest that a critical part of the calculus for making this determination is the individual's convictions about (a) the size of the required attentional investment per subjective unit time, (b) the size of the anticipated investment return, and (c) the availability and potential value of competing targets for attentional investment (Weiss et al. 2020).

To the extent that the beliefs and expectations embedded in the investment process are subject to distortion through contextual manipulations (e.g., via misinformation), it should be possible to influence the feelings of boredom even when the stimulus conditions and task demands remain objectively unchanged. Indeed, several studies suggest that this is the case. For example, London and Monello (1974) demonstrated that individuals are more inclined to rate tasks as more boring when clock time is manipulated to appear as if it is passing more slowly than expected. More recent studies have also confirmed that a positive hedonic response can be induced by creating the illusion of hastened temporal progression and that the induction of a false belief about the boringness of a future task is sufficient to cause the task to be experienced as being more time consuming (Sucala et al. 2010). Additionally, findings from studies by Pallak and Pittman (1972) and others suggest that the conviction that one is unconstrained while performing a boredom-inducing task may be sufficient to inhibit the usual illusion of temporal slowing, although the interpretation of the results from some of these studies has not always been straightforward (see Toutwine and O'Neil [1981] as an example)

An IAIT

Emily Weiss, one of my doctoral students, and I have attempted to capture this slightly more elaborated functional conceptualization of boredom using the IAIT (Weiss et al. 2020). The IAIT, which incorporates the basic processing elements described above, posits that state boredom is the subjective manifestation of the opportunity costs that accrue when attentional resources invested in a task under conditions of subjective constraint fail to provide the expected or desired return on investment. In other words, boredom always involves the feeling that time and attentional resources that could otherwise be used more productively are being squandered. Attention (broadly defined) and subjective time are thus conceptualized as psychological commodities that can be invested, divested, hedged, devalued, lost, and even misappropriated in our ongoing transactions with our environments. It is through this framework that I will endeavor to explore boredom's impact on moral behavior.

We are, of course, aware of the danger of leaning too heavily on an economic/investment metaphor to describe psychological processes, and readily concede that there are several alternative models of boredom to be found in the literature that are well articulated and already enjoy substantial empirical support (see Westgate and Wilson [2018], for a description of their MAC theory of boredom and a thorough review of many of the alternative theories). And it is not our contention that any of the alternative models are any less capable of accounting for what I will have to say in the following pages. However, even though the IAIT has not yet been subjected to rigorous empirical scrutiny, we believe that it is a framework that is compatible with most of the important observations that have been made about boredom in the research literature, and also hospitable to the broad diversity of perspectives that have been put forward to account for those observations. Additionally, the IAIT is relatively easy to reconcile with the dynamic and cognitive-behavioral models that clinicians use to formulate their understanding of clinical dysfunction, especially with respect to the management of negative emotions, thus making it particularly appealing as an organizing instrument for this chapter. Below are some of the key observations and widely held assumptions in the boredom literature that we have tried to accommodate and incorporate into the IAIT. Specifically, the IAIT posits the following:

a. The processes associated with the management and allocation of attentional resources are central to the subjective experience of boredom (see Damrad-Frye and Liard 1989; Danckert and Allman 2005; Eastwood et al. 2012; Zakay 2014).
b. Boredom is an emotion, and thus has a function, an evolutionary purpose, which is tied to the proximal goal of optimizing the attentional allocation process (see Bench and Lench 2013; Elpidorou 2014), as well as the more distal goal of improving adaptive fitness through the search for new information that can be readily integrated with what we already know (see Bench and Lench 2013).
c. Boredom has a signaling function that indicates that the optimization process is being frustrated and that attentional processes should be invested elsewhere or a different mode of engagement with the current environment/task needs to be adopted (see Elpidorou 2014, 2017). This optimization process has variously been referred to as the putative

self-regulatory function of boredom (see Elpidorou 2014; Moynihan, Igou, and Van Tilburg 2017a).

d. The optimization failure that is reflected in the experience of boredom is in large part due to the constraints placed on the desire to reallocate underperforming attentional resources. The constraints can be internal or external in origin. Often, they exist in the form of the abstract social rules and conventions that govern and regulate everyday social behavior, but they can also be natural, physical constraints like a snowstorm or a pandemic that forces us to remain indoors for an extended period (see Chin et al. 2017; Daschmann, Goetz, and Stupnisky 2011; Toutwine and O'Neil 1981).

e. The feeling of state boredom is the subjective manifestation of the opportunity costs that accrue when attentional resources invested in a task or stimulus under conditions of subjective constraint fail to provide the expected or desired return on investment (see Kurzban et al. 2013).

f. Attentional processing requires time, and as such the potential psychological cost or value associated with the utilization and allocation of attentional resources is partly determined by the amount of perceived time invested in attending to a task or stimulus (see Danckert and Allman 2005; London and Monello 1974; Watt 1991; Zakay 2014).

g. We agree with Westgate and Wilson (2018) that it is possible for us to become bored with our own thoughts, and we contend that a model of boredom in which thoughts, memories, and perceptual representations are constantly vying for attentional investment is consistent with this observation. As is made clear later in the chapter, this point is particularly relevant to the putative relationship between boredom and substance use.

h. Boredom is believed to be a negative emotion, and like other negative feeling states it is assumed that humans (and other species) are incentivized to either avoid or minimize exposure to conditions that are likely to lead to its occurrence/recurrence (see Havermans et al. 2015; Wilson et al. 2014)

i. Boredom can be mitigated by the creation of "meaning" (see Van Tilburg and Igou 2012, 2013; Van Tilburg, Igou, and Sedikides 2013; Westgate and Wilson 2018), a construct that is difficult to define. However, engagement with a task that is experienced as "meaningful" as opposed to one that is boring always seems to involve the conviction that even when there is little in the way of near-term return on investment, there is the possibility of obtaining later outcomes that are perceived to be relevant to the individual's personal goals, values, and perceived standing in the community. As such, the relationship between boredom and meaning hinges on the drive to preserve a continued sense of self (see Van Tilburg and Igou 2011a, 2011b).

j. Boredom is affected by beliefs and expectations. Altering what individuals believe about the parameters of their attentional allocations and the constraints surrounding them can affect the experience of temporal progression, the intensity of feelings of boredom, the perceived distribution of attentional resources, and the attributions about the source of one's feelings of boredom (see Damrad-Frye and Laird 1989; London and Monello 1974; Sucala 2010).

k. Boredom experiences promote learning, especially regarding their management. Some of the acquired boredom management strategies are limited to the identification, anticipation, and avoidance of future boring environments and tasks. More sophisticated strategies tend to involve acquired skills devoted to the approach, tolerance, and reframing of boredom-inducing conditions so that engagement is more likely. The mitigation of boredom through meaning-making (see Van Tilburg and Igou, 2013; Van Tilburg, Igou, and Sedikides 2013; Westgate and Wilson 2018) is an example of this latter type of boredom management. We also conjecture that it would be difficult to persevere on the acquisition of difficult-to-learn skills (especially in educational settings) without the benefit of the more sophisticated types of boredom management strategies.

Boredom: Self- and Social-Regulation

A functional definition of boredom, of which the IAIT is one of many possible derivatives, is consistent with the idea that boredom serves a self-regulatory purpose, a view that is widely shared by a number theorists (e.g., Elpidorou 2014; Moynihan, Igou, and Van Tilburg 2017; Todman 2013; Westgate and Wilson 2018). Although there have been important and subtle differences in the way this self-regulatory function has been described in the literature, there seems to be general agreement that without feelings of boredom to guide us, it would be difficult to construct and maintain a life that is both meaningful and purposeful (Elpidorou 2014; Van Tilburg and Igou 2011a). Prodded by feelings of boredom, and perhaps even more frequently, the anticipation of boredom, we are incentivized to constantly update what we think we know about ourselves and the world that we inhabit, but only to the extent that the new experiences are interpretable based on what we already know, believe, and value (e.g., Csikszentmihalyi 2000; Vygotsky 1980).

However, boredom also serves a social-regulatory function. It can be argued that the members of a given community share certain assumptions about boredom that are likely to influence the way they perceive, evaluate, and respond to the choices made by other individuals in the same community. For example, most of us have a pretty good sense of the conditions that tend to provoke feelings of boredom in the average person, and we assume that as adults with agency we can choose to avoid or at least limit our exposure to circumstances that are likely to provoke boredom. We probably also believe that we can recognize expressions of boredom in other people, especially among people who we know well. And we certainly have an opinion as to when, where, how, and for how long individuals should be expected to tolerate their boredom and the strategies that they might use to mitigate its severity. Collectively, all these assumptions, I would argue, act through the connective threads of the social fabric to influence the way we make attributions about the behaviors and motivations of not only other individuals but also groups of individuals who happen to share certain (relevant and irrelevant) characteristics. To the extent that these attributions contribute to erroneous judgments about capacities and potentialities, they can also potentially bring about flawed social policies that ultimately lead to disparities in the way social resources are allocated. After all, while it is unusual for someone to be accused of consciously choosing to be anxious or depressed (except under artificial circumstances such as in a theatrical performance), that is not the case with an emotion like boredom or anger. Adults (and even young children in some contexts) are assumed to have some control over the conditions that trigger and sustain feelings of boredom, and if we are frequently bored or bored for an extended period, it is not unusual for others to attribute our boredom to a conscious choice that is indicative of some type of self-regulatory failure. Lastly, the extent to which these types of negatively valenced attributions are likely to be erroneous and consequential for an individual's social standing suggests that boredom's putative social-regulatory function is inextricably intertwined with the notion of social justice.

2. INDIVIDUAL MORAL DECISION-MAKING VS. SOCIAL JUSTICE AND EQUITY

Although boredom and the propensity to become bored probably do influence the way individuals make morally relevant choices (e.g., Barbalet 1999; Ferrell 2004; Van Tilburg and Igou 2017), the less well-traveled terrain surrounding the question of what is the nature of the relationship between boredom and the broader notion of social justice also needs to be acknowledged. The history of human civilization is replete with examples in which disparities in power and wealth are matched by equally wide disparities in both physical and emotional health. Overall mental health and even subjective well-being are positively correlated with socioeconomic status (SES) in most Western industrialized countries (e.g., Pickett and Wilkinson 2015; Sturm and Gresenz 2002; Wilkinson and Pickett 2017), and the overwhelming majority of longitudinal studies conducted to date have reported a positive relationship between income inequality and the risk of depression (e.g., Patel 2018). Although direct evidence of a similar inverse association between the prevalence of boredom and SES is far more limited (e.g., Markey 2014), there is an abundance of indirect evidence, primarily in the form of robust positive associations between depression, measures of trait boredom (Goldberg, et al. 2011; Harris 2000), and the prevalence of state boredom (e.g., Krotava and Todman 2017; Maple 2020).

If it is indeed the case that the prevalence of boredom is inversely related to SES, there are some intriguing implications to consider. For example, if boredom is a symptom of the frustrated need to search for potentially more lucrative targets for attentional investment, one could conjecture that any association between higher rates of boredom and low SES should, in part, be attributable to class-conditioned inequities in access to potential targets. One could further speculate that this disparity—which is particularly salient in areas like access to recreation, freedom to travel, and educational resources— would be prone to different causal interpretations, depending upon where one happens to be on the class divide. For some low SES individuals, for example, the perceived constraints that preclude them from investing attentional resources in certain experiences (except vicariously) could be judged to be arbitrary and inherently unfair, thereby justifying a decision to violate those constraints, even if it also means violating certain laws or cultural taboos. Indeed, for some, to be trapped in a life of excessive sameness when others have seemingly endless access to the new and interesting is akin to being unjustly punished.

On the contrary, for some high SES individuals, the low SES individuals who are frequently bored have only themselves to blame. They would argue that there is an abundance of alternative, prosocial experiences in low-income environments that are available for attentional investment, especially if individuals are willing to accept the necessary short-term investment losses (i.e., tolerate/manage their boredom) that are necessary for realizing long-term investment gains. They might also contend that many high SES individuals, their preexisting advantages notwithstanding, endured frequent and protracted periods of boredom (especially during school-age years) on the gamble that their investments would eventually yield a positive and significant return.

Let us take the fictional case of Alex as an example:

Alex is fifteen years of age and lives in public housing with his unemployed, single mother, and his three younger sisters. He attends the local high school, located about twenty minutes from his home. Although he has an older brother who has had some scrapes with the law, no one in his family has been convicted or imprisoned, and he has been able to resist the frequent temptation to join one of the neighborhood gangs. At school, he is a middling student and even though he is frequently bored, he attends all his classes and is not a truant. Still, he is constantly reminded of the fact that very few students in his high school go on to college and almost everyone who graduates, ends up in a low paying job or is unemployed. Trying to get his homework done in his family's small, noisy apartment is near impossible, so he tends to make only a token effort to study, and only when he has an upcoming test. Because he is only an average student and the classes are large, no faculty member has taken a special interest in his academic career, and he seldom receives encouragement from any of his teachers. Similarly, his mother is relatively indifferent to his academic progress and does not communicate, either in word or deed, how and why a commitment to success in school might eventually lead to a rewarding future. The same sentiment is frequently expressed by his neighborhood friends, many of whom are chronically truant or have already dropped out. He is teased constantly about his apparent conscientiousness and made to feel like a failure for the fact that he seems to have very little to show for it. Perhaps, not surprisingly, Alex feels trapped and demoralized. He is constrained daily by conditions that demand that he remain bored for much of the time he is in school or at home working on his homework assignments. But, unlike his wealthy suburban counterparts, he is denied access to the type of imagined positive future that would provide "meaning" to his experience and the promise of deferred compensation for his sacrifice.

Alex's story highlights the important yet paradoxical motivational role that boredom plays in the enterprise of learning. Mastering difficult and unfamiliar tasks often requires a willingness to withstand periods of sustained boredom in order to discover strategies that can make a seemingly intractable or redundant task more engaging. Since the alternative is to give up prematurely or to avoid the situation altogether, a reasonable question to ask is why do some individuals choose to privilege the strategies of early disengagement and avoidance in school settings, while others do not. While both types of reactions to boredom are likely to lead to learning, the strategies of avoidance and early disengagement are restricted to the identification and cataloging of tasks and environments that promote boredom. To be sure, this is useful information to have, but probably not particularly helpful (and probably quite the opposite) in formal school settings. By contrast, boredom management strategies that encourage tolerance of boredom and its mitigation through the reframing of a task so that engagement becomes possible (i.e., attentional investment becomes more attractive) encourages a different type of learning in which the individual discovers how to transform the nature and meaning of a growing range of tasks and conditions so that they are experienced as less boring. In so doing, the individual can reduce the range and scope of potentially boring tasks and conditions that would otherwise have to be reflexively avoided. Moreover, boredom management strategies that involve tolerance and mitigation would also enhance the individual's perceived capacity to manage similar challenges in the future (i.e., self-efficacy).

But does someone like Alex have a reason to believe that it matters which types of boredom management strategies he chooses to employ concerning his school-related tasks? He is trying to be a conscientious student, but he is also frequently bored, suggesting that even though he has managed to resist the temptation to engage in full-scale avoidance measures he has not yet learned how to tolerate and mitigate his boredom and thus remains inclined to quickly disengage from his school-related activities.

I would like to argue that the problems that individuals like Alex have in school settings stem in part from the existence of two types of interlocking social disparities. One disparity is the range and quality of the potential attentional investment opportunities that low and high SES individuals typically have access to outside of formal educational settings (e.g., recreation and travel). The other is the disparity in the skills and strategies that low and high SES individuals are required to have at their disposal to manage their current and anticipated boredom effectively. In other words, if you are a low SES individual you will have to do a lot more (in terms of boredom management) with a lot less (i.e., fewer investment opportunities) for you to be convinced that your investments will likely yield results that are both personally rewarding and, crucially, socially syntonic. I, therefore, suggest that economic and social deprivation limits the opportunities not only for attentional investment but also to acquire the skills necessary for effectively mining the available opportunities. And to the degree that these skills precede and undergird the learning that occurs in formal educational settings—a topic that I will return to later in this chapter—the problem of achievement disparities is likely to be only further compounded and institutionalized. So, what are these boredom management skills? It is to that question that I now turn.

3. COPING, TOLERANCE, AND MISMANAGEMENT

What does it mean to cope effectively with boredom? Indeed, the very suggestion that it is something that needs to be coped with or tolerated suggests that in an ideal world, boredom, like a disease or disability, would not exist—something that seems absurd if we are to accept the notion that boredom has an evolutionary purpose. Still, boredom is widely conceived as a feeling state that should be avoided if possible, minimized or mitigated if unavoidable, and tolerated only if necessary. It is my contention, however, that much of what makes boredom adaptive is in fact how well these boredom management strategies of avoidance, mitigation, and tolerance are brought to bear in the transactions of daily life. I would further contend that our expertise in this area is very much dependent on our capacity to accurately identify and diagnose the causal factors associated with both the boredom that we are currently experiencing and the boredom that we anticipate in the future. In short, boredom may be an invaluable tool in our self- and social-regulatory strivings, but its effectiveness is very much dependent on our ability to use it skillfully and in a manner that is consistent with societal expectations. Although there have been many prior attempts to catalog the various ways in which individuals might attempt to cope with boredom, most of this research has focused on specific settings (e.g., schools) and, for the most part, is informed by models of boredom that differ substantially from the IAIT (e.g., Nett, Gotz, and Daniels 2010). The following is a summary of what I believe are some of the more important strategies that are both commonly implicated in the mismanagement of boredom and consistent with IAIT. It is argued that when these strategies are overused or misapplied, then functional and even moral consequences are likely to ensue.

Avoidance-Coping: The Risk of Overreliance

There is probably little disagreement with the claim that boredom is not only ubiquitous but also more common than probably most other negative emotions. For example, a survey by the National Center on Addiction and Substance Abuse (2003) revealed that as much as 91 percent of school-aged children reported experiencing boredom at some point in their daily lives. Another survey suggested an even greater percentage of around 98 percent (Yazzie-Mintz 2007). These and other similar findings would seem to underscore the view that in modern societies where occupational activities are often highly routinized and detached from the needs and wants of the individual (i.e., lacking meaning), it may be impossible to avoid potentially boredom-inducing environments for very long. Still, there is no disputing that like most negative emotions, boredom promotes learning that will ultimately help the individual to minimize its recurrence. Hence, a common and often effective strategy for managing boredom is a studied avoidance of those conditions that we come to associate, consciously and unconsciously, with past feelings of boredom (i.e., specific conditions of constraint and low investment return).

However, there are obvious and important limitations to the use of avoidance-coping. Avoidance, much like the role it plays in the maintenance of phobic fears, discourages engagement with an aversive situation and thus, ironically, constrains and limits the individual's options for future engagement. The individual who adheres to avoidance as their preferred boredom management strategy is at greater risk of prematurely foreclosing on the opportunity to learn new ways of engaging with boring situations that could potentially lead to better returns on future attentional investments. Avoidance is, therefore, an inefficient management strategy if the goal is to improve one's investment prowess.

Even so, I suspect that for most individuals, most of the time, the reliance on avoidance to cope with potentially boring experiences does not result in significant complications. Indeed, the reason why most phobic fears seldom come to clinical attention is that most of us can easily arrange our lives in such a way that we do not have to confront our fears. If we are afraid of heights, then we do not visit high places, and life goes on relatively smoothly. So too with boredom, most of the things that we designate as boring we probably can avoid without significant consequences. However, there are undoubtedly limits as to how often avoidance can be employed to manage boredom without causing problems for the individual. I strongly suspect that in every culture there exists certain environments and tasks for which engagement is necessary, but which also poses a risk for boredom induction. For example, persistent avoidance of formal educational settings would probably be a recipe for failure.

Avoidance-coping can come in many guises and trying to enumerate a list of the possible types of avoidance-coping would probably be pointless. However, using the IAIT as the framework, I would like to propose that all avoidance-coping strategies involve an active resistance to investing attentional resources of any amount, for any period, in a specific focal task or experience. And if an investment is made because it is unavoidable or inadvertent, attempts are made to withdraw the investment in its entirety once conditions (constraints) permit. How the actual avoidance is accomplished, however, would depend on the context and the resources available to the individual, but it can be assumed that all effective avoidance strategies would make it possible for the individual to neutralize or eliminate the perceived constraints that obligate attentional investment. This is done by either anticipating them and avoiding them entirely or by degrading the perceived constraints in some way so that it is possible to easily divest and reinvest in another target.

Resource Sharing Mitigation: Misalignment of Strategy and Context

Of course, avoidance is not the only strategy at our disposal in attempting to manage boredom. We often deploy other methods of mitigation, alone or in combination, that allow us to feel less bored or bored for a shorter period while engaged with a boring task or stimulus. Many of these mitigation strategies often involve engagement with a concurrent task or stimulus while also remaining invested in the focal task or stimulus (or alternatively, alternating the deployment of attentional resources between the two tasks). These concurrent activities could be either covert (e.g., daydreaming) or more commonly, overt, as in the case of listening to music while driving or jogging.

In terms of the IAIT, this approach to boredom management could be described as something akin to diversifying an investment portfolio. By distributing some of the available attentional resources to non-focal stimuli or tasks that are believed (based on experience) to provide a reliably good return on investment, the expected loss on the investment in the focal task is at least partially offset. Of course, this presumes that we can always be sure that our allocation decisions will maximize our return while not significantly impairing our success on the focal task and that our decision to partition attentional investments will not violate the constraints associated with the focal task or stimulus (e.g., texting while driving).

However, much like avoidance-coping, resource-sharing mitigation strategies can be overused and even more often, misapplied, thus causing us to select a cure that is sometimes worse than the disease. While it is probably true that there is no resource sharing boredom management strategy that is appropriate for all situations, it is equally true that some strategies will be more appropriate than others in a given context (e.g., listening to the radio vs. texting while driving). It is also true that some strategies, like consuming alcohol while driving, are seldom appropriate as a regular choice for boredom management.

Self-Diagnostics and Causal Modeling: Attribution Errors

We frequently make inferences about the sources of our current and future boredom, and in some instances, we are wrong, especially when the environmental context is multidimensional, complex, or ambiguous. Damrad-Frye and Laird (1989) demonstrated this point in a now-classic study in which the researchers read a journal article to participants who were simultaneously exposed to sounds from an adjacent room that was either very loud (i.e., highly distracting), inaudible (i.e., non-distracting), or barely audible (faintly distracting). The researchers found that participants in the barely audible condition rated the article to be more boring than those in the other two conditions and offered the following explanation: participants in the barely audible condition were more likely to underestimate the drain on attentional resources caused by the faintly distracting stimulus, and thus were more likely to misattribute their lack of engagement with the task—à la Self Perception Theory (Bem 1972)—to the inherent boringness of the task itself. In other words, per IAIT, participants underestimated their attentional investment in the processing of the competing stimulus (i.e., the barely audible sounds) and overestimated their investment in the processing of the article content, causing them to expect more in terms of a return on latter investment (e.g., greater ease of comprehension).

In addition to highlighting the previously mentioned danger of resource sharing as a management strategy (i.e., the risk of miscalculating the relative attentional allocation amounts), it is not difficult to imagine how this type of error could lead to problems in settings where accurate sourcing of one's boredom is critical for success. For example, a young student might come to misattribute her feelings of boredom in a math or history class to the subject matter rather than to the instructor or the method of instruction. This failure to accurately diagnose the source of one's boredom, I would conjecture, increases the chance that an individual would elect to utilize an ill-suited boredom management strategy. This, in turn, would probably further limit the opportunities to correct the initial attribution error (e.g., the avoidance of math classes rather than droning math teachers).

One could imagine that our fictional low SES student, Alex, described above, might be particularly vulnerable to this type of attribution error. Even more troubling is the possibility that he might conclude that his frequent boredom in the classroom (and at home) is not due to the conditions under which he is asked to perform the student role, but rather due to an inborn limitation on his ability to engage with the subject matter.

Boredom Tolerance Coping: Unwillingness or Inability to Endure Feelings of Boredom

Most human beings have a pretty good idea of the kinds of situations that are likely to cause them to experience a negative emotional state like sadness and anxiety. It is also true that we often make use of this knowledge to intentionally place ourselves in situations that are likely to provoke one of these negative emotional states, albeit in highly contrived, time limited, and controlled environments (e.g., sad movies, roller coasters, and horror movies). And though this tendency for sporadic self-exposure to stimuli that induce negative emotions does not apply to all negative emotions (e.g., shame and guilt), boredom seems to occupy a rather curious no man's land for intentional self-exposure.

As noted earlier, in modern societies where behavioral constraints, social rules, and repetitive routines are the norm, exposure to boredom-inducing conditions is probably unavoidable. And all societies probably share the view that the ability to anticipate, avoid, or mitigate the conditions that precipitate boredom is a hallmark of psychological maturity and effective self-regulation. Still, there are instances where recourse to avoidance and resource sharing mitigation strategies is not possible, but we are still expected to subject ourselves to a potentially boredom-inducing situation without the promise of a near-term return on their investment. This fact, however, does not prevent us from establishing expectations about the possibility of future dividends. Indeed, IAIT predicts that beliefs about even distant, long-term returns on an attentional investment, regardless of their accuracy, should have an impact on how a boredom-inducing task or environment is experienced in the present.

There is no denying that we frequently engage in boredom-inducing activities that would be painfully boring were it not for the expectation of some sort of deferred compensation. Common examples would be activities like choosing to stand in a long line for hard-to-get theater tickets or sitting for fifteen minutes, half-dressed in your doctor's examination room waiting to be seen. I also suspect, however, that one of the most common long-term investment dividends might be something as simple as social affirmation and gratitude from others. And if I am right, then it seems reasonable to assume that we might also be inclined to make attributions in moral terms about an individual's generosity or lack thereof, based on their apparent willingness or unwillingness to tolerate certain types of social situations that are potentially boring. The wayward teenager who is unwilling to spend several hours on a weekend with an elderly grandparent listening to "boring" stories that they have heard many times before is seen as callous and immature. So too is the young parent who opts to watch television rather than play "boring" games with their restless two-year-old daughter or read "boring" children's books to their three-year-old son.

It probably has not gone unnoticed that it is possible to consider boredom tolerance coping to be a special type of boredom mitigation strategy in which the expectation of a relatively meager return in the near term on an attentional investment is moderated by the expectation of a much larger return in the future. Consequently, any factor that permits an individual to imagine that their sacrifice of attentional resources per subjective unit time will eventually yield dividends should in theory (a) incentivize the individual to persist with the boring task and (b) cause the experience of boredom to feel less aversive. In short, boredom tolerance is likely to be successful as a management strategy when the boring task is made meaningful by the individual's faith in the future and the conviction that their sacrifice will not go for naught (Kurzban et al. 2013).

The idea that current and anticipated boredom might be lessened and better tolerated when there is an accompanying conviction that the investment will yield a future reward is consistent with much of what we already know about the interrelationships between the constructs of boredom, purpose/meaning in life, and religious conviction. For example, there is an abundance of evidence indicating that lack of self-reported meaning in life is associated with a higher incidence of future boredom and that the experience of boredom invariably triggers a search for more meaningful, but not necessarily more adaptive, modes of engagement (e.g., Fahlman et al. 2009; Van Tilburg and Igou 2012; Van Tilburg et al. 2013). In one of the more comprehensive explorations of this topic, Van Tilburg and colleagues provided evidence to suggest that highly religious individuals (compared to less religious individuals) are more likely to report a lower prevalence of state boredom and less prone to become bored when subjected to a boredom-inducing task (Van Tilburg et al. 2019). Importantly, the researchers were also able to confirm that compared to nonreligious individuals, religious conviction appeared to be prophylactic for boredom. Specifically, highly religious individuals, when bored, demonstrated less of a need to search for meaning (as measured by the Search for Meaning scale [Steger et al. 2006]) than nonreligious individuals (Van Tilburg et al. 2019).

It is also worth mentioning that from the perspective of IAIT, religious convictions occupy a unique place among the types of beliefs that are theorized to facilitate boredom tolerance coping. Since religious convictions are invariably non-falsifiable, they would confer the special benefit of allowing for an almost unbounded confirmatory cognitive bias to (mis)construe all future instances of good fortune as deferred compensation for successfully tolerating boredom in the past (Alós-Ferrer and Hügelschäfer 2012).

Boredom and the Misuse of Psychoactive Substances

The prescription that individuals who are in recovery from addiction to a psychoactive substance should avoid extended periods of boredom is so common in clinical settings that it is surprising how little empirical research has been done to explore boredom's presumed relationship to the risk of relapse. Of course, it makes sense that an emotional state that is hypothesized to serve a key self-regulatory function should prove also to be a potent signal for the need for some sort of allostatic adjustment. And there is quite a bit of correlational evidence to indicate that there is a robust positive association between trait boredom and alcohol use, as well as other potentially addictive substances (Iso-Ahola and Crowley 1991; Johnston and O'Malley 1986; Orcutt 1984; Pettiford et al. 2007; Todman 2007). There is also some evidence to suggest that the frequency of state boredom episodes is associated with higher rates of substance use, even when differences in trait boredom are controlled for statistically (Krotava and Todman 2017; Maple 2020). Unfortunately, we know far less about how or why boredom or the predisposition to be bored increases the risk of relapse, and it is even less clear if boredom plays a role at all in the transition from a pattern of experimentation and casual use to one of habitual use.

The fact that there is a positive association between boredom and the use of psychoactive substances, some of which are illegal without medical authorization, leads to the inescapable statistical conclusion that bored individuals are disproportionately inclined to engage in an illegal, and, some would say, immoral activity. And to be sure, the habitual use of certain types of substances can lead to enormous personal and social costs that make the condemnation of uncontrolled consumption understandable, even when it does not result in obvious untoward consequences. However, the fact that social and legal penalties for substance misuse are often inequitably administered at the expense of disadvantaged populations (e.g., Carson and Sabol 2011; Cooper 2015) suggests that the alleged sins of personal irresponsibility on the part of the substance users are more than offset by legitimate concerns about the justness of society's response to the problem. Furthermore, most addictions involve legal substances such as alcohol and tobacco, something that underscores the fact that for many, it is not just the type of substance involved, but also the dysregulation that addictive behavior implies that provides the taint of deviance and amorality. Hence, the question that seems to present itself at this juncture is how and to what extent is the dysregulation observed in addictive behavior reflective of the functioning of the regulatory system associated with the management of boredom.

Before the introduction of the medical model of addiction in the twentieth century, the dominant paradigm of understanding addictive behavior was the so-called moral model of addiction, which attributed addictive behavior to a weakness of character or will (see Heather 2017). Individuals chose to expose themselves to addictive substances and had only themselves to blame for their plight; a view that is still prevalent among the lay population (Heather 2017). Interestingly, a similar attitude is often expressed about the behavior that is attributed to feelings of boredom. As noted previously, it is assumed that as competent adults we should be able to manage our boredom effectively (essentially, "just say no" to our boredom). Excessive complaints of boredom are therefore often interpreted as evidence of a regulatory failure brought about by a willful decision not to engage in an alternate, prosocial activity.

Also interesting is the fact that several prominent theories suggest that addiction may be a problem of failed self-regulation and that the addicted individual comes to rely on an exogenous substance for maintaining homeostasis (e.g., Koob and Schulkin 2019). A detailed review of this literature is beyond the scope of this chapter, but suffice to say, it is not unreasonable to speculate that the boredom management system, given its self-regulatory function, would be easily seduced by the outsized, near-term investment returns that psychoactive substances tend to provide. But for some, the allure may be so compelling that many older investment targets with respectable but decidedly smaller rates of return (e.g., hobbies or relationships) would eventually cease to attract attentional resources (essentially becoming boring) as the individual became convinced that their substance-using activity was both sufficient and necessary for good self-regulation.

This would explain both the high correlation between measures of boredom and substance use rates and the reason why the minimization of boredom is so strongly encouraged in almost all treatment settings. And it also makes sense from the perspective of IAIT. If the activity of using substances promises to provide the largest return in the near term for the addicted individual, it seems logical to assume that the greater the availability and number of perceived high yield alternative investments (e.g., engaging with hobbies, going to the movies, etc.) the greater the likelihood of at least moderating use. In practice, however, as most clinicians will attest, it is never that easy. Most addictive substances are potent investment vehicles because they always promise a big, proximal return on investment that tends to dwarf the returns from most other activities that the individual is likely to engage in. This means that boredom avoidance-coping would almost certainly fail at some point. Moreover, to ensure that the individual does not yield to the temptation to divest from the selected activity too quickly, stringent internal constraints on the alternate activity would have to be imposed, which would further increase the feelings of boredom. It is perhaps then not surprising why abstinence as a treatment goal is often so difficult to maintain (Lozano, Stephens, and Roffman 2006).

Resource sharing coping as a boredom mitigation strategy might fare better if moderated or controlled use is to be considered a viable treatment goal (e.g., Heather and Robertson 1981; Marlatt and Witkiewitz 2002). For some individuals, it might be possible to partially invest in the preferred substance use activity, while also maintaining investments in a range of alternate, pro-social activities. However, some substances are more amenable to this type of boredom management than others. Drugs of abuse vary considerably in their proximal and distal neuropsychological and psychosocial effects, and many drugs remain illegal, thus risking involvement with the criminal justice system.

Although the boredom tolerance coping strategy might seem to be an unlikely option for an addicted individual, it is compatible with the psychological mechanisms that are believed to be in play in programs like Alcohol Anonymous (AA; Galanter 2016). In such programs, individuals are encouraged to invest in the AA community of which they are a member. Importantly, this investment is given "meaning" by the AA member's commitment to pursue a series of progressive steps or goals that connect the current self to the hoped-for self that is often couched in religious or spiritual terms (Galanter 2005, 2016). To the extent that this echoes the aforementioned research findings on boredom and meaning (and religiosity) it also reinforces the argument that if boredom, and the dysregulation that it represents, can be reliably controlled, it might also be possible to reduce the use of a substance.

Finally, what about the cravings and the intrusive thoughts about the addictive substance? Per IAIT, thoughts and other internal states are fair game as targets for attentional investment, so one would assume that non-drug-related thoughts would probably find it difficult to compete for attentional resources, especially in environments where drug-related cues are present (e.g., in bar or restaurant). In a study of the binge cycle of cocaine users, Gawin and Kleber (1986) describe a period between one and ten weeks after the end of a binge during which the cocaine addict begins to experience intense feelings of boredom, anhedonia, and anxiety. During this same period, drug-related cues (triggers) become particularly salient, and it becomes difficult not to think about the drug. Gawin and Kleber (1986) suggest that this period of intense boredom and anxiety represents the period of greatest risk of relapse for binging cocaine users. I would posit that it is also a time when the self-regulatory system, of which boredom is a part, declares that there are no other viable investment options available other than cocaine use and that one should act accordingly. Interestingly, this putative "hijacking" of the self-regulatory system by a substance parallels the process that Berridge and Robinson (2016) describe with respect to the dopamine-mediated "wanting system" in their Incentive-Sensitization Theory of addiction.

Can the Incidence Rate of Boredom Be Too Low?

In discussing their findings from their boredom and religiosity study, Van Tilburg and his colleagues make the important point that a potential drawback to the boredom-mitigating power of religiosity is that it might result in less motivation for change, even when there is an adaptive advantage to do so (e.g., Van Tilburg et al. 2019). This observation seems not only right to me but also raises the more fundamental question of whether there is such a thing as an optimal range for the incidence and prevalence of boredom. Is it possible to have too few experiences of boredom or to not experience boredom intensely enough? This is the issue that I turn to next, as I believe that there are implications for both social regulation and moral functioning.

One of the many seeds of confusion that may have been sown by the tendency to conflate the observed correlates of trait boredom with the correlates of state boredom is the widely held assumption that lower than average rates of state boredom are always adaptive. However, not only is this assumption largely unproven, but there is also an abundance of examples where the presumed adaptive value of an emotional state is diminished when the frequency with which it is elicited is deemed insufficient. For example, the emotions of guilt and shame play important roles in the regulation of prosocial behavior in human communities by reigning in the self-interested and potentially disruptive strivings of the individual; and an abundance of shamelessness and remorselessness is not, by any stretch of the imagination, considered desirable for a fair and just society. So too might be the case with boredom, but there are no empirical studies or serious theoretical discussions in the literature (at least that I am aware of) that have attempted to address this issue.

Are there instances where too low a level of subjective boredom could be a liability? And, if so, what are some of the possible implications for individual moral decision-making and, more broadly, the issues of social regulation and social justice? Two possible candidates come to mind, both of which rest on the characterization of boredom that is being employed in this chapter (IAIT), which posits that perceived constraints (internal or external in origin) on the desire to reinvest attentional resources elsewhere are central to the subjective experience of boredom. Assuming that there is some truth to this conjecture, we can speculate that there are several possible ways in which lower than normal rates of state boredom might result in problematic forms of self- and social-regulation.

Constraint Hypersensitivity and Extreme Boredom Aversion: Antisocial Coping

This first example follows from comments that were made earlier about the risks of an overreliance on the strategy of avoidance and/or the chronic misalignment of other mitigation strategies. If the experience of boredom teaches us that certain tasks and environments are no longer worth the investment of our attention, it seems reasonable to assume that most individuals eventually develop a capacity to anticipate, mitigate, and, if necessary, avoid the tasks and environments that are likely to make them bored. This seems to be an adaptive response that comports with the presumed function of boredom, but as I explained above, there are probably instances where the overuse and misapplication of management strategies are so extreme that the incidence of state boredom is severely reduced. In other words, some individuals may be so averse to the constraints that restrict their autonomy to reinvest their attentional resources that they may go to extraordinary and potentially morally questionable lengths to avoid potentially boring experiences. As an example, take the case of Murray:

> Murray is a courier for a company in Manhattan, New York. He makes deliveries on a bike, weaving through busy New York traffic, often traveling the wrong way on one-way streets. He has known since childhood that he is easily bored and strenuously avoids the kinds of activities that tend to make him bored. He has been in numerous accidents, some of them involving injuries to pedestrians, but reports that he is seldom bored. When he is not working, he is either sleeping or out clubbing with friends in lower Manhattan.

There are two things of note about the case of Murray. First, his decision to skirt the law and his seeming disregard for the risks that his behavior poses to others could be construed as immoral behavior. It is also true that his immoral acts are a consequence of a lifestyle and the choices that he has made to ensure that he is rarely bored. Second, underscoring the point made earlier about the dangers of conflating trait boredom with state boredom, Murray himself acknowledges that he has long recognized that he is easily bored. Hence, he has devised ways to make sure that this vulnerability does not materialize in the form of a life filled with boredom.

Does Murray owe it to his fellow citizens to tolerate the discomforts that come with boredom rather than engaging in behaviors that put others at risk? Perhaps, and some would even be tempted to declare that Murray's apparent failure to learn from the consequences of his frequent rule-breaking is evidence of antisocial traits, especially concerning what appears to be an absence of empathy for others.

Indeed, there is ample evidence to suggest that individuals with high levels of trait boredom are more likely than those with low trait boredom to exhibit traits similar to those observed in antisocial personality disorder (APD), such as impulsivity and aggression (Dahlen 2005; Rupp and Vodanovich 1997; Watt and Vodanovich 1992). Additionally, contemporary research on the Psychopathy Checklist-Revised (Hare and Neumann 2006), developed to identify APD in incarcerated offenders, has consistently yielded a two-factor model solution, with one of the factors being an "impulsive-antisocial factor." This factor includes traits such as boredom proneness, impulsivity, irresponsibility, and aggressiveness (Harpur, Hare, and Hakstian,1989). However, the clinical diagnosis of APD requires far more than a proclivity to avoid boredom at the expense of antisocial outcomes, and the boredom avoidance behavior that is being described is readily visible in the everyday decision-making of a wide variety of people, most of whom do not meet the diagnostic criteria for APD.

The point that is being made here is that for at least some individuals antisocial behavioral outcomes may not be the result of simply being unable to learn from the consequences of their transgressive acts. I would hazard to guess that there is a nontrivial number of individuals, like Murray, who are largely motivated by the desire to avoid a fate that they believe to be even more aversive than social censure or even physical pain, and that is the prospect of being subjected to constraint and the boredom that it engenders. Hence, it is not that Murray is unable to experience empathy and remorse for the countless number of elderly ladies that he has caused to fall to the pavement as they tried to avoid being injured by his oncoming bike. He probably does. Rather, it is that the distress of boredom exceeds that of almost all other negative emotions and thus motivates many of his choices, moral or otherwise.

Timothy Wilson and colleagues conducted a series of studies in which they explored the question of what is the experience of individuals who are asked to sit alone in a featureless room for fifteen minutes with nothing to occupy themselves other than their thoughts. Surprisingly, or perhaps not, most individuals in the study found the experience to be particularly aversive. So much so, that in one of the studies a sizeable percentage of the participants opted to self-administer a painful electric shock at least once during the fifteen minutes, rather than simply letting their thoughts wander for the duration. Although Wilson et al. (2014) did not measure boredom directly, other studies have confirmed that the decision to self-shock is indeed correlated with reported boredom levels (e.g., Havermans et al. 2014) and as such supports the argument that for some individuals the experience of boredom and the constraints that promote it can be experienced as being so aversive that they are inclined to make decisions that are potentially harmful to their self-interests. Although I am not aware of any studies that have been done to test the logical and morally relevant extension of this observation, I would like to propose that boredom and its supporting constraints might be capable of precipitating very similar decisions that could conceivably result in causing harm to other individuals. The case of Murray in which misapplied boredom management strategies have coalesced into a way of living that is potentially harmful to others is an example of how this might be manifested in the real world.

An argument could be made that because Murray would probably register as being highly boredom prone on a measure of trait boredom, his real problem is not that he experiences too little state boredom but rather that he is excessively boredom prone. This is a valid point but it also misses a more critical one, which is that much of Murray's problematic behavior is motivated not by his high rates of subjective boredom but rather by his desire to retain his unusually low rate of boredom and the strategies that he feels compelled to employ to make that happen.

Unlike Murray, most individuals with high levels of trait boredom also have a higher than average incidence of state boredom (e.g., Maple 2020; Todman 2013), suggesting that they are less inclined to rely (at least exclusively) on the extreme avoidance/mitigation solutions that Murray seems to prefer. It also suggests that unlike Murray, these individuals are more likely to live lives that are marked by high levels of subjective distress that are relatively unproblematic in terms of social and moral transgressions. It may also partially explain why the two most widely used measures of trait boredom, the Boredom Proneness Scale (BPS; Farmer and Sundberg 1986) and the Boredom Susceptibility Scale (BSS; Zuckerman 1979), share only a modest positive correlation (e.g., Mercer-Lynn et al. 2013), suggesting that they measure different types of vulnerability to boredom. Research on this point seems to support this conjecture. For example, the BPS is highly correlated with measures of depression and neuroticism, reflecting the dysphoria that often characterizes individuals with certain types of high trait boredom. The BSS, on the other hand, tends to capture the individuals who are motorically impulsive and in constant need of stimulation and are closer to the type of high trait boredom individual that Murray appears to represent (Mercer-Lynn et al. 2013)

Social Constraint Insensitivity and Schizoid Adaptation

A second scenario in which low rates of boredom might occur is when individuals are insensitive to or fail to recognize a significant number of constraints that typically restrict attentional investment options. This lack of sensitivity could, in theory, cause an individual to report less boredom.

Admittedly, I have no direct empirical evidence to cite in support of this conjecture other than the observation that many of the constraints that enjoin us to remain invested in an interest-depleted situation are abstract social rules of behavior. Indeed, these are exactly the types of constraints that are typically employed by researchers to induce boredom in a laboratory setting: A social contract is established, usually reinforced by a financial inducement, that obligates the participant to invest in a monotonous task for a finite period and to resist the temptation to invest their attentional resources elsewhere. The boredom that study participants experience is thus a product of both the monotonous task and the constraints that the implicit social contract imposes on attentional divestment. Indeed, the aforementioned experiment by Wilson et al. (2014) is notable in that the only unconstrained investment option that was afforded to the participants was to shock themselves. But what if an additional investment option had been made available (e.g., the option to throw darts at the wall)? IAIT suggests that the self-shock rates would be substantially lower. Similarly, when we have lost interest in a conversation, the same type of social contract in the form of good manners tends to inhibit us from yawning loudly and conspicuously turning our attention to composing messages on our mobile phones. Violating those expectations would probably be interpreted by most as evidence of social ineptness, childish immaturity, or worse. Yet, interestingly, it would also probably result in a net reduction in the prevalence of state boredom.

An individual who is largely insensitive to many important social constraints could, like Murray, quite possibly report that they are not frequently bored, and when they are bored, it is usually only briefly. But what would such a person look like? Well, they might be perceived as somewhat odd, not unlike someone with schizoid-like traits (American Psychiatric Association 2013). These individuals are usually indifferent to praise and criticism, derive

little pleasure from relationships with others, and have little or no interest in engaging in most types of social interactions (American Psychiatric
Association 2013). They are therefore less attuned to social convention and
less well regulated by the expectations and needs of others. And because
they are socially anhedonic and effectively blind to many of the explicit and
implicit constraints that structure most social transactions, they are also more
likely to violate those constraints if preemptive avoidance is not possible.

A common assumption is that the aversion to social intimacy that is
observed among individuals with schizoid-like traits rests on feelings of
anxiety and fear, but I would like to suggest that much of the lack of reactiv-
ity and indifference to social reinforcers has more in common with feelings
of boredom—a conjecture that is consistent with the positive, albeit modest, association that has been observed between measures of anhedonia and
boredom (Goldberg et al. 2011; Todman et al. 2008). And I suspect schizoid
individuals would be quick to conclude that their attentional investments in
human relationships are being wasted and should be invested elsewhere (e.g.,
in technology and solitary pursuits). Alas, it is not that they do not want to
invest their attentional resources in situations and tasks that are likely to yield
a good return on that investment, but social transactions for the schizoid individual do not qualify as a good investment.

To be clear, though, if forced by common functional and instrumental needs
(e.g., the need to make a living) to invest in social relationships for extended
periods (e.g., a job that necessitates frequent interactions with customers),
schizoid individuals would most likely report that they are frequently and
intensely bored. However, for those individuals who can find avocations and
occupations (e.g., a security guard on the night shift, a home-based software
developer) that are largely solitary, then the expectation would be that, like
Murray, they would report having a fairly low prevalence of boredom, despite
remaining at an elevated risk for boredom in social settings.

But what are the moral implications that follow from these examples?
Well, to reiterate, the claim that is being made here is that effective self- and
social-regulation are contingent upon an optimal range of state boredom
experiences. Boredom rates that are too high or too low are probably markers
for an increased risk for self- and social-regulatory failures that can be both
functional and moral. In the case of Murray, I tried to argue that there are
individuals—possibly a relatively small number—who have adapted to their
hyper-aversion to subjective constraint and the boredom that it engenders
by misapplying and over-relying on avoidance and other extreme boredom
mitigation strategies while eschewing the strategy of boredom tolerance.
Consequently, they are often too easily captured by competing targets of
attentional investment, many of which are proscribed by social convention
and, in many instances, the law.

The moral dilemma for individuals like Murray is how do they satisfy their desperate need for autonomy without making decisions that are likely to put others and themselves at risk. From the perspective of others in the community, however, Murray's behavior indicates an intentional disregard for the rules. And the fact that he is unwilling to tolerate even a modicum of boredom in anticipation of future compensation for his current investments, especially in the form of social approval, indicates to others that his motives are undeniably selfish and deserving of condemnation.

If this is a fair assessment of Murray, we should recall that he probably does experience regret and remorse, and he can feel shame and guilt. It is just that they are not nearly enough to discourage him from acting on his much more acute aversion to the painful experience of boredom. For example, what would our position be if instead of the avoidance of boredom Murray's behavior was motivated by the fact that he needs the money to pay for his mother's heart medication and his rate of pay is based on how quickly he delivers his packages? Most of us I suspect would be far more sympathetic to this altruistic construal of Murray's behavior primarily because it is perceived as selfless whereas the boredom-fueled construal connotes selfishness. But what would we make of an individual who is motivated by both boredom and the need to provide for his sick mother?

I also tried to make the case that there are probably some individuals with schizoid-like traits who manifest unusually low rates of state boredom. In contrast to the APD-like case of Murray, I suggested that these individuals lack sufficient sensitivity to the abstract social constraints that normally inhibit certain contextually inappropriate boredom management responses (e.g., overt expressions of attentional disengagement) and as a consequence, judgments of disapproval by others are likely to occur. Since the most probable misattribution for such behavior is that it is a deliberate attempt to cause harm (by giving insult through disregard for the feelings of others), it would not be unreasonable to assume that some might view the behavior as morally deviant.

This type of harsh assessment of the schizoid individual's inability to disguise their disinterest in social relationships (i.e., excessive avoidance and misaligned resource sharing) is particularly likely to occur in school environments where social capital is fiercely coveted, and lack of social conformity is frequently met with hostility and marginalization.

Although the experiences of schizoid individuals in school settings are probably not generalizable to most children, this is not to say that school settings do not present a formidable adaptive challenge for most children. School environments are highly routinized and constraining institutions that present particularly unique challenges concerning the boredom management skills that are needed to navigate them successfully. Additionally, there are reasons to believe that this level of expertise may be difficult to attain without access to certain types of learning opportunities in the home. This, therefore, brings me to the final section of this chapter in which I try to build on the argument that school environments may be unheralded engines of boredom-induced social dysregulation among low SES students, and by extension, contributors to a pernicious form of social injustice.

4. BOREDOM AND SCHOOL ENVIRONMENTS

Formal educational settings and their collateral chores, such as homework, are notorious vectors for boredom promotion in adolescents and teenagers, and boredom is one of the factors frequently cited by students when trying to explain their decision to drop out of school (e.g., Irving and Parker-Jenkins 1995; Wegner et al. 2008). And if failing to complete high school is predictive of a less successful adult life (at least in modern Westernized societies) it is perhaps worth taking a moment to look at the various ways in which school environments and the high levels of boredom that they can engender might be contributing to systemic inequities in social mobility.

School environments vary along several instructional and curricular dimensions but in all cases, the students are expected to invest their attentional resources into two complementary tasks: exploring and imputing things that they do not yet know (even if they do not fully grasp the potential utility) and practicing things that they do know in order to promote greater mastery, fluency, and expertise. In other words, attending to the new and eventually integrating it with the practiced and familiar. School environments are therefore by design environments that impose constraints on attentional processing and limit autonomy in terms of the strategies that might be deployed by students to minimize the feeling that their attentional resources are being squandered (i.e., boredom).

In well-engineered school environments, boredom is held at bay by structuring the curricula and activity schedules to ensure that the balance between the new and the familiar is kept in a range that maximizes the probability of sustained engagement for the maximum number of students. However, in most large school systems in the United States, especially in urban, underresourced school systems, such curricular engineering is difficult to execute and sustain. For example, Zachary Jason, reporting in the *Harvard Education Magazine*, noted that when teens in a 2004 Gallup poll were asked "to select the top three words that describe how they feel in school from a list of 14 adjectives, 'bored' was chosen most often, by half the students," and "only 2 percent said they were never bored" (Jason 2017).

Jason's commentary underscores the sad fact that too many students in our school systems are confronted with chronically unengaging school environments for which avoidance, either overtly (i.e., truancy and dropping out) or covertly (e.g., daydreaming or concurrently engaging with other off-task activities), is the only realistic solution for a nontrivial minority. This phenomenon, as Jason's article suggests, is well documented and is not in serious dispute. However, what is also notable about the statistics cited by Jason is that the complaints of boredom are not limited to children from low SES homes, even though they fare significantly less well than their high SES counterparts in terms of dropout rates and the like (e.g., Winding and Andersen 2015). Perhaps then the question that needs to be asked is how are children from low SES households likely to manage and experience their school-induced boredom differently than children from high SES households. Part of the answer to this question, I believe, is that some low SES students may experience their boredom as evidence of a type of victimization, and thus justification for adopting more extreme boredom management strategies.

If attention and psychological time are resources that have value and each of us has a proprietary relationship to our psychological resources, one could conjecture that there are circumstances in which we might come to feel that we have been cheated out of those resources by some sort of deliberate action or scheme on the part of others. Schools may be such a circumstance for many children. If boredom can be construed as a subjective marker that attentional resources and time are being squandered, then one way that this might occur is by the process of misappropriation through the unreasonable or unjustified constraints imposed by others. Indeed, one of the central tenants of the IAIT is that bored individuals not only feel constrained by the choices that they are afforded but are also convinced that they are being prevented from searching for something better, even if no such alternative exists at the time. Consistent with this claim are studies by Pallak and Pittman (1972) and others (e.g., Chin et al. 2017, Fisher 1993) that suggest that the mere belief that one is free to attend elsewhere during the performance of a monotonous task may be sufficient to reduce the amount of boredom reported. These findings suggest that one's response to a potentially boredom-inducing situation and whether one reverts to avoidance as a solution—rather than boredom tolerance coping or an appropriate resource sharing strategy—depends in large part on how one interprets the constraints (e.g., Larson 1987). If they are interpreted not as attempts to limit choice and agency but rather as guidelines for an attentional investment strategy that has a proven track record for producing substantial returns on investment—despite the short-term losses—then the discomfort associated with academic boredom, like the physical distress that athletes endure during training, becomes meaningful, goal directed, worthwhile and ego-syntonic (Moynihan, Igou, and Van Tilburg 2017b).

Notice, however, this willingness to accept short-term attentional investment loses (boredom) assumes that all students share equally in the belief
that the future investment returns will materialize. This is not the case. In
households at the bottom of the socioeconomic ladder (like our fictional
student Alex), there is often little evidence to indicate that the ability to
tolerate boredom in school has ever yielded much of a return. Sadly, for
many of these individuals, the constraints of school environments are seldom
experienced as necessary mechanisms to facilitate learning. Rather they are
felt to be tools that are used by the powerful to misappropriate a valuable
possession. This conjecture is consistent with the findings of Kanevsky and
Keighley (2003) who reported that some of the bored students in their study
described their underachievement and disengagement as an "honorable
action in response to . . . their growing sense of moral indignation" to an
environment that they experienced as being overly constraining and uncar-
ing (20).

If the putative differences in boredom management choices contribute to
the decisions that eventually lead to poorer academic outcomes of low SES
students, the next question that may be worth asking is whether there is reason to believe that these poor management choices could be used by others
to make attributions about the abilities and potentialities of such students.
Evangeline Lehr and I conducted a study with a sample of young children
attending an afterschool program in New York City that partially touched on
this question (Lehr and Todman 2009). Two findings from the study are relevant. First, we found that even among children as young as nine years of age,
there was a significant positive association between the self-reported rates of
boredom over the preceding two weeks and scores on the citywide academic
tests in reading and mathematics. Perhaps even more surprising was the finding that adult teachers in the afterschool program who were kept blind to the
differences in the students' academic test scores, as well as their scores on the
boredom measure, tended to rate the children who reported more boredom in
their daily lives as having fewer positive personal attributes, even after statistically controlling for differences in academic scores. Interestingly, there
were no differences in the number of negative attributes endorsed.

While the sample was admittedly small and it is only a single study, the
implication is that boredom management-associated behaviors and decisions,
even among very young school children, might be capable of influencing
attributions and appraisals made by teachers and others in a school setting. Although the negative bias might be subtle and unconscious, if it is
real, it raises the possibility that the less positive attributions and appraisals
could also result in the inequitable allocation of instructional attention and
resources to the very same children who may already be resentful of being
victims of misappropriation.

Most of us are familiar with the well-worn anecdotes about the unusually bright child who performs poorly in school and is mistakenly assumed to be "slower" than the other children until the realization that she was insufficiently challenged by her school assignments (Peckrun et al. 2010). However, there are countless other children in impoverished school districts where there is a similar level of disengagement, but not because the subject matter is overly familiar (as in the case of the aforementioned prodigy) but rather because the new subject matter has become too unfamiliar to be assimilated due to a history of chronic underinvestment of attentional resources in the earlier foundational subject matter (Vogel-Walcutt et al. 2012). And the point to appreciate here, of course, is that in both the case of the prodigy and the average child in an overcrowded classroom in an underfunded school system, there is the ever-present temptation to view boredom in the school environment as evidence of a lack of ability, and, more problematically, lack of potential.

This common and reflexive interpretation of boredom and the associated avoidance behaviors is thus a way for society's more fortunate to perform the following inferential gymnastic routines: (1) If student x complains of boredom and does poorly in school it is probably because she is not smart enough to keep up with the classwork; or (2) If student x engages in excessive amounts of boredom avoidance behaviors he most probably lacks the self-discipline and strength of character necessary to resist the temptation to invest his attentional resources elsewhere (e.g., skipping school to go to the movies with friends). Two further inferences frequently follow from this latter point of view. The first is a manifestation of the tacit just world belief (Lerner 1980; Furnham 2003) that the truant or chronically unengaged student deserves to fail. The second is the equally familiar assertation that the primary caregivers and the home environment failed to impose the types of stringent attentional constraints that would discourage disengagement from the school environment and force the child to preferentially invest in the activities of the school. In other words, in addition to reinforcing the attentional constraints imposed in the school environment, caretakers of school-aged children are also expected to promote a certain degree of tolerance for the discomfort of boredom and to instill the belief that short-term investment losses (e.g., memorizing organic chemistry formulae) will be rewarded by long-term investment gains (i.e., through the ever-widening opportunities for potentially lucrative attentional investment that come with the social markers of a successful student).

If this sounds a lot like learning to delay gratification or the phenomenon of temporal discounting (Bickel, Odum, and Madden 1999; Doyle 2013) that is because the similarity is real. However, unlike delay of gratification and temporal discounting, both of which involve actively resisting something in the present that is perceived to be desirable, boredom, per IAIT (Weiss et al. 2020), always involves engagement in an activity in the present that is perceived to be providing a poor return on the attentional investment, and thus subjectively unappealing. What is being resisted (or constrained by an external injunction of some sort) is the temptation to reinvest attention into a contemporaneous activity with a potentially higher return on the same investment. Consequently, what school environments require of students is not only to learn to tolerate boredom—in the sense that they should resist the temptation to divest in attention on school-related tasks despite the short-term investment losses—but also to commit to the belief that it is an investment strategy that will be rewarded in the proximal and distal future. However, this is far easier to commit to if one is lucky enough to live in a home where the connection between boredom tolerance coping and academic success can be modeled and also reinforced by a slate of proximal experiential investment options (e.g., vacations, expensive hobbies, social and cultural events, internships, etc.). Unfortunately, for the less fortunate, the conviction and commitment to boredom tolerance coping as an essential ingredient in educational success (and ultimately, social mobility) are far more difficult to sustain.

5. CONCLUSION

The proposition that the feeling state of boredom can sometimes precede decisions that result in an amoral choice of action is probably not a controversial claim. However, if an emotional state, such as boredom, is likely to bias an individual's decision-making in a way that may be socially transgressive, can we and should we fault an individual for (a) being insufficiently aware of the relationship between boredom and the risk of engaging in morally questionable decision-making, (b) not doing enough to avoid or limit exposure to conditions that are likely to provoke feelings of boredom, and (c) being insufficiently skilled at mitigating the potential impact of boredom on moral decision-making if the boredom-provoking conditions are unavoidable? I attempted to tackle these and related questions through an examination of hypothetical scenarios in which boredom's presumed self-regulatory and social-regulatory functions are likely to misfire, potentially leading to several morally consequential outcomes.

An effort was made to distinguish the role of boredom in the precipitation of potentially immoral acts by an individual vs. the social justice and equity-relevant attributions that members of a community are likely to make about an individual whose problematic behavior has been judged to be motivated by boredom. Through the lens of the IAIT, I have made the case, with several examples, that these attributions invariably assume that the individual is not only deficient but also is acting intentionally to be transgressive and should be condemned.

I also tried to draw attention to the claim that a critical part of human socialization is learning how to manage boredom, and students should not be penalized for being less than proficient. Yet, that is precisely what happens when children, especially from less privileged demographic groups in certain types of school environments, are identified as being too willing to divest their attentional investment in an educational activity. If education about the capacity and necessity to manage boredom is believed to begin in the same place as the capacity to delay gratification (the home), then we should calibrate accordingly our expectations for children who come from homes where the teaching and modeling of boredom tolerance coping do not occur.

Finally, the remarks in this chapter must also be contextualized by the fact that I am writing at a time when most of the world is in the throes of the COVID-19 pandemic. Across the globe, entire populations have been obliged to shelter at home for extended periods and to forgo most types of everyday social interactions. Following closely on the heels of this broad and persistent constraint on personal autonomy have been two widescale social movements, both notable for their moral implications. The first is a determined revolt by some against the recommended social distancing and other antiviral transmission precautions despite the grave risks that such violations might pose to the self and others. The second is the emergence of widespread protests and other acts of civil disobedience directed at perceived sources of institutional inequality and injustice and triggered in large part by viral videos of blatant acts of police brutality against mostly, but not exclusively, people of color.

Is it possible the COVID-19-related constraints on normal social activity served to amplify the search for a better attentional investment return than the rapidly diminishing returns provided by social media, Netflix, Zoom calls, and the once-a-week trips to the supermarket? If so, one could also speculate that the decision about which of the two movements to join might have been determined by its resonance with one's beliefs or ideology (Van Tilburg and Igou 2011a, 2017). Importantly, IAIT would predict that even if individuals returned to their homes and submitted once again to the lockdown constraints, they would probably be less bored by virtue of the fact they would be better equipped to engage in boredom tolerance coping.

Although it is difficult to discern at this time whether the frequency and duration of boredom in the community at large have increased dramatically during the long periods of social distancing and sheltering at home—much less whether such a rise has contributed to the two aforementioned transgressive social movements and reactions—it is, nonetheless, a contextual reality that has to be acknowledged.

REFERENCES

Alós-Ferrer, Carlos and Sabine Hügelschäfer. 2012. "Faith in Intuition and Behavioral Biases". *Journal of Economic Behavior and Organization* 84: 182–92. https://doi .org/10.1016/j.jebo.2012.08.004.

American Psychiatric Association. 2013. *Diagnostic and Statistical Manual of Mental Disorders* (5th ed.). Arlington, VA: Author.

Barbalet, Jack M. 1999. "Boredom and Social Meaning". *British Journal of Sociology* 50, no. 4: 631–46. https://doi.org/10.1111/j.1468-4446.1999.00631.x.

Bem, Daryl J. 1972. "Self-Perception Theory". *Advances in Experimental Social Psychology* 6, no. 1: 1–62.

Bench, Shane W., and Heather C. Lench. 2013. "On the Function of Boredom". *Behavioral Sciences* 3, no. 3: 459–72.

Berridge, Kent C., and Terry E. Robinson. 2016. "Liking, Wanting, and the Incentive-Sensitization Theory of Addiction." *The American Psychologist* 71, no. 8: 670–9. https://doi.org/10.1037/amp0000059.

Bickel, Warren K., Amy L. Odum, and Gregory J. Madden 1999. "Impulsivity and Cigarette Smoking: Delay Discounting in Current, Never, and Ex-Smokers." *Psychopharmacology* 146, no. 4: 447–54. https://doi.org/10.1007/PL000 05490.

Carson E. Ann, and William J. Sabol. 2012. *Prisoners in 2011*. U.S. Department of Justice: Bureau of Justice Statistics. http://www.bjs.gov/content/pub/pdf/p11.pdf. NCJ 239808.

Chin, Alycia, Amanda Markey, Saurabh Bhargava, Karim S. Kassam, and George Loewenstein. 2017. "Bored in the USA: Experience Sampling and Boredom in Everyday Life." *Emotion* 17, no. 2: 359–68. http://dx.doi.org/10.1037/emo0000232.

Cooper Hannah L. F. 2015. "War on Drugs Policing and Police Brutality." *Substance Use and Misuse*. 50, no. (8–9): 1188–94.

Csikszentmihalyi, Mihaly. 2000. *Beyond Boredom and Anxiety*. San Francisco, CA: Jossey-Bass.

Dahlen, Eric R., Ryan C. Martin, Katie Ragan, and Myndi M. Kuhlman. 2005. "Driving Anger, Sensation Seeking, Impulsiveness, and Boredom Proneness in the Prediction of Unsafe Driving." *Accident Analysis & Prevention* 37, no. 2: 341–48.

Damrad-Frye, Robin, and James D. Laird. 1989. "The Experience of Boredom: The Role of the Self-Perception of Attention." *Journal of Personality and Social Psychology* 57, no. 2: 315–20.

Danckert, James A., and Ava-Ann A. Allman. 2005. "Time Flies When You're Having Fun: Temporal Estimation and the Experience of Boredom." *Brain and Cognition* 59, no. 3: 236–45.

Daschmann, Elena C., Thomas Goetz, and Robert H. Stupnisky. 2011. "Testing the Predictors of Boredom at School: Development and Validation of the Precursors to Boredom Scales." *British Journal of Educational Psychology* 81, no. 3: 421–40. http://doi.org/10.1348/000709910X526038.

Doyle, John R. 2013. "Survey of Time Preference, Delay Discounting Models." *Judgment and Decision Making*, 82: 116–35.

Eastwood, John D., Alexandra Frischen, Mark J. Fenske, and Daniel Smilek. 2012. "The Unengaged Mind: Defining Boredom in Terms of Attention." *Perspectives on Psychological Science* 7, no. 5: 482–95. http://doi.org/10.1177/1745691612456044.

Elpidorou, Andreas. 2014. "The Bright Side of Boredom." *Frontiers in Psychology*, 5: 1245. http://doi.org/10.3389/fpsyg.2014.01245.

Elpidorou, Andreas. 2018. "The Good of Boredom." *Philosophical Psychology* 31, no. 3: 323–51.

Fahlman, Shelley A., Kimberley B. Mercer, Peter Gaskovski, Adrienne E. Eastwood, and John D. Eastwood. 2009. "Does a Lack of Life Meaning Cause Boredom? Results from Psychometric, Longitudinal, and Experimental Analyses." *Journal of Social and Clinical Psychology* 28, no. 3: 307–40.

Farmer, Richard, and Norman D. Sundberg. 1986. "Boredom Proneness—The Development and Correlates of a New Scale." *Journal of Personality Assessment* 50, no. 1: 4–17.

Ferrell, Jeff. 2004. "Boredom, Crime and Criminology." *Theoretical Criminology* 8, no.3: 287–302.

Fisher, Cynthia. D. 1993. "Boredom at Work: A Neglected Concept." *Human Relations* 46, no.3: 395–417. http://doi.org/10.1177/001872679304600305.

Furnham, Adrian 2003. "Belief in a Just World: Research Progress Over the Past Decade." *Personality and Individual Differences* 345, no. 5: 795–817.

Galanter, Marc. 2005. *Spirituality and the Healthy Mind: Science, Therapy, and the Need for Personal Meaning*. Oxford: Oxford University Press.

Galanter, Marc. 2016. *What is Alcoholics Anonymous? A Path from Addiction to Recovery*. New York: Oxford University Press.

Goldberg, Yael K., John D. Eastwood, Jennifer LaGuardia, and James Danckert. 2011. "Boredom: An Emotional Experience Distinct from Apathy, Anhedonia, or Depression." *Journal of Social and Clinical Psychology* 30, no. 6: 647–66.

Hare, Robert D., and Craig S. Neumann. 2006. "The PCL-R Assessment of Psychopathy: Development, Structural Properties, and New Directions." In *Handbook of Psychopathy*, edited by Christopher J. Patrick, 58–88. New York: Guilford.

Harpur, Timothy J., Robert D. Hare, and A. Ralph Hakstian. 1989. "Two-Factor Conceptualization of Psychopathy: Construct Validity and Assessment Implications." *Psychological Assessment: A Journal of Consulting and Clinical Psychology* 1, no. 1: 6–17.

Harris, Mary B. 2000. "Correlates and Characteristics of Boredom Proneness and Boredom." *Journal of Applied Social Psychology* 303, no.3: 576–98.

Havermans, Remco C., Linda Vancleef, Antonis Kalamatianos, and Chantal Nederkoorn. 2015. "Eating and Inflicting Pain Out of Boredom." *Appetite* 85: 52–7.

Heather Nick, and Ian Robertson . 1981. *Controlled Drinking*. London: Methuen.

Heather, Nick. 2017. "Q: Is Addiction a Brain Disease Or a Moral Failing? A: Neither." *Neuroethics* 10, no. 1: 115–24.

Irving, Barrie Anthony, and Marie Parker-Jenkins. 1995. "Tackling Truancy: An Examination of Persistent Non-Attendance Amongst Disaffected School Pupils and Positive Support Strategies." *Cambridge Journal of Education* 25, no. 2: 225–35.

Iso-Ahola, Seppo E., and Edward D. Crowley. 1991. "Adolescent Substance Abuse and Leisure Boredom." *Journal of Leisure Research* 23, no. 3: 260–71.

Iso-Ahola, Seppo E., and Ellen Weissinger. 1987. "Leisure and Boredom." *Journal of Social and Clinical Psychology* 53, no. 3: 356–64.

Jason, Zachary, 2017. "Bored Out of Their Minds." *Harvard Education Magazine.* https://www.gse.harvard.edu/news/ed/17/01/bored-out-their-minds.

Johnston, Lloyd D., and Patrick M. O'Malley. 1986. "Why Do the Nation's Students Use Drugs and Alcohol? Self-Reported Reasons from Nine National Surveys." *Journal of Drug Issues* 16, no. 1: 29–66.

Kanevsky, Lannie, and Tacey Keighley. 2003. "To Produce Or Not to Produce? Understanding Boredom and the Honor in Underachievement." *Roeper Review* 261, no. 1: 20–28.

Koob, George F., and Jay Schulkin. 2019. "Addiction and Stress: An Allostatic View." *Neuroscience & Biobehavioral Reviews* 106: 245–62.

Krotava, Iryna, and McWelling Todman. 2014. "Boredom Severity, Depression and Alcohol Consumption in Belarus." *Journal of Psychology and Behavioral Science* 2, no. 1: 73–83.

Kurzban, Robert, Angela Duckworth, Joseph W. Kable, and Justus Myers. 2013. "An Opportunity Cost Model of Subjective Effort and Task Performance." *The Behavioral and Brain Sciences* 36, no. 6: 661–679.

Larson, Richard C. 1987. "Perspectives on Queues: Social Justice and the Psychology of Queueing." *Operations Research* 35, no. 6: 895–905. http://www.jstor.org/stable/171439.

Lehr, Evangeline, and McWelling Todman. 2009. "Boredom and Boredom Proneness in Children: Implications for Academic and Social Adjustment." In *Self-Regulation and Social Competence: Psychological Studies in Identity, Achievement and Work-Family Dynamics*, edited by McWelling Todman, 79–90. Athens: ATNIER Press

Lerner, Melvin J. 1980. *The Belief in a Just World: A Fundamental Delusion. Perspectives in Social Psychology.* New York: Plenum Press.

London, Harvey, and Monello, Lenore. 1974. "Cognitive Manipulation of Boredom." In *Thought and Feeling: Cognitive Alteration of Feeling States*, edited by Harvey London and Richard E. Nisbett, 74–84. Oxford: Aldine.

Lozano, Brian E., Robert S. Stephens, and Roger A. Roffman. 2006. "Abstinence and Moderate Use Goals in the Treatment of Marijuana Dependence." *Addiction* 101, no. 11: 1589–97.

Maple, Emily. 2020. *Boredom Awareness and Alcohol Use: An Intervention.* New School for Social Research Dissertations. Paper 170.

Markey, Amanda Rose. 2018. *Three Essays on Boredom.* Carnegie Mellon University. Thesis. https://doi.org/10.1184/R1/6723896.v1.

Marlatt, G. Alan, and Katie Witkiewitz. 2002. "Harm Reduction Approaches to Alcohol Use: Health Promotion, Prevention, and Treatment." *Addictive behaviors* 27, no. 6: 867–86.

Mercer-Lynn, Kimberley B., David B. Flora, Shelley A. Fahlman, and John D. Eastwood. 2013. "The Measurement of Boredom: Differences Between Existing Self-Report Scales." *Assessment* 20, no. 5: 585–96.

Moynihan, Andrew B., Eric R. Igou, and Wijnand A.P. van Tilburg. 2017a. "Boredom Increases Impulsiveness: A Meaning-Regulation Perspective." *Social Psychology* 48, no. 5: 293–309.

Moynihan, Andrew B., Eric R. Igou, and Wijnand A.P. van Tilburg. 2017b. "Free, Connected, and Meaningful: Free Will Belief Promotes Meaningfulness Through Belongingness." *Personality and Individual Differences* 107: 54–65.

Nett, Ulrike E., Thomas Goetz, and Lia M. Daniels. 2010. "What to Do When Feeling Bored?: Students' Strategies for Coping with Boredom." *Learning and Individual Differences* 20, no. 6: 626–38.

Orcutt, James D. 1984. "Contrasting Effects of Two Kinds of Boredom on Alcohol Use." *Journal of Drug Issues* 14, no. 1: 161–73.

Pallak, Michael S., and Thane S. Pittman. 1972. "General Motivational Effects of Dissonance Arousal." *Journal of Personality and Social Psychology* 21, no. 3: 349–58.

Patel, Vikram, Jonathan K. Burns, Monisha Dhingra, Leslie Tarver, Brandon A. Kohrt, and Crick Lund. 2018. "Income Inequality and Depression: A Systematic Review and Meta-Analysis of the Association and a Scoping Review of Mechanisms." *World Psychiatry* 17, no. 1: 76–89.

Pekrun, Reinhard, Thomas Goetz, Lia M. Daniels, Robert H. Stupnisky, and Raymond P. Perry. 2010. "Boredom in Achievement Settings: Exploring Control–Value Antecedents and Performance Outcomes of a Neglected Emotion." *Journal of Educational Psychology* 102, no. 3: 531–49.

Pettiford, Jasmine, Rachel V. Kozink, Avery M. Lutz, Scott H. Kollins, Jed E. Rose, and F. Joseph McClernon. 2007. "Increases in Impulsivity Following Smoking Abstinence are Related to Naseline Nicotine Intake and Boredom Susceptibility." *Addictive behaviors* 32, no. 10: 2351–57.

Pickett Kate E., and Richard G. Wilkinson. 2015. "Income Inequality and Health: A Causal Review. *Social Science and Medicine* 128: 316–26.

Rupp, Deborah E., and Stephen J. Vodanovich. 1997. "The Role of Boredom Proneness in Self-Reported Anger and Aggression." *Journal of Social Behavior and Personality* 12, no. 4: 925–36.

Steger, Michael F., Patricia Frazier, Shigehiro Oishi, and Matthew Kaler. 2006. "The Meaning in Life Questionnaire: Assessing the Presence of and Search for Meaning in Life." *Journal of Counseling Psychology* 53, no. 1: 80–93.

Sturm, Roland, and Carole Roan Gresenz. 2002. "Relations of Income Inequality and Family Income to Chronic Medical Conditions and Mental Health Disorders: National Survey." *BMJ* 324: 20.

Sucala, Madalina L., Simona Stefan, Aurora Szentagotai-Tatar, and Daniel David. 2010. "Time Flies When You Expect to Have Fun. An Experimental Investigation of the Relationship Between Expectancies and the Perception of Time Progression." *Cognition, Brain, Behavior* 14, no. 3: 231–41.

The National Center on Addiction and Substance Abuse at Columbia University. 2003. *National Survey of American Attitudes on Substance Abuse VIII: Teens and Parents*. New York, NY: Columbia University.

Todman, McWelling. 2003. "Boredom and Psychotic Disorders: Cognitive and Motivational Issues." *Psychiatry* 66: 146–67. http://doi.org/10.1521/psyc.66.2.146.20623.

Todman, McWelling. 2007. "Psychopathology and Boredom: A Neglected Association." In *Psychological Science: Research, Theory and Future Directions*, edited by Kostas Andrea Fanti, 145–60. Athens, Greece: ATINER Press.

Todman, McWelling. 2013. "The Dimensions of State Boredom: Frequency, Duration, Unpleasantness, Consequences and Causal Attributions." *Educational Research International* 1, no. 1: 32–40.

Todman, McWeeling, Daniel Shepuk, Kristin Nelson, Jason Evans, Robert Goldberg, and Evangeline Lehr. 2008, "Boredom, hallucination-proneness and hypohedonia in Schizophrenia and Schizoaffective Disorder." In *Schizoaffective Disorder: International Perspectives on Understanding, Intervention and Rehabilitation*, edited by Kam-Shing Yip. New York: Nova Science Publications.

Troutwine, Robert, and Edgar C. O'Neal. 1981. "Volition, Performance of a Boring Task and Time Estimation." *Perceptual and Motor Skills* 52, no. 3: 865–66. http://dx.doi.org/10.2466/pms.1981.52.3.865

Van Tilburg, Wijnand A.P., and Eric R. Igou. 2011a. "On Boredom and Social Identity: A Pragmatic Meaning-Regulation Approach." *Personality and Social Psychology Bulletin* 37, no. 2: 1679–92.

Van Tilburg, Wijnand A.P., and Eric R. Igou. 2011b. "On the Meaningfulness of Existence: When Life Salience Boosts Adherence to Worldviews." *European Journal of Social Psychology* 41, no. 6: 740–50.

Van Tilburg, Wijnand A.P., and Eric R. Igou. 2012. "On Boredom: Lack of Challenge and Meaning as Distinct Boredom Experiences." *Motivation and Emotion* 36, no. 2: 181–94.

Van Tilburg, Wijnand A.P., and Eric R. Igou. 2013. "On the Meaningfulness of Behavior: An Expectancy X Value Approach." *Motivation and Emotion* 37, no. 3: 373–88.

Van Tilburg, Wijnand A.P., Eric R. Igou, and Constantine Sedikides. 2013. "In Search of Meaningfulness: Nostalgia as an Antidote to Boredom." *Emotion* 13, no. 3: 450–61.

Van Tilburg, Wijnand A.P., and Eric R. Igou. 2017. "Can Boredom Help? Increased Prosocial Intentions in Response to Boredom." *Self and Identity* 16, no. 1: 82–96.

Van Tilburg, Wijnand A.P., Eric R. Igou, Paul J. Maher, Andrew B. Moynihan, and Dawn G. Martin. 2019. "Bored like Hell: Religiosity Reduces Boredom and Tempers the Quest for Meaning." *Emotion* 19, no. 2: 255–69. https://doi.org/10.1037/emo0000439.

Vogel-Walcutt, Jennifer J., Logan Fiorella, Teresa Carper, and Sae Schatz. 2012. "The Definition, Assessment, and Mitigation of State Boredom Within Educational Settings: A Comprehensive Review." *Educational Psychology Review* 24, no. 1: 89–111.

Vygotsky, Lev S., 1980. "Interaction between learning and development". In *Mind in society: The development of higher psychological processes*, edited by Michael Cole, Vera John-Steiner, Sylvia Scribner, and Ellen Souberman, 79–91. Cambridge, MA: Harvard University Press.

Watt, John D. 1991. "Effect of Boredom Proneness on Time Perception." *Psychological Reports*, 69, no. 1: 323–27.

Watt, John D., and Stephen J. Vodanovich. 1992. "Relationship Between Boredom Proneness and Impulsivity." *Psychological reports* 70, no. 3: 688–90.

Wegner, Lisa, Alan J. Flisher, Perpetual Chikobvu, Carl Lombard, and Gary King. 2008. "Leisure Boredom and High School Dropout in Cape Town, South Africa." *Journal of Adolescence* 31, no. 3: 421–31.

Wegner, Lisa, and Alan J. Flisher. 2009. "Leisure Boredom and Adolescent Risk Behaviour: A Systematic Literature Review." *Journal of Child and Adolescent Mental Health* 21, no. 1: 1–28.

Weiss, Emily, McWelling Todman, M., Özge Pazar, Sophia Mullens, Kristin Maurer, Alexandria Romano. 2020. "Boredom and the Illusion of Temporal Slowing: An Integrated Attentional Investment Model". Unpublished manuscript. Department of Psychology, New School for Social Research.

Westgate, Erin C., and Timothy D. Wilson. 2018. "Boring Thoughts and Bored Minds: The MAC Model of Boredom and Cognitive Engagement." *Psychological Review* 125, no. 5: 689–713.

Wilkinson, Richard, and Kate Pickett. 2017. "Inequality and Mental Illness." *The Lancet Psychiatry* 4, no. 7: 512–13.

Wilson, Timothy D., David A. Reinhard, Erin C. Westgate, Daniel T. Gilbert, Nicole Ellerbeck, Cheryl Hahn, Casey L. Brown, and Adi Shaked. 2014. "Just Think: The Challenges of the Disengaged Mind." *Science* 345 (6192): 75–77.

Winding, Trine Nøhr, and Johan Hviid Andersen. 2015. "Socioeconomic Differences in School Dropout Among Young Adults: The Role of Social Relations." *BMC public health* 15, no. 1: 1–11.

Yazzie-Mintz, Ethan. 2007. "Voices of Students on Engagement: A Report on the 2006 High School Survey of Student Engagement." Center for Evaluation and Education Policy, Indiana University. https://eric.ed.gov/?id=ED495758.

Zakay, Dan. 2014. "Psychological Time as Information: The Case of Boredom." *Frontiers in Psychology* 5: 917. https://doi.org/10.3389/fpsyg.2014.00917

Zuckerman, Marvin. 1979. *Sensation Seeking: Beyond the Optimal Level of Arousal*, Hillsdale, NJ: Erlbaum.

Chapter 7

Boredom and Poverty

A Theoretical Model

Andreas Elpidorou

Most of us are affected by boredom—maybe not everywhere or not all the time, but at least somewhere and some of the time (Chin et al. 2017; Goetz et al. 2014; Larson and Richards 1991; Smith et al. 2015; Weybright et al. 2020). The prevalence of boredom is important. It signals our susceptibility to it and suggests that boredom is a widespread psychological phenomenon. The psychological reality of boredom has been underscored by work in the affective sciences. From psychoanalytical accounts of boredom (e.g., Fenichel 1951; Greenson 1953) to descriptions of boredom as a state of nonoptimal arousal (e.g., Barmack 1938; Berlyne 1960), and from cognitive (e.g., Eastwood et al. 2012; Fisher 1993; Hill and Perkins 1985; Tam et al. in press) and existential theories (e.g., Maddi 1970; Van Tilburg and Igou 2012) of boredom to neurophysiological models of boredom (e.g., Danckert and Merrifield 1980; Mathiak 2013), a rich and productive research program has affirmed the importance and existence of boredom as a psychological phenomenon. What is more, research shows that whether or not we experience boredom does not depend merely nor invariably on some objective features of our situation. Rather, the experience of boredom is more reliably correlated with our subjective standing: how features of our situation are appraised by us, given our psychological resources and physiological states (Barbalet 1999; Eastwood et al. 2012; Fisher 1993; Martin, Sadlo, and Stew 2006; Mercer-Lynn, Bar, and Eastwood 2014).

Nonetheless, the success and attention that this paradigm of research has received over the past few decades should not mislead us to think that boredom is merely a personal issue, that is, an emotion or affective state whose social and historical context is a superficial feature that we can ignore when trying to understand its nature. Boredom is as much personal as it is social (see also Ohlmeier et al. 2020). Indeed, there are at least two different senses in which boredom is social. First, insofar as the experience of boredom is prompted (but not necessitated) by situational features and those features are influenced by our social standing, the experience of boredom is influenced by our social standing. No one would deny that boredom is social in this sense. Still, many discussions of boredom tend to focus on its proximal antecedents, ignoring its more distal determinants. To properly understand the social character of boredom we need to examine the structures that give rise to those proximal antecedents. Different social structures and institutions will give rise to different rates of the experience of boredom. Moreover, attempts to alleviate boredom would be ineffective if the structural factors remain unchanged. Second, boredom appears to be social in an additional, perhaps even stronger sense: the very experience of boredom is socially determined. Lest I be misunderstood, I should clarify that the claim of social determination of the experience of boredom does not vitiate the biological basis of boredom. Nor does it entail that boredom lacks an evolutionary history. What the claim of social determination entails is that the very character of boredom, and not just its frequency, is shaped by the dominant social forces that surround us. Depending on our social condition, boredom will be experienced differently.

My aim in this chapter is to take seriously the social character of boredom in both of the aforementioned senses. To that end, I articulate the ways in which our social standing, and particularly our socioeconomic status (SES), affects, even transforms, the experience of boredom. Even if boredom can be said to be *democratic*, in the sense that it can potentially affect all of us, it does not actually affect all of us in the same way. Boredom, I argue, is unjust—some groups are disproportionately negatively impacted by boredom through no fault of their own. Depending on our social position and self and others' perceptions of our SES, we can experience it more frequently, more intensely, and in ways that either leave us incapable of alleviating it or push us to harmful and maladaptive responses to it. Hence, seen in a socioeconomic light, boredom can become a serious threat to our physical and psychological well-being. Insofar as freedom to pursue and achieve one's well-being is essential to human life and a primary concern of contemporary liberal societies, boredom should be considered to be a social justice issue. The disproportionately negative effects of boredom on lower SES groups indicate the profound ways that boredom affects individuals and further disadvantages those who are already in marginalized positions. Contrary to many historical accounts, boredom is not only the experience of the elite, the wealthy, or those with ample free time. In our current political, social, and economic climate, boredom is primarily the experience of the less privileged, the disadvantaged, and the marginalized.

1. SOCIAL CLASS

Social class does not exist naturally in the world, disconnected from our concerns, institutions, and opinions. Consequently, there is no fact independent of human practices and beliefs that determines class membership. All the same, within our intersubjective context, social class is both a powerful and an effective determinant of human action and existence in general. Our income and wealth, food and medical care, neighborhood and housing, education, participation in cultural and social institutions, and relationships, just to name a few, are linked to and determined by our economic and social status. Thus, even if social class is not "deep" in a metaphysical or biological sense—neither a "furniture" of the world nor a biological given—it is real through and through. It has causal significance and power; it relates to our past and shapes our present and future.

There are both objective and subjective indexes of SES. The former is an indicator of the social class of an individual based on some discernible and quantifiable feature of that individual. For instance, a classic Marxist analysis of class utilizes an objective indicator of social class because it divides society into two social classes—the bourgeoisie and the proletariat—depending on who owns the means of production. More recently, researchers have shifted away from using ownership of means of production as a determinant of social class. Objective SES is now generally determined in terms of income and financial resources, educational attainment, occupation, or participation in various social institutions (Oakes and Rossi 2003). In addition to objective measures, researchers also utilize subjective measures of SES. These measures assess individuals' perceptions of their class membership and relationship to others. A widely used measure of subjective SES gives individuals a drawing of a ladder and asks them to place an "X" on the rung where they think they stand relative to other people in either their country or community (Adler et al. 2000; Goodman et al. 2001). There is clear evidence that both objective and subjective assessments of SES are necessary and valid: they are only moderately correlated with each other and they independently predict different class-related outcomes (Adler et al. 2000; Goodman et al. 2001).

Studies have demonstrated the many and profound ways in which social class shapes our lives. Material resources (or lack thereof) affect one's social opportunities, marriage and relationship prospects, educational attainment, and access to social institutions (Bourdieu 1985; Fiske and Markus 2012; Lareau 2011; Manstead 2018; Shafer and James 2013; Stephens, Fryberg, and Markus 2011). In addition, class membership affects physical and psychological well-being (Adler et al. 1994). Lower-class individuals are more vulnerable to physical disease and at a greater health risk (Adler et al. 2000; Cohen et al. 2008). They also experience lower subjective well-being, more negative moods, and more chronic stress relative to those belonging to higher social classes (Sapolsky 2005; Diener and Suh 1997; Gallo and Matthews 2003; Howell and Howell 2008; Vliegenthart et al. 2016). There are also discernible cultural differences between members of different social classes. Manners and etiquette (Bourdieu 1975; Elias 1978), aesthetic and gustatory preferences (Snibbe and Markus 2005), language use (Bernstein 1971), parenting strategies (Lareau 2011), even one's accepted norms and expectations turn out to be class specific (Stephens et al. 2012). Lastly, social class has been shown to affect or impact the construction of one's self (Kraus et al. 2012), prejudices and prosocial actions (Manstead 2018), and behaviors in educational contexts (Lareau 2011; Stephens et al. 2012).

Without a doubt, social class is a powerful determinant of one's existence—it affects our lives in numerous and significant ways, ones that are often invisible to us and are entrenched in historical and social institutions. In light of the effects of social class and specifically the dangers and harms that members of lower classes face on account of their class membership one might question the importance of examining the issue of boredom. Compared to everything else that low SES individuals have to endure, isn't boredom a trivial matter?

It is not. As a chronic condition or a propensity to experience boredom in a wide range of situations, boredom is far from trivial. Decades of research has documented the numerous harms and dangers that *boredom proneness* (a conceptualization and operationalization of one's propensity to experience boredom; Farmer and Sundberg 1986) poses. Although there are well-founded concerns with both the theoretical framework of boredom proneness and the psychometric properties of instruments assessing it (Gana, Broc, and Bailly 2019; Struk et al. 2017; Vodanovich 2003; Tam, Van Tilburg, and Chan 2021), research employing measures of boredom proneness shows that it is a serious threat to one's well-being. Individuals who score high on measures of boredom proneness report lower life meaning (Fahlman et al. 2019), lower life and job satisfaction (Farmer and Sundberg 1986), and poorer interpersonal relationships (Leong and Schneller 1993; Tolor 1989; Watt and Vodanovich 1999) compared to individuals who score low on such measures. Moreover, as measured by boredom proneness, the propensity to experience boredom often has been positively correlated, on the one hand, with depression (Ahmed 1990; Farmer and Sundberg, 1986; Goldberg et al. 2011; Malkovsky et al. 2012), loneliness (Farmer and Sundberg 1986), and hopelessness (Farmer and Sundberg 1986), and on the other hand, with anger and aggression, and hostility (Dahlen et al. 2004; Gana and Akremi 1998; Gordon et al. 1997; Rupp and Vodanovich 1997). Lastly, boredom proneness has been linked to a host of maladaptive behaviors. Boredom-prone individuals are more likely to engage in risk-taking activities (Dahlen et al. 2005; Kass et al. 2010) and are more prone to problem gambling (Blaszczynski, McConaghy, and Frankova 1990, but see Mercer and Eastwood 2010), and drug and alcohol abuse (LePera 2011; Paulson, Coombs, and Richardson 1990) than those who are not prone to boredom.

Thus, if individuals in lower social classes are more likely to experience prolonged or more frequent boredom, then such an increased likelihood is an indication that they are also in danger to inherit the harms associated with boredom proneness. In section 3, I will complete this argument by offering reasons that suggest that an increase in boredom will be associated with lower SES. But boredom matters for individuals of low SES not just because of a potential increase in the frequency of the experience of boredom. As I will show in sections 4 and 5, our current understanding of boredom reveals that lower SES individuals are in a disadvantageous position when dealing with boredom. Hence, low SES individuals are doubly threatened by boredom: they are more likely to experience it more often and are less likely to be able to escape from it.

2. BOREDOM AND POVERTY: AN INTERACTIONIST MODEL

Boredom is an experientially unpleasant state that involves a strong desire to engage in an alternative situation (Eastwood et al. 2012; Elpidorou 2014; Fahlman et al. 2013). The state of boredom has been associated both with attentional difficulties and negative appraisals of one's situation (Eastwood et al. 2012; Tam et al. in press; Van Tilburg and Igou 2017a; Westgate and Wilson 2018). On the one hand, during boredom one is experiencing an inability to engage in a satisfactory manner with the situation at hand. On the other hand, bored individuals find their situations to be lacking in meaning (Van Tilburg and Igou 2012), monotonous or repetitive (Thackray, Bailey, and Touchstone 1977), affording inadequate control (Caldwell et al. 1999; Martin, Sadlo, and Stew 2006; Shaw, Caldwell, and Kleiber 2006; van Hooft and van Hooff 2018), or nonoptimally challenging or stimulating (Csikszentmihalyi 1975; Daschmann, Goetz, and Stupnisky 2011). Although there are additional aspects to the experience of boredom as well as disagreements about the centrality and exact role of those aspects, it is widely accepted that boredom is a state of perceived dissatisfaction with our situation (Elpidorou 2018a). It is both a bothersome reminder that we find ourselves in a situation for which there is a perceived mismatch between our desired engagement and actual engagement, and a motivating force that compels us to make its presence go away.

Boredom, we might say, is an aversively felt warning that we have found ourselves in an unsatisfactory situation. But that is not all. Because of its volitional, cognitive, and experiential character, boredom also calls on us to move out of our current state of discontent and into one that is either in line with our interests and preferences or engaging and stimulating in the right way (Bench and Lench 2013; Elpidorou 2020, 2021; Kurzban et al. 2013). Despite this inherent push that boredom carries, boredom cannot guarantee that one would be able to alleviate one's feelings of boredom. Boredom is a push for a change but not the assurance of one. This aspect of boredom becomes obvious when we consider the effects of boredom within occupational and educational contexts. Bring to mind a seemingly never-ending work shift or a mandatory meeting. The boredom they induce is inescapable. Or think of workers in factories, secretaries inputting data, or students attending a lecture that is beyond their comprehension. They are often bored and forced to remain so until their work or class concludes. Hence, the very experience of boredom will not suffice to get us out of our discontent. We must also have the resources, freedom, and energy to do so.

Even when with our help boredom succeeds in realizing change, it is not necessarily for the better. As it has been widely discussed in the literature, our responses to boredom vary: they can be beneficial or harmful, moral or immoral, profound or mundane (Elpidorou 2017, 2020; Van Tilburg and Igou 2017b). Boredom is an instigator of change—a felt provocation, we could say, to take action and to respond to a crisis of agency. Through its affective, cognitive, volitional, and psychological concomitants, it calls on us to do something other than what we are currently doing. All the same, it is limited in at least two ways. First, it never reveals to us what that something else is that we should be doing. While bored, subjects report a strong desire to do something other than what they are currently doing without however being able to readily identify what that is (Fahlman et al. 2013; Todman 2003). Second, the experience of boredom does not fabricate opportunities when those do not exist. Thus, without access to the right resources of alternative engagement, and without guidance as to what might be worth pursuing, it is easy to choose the wrong way out of boredom. It is no surprise that maladaptive responses to boredom are common. This is especially true for subjects who find themselves often in the grips of boredom, distressed and bedraggled by its force. Binge drinking, drug use, gambling, mindless eating, self-harm, even disobeying social distancing measures are all appropriate, in some sense, responses to the doldrums of life. They might not serve a greater purpose. They might even hinder one's chances for self-improvement and lead us back to boredom. Yet they offer a much-needed respite from the pains of ennui.

The aforementioned description of boredom suggests that if an agent lacks the material and psychological resources to properly respond to its onset, boredom can become both a burden to bear and a threat to the agent's well-being. The capacity to respond to boredom is undermined and one is less likely to alleviate it in productive ways. In this way, boredom may become unjust. It can affect most severely those who, because of their social and material standing, will have a hard time escaping productively out of boredom.

It is time to offer a theoretical model in support of the previously raised contention that SES is an important determinant both of the experience of boredom and of our responses to it. The model on offer predicts that individuals in low SES are at a severe disadvantage when it comes to boredom. Specifically, and as depicted in Figure 7.1, the model proposes three distinct "pathways" by which poverty and low SES interact with boredom. First, our material conditions affect the antecedents and thus frequency of boredom. Being a member of a low socioeconomical class, the model proposes, makes the experience of boredom more frequent because it puts subjects in situations that are known elicitors of boredom. Second, social status also affects the very experience of boredom: boredom is felt differently by individuals of low SES compared to those of high SES. Third, and finally, our responses to boredom are affected by our social status. In particular, individuals of low SES will have difficulties either alleviating or responding to boredom in productive and potentially beneficial manners. In my explication of this theoretical model, I focus primarily on making a case for the existence of the first pathway. In light of the many documented harms that boredom proneness

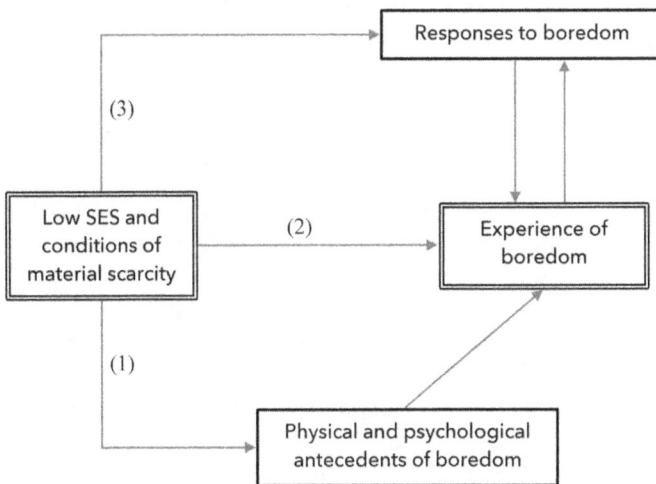

Figure 7.1 An interactionist model of the influence of poverty on boredom. SES affects the frequency of boredom (pathway 1), the experience of boredom (pathway 2), and our ability to respond to boredom (pathway 3). The manner in which we experience boredom influences and is influenced by our ability to respond to the onset of boredom.

poses to individuals, knowing whether such a pathway exists is of crucial importance. The second and third proposed pathways are also important, yet a full articulation of their workings would have to be the aim of a separate project. All the same, I do provide empirical evidence in support of their existence and role in the experience of boredom.

Before I turn to a discussion of how social class (and specifically, low SES) interacts with boredom, it is crucial to mention an important limitation with the proposed model and approach that I take in this chapter. The proposed model, which is based on available literature, treats SES as a monolithic category. In doing so, it fails to distinguish between the various ways in which one's SES interacts with race, gender, age, sexual orientation, gender identity, physical ability, ethnicity, nationality, religion, and other components of one's identity and determinants of group membership. Unfortunately, the empirical and conceptual literature upon which the model is based is not sufficiently intersectional (sometimes, it is not intersectional at all) to permit an investigation into the ways in which different group memberships interact with SES. This shortcoming calls for greater nuance in research programs moving forward. Having said that, the proposed model not only makes a strong case for the influence of SES on the experience of boredom but also paves the way for an intersectional analysis (Crenshaw 1989, 1991). It is of tremendous importance to determine precisely how low SES individuals of different groups experience boredom on the basis of their multiple identities. To get closer to such an intersectional analysis we must first offer an empirically supported model of how boredom and social class interact. This is the task that I undertake in this chapter.

3. FROM POVERTY TO BOREDOM

To understand how social class membership relates to the occurrence and frequency of boredom, we first need to discuss the antecedents of boredom. When and where does boredom arise? A survey of the literature shows that boredom is likely to arise in a variety of situations (Elpidorou 2018a). These include situations where one is faced with repetitive or monotonous tasks (De Chenne and Moody 1988; Hill and Perkins 1985; O'Hanlon 1981; Thackray, Bailey, and Touchstone 1977), nonoptimally challenging tasks (Daschmann, Goetz, and Stupnisky 2011; Pekrun et al, 2010), or conditions of constraint (Eastwood et al. 2012; Fahlman et al. 2013; Fenichel 1951; Geiwitz 1966; Hill and Perkins 1985; Todman 2013). Situations which involve a sense of meaninglessness (Barbalet 1999; Fahlman et al. 2009; Van Tilburg and Igou 2012), the perception of feeling stuck (Brissett and Snow 1993), or an inability to find flow in one's activities (Csikszentmihalyi 1975) have also been reported

as elicitors of boredom. Moreover, boredom also arises when one's attentional resources are scarce or unavailable (Eastwood et al. 2012; Tam et al. in
press; Van Tilburg and Igou 2017a; Westgate and Wilson 2018), when one is
fatigued (Martin, Sadlo, and Stew 2006; Milyavskaya et al. 2019), or when
one perceives oneself as not being in control of a situation (Troutwine and
O'Neal 1981; Shaw, Caldwell, and Kleiber 2006; van Hooft and van Hooff
2018). These antecedents of boredom might appear to be a sundry list of
conditions (both objective and psychological) that often give rise to boredom.
Yet noting all these conditions is helpful for it makes evident the variety of
factors that can elicit boredom. Most importantly, the list allows us to directly
examine the influence of social class on the experience of boredom. If social
class makes the presence of elicitors or antecedents of boredom more likely,
then it has an effect on the frequency of the experience of boredom. In what
follows, I focus on what I take to be the three most significant antecedents of
boredom—the presence of constraint, attentional difficulties, and perceived
meaninglessness—and examine how each one relates to poverty.

Boredom and Constraint

The term "constraint" refers not only to situations that place physical limitations on us but also to situations that give rise to feelings of constraint or to
the perception of lack of autonomy, lack of choice, or lack of agency. The
boredom literature reports a close relationship between the presence of constraint and the experience of boredom.

Some theorists have included constraint in their theoretical explications of
the character of boredom. For instance, Geiwitz (1966) analyzed boredom in
terms of four dimensions, one of which was constraint. Fenichel famously
quipped that boredom "arises when we must not do what we want to do, or
must do what we do not want to do" (1951, 359). In addition to accounts
of boredom that have made constraint a constitutive part of the experience
of boredom, many others have claimed it to be a cause of boredom. Fisher
(1993) reported that organizational constraints are a cause of workplace boredom. Martin, Sadlo, and Stew (2006) and Steinberger, Moeller, and Schroeter
(2016) provided evidence supporting a link between constraints and boredom
during work. Iso-Ahola and Weissinger (1990) found that the presence of
constraints contributes to the perception of boredom in leisure. Troutwine and
O'Neal (1981) noted that choice (and thus the absence of constraint) reduces
boredom. Scerbo (2001) argued that constraint is one of the factors that
explains high levels of boredom during vigilance tasks. Perceived autonomy
or lack of control has also been found to play a causal role in the experience
of boredom. Within an academic context, Tze, Klassen, and Daniels (2014)
found that low perceived autonomy resulted in higher levels of student

boredom. For adolescents, perceived lack of control was predictive of the experience of boredom during free time (Caldwell, Smith, and Weissinger 1992) and lack of choice was positively associated with boredom (Shaw, Caldwell, and Kleiber 1996). Van Hooft and van Hooff (2018) reported that subjects who were assigned to a low autonomy condition and were asked to perform a number of tasks experienced the tasks as more boring than individuals in a high autonomy condition (see also Reijseger et al. 2013; van Hooff and van Hooft 2017). Even though the precise psychological mechanism by which constraint leads to boredom remains unclear, it is evident that the presence of constraint is an important antecedent of boredom.

Poverty and Constraint

Objective measures of poverty—income, education level, parents' wealth, and so on—are metrics of freedom and constraint. Having more income allows one more freedom—as a consumer, citizen, parent, or an individual. Higher educational attainment is often a "passport" to more jobs. In general, one's economic, social, and cultural participation and residential and professional choices are a factor of one's economic status such that, other things being equal, the less wealthy one is the more restricted one's set of choices and freedoms becomes. Direct support for the existence of a close relationship between objective measures of SES and constraint is provided by findings documenting a positive association between income and increased reports of personal control in various domains of life (Johnson and Krueger 2005), a positive association between income and general perception of mastery (Lachman and Weaver 1998), and a negative association between income and perception of life constraints (Lachman and Weaver 1998).

Other approaches to poverty corroborate the intimate connection between poverty and lack of choice. Under a subjective understanding of SES, one has to indicate one's economic status in relationship to others in one's country or community. Although measures of subjective SES do not explicitly address issues of freedom and constraint, it is reasonable to assume that an individual's reasoning for indicating their relative socioeconomical position is affected by a comparative analysis of their own freedoms to those of others. The strong association between subjective SES and financial security is one reason to think that this is the case (Singh-Manoux, Marmot, and Adler 2005). Moreover, in an unpublished study, Snibbe and colleagues asked participants to narrate how they reasoned their place on the SES ladder. They reported that the most frequent criterion used by participants was material wealth (90 percent of participants), followed by occupation (72 percent) and education (62 percent) (Snibbe, Stewart, and Adler 2007). Such a result shows that our subjective perceptions of our SES are closely connected to objective measures which in turn relate to freedom and constraint. It is important to note that when individuals were asked to rank how they stand in their *communities* and not in their country, individuals used very different criteria to indicate their relative position. The most frequently used criterion was the ability to participate in giving activities (Snibbe, Stewart, and Adler 2007). This criterion is also reflective of one's freedom. How much one can help others is directly related to one's real or perceived freedom and lack of constraints.

Lastly, the link between poverty, on the one hand, and constraint and lack of freedom, on the other hand, becomes a definitional one, if one accepts a capabilities approach to poverty (e.g., Nussbaum 2000; Sen 1999, 2000). According to the capabilities approach, poverty is not defined as lack of income or of some other resource but as the deprivation of basic capabilities (Sen 1992). Sen (2000), for instance, holds poverty to be "a capability deprivation (that is poverty is seen as the lack of the capability to live a minimally descent life)" (4). Poverty, understood as lack of freedom, is thus inextricably bound to constraints. Individuals in poverty are subject to various forms of constraints or unfreedom: little or no access to health care, undernutrition, lack of clean water, premature morbidity, illiteracy, lack of participation in social activities, and diminishment of personal freedom and the use of skills. Hence, poverty is fundamentally an obstacle to individuals' exercise of their capabilities.

Boredom and Attention

A close relationship between boredom and attention is well supported in the literature (for helpful discussions, see Eastwood et al. 2012; Hunter and Eastwood 2013; Tam et al. in press). It has been reported that individuals with a propensity to experience boredom report a difficulty with everyday attentional tasks (e.g., Carriere et al. 2008; Cheyne, Carriere, and Smilek 2006; Malkovsky et al. 2012) and tend to perform poorly on attention-based laboratory tasks (e.g., Hamilton, Haier, and Buchsbaum 1984; Sawin and Scerbo 1995). In addition, impairments of attention have been linked to increases in the experience of boredom. For instance, individuals with mild traumatic brain injury report attentional difficulties in everyday activities and perform more errors in attentional tasks (Dockree et al. 2006; Slovarp, Azuma, and LaPointe 2012; Ziino and Ponsford 2006). They also report the frequent experience of boredom (Kreutzer, Seel, and Gourley 2001) and tend to score higher on measures of boredom proneness (Goldberg and Danckert 2013). What is more, the experience of boredom has been found to be associated with poor performance in tasks that require sustained attention (Pattyn et al. 2008; Scerbo 1998; Thackray, Bailey, and Touchstone 1977). Lastly, there are theoretical accounts of boredom that render attention (or attentional difficulties) an essential part of the experience of boredom. In fact, early accounts of boredom highlighted the importance of attentional difficulties in the experience of boredom going so far as to define boredom as the consequence of the "effortful maintenance of attention" (Leary, Canfield, and Coe 1986, 988. See also Damrad-Frye and Laird 1989; Hamilton 1981). More recently, Eastwood and colleagues (2012) have proposed a detailed and empirically grounded theoretical account of boredom that purports to explain its experiential components in terms of attentional mechanisms. Investigations into the cognitive appraisals of boredom corroborate the existence of an intimate connection between boredom and attentional difficulties (Smith and Ellsworth 1985; Van Tilburg and Igou 2017a).

The reported findings do not allow us to draw any definitive conclusions about the exact role of attentional difficulties in boredom. Indeed, it is still unclear whether attentional difficulties are the cause of boredom, an essential component of boredom, or the consequence of the experience of boredom. Although we cannot rule out the last option, it would be unreasonable to conclude that attentional issues are *always* the consequence of boredom. In fact, both available evidence (Hunter and Eastwood 2018) and theoretical models of boredom (Eastwood et al. 2012; Tam et al. in press) support the claim that attentional difficulties can give rise to boredom.

Poverty and Attention

The literature on boredom paints a clear enough picture about attention: the two are closely related. When we turn to the issue of how poverty and attention are related, however, the picture becomes fuzzier.

A growing number of researchers are becoming interested in the psychological differences between wealthy and poor individuals. In part, this interest can be explained by a movement in psychology and economics that aims to explain behavioral differences of individuals from different social classes on account of psychological or personal differences. Moreover, research on how conditions of material scarcity affect the psychology of individuals could give rise to novel avenues of research, hypotheses, and solutions to the seemingly counterproductive behaviors that have been associated with poverty (e.g., borrowing at high interest rates or spending money on lottery) (Banerjee and Duflo 2007; Blalock, Just, and Simon 2007; Haisley, Mostafa, and Loewenstein 2008). In their influential work, Mullainathan and Shafir (2013) proposed that poverty gives rise to a scarcity mindset that affects decision-making and behavior. The basic idea behind their theoretical model is that individuals who find themselves in conditions of scarcity need to think about money, budgets, expected and unexpected needs, and demands constantly.

These thoughts tax the individuals and consume their cognitive resources. As a result, poor individuals are left with fewer available cognitive resources for non-scarcity-related demands and tasks. Ultimately, conditions of material and financial scarcity adversely affect the psychology of poor individuals and as a result, such individuals tend to make choices that may further economically disadvantage them.

The scarcity theory or approach has given rise to a number of specific hypotheses concerning the psychological mechanisms that are meant to be responsible for the behavioral choices of poor individuals (Dean, Schilbach, and Schofield 2017; de Bruijn and Antonides 2021; Schilbach, Schofield, and Mullainathan 2016). Here, I focus on two claims that proponents of the scarcity approach have advanced and that directly pertain to the issue of attention. First, it has been argued that poverty directs our attention to scarcity-related issues and in doing so, leads us to neglect non-scarcity-related issues. Second, it is theorized that scarcity has an adverse effect on mental bandwidth, or "the brain's ability to perform the basic functions that underlie higher-order behavior and decision-making" (Schilbach, Schofield, and Mullainathan 2016, 435). Given boredom's connection to attention, both claims are important. If poverty causes a shift in our attention, then this shift could be responsible for the experience of boredom—situations that otherwise would have captured our attention, they now fail to do so and thus elicit the experience of boredom. Moreover, if poverty reduces mental bandwidth—which includes both cognitive capacity (the ability to solve problems and reason in a logical fashion) and executive control (the ability to manage cognitive activities, including attention)—then boredom could arise because of such decreases in mental bandwidth: in conditions of material scarcity, we lack the psychological resources to engage in a satisfactory manner with our tasks and situations.

The first claim—that is, that a scarcity mindset leads to attentional shifts—appears to be supported by empirical evidence. Studies by Shah and colleagues (2012) and Zhao and Tomm (2017) show that the perception of scarcity influences attentional allocation: attention is moved to, or "grabbed" by, scarcity-related concerns (see also Lichand and Mani 2020). Shah et al. (2018) reported that lower-income individuals are more likely to think about the costs of their activities, and that such thoughts are both persistent and spontaneous. Furthermore, the studies by Shah et al. (2012) and Zhao and Tomm (2017) also lend support to the claim that an attentional focus on scarcity issues leads to a neglect of other information (but see Shah, Mullainathan, and Shafir 2019 for an attempted replication study and de Bruijn and Antonides 2021 for some methodological concerns). The proposed attentional effects of a scarcity mindset are consistent with (although not directly supported by) findings showing that children's performance on attention tasks is negatively correlated with their parents' SES (Lengua et al. 2014; Razza, Martin, and Brooks-Gunn 2010, 2012; Ruberry et al. 2016; but also see Bernier et al. 2015).

The second claim of the scarcity approach holds that financial hardship and a scarcity mindset induce thoughts and concerns that preoccupy and tax low-income participants so much so that their available mental bandwidth for other tasks is reduced. In particular, scarcity is thought to affect both cognitive capacity and executive control (Mani et al. 2013; Mullainathan and Shafir 2013; Schilbach, Schofield, and Mullainathan 2016). Support for this hypothesis was initially provided by Mani and colleagues (2013) who in both a lab study and a field experiment offered evidence for the causal effects of poverty on both cognitive capacity and executive control. Previously, Spears (2011) reported corroborating findings. However, ensuing work has delivered mixed results. First, two studies that attempted to replicate the reported effects of poverty on cognitive capacity found no causal connection between the two (Dalton, Nhung, and Rüschenpöhler 2019; Fehr, Fink, and Kelsey 2019). Second, follow-up studies exploring the impact of poverty on executive control were inconclusive. Two of them (Fehr, Fink, and Kelsey 2019; Carvalho, Wang, and Meier 2016) failed to find any support for Mani et al.'s claim that poverty affects executive control. Two other studies, however, did find evidence confirming the Mani et al.'s claim that poverty has an effect on executive control (Ong, Theseira, and Ng 2019; Lichand and Mani 2020).

Taking these studies into consideration, we can conclude that there is support for the claim that scarcity affects attentional allocation: individuals in scarcity conditions pay more attention to scarcity-related concerns. However, evidence in support of poverty's effects on mental bandwidth is mixed and thus, at this point, inconclusive. Having said that, it is important to note that monetary worries are not the only threats to cognitive capacity and executive control. Malnutrition (Schofield 2014), sleep deprivation (Lim and Dinges 2010), and chronic pain (Moriarty, McGuire, and Finn 2011)—conditions which are common among low SES individuals—also impair cognitive function. Moreover, regardless of the validity of the scarcity approach, it is worth noting that studies involving both adults and young children have found that there is a positive correlational relationship between SES and better cognitive outcomes (e.g., Holmes and Kiernan, 2013; Jenkins et al. 2013; Pina et al., 2014; Razza, Martin, and Brooks-Gunn 2012; Torres, 2013). All in all, extant findings point to the existence of a relationship between poverty and attention (poverty influences the manner in which we allocate attention) and at the same time force us to take seriously the possibility that poverty might even causally affect decision-making and cognitive capacities.

Boredom and Meaning

Just like its connection to attention, boredom's connection to meaning is well documented. On the one hand, lack of perceived meaning has been proposed to be a cause of boredom. For instance, Barbalet (1999) advances a sociological account of boredom that treats boredom as both a signal of perceived meaninglessness and a drive to seek meaning. For Barbalet, perceived meaninglessness appears to be both an antecedent or cause of boredom and an essential part of its experience. This theoretical model of boredom has found empirical support. Chan et al. (2018) reported data confirming that the perception of meaninglessness gives rise to state boredom. In addition, Westgate and Wilson (2018) have argued that there is a type of boredom that arises out of the perception of meaninglessness. On the basis of their experimental work, they concluded that perceived meaninglessness is a sufficient but not a necessary condition of boredom.

Further support for the close relationship between boredom and lack of meaning is found in studies that demonstrate a correlational relationship between the presence of state and trait boredom and perceived meaninglessness. Subjects in a high boredom condition report a greater sense of meaninglessness than subjects in a low boredom condition (Van Tilburg and Igou 2011, 2017a). Moreover, Fahlman et al. (2009) found that participants in a meaningless condition report greater boredom than those in a meaningful condition. Importantly, Fahlman and colleagues found a bidirectional relationship between boredom and perceived lack of meaning in life—life meaning was a significant predictor of changes of boredom across time and vice versa. A study by Anusic, Lucas, and Donnellan (2017) (reported in Chan et al. 2018) found that activities associated with high levels of meaning are associated with low ratings of boredom, negative affect, and loneliness. Lastly, there are experimental studies that strongly suggest that a perception of meaninglessness is an important element of boredom. Van Tilburg and Igou (2012) showed that state boredom can be distinguished from sadness, anger, and frustration on the basis of the fact that only boredom involves thoughts about lack of meaning in one's situation. Van Tilburg and Igou (2017a) extended this finding beyond state boredom to both trait boredom and lay conceptualizations of boredom.

Poverty and Meaning

From a theoretical perspective, the relationship between poverty and perceived meaninglessness is an intimate one. As social beings, we derive meaning from our participation in social activities. Yet, the poor are marginalized and often excluded from such participation. For instance, poor individuals cannot afford to participate in cultural life, are politically disenfranchised, and are even redlined. Previous work has shown that a sense of belonging and anticipated social support are positively associated with meaning in life (Hicks and King 2009; Hicks, Schlegel, and King 2010; Krause 2007; Lambert et al. 2013; Stavrova and Luhmann 2016). Moreover, experiments that have placed individuals in conditions of social exclusion have found that excluded individuals rate their activities as less meaningful than individuals in a control condition (King and Geise 2011; Stillman et al. 2009; Twenge, Catanase, and Baumeister 2003).

The relationship between poverty and perceived meaninglessness is not merely a theoretical one. There is evidence suggesting that poverty is associated with feelings or perceptions of meaninglessness. An analysis of data from the World Values Survey (1980–2008) from forty-three countries showed that low income predicted increased feelings of meaninglessness (Haushofer 2013). Corroborating evidence is found in studies showing that the level of independence in activities is positively related with meaning in life (Koren and Lowenstein 2008) and that the inability to fulfill important social roles is negatively related to a sense of meaningfulness in one's life (Krause 2004) for older adults. Poor individuals will presumably lack independence, power, and control over their lives, and because of the various and severe financial constraints that they face, they will be less likely to be in a position to execute their desired social roles.

Furthermore, both the amount of work meaning and how it is experienced appear to differ depending on one's social class. Work by Hackman and colleagues (Hackman and Lawler 1971; Hackman and Oldham 1975) found that job characteristics such as task significance, task identity, skill variety, autonomy, and feedback from the job, influence one's psychological states, including the experience of meaningfulness. Many low-paying jobs lack characteristics such as autonomy, task significance, and skill variety (Ehrenreich 2010). The absence of these characteristics should thus contribute to a sense of meaninglessness. Allan and colleagues (2013) empirically tested the relationship between work meaning and social class. They found that individuals belonging to higher social classes were more likely to experience work meaning than individuals in lower social classes. Importantly, they also found that volition ("a perceived capacity to make occupational choices") and financial constraints fully mediated the reported relationship between social class and meaning (Allan, Autin, and Duffy 2014, 546).

Lastly, important work on homelessness and boredom reveals a direct link between poverty, lack of meaning, and boredom. Research has shown that homeless individuals experience difficulties in participating in social activities. They are either excluded and are thus forced to spend their time on their own, or they are given the opportunity to participate in some activities while being subjected to strict institutional requirements (Marshall, Lysaght, and Krupa 2017; O'Neill 2017). Researchers have documented how such an exclusion from meaningful engagement results in the profound and chronic experience of boredom (Marshall et al. 2019; O'Neill 2017; Marshall, Roy et al., 2020; Marshall, Keogh-Lim et al. 2020). Indeed, a growing body of work makes it clear that homeless individuals experience boredom on account of the social exclusion that they are subjected to *because of their social class*. This research has shown not just how central and profound boredom becomes in their lives but also how it may threaten their well-being by leading them to a variety of maladaptive behaviors (Marshall et al. 2019; O'Neill 2017; Marshall, Roy et al., 2020; Marshall, Keogh-Lim et al. 2020).

Conclusion: Poverty as the Ground of Boredom

The foregoing considerations provide ample evidence in support of the claim that conditions of material scarcity will be associated with an increase in the experience of boredom. Poverty is related to the experience of constraint and lack of freedom, to attentional shifts and cognitive difficulties, and to perceived meaninglessness. Any one of those conditions on its own would be capable of eliciting the experience of boredom. Together they are bound to completely transform the day-to-day experiences of individuals from lower social classes making these individuals much more susceptible to the experience of boredom. Such a conclusion is in line with published findings that demonstrate a relationship between high rates of boredom and lower SES (Chin et al. 2017; Martz et al. 2018; Willging, Quintero, and Lilliott 2014; Jervis et al. 2003).

4. POVERTY AND THE EXPERIENCE OF BOREDOM

The second proposed mechanism of how poverty interacts with boredom concerns the effects of SES on the subjective experience of boredom. Specifically, the model predicts that individuals in low SES are likely to experience boredom differently than those who are wealthy and more financially secure.

If poverty is related to an increase in the situational and psychological elicitors of boredom, then it will also bring about a change in the character of the experience of boredom. Theoretical and experimental work suggests that individuals are capable of recalling and encoding frequency information regarding their affects (Diener, Sandvik, and Pavot 2009; Hasher and Zacks 1984). Hence, changes in the frequency of the experience of an emotion will lead to noticeable experiential changes. First, from a subjective point of view, there will be an important difference between experiencing boredom sparingly and as response to particular situational features compared to experiencing it frequently or even chronically (Bargdill 2000; Elpidorou 2017). This conclusion is supported by research demonstrating a positive correlational relationship between boredom proneness, on the one hand, and depression, anxiety, anger, and apathy, on the other hand. Second, the experience of boredom is aversive: it is related to feelings of restlessness, tiredness, and frustration, and to a felt inability to find satisfactory engagement (Martin, Sadlo, and Stew 2006; Harris 2000); moreover, boredom's presence correlates with other negative emotions and arises as a part of a network of similarly valenced emotions and affective states (Chin et al. 2017; Martin, Sadlo, and Stew 2006). For individuals in low SES, boredom's negative experience will also be accompanied by feelings of lack of autonomy and constraint and the perception of meaninglessness. As a result, the more frequent the experience of boredom becomes the more one will experience other negative emotions and be subjected to unfulfilled desires and negative thoughts about one's self and situation.

In addition, the interactionist model predicts that poor individuals' experience of boredom is likely to be colored by the phenomenological experience of stress and affected by stress's physiological correlates. "Stress" can be used as a general term to refer to the body's physiological response to the disruption of its homeostatic balance (Sapolsky 2005). Those disruptions can come in the form of physical stressors (e.g., pain, hunger) or psychosocial stressors (e.g., the anticipation of an imminent hardship or the perception of a slight against oneself). Although our body is capable of adequately responding to physical and often psychosocial stressors that are short in duration, prolonged or chronic stressors can become pathogenic (Blanch, Shern, and Staverman 2014; Sapolsky 2005). Research has found that prolonged activation of the body's stress response systems results in several long-term and negative health, social, and even cognitive outcomes (McEwen 2000; Sapolsky 2005; Shanks and Robinson 2013).

Theoretical articulations of the conditions in which individuals are at a high risk to experience chronic stress are suggestive of a strong and close relationship between poverty and chronic stress. Sapolsky (2005) noted that chronic stress is likely to occur when the following conditions are persistently present in an individual's life: (a) there is the perception of little or no control over one's stressors, (b) there is a lack of predictive knowledge about the stressors that one faces, and (c) there is an inability to vent or to find productive outlets for one's frustration experienced during stress. Although Sapolsky names additional conditions that may contribute or give rise to chronic stress, the aforementioned three suffice to show that low SES individuals are at a high risk of experiencing chronic stress. Their jobs and occupations meet condition (a); their lack of resources, unreliable housing, broken appliances, damaged cars, and so on, contribute to condition (b); and their exclusion from social participation leads to (c). But it is not just these theoretical reasons that support the claim that conditions of poverty will lead to (or be associated with) chronic stress. Numerous studies have experimentally confirmed the existence of a relation between the two. Indeed, a recent review has found that over 80 percent of the studies examining the relationship between poverty and stress found that income is either predictive or partially predictive of physical stress, measured either by individual biomarkers (e.g., cortisol levels) or by a cumulative biomarker (allostatic load) (Brisson et al. 2020). Moreover, Haushofer and Fehr (2014) summarize and discuss findings revealing a relationship between poverty and both physical and psychological stress. (See also Evans and English 2002 for evidence in support of the existence of a connection between poverty and psychosocial stress.)

In sum, the boredom of low SES individuals will not be just more frequent, but it will also be more severe than that of high SES individuals.

5. RESPONSES TO BOREDOM IN POVERTY

Limited Resources

At its core, boredom involves a desire for an alternative form of engagement. Consequently, we can alleviate feelings of boredom if we are able to fulfill this desire. Often the need for alternative engagement will be satisfied by switching activities. For example, we get rid of the boredom of work with a break; we assuage the tedium of being alone by going for a walk or talking to friends. At other times the need for stimulating engagement can be fulfilled not by a change in activities but by changing either behaviorally or cognitively the manner in which we approach our current task. For instance, we might cognitively reappraise a boring lecture as significant and thus motivate ourselves to engage with it (Tze, Klassen, and Daniels 2014). Or we might make a shift more enjoyable by talking to others while preforming it or by turning it into a game (Hamilton, Haier, and Buchsbaum 1984; Elpidorou 2020).

How we respond to the presence of boredom thus depends on the type of opportunities that are available to us. And the more opportunities for alternative engagement we have, the better we will be able to deal with boredom when it arises. Individuals with jobs that afford them frequent breaks, freedom, autonomy, and a sense of meaningfulness will not only experience boredom less often, but they will also be better equipped to deal with it when it arises compared to those whose job includes none of those perks. Students who are grappling with boredom while doing homework will be tempted to give it up and turn their attention to less effortful or more exciting projects to the detriment of their academic success, unless they have someone with them to help them with homework, instill in them the significance of doing homework, or motivate them to persist in their work. Individuals living in dangerous neighborhoods often cannot respond to boredom by going for a walk, socializing with neighbors, or exercising. In general, living on a tight budget restricts what one can do and how one can respond to boredom—there is no time for hobbies, visiting museums, and traveling, and no resources for projects of self-care. It is evident thus that the fewer financial resources one possesses, the fewer choices one has as to how to respond to boredom. Even though boredom could propel one into activities that are meaningful, creative, or even beneficial for oneself (Elpidorou 2020), this is less likely to happen for individuals of low SES. The privilege of boredom—the ability to use boredom productively as an opportunity for self-growth—is a privilege that depends on one's SES.

Psychological Obstacles

Lack of access to alternative engagement makes it harder for individuals of low SES to alleviate their boredom. The same is likely to occur because of known influences of poverty on both perceived response efficacy and self-regulation (Sheehy-Skeffington and Rea 2017).

First, boredom has been related to agency. Specifically, boredom has been characterized as a crisis of agency (Danckert and Eastwood 2020; Eastwood et al. 2012; Eastwood and Gorelik this book) or as involving a "disordered agency" (Eastwood et al. 2012, 488). What this means is that the experience of boredom involves a difficulty in articulating what the bored subject would like to do (see also Fahlman et al. 2013 and Fenichel 1951). In other words, although bored individuals are well aware that they do not want to be doing what they are currently doing, they are not sure what alternative activity will assuage their boredom. As Eastwood and Gorelik (this book) make clear, this crisis of agency explains why it is so difficult for bored individuals to alleviate their feelings of boredom on their own. Such a crisis of agency could also be a key mechanism in understanding why the frequent or chronic experience of boredom (as operationalized by boredom proneness) leads to a variety of maladaptive behaviors. In an attempt to escape boredom, one might find recourse to activities that are easy, novel, or exciting (e.g., Bench and Lench 2019), and not to activities that are beneficial to oneself.

Poverty and conditions of material scarcity will contribute to and worsen this disruption of agency characteristic of boredom. A number of cross-sectional studies involving large samples of adults have found a consistent relationship between SES and perceived response efficacy. Perceived response efficacy is the extent to which an individual believes that external and personal events are the product of their behavior instead of the result of circumstances over which they have little or no control. Studies have found that lower SES is associated both with a weaker belief that external and personal events are the result of personal actions and with a stronger belief that such events are determined by factors that are not within the control of the subjects (Bodovski 2014; Greene and Murdock 2013; Kiviruusu et al. 2013; Prawitz, Kalkowski, and Cohart 2013. See also Hsieh and Huang 2014; Murray and Rodgers 2012). Such findings strongly suggest that, for low SES individuals, the crisis of agency experienced in boredom will be more pronounced and harder to be resolved. Subjects of low SES are thus at an increased risk of being unable to escape boredom or to protect themselves from the temptations that boredom poses.

Second, one's ability to regulate one's behavior will be crucial to how one deals with and responds to the onset of boredom. Self-regulation is a complex psychological process that permits agents to control their goal-oriented behavior. It is, in other words, a capacity to regulate (either maintain or change) one's behavior, responses, and inner states. It is clear that the effective pursuit of goals involves the successful exercise of self-regulation. Such an exercise of self-regulation is thought to involve three components (Baumeister and Heatherton 1996): (a) the acceptance of standards of thought, feelings, and action that are meant to guide behavior; (b) the monitoring of how actual states of the self compare to one's standards; and (c) the ability to control and change one's actual states (behavioral or psychological) when those do not meet the accepted standards. Failures of self-regulation have been implicated in a number of social and personal problems, and, conversely, success in self-regulation has been linked to improved well-being (Moffitt et al., 2011; Tangney, Baumeister, and Boone 2004.)

Extant literature suggests a close relationship between boredom and self-regulation—especially the aspect of self-regulation that involves the ability to control one's impulses and to change one's states to better match one's standards ("self-control"). From a theoretical perspective, it has been proposed that boredom proneness might be a dysfunction of state boredom insofar as it involves an inability to engage properly in goal-oriented behavior (Elpidorou 2018b; see also Struk, Scholer, and Danckert 2016). In addition, models of boredom that emphasize the role of attentional mechanisms can also explain why some individuals have a higher tendency to experience boredom than others by appealing to self-regulatory failures (Struk, Scholer, and Danckert 2016). Specifically, a difficulty to regulate attention in a way that yields satisfactory engagement could lead to an increase in the experience of boredom. Finally, there are empirical findings that both directly and indirectly reveal a connection between self-regulation and boredom. On the one hand, there is a reported association between higher level of self-control and lower levels of boredom proneness (Isacescu and Danckert 2018; Isacescu, Struk, and Danckert 2017; see also Struk, Scholer, and Danckert 2016). On the other hand, boredom proneness has been linked to behaviors that are indicative of poor self-regulation and self-control (e.g., Mercer-Lynn et al. 2013).

The connection between boredom and self-regulation entails that our responses to boredom will be affected by our ability to regulate and control our selves. In the case of poverty, we have good reasons to think that poverty will affect self-regulation. Studies involving young children show that their self-regulatory abilities are adversely affected by poverty (Noble et al. 2005; Raver, Blair, and Willoughby 2013; Rhoades et al. 2011) and that improvement in SES (e.g., moving to a better neighborhood) leads to an improvement in self-regulation (Roy, McCoy, and Raver 2014) (for additional discussion, see Hackman and Farah 2009). SES and self-regulatory abilities have also been found to be positively correlated both in teenagers (Freeney and O'Connell 2010; Vettenburg et al. 2013) and in adults. Regarding adults, studies show that those lower in SES report a lesser ability to resist impulses and a greater tendency to procrastinate than those higher in SES (Chow 2011; Johnson, Richeson, and Finkel 2011). Such findings demonstrate that one's SES, by influencing self-regulation, can place one in a disadvantageous position when dealing with boredom. Obstacles to self-regulation will make it harder for individuals to respond to boredom in productive ways and easier for them to either remain in boredom (Struk, Scholer, and Danckert 2016) or to give in to maladaptive responses.

6. CONCLUSION

In this chapter, I advanced a model that attempts to explicate the ways in which poverty interacts with boredom. Specifically, I have argued that it is likely that poverty makes boredom more frequent, changes its experience, and affects the ways that we can respond to it. Thus, poverty does not only invite boredom but can also corrode our ability to productively respond to it. Poverty restricts our responses to boredom, takes a toll on our self-regulatory abilities, and may even affect mental and cognitive functioning. In doing so, it has the capacity to derail our coping mechanisms and to even further solidify our vulnerability to boredom.

The model that I offered is theoretical: it synthesizes literature on poverty and boredom in order to suggest ways as to how the two interact. It is also speculative and thus in need of empirical confirmation or disconfirmation. All the same, the proposed model shows that accounts of boredom ought to take SES seriously—both as a potential contributor to boredom and as a formidable obstacle to our ability to respond to boredom efficiently and beneficially. It also demonstrates, I believe, that boredom is a serious matter even within the context of poverty. Although boredom is a potential threat to everyone's well-being, it poses an especially grave danger to individuals of low SES. In poverty, boredom can become cruel and unjust—a scourge that afflicts most severely those who are the least capable of dealing with it.

REFERENCES

Adler, Nancy E., Elissa S. Epel, Grace Castellazzo, and Jeannette R. Ickovics. 2000. "Relationship of Subjective and Objective Social Status with Psychological and Physiological Functioning: Preliminary Data in Healthy, White Women." *Health Psychology*, 19, no. 6: 586–92. https://doi.org/10.1037/0278-6133.19.6.586.

Adler, Nancy E., Thomas Boyce, Margaret A. Chesney, Sheldon Cohen, Susan Folkman, Robert L. Kahn, and S. Leonard Syme. 1994. "Socioeconomic Status and Health: The Challenge of the Gradient." *American Psychologist* 49, no. 1: 15–24. https://doi.org/10.1037/0003-066X.49.1.15.

Ahmed, S. M. S. 1990. "Psychometric Properties of the Boredom Proneness Scale." *Perceptual and Motor Skills* 71, no. 3: 963–66. https://doi.org/10.2466/pms.1990.71.3.963.

Allan, Blake A., Kelsey L. Autin, and Ryan D. Duffy. 2014. "Examining Social Class and Work Meaning Within the Psychology of Working Framework." *Journal of Career Assessment* 22, no. 4: 543–61. https://doi.org/10.1177/1069072713514811.

Anusic, Ivana, Richard E. Lucas, and M. Brent Donnellan. 2017. "The Validity of the Day Reconstruction Method in the German Socio-Economic Panel Study." *Social Indicators Research* 130, no. 1: 213–32. https://doi.org/10.1007/s11205-015-1172-6.

Banerjee, Abhijit V., and Esther Duflo. 2007. "The Economic Lives of the Poor." *Journal of Economic Perspectives* 21, no. 1: 141–68. https://doi.org/10.1257/jep.21.1.141.

Barbalet, Jack M. 1999. "Boredom and Social Meaning." *The British Journal of Sociology* 50, no. 4: 631-46. https://doi.org/10.1080/000713199358572.

Bargdill, Richard. 2000. "The Study of Life Boredom." *Journal of Phenomenological Psychology* 31, no. 2: 188–219. https://doi.org/10.1163/15691620051090979.

Barmack, Joseph E. 1938. "The Effect of Benzedrine Sulfate (benzyl methyl carbinamine) Upon the Report of Boredom and Other Factors." *The Journal of Psychology* 5, no. 1: 125–33. https://doi.org/10.1080/00223980.1938.9917557.

Baumeister, Roy F., and Todd F. Heatherton. 1996. "Self-regulation Failure: An Overview." *Psychological Inquiry* 7, no. 1: 1–15. https://www.jstor.org/stable/1449145.

Bench, Shane W., and Heather C. Lench. 2013. "On the Function of Boredom." *Behavioral Sciences* 3, no. 3: 459–72. https://doi.org/10.3390/bs3030459.

Bench, Shane W., and Heather C. Lench. 2019. "Boredom as a Seeking State: Boredom Prompts the Pursuit of Novel (Even Negative) Experiences." *Emotion* 19, no. 2: 242–54. https://doi.org/10.1037/emo0000433.

Berlyne, Daniel E. 1960. *Conflict, Arousal and Curiosity*. New York, NY: McGraw-Hill.

Bernier, Annie, Miriam H. Beauchamp, Stephanie M. Carlson, and Gabrielle Lalonde. 2015. "A Secure Base from Which to Regulate: Attachment Security in Toddlerhood as a Predictor of Executive Functioning at School Entry." *Developmental Psychology* 51, no. 9: 1177–89.

Bernstein, Basil. 1971. *Class, Codes and Control* (Vol. 1). London: Routledge & Kegan Paul.

Blalock, Garrick, David R. Just, and Daniel H. Simon. 2007. "Hitting the Jackpot or Hitting the Skids: Entertainment, Poverty, and the Demand for State Lotteries." *American Journal of Economics and Sociology* 66, no. 3: 545–70. https://doi.org/10.1111/j.1536-7150.2007.00526.x.

Blaszczynski, Alex, Neil McConaghy, and Anna Frankova. 1990. "Boredom Proneness in Pathological Gambling." *Psychological Reports* 67, no. 1: 35–42. https://doi.org/10.2466/pr0.1990.67.1.35.

Bodovski, Katerina. 2014. "Adolescents' Emerging Habitus: The Role of Early Parental Expectations and Practices." *British Journal of Sociology of Education* 35, no. 3: 389–412. https://doi.org/10.1080/01425692.2013.776932.

Bourdieu, Pierre. 1985. "The Social Space and the Genesis of Groups." *Theory and Society* 14, no. 6: 723–44. https://doi.org/10.1007/BF00174048.

Brissett, Dennis, and Robert P. Snow. 1993. "Boredom: Where the Future Isn't." *Symbolic Interaction* 16, no. 3: 237–56. https://doi.org/10.1525/si.1993.16.3.237.

Brisson, Daniel, Sarah McCune, Jennifer H. Wilson, Stephanie Rachel Speer, Julie S. McCrae, and Katherine Hoops Calhoun. 2020. "A Systematic Review of the Association Between Poverty and Biomarkers of Toxic Stress." *Journal of Evidence-Based Social Work* 17, no. 6: 696–713. https://doi.org/10.1080/26408066.2020.1769786.

Caldwell, Linda L., Edward A. Smith, and Ellen Weissinger. 1992. "The Relationship of Leisure Activities and Perceived Health of College Students." *Loisir et société/ Society and Leisure* 15, no. 2: 545–56. https://doi.org/10.1080/07053436.1992.10715431.

Caldwell, Linda L., Nancy Darling, Laura L. Payne, and Bonnie Dowdy.1999. "'Why Are You Bored?': An Examination of Psychological and Social Control Causes of Boredom Among Adolescents." *Journal of Leisure Research* 31, no. 2: 103–21. https://doi.org/10.1080/00222216.1999.11949853.

Carriere, Jonathan S. A., J. Allan Cheyne, and Daniel Smilek. 2008. "Everyday Attention Lapses and Memory Failures: The Affective Consequences of Mindlessness." *Consciousness and Cognition* 17, no. 3: 835–47. https://doi.org/10.1016/j.concog.2007.04.008.

Carvalho, Leandro S., Stephan Meier, and Stephanie W. Wang. 2016. "Poverty and Economic Decision-Making: Evidence from Changes in Financial Resources at Payday." *American Economic Review* 106, no. 2: 260-84. https://www.jstor.org/stable/43821452.

Chan, Christian S., Wijnand A. P. van Tilburg, Eric R. Igou, Cyanea Y. S. Poon, Katy Y. Y. Tam, Venus U. T. Wong, and S. K. Cheung. 2018. "Situational Meaninglessness and State Boredom: Cross-Sectional and Experience-Sampling Findings." *Motivation and Emotion* 42, no. 4: 555–65. https://doi.org/10.1007/s 11031-018-9693-3.

Cheyne, James Allan, Jonathan S. A. Carriere, and Daniel Smilek. 2006. "Absent-Mindedness: Lapses of Conscious Awareness and Everyday Cognitive Failures." *Consciousness and Cognition* 15, no. 3: 578–92. https://doi.org/10.1016/j.concog .2005.11.009.

Chin, Alycia, Amanda Markey, Saurabh Bhargava, Karim S. Kassam, and George Loewenstein. 2017. "Bored in the USA: Experience Sampling and Boredom in Everyday Life." *Emotion* 17, no. 2: 359–68. https://doi.org/10.1037/emo0000232.

Chow, Henry P. H. 2011. "Procrastination Among Undergraduate Students: Effects of Emotional Intelligence, School Life, Self-Evaluation, and Self-Efficacy." *Alberta Journal of Educational Research* 57, no. 2: 234–40.

Cohen, Sheldon, Cuneyt M. Alper, William J. Doyle, Nancy Adler, John J. Treanor, and Ronald B. Turner. 2008. "Objective and Subjective Socioeconomic Status and Susceptibility to the Common Cold." *Health Psychology,* 27, no. 2: 268–74. https ://doi.org/10.1037/0278-6133.27.2.268.

Crenshaw, Kimberlé W. 1989. "Demarginalizing the Intersection of Race and Sex: A Black Feminist Critique of Antidiscrimination Doctrine, Feminist Theory, and Antiracist Politics." *University of Chicago Legal Forum* 1, no. 8: 139–67. http://chi cagounbound.uchicago.edu/uclf/vol1989/iss1/8.

Crenshaw, Kimberlé W. 1991. "Mapping the Margins: Intersectionality, Identity Politics, and Violence Against Women of Color." *Stanford Law Review 43*, no. 6: 1241–99.

Csikszentmihalyi, Mihaly. 1975. *Beyond Boredom and Anxiety.* San Francisco, CA: Jossey-Bass.

Dahlen, Eric R., Ryan C. Martin, Katie Ragan, and Myndi M. Kuhlman. 2004. "Boredom Proneness in Anger and Aggression: Effects of Impulsiveness and Sensation Seeking." *Personality and Individual Differences* 37, no. 8: 1615–27. https://doi.org/10.1016/j.paid.2004.02.016.

Dahlen, Eric R., Ryan C. Martin, Katie Ragan, and Myndi M. Kuhlman. 2005. "Driving Anger, Sensation Seeking, Impulsiveness, and Boredom Proneness in the Prediction of Unsafe Driving." *Accident Analysis & Prevention* 37, no. 2: 341–48. https://doi.org/10.1016/j.aap.2004.10.006.

Dalton, Patricio S., Nguyen Nhung, and Julius Rüschenpöhler. 2020. "Worries of the Poor: The Impact of Financial Burden on the Risk Attitudes of Micro-Entrepreneurs." *Journal of Economic Psychology* 79: 102198. https://doi.org/10.1 016/j.joep.2019.102198.

Damrad-Frye, Robin, and James D. Laird. 1989. "The Experience of Boredom: The Role of the Self-Perception of Attention." *Journal of Personality and Social Psychology* 57, no. 2: 315–20.

Danckert, James, and Colleen Merrifield. 2018. "Boredom, Sustained Attention and the Default Mode Network." *Experimental Brain Research* 236, no. 9: 2507–18. https://doi.org/10.1007/s00221-016-4617-5.

Danckert, James, and John Eastwood D. 2020. *Out of My Skull: The Psychology of Boredom.* Cambridge, MA: Harvard University Press.

Daschmann, Elena C., Thomas Goetz, and Robert H. Stupnisky. 2011. "Testing the Predictors of Boredom at School: Development and Validation of the Precursors to Boredom Scales." *British Journal of Educational Psychology* 81, no. 3: 421–40. https://doi.org/10.1348/000709910X526038.

de Bruijn, Ernst-Jan, and Gerrit Antonides. 2021. "Poverty and Economic Decision Making: A Review of Scarcity Theory." *Theory and Decision*: 1–33. https://doi.org/10.1007/s11238-021-09802-7.

De Chenne, Timothy K., and Andrea J. Moody. 1988. "Boredom: Theory and Therapy." *The Psychotherapy Patient* 3, no. 3–4: 17–29. https://doi.org/10.1300/J358v03n03_03.

Dean, Emma Boswell, Frank Schilbach, and Heather Schofield. 2017. "Poverty and Cognitive Function." In *The Economics of Poverty Traps*, edited by Christopher B. Barrett, Michael Carter, Jean-Paul Chavas, and Michael R. Carter, 57–118. Chicago: University of Chicago Press.

Diener, Ed, and Eunkook Suh.1997. "Measuring Quality of Life: Economic, Social, and Subjective Indicators." *Social Indicators Research* 40, no. 1: 189–216. https://doi.org/10.1023/A:1006859511756.

Diener, Ed, Ed Sandvik, and William Pavot. 2009. "Happiness is the Frequency, Not the Intensity, of Positive Versus Negative Affect." In *Assessing Well-Being*, edited by Ed Diener, 213–31. Dordrecht: Springer.

Dockree, Paul M., Mark A. Bellgrove, Fiadhnait M. O'Keeffe, Pauline Moloney, Lina Aimola, Simone Carton, and Ian H. Robertson. 2006. "Sustained Attention in Traumatic Brain Injury (TBI) and Healthy Controls: Enhanced Sensitivity with Dual-Task Load." *Experimental Brain Research* 168, no. 1–2: 218–29. https://doi.org/10.1007/s00221-005-0079-x.

Eastwood, John D., Alexandra Frischen, Mark J. Fenske, and Daniel Smilek. 2012. "The Unengaged Mind. Defining Boredom in Terms of Attention." *Perspectives on Psychological Science* 7, no. 5: 482–95. https://doi.org/10.1177/1745691612456044.

Ehrenreich, Barbara. 2010. *Nickel and Dimed: On (Not) Getting by in America.* New York: Metropolitan Books.

Elias, Norbert. 1978. *The Civilizing Process: The History of Manners.* New York, NY: Urizen Books.

Elpidorou, Andreas. 2014. "The Bright Side of Boredom." *Frontiers in Psychology* 5: 1245. https://doi.org/10.3389/fpsyg.2014.01245.

Elpidorou, Andreas. 2017. "The Moral Dimensions of Boredom: A Call for Research." *Review of General Psychology* 21, no. 1: 30–48. https://doi.org/10.1037/gpr0000098.

Elpidorou, Andreas. 2018a. "The Bored Mind is a Guiding Mind: Toward a Regulatory Theory of Boredom." *Phenomenology and the Cognitive Sciences* 17, no. 3: 455–84. https://doi.org/10.1007/s11097-017-9515-1.

Elpidorou, Andreas. 2018b. "The Good of Boredom." *Philosophical Psychology* 31, no. 3: 323–51. https://doi.org/10.1080/09515089.2017.1346240.

Elpidorou, Andreas. 2020. *Propelled: How Boredom, Frustration, and Anticipation Lead Us to the Good Life.* New York: Oxford University Press. https://doi.org/10.1093/oso/9780190912963.001.0001.

Elpidorou, Andreas. 2021. "Is Boredom One or Many? A Functional Solution to the Problem of Heterogeneity." *Mind & Language* 36, no. 3: 491–511. https://doi.org/10.1111/mila.12282.

Evans, Gary W., and Kimberly English. 2002. "The Environment of Poverty: Multiple Stressor Exposure, Psychophysiological Stress, and Socioemotional adjustment." *Child Development* 73, no. 4: 1238–48. https://doi.org/10.1111/1467-8624.00469.

Fahlman, Shelley A., Kimberley B. Mercer-Lynn, David B. Flora, and John D. Eastwood. 2013. "Development and Validation of the Multidimensional State Boredom Scale." *Assessment* 20, no. 1: 68–85. https://doi.org/10.1177/1073191111421303.

Fahlman, Shelley A., Kimberley B. Mercer, Peter Gaskovski, Adrienne E. Eastwood, and John D. Eastwood. 2009. "Does a Lack of Life Meaning Cause Boredom? Results from Psychometric, Longitudinal, and Experimental Analyses." *Journal of Social and Clinical Psychology* 28, no. 3: 307–40. https://doi.org/10.1521/jscp.2009.28.3.307.

Farmer, Richard, and Norman D. Sundberg. 1986. "Boredom Proneness--the Development and Correlates of a New Scale." *Journal of Personality Assessment* 50, no. 1: 4–17. https://doi.org/10.1207/s15327752jpa5001_2.

Fehr, Dietmar, Günther Fink, and Kelsey Jack. 2019. *Poverty, Seasonal Scarcity and Exchange Asymmetries.* No. w26357. National Bureau of Economic Research. www.nber.org/papers/w26357.

Fenichel, Otto. 1951. "On the Psychology of Boredom." In *Organization and Pathology of Thought: Selected Sources*, edited by David Rapaport, 349-61. New York, NY: Columbia University Press.

Fisher, Cynthia D. 1993. "Boredom at Work: A Neglected Concept." *Human Relations*, 46: 395–417. https://doi.org/10.1177/001872679304600305.

Fiske, Susan T. and Hazel Rose Markus. 2012. "Introduction: A Wide-Angle Lens on the Psychology of Social Class." In *Facing Social Class: How Societal Rank Influences Interaction*, edited by Susan T. Fiske and Hazel Rose Markus, 1–11. New York: Russell Sage Foundation.

Freeney, Yseult, and Michael O'Connell. 2010. "Wait for It: Delay-Discounting and Academic Performance Among an Irish Adolescent Sample." *Learning and Individual Differences* 20, no. 3: 231–36. https://doi.org/10.1016/j.lindif.2009.12.009.

Gallo, Linda C., and Karen A. Matthews. 2003. "Understanding the Association Between Socioeconomic Status and Physical Health: Do Negative Emotions Play a Role?." *Psychological Bulletin* 129, no. 1: 10–51. https://doi.org/10.1037/0033-2909.129.1.10.

Gana, Kamel, and Malek Akremi. 1998. "L'échelle de Disposition à l'Ennui (EDE): Adaptation française et validation du Boredom Proneness Scale (BP)." *L'année Psychologique* 98, no. 3: 429–50. https://doi.org/10.3406/psy.1998.28576.

Gana, Kamel, Guillaume Broc, and Nathalie Bailly. 2019. "Does the Boredom Proneness Scale Capture Traitness of Boredom? Results from a Six-Year Longitudinal Trait-State-Occasion Model." *Personality and Individual Differences* 139: 247–53. https://doi.org/10.1016/j.paid.2018.11.030.

Geiwitz, P. James. 1966. "Structure of Boredom." *Journal of Personality and Social Psychology* 3, no. 5: 592–600. https://doi.org/10.1037/h0023202.

Goetz, Thomas, Anne C. Frenzel, Nathan C. Hall, Ulrike E. Nett, Reinhard Pekrun, and Anastasiya A. Lipnevich. 2014. "Types of Boredom: An Experience Sampling Approach." *Motivation and Emotion* 38, no. 3: 401–19. https://doi.org/10.1007/s 11031-013-9385-y.

Goldberg, Yael K., John D. Eastwood, Jennifer LaGuardia, and James Danckert.2011. "Boredom: An Emotional Experience Distinct from Apathy, Anhedonia, or Depression." *Journal of Social and Clinical Psychology* 30, no. 6: 647–66. https://doi.org/10.1521/jscp.2011.30.6.647.

Goldberg, Yael, and James Danckert. 2013. "Traumatic Brain Injury, Boredom and Depression." *Behavioral Sciences* 3, no. 3: 434–44. https://doi.org/10.3390/bs3030434.

Goodman, Elizabeth, Nancy E. Adler, Ichiro Kawachi, A. Lindsay Frazier, Bin Huang, and Graham A. Colditz. 2001. "Adolescents' Perceptions of Social Status: Development and Evaluation of a New Indicator." *Pediatrics* 108, no. 2: e31–e31. https://doi.org/10.1542/peds.108.2.e31.

Gordon, Anne, Ross Wilkinson, Anne McGown, and Slavica Jovanoska. 1997. "The Psychometric Properties of the Boredom Proneness Scale: An Examination of its Validity." *Psychological Studies* 42, no. 2–3: 85–97.

Greene, Carolyn A., and Karla Klein Murdock. 2013. "Multidimensional Control Beliefs, Socioeconomic Status, and Health." *American Journal of Health Behavior* 37, no. 2: 227–37. https://doi.org/10.5993/AJHB.37.2.10.

Greenson, Ralph R. 1953. "On Boredom." *Journal of the American Psychoanalytic Association* 1: 7-21. https://doi.org/10.1177/000306515300100102.

Hackman, Daniel A., and Martha J. Farah. 2009. "Socioeconomic Status and the Developing Brain." *Trends in Cognitive Sciences* 13, no. 2: 65–73. https://doi.org/10.1177/000306515300100102.

Hackman, J. Richard, and Greg R. Oldham. 1975. "Development of the Job Diagnostic Survey." *Journal of Applied psychology* 60, no. 2: 159–70. https://doi.org/10.1037/h0076546.

Hackman, J. Richard, and Greg R. Oldham. 1976. "Motivation Through the Design of Work: Test of a Theory." *Organizational Behavior and Human Performance* 16, no. 2: 250–79. https://doi.org/10.1016/0030-5073(76)90016-7.

Haisley, Emily, Romel Mostafa, and George Loewenstein. 2008. "Myopic Risk-Seeking: The Impact of Narrow Decision Bracketing on Lottery Play." *Journal of Risk and Uncertainty* 37, no. 1: 57–75. https://doi.org/10.1007/s11166-008-9041-1.

Hamilton, Jean A. 1981. "Attention, Personality, and the Self-Regulation of Mood: Absorbing Interest and Boredom." *Progress in Experimental Personality Research* 10: 281–315.

Hamilton, Jean A., Richard J. Haier, and Monte S. Buchsbaum. 1984. "Intrinsic Enjoyment and Boredom Coping Scales: Validation with Personality, Evoked Potential and Attention Measures." *Personality and Individual Differences* 5, no. 2: 183–93. https://doi.org/10.1016/0191-8869(84)90050-3.

Harris, Mary B. 2000. "Correlates and Characteristics of Boredom Proneness and Boredom." *Journal of Applied Social Psychology* 30, no. 3: 576–98. https://doi.org/10.1111/j.1559-1816.2000.tb02497.x.

Hasher, Lynn, and Rose T. Zacks. 1984. "Automatic Processing of Fundamental Information: The Case of Frequency of Occurrence." *American psychologist* 39, no. 12: 1372–88. https://doi.org/10.1037/0003-066X.39.12.1372.

Haushofer, Johannes, and Ernst Fehr. 2014. "On the Psychology of Poverty." *Science* 344, no. 6186: 862–67. https://doi.org/10.1126/science.1232491.

Haushofer, Johannes. 2013. *The Psychology of Poverty: Evidence from 43 Countries.* Princeton, NJ, Princeton University.

Hicks, Joshua A., and Laura A. King. 2009. "Positive Mood and Social Relatedness as Information About Meaning in Life." *The Journal of Positive Psychology* 4, no. 6: 471–82. https://doi.org/10.1080/17439760903271108.

Hicks, Joshua A., Rebecca J. Schlegel, and Laura A. King. 2010. "Social Threats, Happiness, and the Dynamics of Meaning in Life Judgments." *Personality and Social Psychology Bulletin* 36, no. 10: 1305–17. https://doi.org/10.1177/0146167210381650.

Hill, Austin Bradford, and Rachel E. Perkins. 1985. "Towards a Model of Boredom." *British Journal of Psychology* 76, no. 2: 235–40. https://doi.org/10.1111/j.2044-8295.1985.tb01947.x.

Holmes, John, and Kathleen Kiernan. 2013. "Persistent Poverty and Children's Development in the Early Years of Childhood." *Policy & Politics* 41, no. 1: 19–42. https://doi.org/10.1332/030557312X645810.

Howell, Ryan T., and Colleen J. Howell. 2008. "The Relation of Economic Status to Subjective Well-Being in Developing Countries: A Meta-Analysis." *Psychological Bulletin* 134, no. 4: 536–60. https://doi.org/10.1037/0033-2909.134.4.536.

Hsieh, Hui-Hsien, and Jie-Tsuen Huang. 2014. "The Effects of Socioeconomic Status and Proactive Personality on Career Decision Self-Efficacy." *The Career Development Quarterly* 62, no. 1: 29–43. https://doi.org/10.1002/j.2161-0045.2014.00068.x.

Hunter, Andrew, and John D. Eastwood. 2018. "Does state boredom cause failures of attention? Examining the Relations Between Trait Boredom, State Boredom, and Sustained Attention." *Experimental Brain Research* 236, no. 9: 2483–92. https://doi.org/10.1007/s00221-016-4749-7.

Isacescu, Julia, and James Danckert. 2018. "Exploring the Relationship Between Boredom Proneness and Self-Control in Traumatic Brain Injury (TBI)." *Experimental Brain Research* 236, no. 9: 2493–505. https://doi.org/10.1007/s00221-016-4674-9.

Isacescu, Julia, Andriy Anatolievich Struk, and James Danckert. 2017. "Cognitive and Affective Predictors of Boredom Proneness." *Cognition and Emotion* 31, no. 8: 1741–48. https://doi.org/10.1080/02699931.2016.1259995.

Iso-Ahola, Seppo E., and Ellen Weissinger.1990. "Perceptions of Boredom in Leisure: Conceptualization, Reliability and Validity of the Leisure Boredom Scale." *Journal of leisure Research* 22, no. 1: 1–17.

Jenkins, Jade V. Marcus, Donald P. Woolley, Stephen R. Hooper, and Michael D. De Bellis. 2013. "Direct and Indirect Effects of Brain Volume, Socioeconomic Status and Family Stress on Child IQ." *Journal of Child and Adolescent Behavior* 1, no. 2: 1000107. https://doi.org/10.4172/2375-4494.1000107.

Jervis, Lori L., Paul Spicer, and Spero M. Manson. 2003. "Boredom, 'Trouble,' and the Realities of Postcolonial Reservation Life." *Ethos* 31, no. 1: 38–58. https://doi .org/10.1525/eth.2003.31.1.38.

Johnson, Sarah E., Jennifer A. Richeson, and Eli J. Finkel. 2011. "Middle Class and Marginal? Socioeconomic Status, Stigma, and Self-Regulation at an Elite University" *Journal of Personality and Social Psychology* 100, no. 5: 838–52. https://doi.org/10.1037/a0021956.

Johnson, Wendy, and Robert F. Krueger. 2005. "Higher Perceived Life Control Decreases Genetic Variance in Physical Health: Evidence from a National Twin Study." *Journal of Personality and Social Psychology* 88, no. 1: 165–73. https://do i.org/10.1037/0022-3514.88.1.165.

Kass, Steven J., Kristen E. Beede, and Stephen J. Vodanovich. 2010. "Self-Report Measures of Distractibility as Correlates of Simulated Driving Performance." *Accident Analysis & Prevention* 42, no. 3: 874–80. https://doi.org/10.1016/j.aap. 2009.04.012.

King, Laura A., and Aaron C. Geise. 2011. "Being Forgotten: Implications for the Experience of Meaning in Life." *The Journal of Social Psychology* 151, no. 6: 696–709. https://doi.org/10.1080/00224545.2010.522620.

Kiviruusu, Olli, Taina Huurre, Ari Haukkala, and Hillevi Aro. 2013. "Changes in Psychological Resources Moderate the Effect of Socioeconomic Status on Distress Symptoms: A 10-year Follow-Up Among Young Adults." *Health Psychology* 32, no. 6: 627–36. https://doi.org/10.1037/a0029291.

Koren, Chaya, and Ariela Lowenstein. 2008. "Late-Life Widowhood and Meaning in Life." *Ageing International* 32, no. 2: 140–55. https://doi.org/10.1007/s12126 -008-9008-1.

Kraus, Michael W., Paul K. Piff, Rodolfo Mendoza-Denton, Michelle L. Rheinschmidt, and Dacher Keltner. 2012. "Social Class, Solipsism, and Contextualism: How the Rich Are Different from the Poor." *Psychological Review* 119, no. 3: 546–72. https://doi.org/10.1037/a0028756.

Krause, Neal. 2004. "Stressors Arising in Highly Valued Roles, Meaning in Lfe, and the Physical Health Status of Older Adults." *The Journals of Gerontology Series B: Psychological Sciences and Social Sciences* 59, no. 5: S287–97. https://doi.org /10.1093/geronb/59.5.S287.

Krause, Neal. 2007. "Longitudinal Study of Social Support and Meaning in Life." *Psychology and Aging* 22, no. 3: 456–69.

Kreutzer, Jeffrey S., Ronald T. Seel, and Eugene Gourley. 2001. "The Prevalence and Symptom Rates of Depression After Traumatic Brain Injury: A Comprehensive

Examination." *Brain Injury* 15, no. 7: 563–76. https://doi.org/10.1080/02699050116884.

Kurzban, Robert, Angela Duckworth, Joseph W. Kable, and Justus Myers. 2013. "An Opportunity Cost Model of Subjective Effort and Task Performance." *The Behavioral and Brain Sciences* 36, no. 6: 661–79. https://doi.org/10.1017/S0140525X12003196.

Lachman, Margie E., and Suzanne L. Weaver. 1998. "The Sense of Control as a Moderator of Social Class Differences in Health and Well-Being." *Journal of Personality and Social Psychology* 74, no. 3: 763–73.

Lambert, Nathaniel M., Tyler F. Stillman, Roy F. Baumeister, Frank D. Fincham, Joshua A. Hicks, and Steven M. Graham. 2010. "Family as a Salient Source of Meaning in Young Adulthood." *The Journal of Positive Psychology* 5, no. 5: 367–76. https://doi.org/10.1080/17439760.2010.516616.

Lareau, Annette. 2011. *Unequal Childhoods: Class, Race, and Family Life.* Berkeley: University of California Press.

Larson, Reed W., and Maryse H. Richards. 1991. "Boredom in the Middle School Years: Blaming Schools Versus Blaming Students." *American Journal of Education* 99, no. 4, 418–43. https://doi.org/10.1086/443992.

Leary, Mark R., Patricia A. Rogers, Robert W. Canfield, and Celine Coe. 1986. "Boredom in Interpersonal Encounters: Antecedents and Social Implications." *Journal of Personality and Social Psychology* 51, no. 5: 968–75. https://doi.org/10.1037/0022-3514.51.5.968.

Lengua, Liliana J., Lyndsey Moran, Maureen Zalewski, Erika Ruberry, Cara Kiff, and Stephanie Thompson. 2015. "Relations of Growth in Effortful Control to Family Income, Cumulative Risk, and Adjustment in Preschool-Age Children." *Journal of Abnormal Child Psychology* 43, no. 4: 705–20. https://doi.org/10.1007/s10802-014-9941-2.

Leong, Frederick TL, and Gregory R. Schneller. 1993. "Boredom Proneness: Temperamental and Cognitive Components." *Personality and Individual Differences* 14, no. 1: 233–39. https://doi.org/10.1016/0191-8869(93)90193-7.

LePera, Nicole. 2011. "Relationships Between Boredom Proneness, Mindfulness, Anxiety, Depression, and Substance Use." *The New School Psychology Bulletin* 8, no. 2: 15–25.

Lichand, Guilherme; Mani, Anandi 2020. "Cognitive Droughts, Working Paper, No. 341." Zurich: University of Zurich, Department of Economics. http://dx.doi.org/10.5167/uzh-185364.

Lim, Julian, and David F. Dinges.2010. "A Meta-Analysis of the Impact of Short-Term Sleep Deprivation on Cognitive Variables." *Psychological Bulletin* 136, no. 3: 375–89. https://doi.org/10.1037/a0018883.

Maddi, Salvatore R. 1970. "The Search for Meaning." In *The Nebraska Symposium on Motivation,* edited by William J. Arnold and Monte M. Page, 134–83. Lincoln: University of Nebraska Press.

Malkovsky, Ela, Colleen Merrifield, Yael Goldberg, and James Danckert. 2012. "Exploring the Relationship Between Boredom and Sustained Attention."

Experimental Brain Research 221, no. 1: 59–67. https://doi.org/10.1007/s00221 -012-3147-z.

Mani, Anandi, Sendhil Mullainathan, Eldar Shafir, and Jiaying Zhao. 2013. "Poverty Impedes Cognitive Function." *Science* 341, no. 6149: 976–80. https://doi.org/10 .1126/science.1238041.

Marshall, Carrie Anne, Daniel Keogh-Lim, Michelle Koop, Skye Barbic, and Rebecca Gewurtz. 2020. "Meaningful Activity and Boredom in the Transition from Homelessness: Two Narratives." *Canadian Journal of Occupational Therapy* 87, no. 4: 253–64. https://doi.org/10.1177/0008417420941782.

Marshall, Carrie Anne, Laurence Roy, Alyssa Becker, Melanie Nguyen, Skye Barbic, Carina Tjörnstrand, Rebecca Gewurtz, and Sarah Wickett. 2020. "Boredom and Homelessness: A Scoping Review." *Journal of Occupational Science* 27, no. 1: 107–24. https://doi.org/10.1080/14427591.2019.1595095.

Marshall, Carrie Anne, Lisa Davidson, Andrea Li, Rebecca Gewurtz, Laurence Roy, Skye Barbic, Bonnie Kirsh, and Rosemary Lysaght. 2019. "Boredom and Meaningful Activity in Adults Experiencing Homelessness: A mixed-methods study." *Canadian Journal of Occupational Therapy* 86, no. 5: 357–70. https://doi .org/10.1177/0008417419833402.

Marshall, Carrie Anne, Rosemary Lysaght, and Terry Krupa. 2017. "The Experience of Occupational Engagement of Chronically Homeless Persons in a Mid-Sized Urban Context." *Journal of Occupational Science* 24, no. 2: 165–80. https://doi.org /10.1080/14427591.2016.1277548.

Martin, Marion, Gaynor Sadlo, and Graham Stew. 2006. "The Phenomenon of Boredom." *Qualitative Research in Psychology* 3, no. 3: 193–211. https://doi.org /10.1191/1478088706qrp066oa.

Martz, Meghan E., John E. Schulenberg, Megan E. Patrick, and Deborah D. Kloska. 2018. "'I Am So Bored!': Prevalence Rates and Sociodemographic and Contextual Correlates of High Boredom Among American Adolescents." *Youth & Society* 50, no. 5: 688–710. https://doi.org/10.1177/0044118X15626624.

Mathiak, Krystyna Anna, Martin Klasen, Mikhail Zvyagintsev, René Weber, and Klaus Mathiak. 2013. "Neural Networks Underlying Affective States in a Multimodal Virtual Environment: Contributions to Boredom." *Frontiers in Human Neuroscience* 7, 820. https://doi.org/10.3389/fnhum.2013.00820.

McEwen, Bruce S. 1998. "Stress, Adaptation, and Disease: Allostasis and Allostatic Load." *Annals of the New York Academy of Sciences* 840, no. 1: 33–44. https://doi .org/10.1111/j.1749-6632.1998.tb09546.x.

Mercer-Lynn, Kimberley B., David B. Flora, Shelley A. Fahlman, and John D. Eastwood. 2013. "The Measurement of Boredom: Differences Between Existing Self-Report Scales." *Assessment* 20, no. 5: 585–96. https://doi.org/10.1177 /1073191111408229.

Mercer-Lynn, Kimberley B., Rachel J. Bar, and John D. Eastwood. 2014. "Causes of Boredom: The Person, the Situation, or Both?." *Personality and Individual Differences* 56: 122–26. https://doi.org/10.1016/j.paid.2013.08.034.

Mercer, Kimberley B., and John D. Eastwood. 2010. "Is Boredom Associated with Problem Gambling Behaviour? It Depends on What You Mean by 'Boredom.'"

International Gambling Studies 10, no. 1: 91–104. https://doi.org/10.1080/144597 91003754414.

Milyavskaya, Marina, Michael Inzlicht, Travis Johnson, and Michael J. Larson. 2019. "Reward Sensitivity Following Boredom and Cognitive Effort: A High-Powered Neurophysiological Investigation." *Neuropsychologia* 123: 159–68. https://doi.org /10.1016/j.neuropsychologia.2018.03.033.

Moffitt, Terrie E., Louise Arseneault, Daniel Belsky, Nigel Dickson, Robert J. Hancox, HonaLee Harrington, Renate Houts, Richie Poulton, Brent W. Roberts, Stephen Ross, Malcolm R. Sears, W. Murray Thomson, and Avshalom Caspi. 2011. "A Gradient of Childhood Self-Control Predicts Health, Wealth, and Public Safety." *Proceedings of the National Academy of Sciences* 108, no. 7: 2693–98. https://doi.org/10.1073/pnas.1010076108.

Moriarty, Orla, Brian E. McGuire, and David P. Finn. 2011. "The Effect of Pain on Cognitive Function: A Review of Clinical and Preclinical Research." *Progress in Neurobiology* 93 (3): 385–404. https://doi.org/10.1016/j.pneurobio.2011. 01.002.

Mullainathan, Sendhil, and Eldar Shafir. 2013. *Scarcity: Why Having Too Little Mans So Much.* New York: Times Books.

Murray, Terra, and Wendy Rodgers. 2012. "The Role of Socioeconomic Status and Control Beliefs on Frequency of Exercise During and After Cardiac Rehabilitation." *Applied Psychology: Health and Well-Being* 4, no. 1: 49–66. https://doi.org/10.1 111/j.1758-0854.2011.01061.x.

Noble, Kimberly G., M. Frank Norman, and Martha J. Farah. 2005. "Neurocognitive Correlates of Socioeconomic Status in Kindergarten Children." *Developmental Science* 8, no. 1: 74–87. https://doi.org/10.1111/j.1467-7687.2005.00394.x.

Nussbaum, Martha. 2000. *Women and Human Development.* Cambridge: Cambridge University Press.

O'Neill, Bruce. 2017. *The Space of Boredom: Homelessness in the Slowing Global Order.* Durham: Duke University Press.

O'Hanlon, James F. 1981. "Boredom: Practical Consequences and a Theory." *Acta Psychologica* 49, no. 1: 53–82. https://doi.org/10.1016/0001-6918(81)90033-0.

Oakes, J. Michael, and Peter H. Rossi. 2003. "The Measurement of SES in Health Research: Current Practice and Steps Toward a New Approach." *Social Science & Medicine* 56, no. 4: 769–84. https://doi.org/10.1016/S0277-9536(02)00073-4.

Ohlmeier, Silke, Mariusz Finkielsztein, and Holger Pfaff. 2020. "Why We Are Bored: Towards a Sociological Approach to Boredom." *Sociological Spectrum* 40, no. 3: 208–25. https://doi.org/10.1080/02732173.2020.1753134.

Ong, Qiyan, Walter Theseira, and Irene YH Ng. 2019. "Reducing Debt Improves Psychological Functioning and Changes Decision-Making in the Poor." *Proceedings of the National Academy of Sciences* 116, no. 15: 7244–49. https://doi.org/10.1073/pnas.1810901116.

Pattyn, Nathalie, Xavier Neyt, David Henderickx, and Eric Soetens. 2008. "Psychophysiological Investigation of Vigilance Decrement: Boredom or Cognitive Fatigue?" *Physiology & Behavior* 93, no. 1–2: 369–78. https://doi.org/10.1016/j .physbeh.2007.09.016.

Paulson, Morris J., Robert H. Coombs, and Mark A. Richardson. 1990. "School Performance, Academic Aspirations, and Drug Use Among Children and Adolescents." *Journal of Drug Education* 20, no. 4: 289–303. https://doi.org/10.2 190/8J0X-LY6D-PL7W-42FA.

Pekrun, Reinhard, Thomas Goetz, Lia M. Daniels, Robert H. Stupnisky, and Raymond P. Perry. 2010. "Boredom in Achievement Settings: Exploring Control–Value Antecedents and Performance Outcomes of a Neglected Emotion." *Journal of Educational Psychology* 102, no. 3: 531–49.

Pina, Violeta, Luis J. Fuentes, Alejandro Castillo, and Sofia Diamantopoulou. 2014. "Disentangling the Effects of Working Memory, Language, Parental Education, and Non-Verbal Intelligence on Children's Mathematical Abilities." *Frontiers in Psychology* 5: 415. https://doi.org/10.3389/fpsyg.2014.00415.

Prawitz, Aimee D., Julie C. Kalkowski, and Judith Cohart. 2013. "Responses to Economic Pressure by Low-Income Families: Financial Distress and Hopefulness." *Journal of Family and Economic Issues* 34, no. 1: 29–40. https://doi.org/10.1007/ s10834-012-9288-1.

Raver, C. Cybele, Clancy Blair, and Michael Willoughby. 2013. "Poverty as a Predictor of 4-year-Olds' Executive Function: New Perspectives on Models of Differential Susceptibility." *Developmental Psychology* 49, no. 2: 292–304. https:// doi.org/10.1037/a0028343.

Razza, Rachel A., Anne Martin, and Jeanne Brooks-Gunn. 2010. "Associations Among Family Environment, Sustained Attention, and School Readiness for Low-Income Children." *Developmental Psychology* 46, no. 6: 1528–42. https://doi.org /10.1037/a0020389.

Razza, Rachel A., Anne Martin, and Jeanne Brooks-Gunn. 2012. "The Implications of Early Attentional Regulation for School Success Among Low-Income Children." *Journal of Applied Developmental Psychology* 33, no. 6: 311–9. https://doi.org/10 .1016/j.appdev.2012.07.005.

Reijseger, Gaby, Wilmar B. Schaufeli, Maria C. W. Peeters, Toon W. Taris, Ilona Van Beek, and Else Ouweneel. 2013. "Watching the Paint Dry at Work: Psychometric Examination of the Dutch Boredom Scale." *Anxiety, Stress & Coping* 26, no. 5: 508–25. https://doi.org/10.1080/10615806.2012.720676.

Rhoades, Brittany L., Mark T. Greenberg, Stephanie T. Lanza, and Clancy Blair. 2011. "Demographic and Familial Predictors of Early Executive Function Development: Contribution of a Person-Centered Perspective." *Journal of Experimental Child Psychology* 108, no. 3: 638–62. https://doi.org/10.1016/j.jecp.2010.08.004.

Roy, Amanda L., Dana Charles McCoy, and C. Cybele Raver. 2014. "Instability Versus Quality: Residential Mobility, Neighborhood Poverty, and Children's Self-Regulation." *Developmental Psychology* 50, no. 7: 1891–96. https://doi.org/10 .1037/a0036984.

Ruberry, Erika J., Liliana J. Lengua, Leanna Harris Crocker, Jacqueline Bruce, Michaela B. Upshaw, and Jessica A. Sommerville. 2017. "Income, Neural Executive Processes, and Preschool Children's Executive Control." *Development and Psychopathology* 29, no. 1: 143–54. https://doi.org/10.1017/S0954579416 00002X.

Rupp, Deborah E., and Stephen J. Vodanovich. "The Role of Boredom Proneness in Self-Reported Anger and Aggression." *Journal of Social Behavior and Personality* 12, no. 4: 925–36.

Sapolsky, Robert. 2005. "Sick of Poverty." *Scientific American* 293, no. 6: 92–9. https://www.jstor.org/stable/26061262.

Sawin, David A., and Mark W. Scerbo. 1995. "Effects of Instruction Type and Boredom Proneness in Vigilance: Implications for Boredom and Workload." *Human Factors* 37, no. 4: 752–65. https://doi.org/10.1518/001872095778995616.

Scerbo Mark W. 1998. "What's So Boring About Vigilance?" In *Viewing Psychology as a Whole: The Integrative Science of William N. Dember,* edited by Robert R. Hoffman, Michael F. Sherrick, and Joel S. Warm, 145–66. Washington: American Psychological Association.

Scerbo, Mark W. 2001. "Stress, Workload, and Boredom in Vigilance: A Problem and an Answer." In *Stress, Workload, and Fatigue,* edited by Peter A. Hancock and Paula A. Desmond, 267–78. Mahwah: Lawrence Erlbaum Associates Publishers.

Schilbach, Frank, Heather Schofield, and Sendhil Mullainathan. 2016. "The psychological Lives of the Poor." *American Economic Review* 106, no. 5: 435–40. https://doi.org/10.1257/aer.p20161101.

Schofield, Heather. 2014. "The Economic Costs of Low Caloric Intake: Evidence from India." Working paper. Harvard University.

Sen, Amartya. 1999. *Development as Freedom.* Oxford: Clarendon Press.

Sen, Amartya. 2000. *Social Exclusion: Concept, Application and Scrutiny. Social Development Papers No. 1.* Manila, Philippines: Office of Environment and Social Development, Asian Development Bank.

Shafer, Kevin, and Spencer L. James. 2013. "Gender and Socioeconomic Status Differences in First and Second Marriage Formation." *Journal of Marriage and Family* 75, no. 3: 544–564. https://doi.org/10.1111/jomf.12024.

Shah, Anuj K., Jiaying Zhao, Sendhil Mullainathan, and Eldar Shafir. 2018. "Money in the Mental Lives of the Poor." *Social Cognition* 36, no. 1: 4–19. https://doi.org/10.1521/soco.2018.36.1.4.

Shah, Anuj K., Sendhil Mullainathan, and Eldar Shafir. 2012. "Some Consequences of Having Too Little." *Science* 338, no. 6107: 682–685. https://doi.org/10.1126/science.122242.

Shah, Anuj K., Sendhil Mullainathan, and Eldar Shafir. 2019. "An Exercise in Self-Replication: Replicating Shah, Mullainathan, and Shafir (2012)." *Journal of Economic Psychology* 75: 102127. https://doi.org/10.1016/j.joep.2018.12.001.

Shanks, Trina R. Williams, and Christine Robinson. 2013. "Assets, Economic Opportunity and Toxic Stress: A Framework for Understanding Child and Educational Outcomes." *Economics of Education Review* 33: 154–70. https://doi.org/10.1016/j.econedurev.2012.11.002.

Shaw, Susan M., Linda L. Caldwell, and Douglas A. Kleiber. 1996. "Boredom, Stress and Social Control in the Daily Activities of Adolescents." *Journal of Leisure Research* 28, no. 4: 274–92. https://doi.org/10.1080/00222216.1996.11949776.

Sheehy-Skeffington, Jennifer, and Jessica Rea. 2017. *How Poverty Affects People's Decision-Making Processes.* New York: Joseph Rowntree Foundation.

Shern, David L., Andrea K. Blanch, and Sarah M. Steverman. 2016. "Toxic Stress, Behavioral Health, and the Next Major Era in Public Health." *American Journal of Orthopsychiatry* 86, no. 2: 109–23.

Singh-Manoux, Archana, Michael G. Marmot, and Nancy E. Adler. 2005. "Does Subjective Social Status Predict Health and Change in Health Status Better Than Objective Status?" *Psychosomatic Medicine* 67, no. 6: 855–61. https://doi.org/10.1 097/01.psy.0000188434.52941.a0.

Slovarp, Laurie, Tamiko Azuma, and Leonard Lapointe. 2012. "The Effect of Traumatic Brain Injury on Sustained Attention and Working Memory." *Brain Injury* 26, no. 1: 48–57. https://doi.org/10.3109/02699052.2011.635355.

Smith, Aaron, Kyley McGeeney, Maeve Duggan, Lee Rainie, and Scott Keeter. 2015. "U.S. Smartphone Use in 2015." Pew Research Internet Project. Retrieved July 03, 2020. https://www.pewresearch.org/internet/2015/04/01/us-smartphone-use-in -2015/.

Smith, Craig A., and Phoebe C. Ellsworth. 1985. "Patterns of Cognitive Appraisal in Emotion." *Journal of Personality and Social Psychology* 48, no. 4: 813–38.

Snibbe, Alana Conner, and Hazel Rose Markus. 2005. "You Can't Always Get What You Want: Educational Attainment, Agency, and Choice." *Journal of Personality and Social Psychology* 88, no. 4: 703–20. https://doi.org/10.1037/0022-3514.88.4.703.

Snibbe, Alana Conner, Judith Stewart, and Nancy E. Adler. 2007. "Where Do I Stand. How People Determine Their Subjective Socioeconomic Status." Unpublished manuscript.

Spears, Dean. 2011. "Economic Decision-Making in Poverty Depletes Behavioral Control." *The B.E. Journal of Economic Analysis & Policy* 11, no. 1: Article 72.

Stavrova, Olga, and Maike Luhmann. 2016. "Social Connectedness as a Source and Consequence of Meaning in Life." *The Journal of Positive Psychology* 11, no. 5: 470–9.

Steinberger, Fabius, April Moeller, and Ronald Schroeter. 2016. "The Antecedents, Experience, and Coping Strategies of Driver Boredom in Young Adult Males." *Journal of Safety Research* 59: 69–82. https://doi.org/10.1080/17439760.2015.1117127.

Stephens, Nicole M., Stephanie A. Fryberg, and Hazel Rose Markus. 2011. "When Choice Does Not Equal Freedom: A Sociocultural Analysis of Agency in Working-Class American Contexts." *Social Psychological and Personality Science* 2, no. 1: 33–41. https://doi.org/10.1177/1948550610378757.

Stephens, Nicole M., Stephanie A. Fryberg, Hazel Rose Markus, Camille S. Johnson, and Rebecca Covarrubias. 2012. "Unseen Disadvantage: How American Universities' Focus on Independence Undermines the Academic Performance of First-Generation College Students." *Journal of Personality and Social Psychology* 102, no. 6: 1178–97.

Stillman, Tyler F., Roy F. Baumeister, Nathaniel M. Lambert, A. Will Crescioni, C. Nathan DeWall, and Frank D. Fincham. 2009. "Alone and Without Purpose: Life Loses Meaning Following Social Exclusion." *Journal of Experimental Social Psychology* 45, no. 4: 686–94. https://doi.org/10.1016/j.jesp.2009.03.007.

Struk, Andriy A., Abigail A. Scholer, and James Danckert. 2016. "A Self-Regulatory Approach to Understanding Boredom Proneness." *Cognition and Emotion* 30, no. 8: 1388–401. https://doi.org/10.1080/02699931.2015.1064363.

Struk, Andriy A., Jonathan S. A. Carriere, J. Allan Cheyne, and James Danckert. 2017. "A Short Boredom Proneness Scale: Development and Psychometric Properties." *Assessment* 24, no. 3: 346–59. https://doi.org/10.1177/1073191115609996.

Tam, Katy Y.Y., Wijnand A.P. Van Tilburg, and Christian S. Chan. 2021. "What Is Boredom Proneness? A Comparison of Three Characterizations." *Journal of Personality*. Early View. https://doi.org/10.1111/jopy.12618.

Tam, Katy, Wijnand A. P. Van Tilburg, Christian Chan, Eric Igou, and Hakwan Lau. In press. "Attention Drifting In and Out: The Boredom Feedback Model." *Personality and Social Psychology Review*. Advance online publication.

Tangney, June P., Roy F. Baumeister, and Angie Luzio Boone. 2004. "High Self-Control Predicts Good Adjustment, Less Pathology, Better Grades, and Interpersonal Success." *Journal of Personality* 72, no. 2: 271–324. https://doi.org /10.1111/j.0022-3506.2004.00263.x

Thackray, Richard I., J. Powell Bailey, and R. Mark Touchstone. 1977. "Physiological, Subjective, and Performance Correlates of Reported Boredom and Monotony While Performing a Simulated Radar Control Task." In *Vigilance: Theory, Operational Performance and Physiological Correlates*, edited by Robert Mackie, 203–16. New York: Plenum.

Todman, McWelling. 2003. "Boredom and Psychotic Disorders: Cognitive and Motivational Issues." *Psychiatry: Interpersonal and Biological Processes* 66, no. 2: 146–67. https://doi.org/10.1521/psyc.66.2.146.20623.

Tolor, Alexander. 1989. "Boredom as Related to Alienation, Assertiveness, Internal-External Expectancy, and Sleep Patterns." *Journal of Clinical Psychology* 45, no. 2: 260–5. https://doi.org/10.1002/1097-4679(198903)45:2<260::AID-JCL P2270450213>3.0.CO;2-.

Torres, D. Diego. 2013. "Understanding How Family Socioeconomic Status Mediates the Maternal Intelligence–Child Cognitive Outcomes Relationship: A Moderated Mediation Analysis." *Biodemography and Social Biology* 59, no. 2: 157–77. https ://doi.org/10.1080/19485565.2013.833804.

Troutwine, Robert, and Edgar C. O'Neal. 1981. "Volition, Performance of a Boring Task and Time Estimation." *Perceptual and Motor Skills* 52, no. 3: 865–6. https:// doi.org/10.2466/pms.1981.52.3.865.

Twenge, Jean M., Kathleen R. Catanese, and Roy F. Baumeister. 2003. "Social Exclusion and the Deconstructed State: Time Perception, Meaninglessness, Lethargy, Lack of Emotion, and Self-Awareness." *Journal of Personality and Social Psychology* 85, no. 3: 409–23. https://doi.org/10.1037/0022-3514.85.3.409.

Tze, Virginia MC, Robert M. Klassen, and Lia M. Daniels. 2014. "Patterns of Boredom and Its Relationship with Perceived Autonomy Support and Engagement." *Contemporary Educational Psychology* 39, no. 3: 175–87. https://doi.org/10.1016/j .cedpsych.2014.05.001.

van Hooft, Edwin A. J., and Madelon L. M. van Hooff. 2018. "The State of Boredom: Frustrating or Depressing?" *Motivation and Emotion* 42, no. 6: 931–46. https://doi .org/10.1007/s11031-018-9710-6.

Van Tilburg, Wijnand A. P., and Eric R. Igou. 2011. "On Boredom and Social Identity: A Pragmatic Meaning-Regulation Approach." *Personality and Social Psychology Bulletin* 37, no. 12: 1679–91. https://doi.org/10.1177/0146167211418530.

Van Tilburg, Wijnand A.P., and Eric R. Igou. 2012. "On Boredom: Lack of Challenge and Meaning as Distinct Boredom Experiences." *Motivation and Emotion* 36, no. 2: 181–94. https://doi.org/10.1007/s11031-011-9234-9.

Van Tilburg, Wijnand A.P., and Eric R. Igou. 2017a. "Boredom Begs to Differ: Differentiation from Other Negative Emotions." *Emotion* 17, no. 2: 309–322. https://doi.org/10.1037/emo0000233.

Van Tilburg, Wijnand A.P., and Eric R. Igou. 2017b. "Can Boredom Help? Increased Prosocial Intentions in Response to Boredom." *Self and Identity* 16, no. 1: 82–96. https://doi.org/10.1080/15298868.2016.1218925.

Vettenburg, Nicole, Ruben Brondeel, Claire Gavray, and Lieven J.R. Pauwels. 2013. "Societal Vulnerability and Adolescent Offending: The Role of Violent Values, Self-Control and Troublesome Youth Group Involvement." *European Journal of Criminology* 10, no. 4: 444–61. https://doi.org/10.1177/1477370812470777.

Vliegenthart, J., Gerard Noppe, E. F. C. Van Rossum, J. W. Koper, Hein Raat, and E. L. T. Van den Akker. 2016. "Socioeconomic Status in Children is Associated with Hair Cortisol Levels as a Biological Measure of Chronic Stress." *Psychoneuroendocrinology* 65: 9–14. https://doi.org/10.1016/j.psyneuen.2015.11.022.

Vodanovich, Stephen J. 2003. "Psychometric Measures of Boredom: A Review of the Literature." *The Journal of Psychology* 137, no. 6: 569–95. https://doi.org/10.1080/00223980309600636.

Watt, John D., and Stephen J. Vodanovich. 1999. "Boredom Proneness and Psychosocial Development." *The Journal of Psychology* 133, no. 3: 303–14. https://doi.org/10.1002/(SICI)1097-4679(200001)56:1<149::AID-JCLP14>3.0.CO;2-Y.

Westgate, Erin C., and Timothy D. Wilson. 2018. "Boring Thoughts and Bored Minds: The MAC Model of Boredom and Cognitive Engagement." *Psychological Review* 125, no. 5: 689–713. https://doi.org/10.1037/rev0000097.

Weybright, Elizabeth H., John Schulenberg, and Linda L. Caldwell. 2020. "More Bored Today Than Yesterday? National Trends in Adolescent Boredom from 2008 to 2017." *Journal of Adolescent Health* 66, no. 3, 360–5. https://doi.org/10.1016/j.jadohealth.2019.09.021.

Willging, Cathleen E., Gilbert A. Quintero, and Elizabeth A. Lilliott. 2014. "Hitting the Wall: Youth Perspectives on Boredom, Trouble, and Drug Use Dynamics in Rural New Mexico." *Youth & Society* 46, no. 1: 3–29. https://doi.org/10.1177/0044118X11423231.

Zhao, Jiaying, and Brandon M. Tomm. 2017. "Attentional Trade-Offs Under Resource Scarcity." In *Augmented Cognition. Enhancing Cognition and Behavior in Complex Human Environments* (Lecture Notes in Computer Science, vol 10285), edited by Dylan D. Schmorrow and Cali M. Fidopiastis, 78–97. Cham: Springer. https://doi.org/10.1007/978-3-319-58625-0_6.

Ziino, Carlo, and Jennie Ponsford. 2006. "Vigilance and Fatigue Following Traumatic Brain Injury." *Journal of the International Neuropsychological Society: JINS* 12, no. 1: 100–10. https://doi.org/10.1017/S1355617706060139.

Chapter 8

The Epistemic Benefits of Irrational Boredom

Lisa Bortolotti and Matilde Aliffi

1. INTRODUCTION

Bernard Williams argues against the idea that an immortal life would be desirable. People who continue to exist for a very long time can only have a certain number of experiences they wish to have, given their interests and life goals (Williams 1973). Once they have satisfied those interests and reached those goals, they would be afflicted by boredom. For their long lives to continue to be exciting, people's interests and life goals would have to change. But people would not preserve their identity if their interests and life goals changed. Thus, for Williams, a person's immortality is either undesirable due to inevitable boredom or impossible due to the psychological constraints on personal identity. Williams's position has been criticized for conflating different meanings of boredom—the everyday boredom that emerges from lack of stimuli and an existential boredom that is closer to a character trait or a persistent feature of one's experience. Also, his position underestimates the capacity people have to pursue different interests and life goals without compromising their identity (Bortolotti and Nagasawa 2009).

If we reject Williams's constraints on personal identity, we can further explore the possibility that boredom conveys valuable information, warning people that their interests and life goals may no longer be the same, that they are evolving. What if one of the functions of boredom, as it has been convincingly argued by Andreas Elpidorou (Elpidorou 2018a; 2018b; 2020), was to motivate people to shape their lives in accordance with information about changed interests and life goals? It would make sense then to acknowledge that boredom has benefits for agents, benefits that can be cashed out in epistemic terms, and in particular in terms of enhanced self-knowledge. Let us consider an intriguing case.

Samy Kamkar became famous as a computer hacker and a security researcher. He dropped out of high school when he was a teenager and started working in software and programming. In an interview for the podcast *Darknet Diaries* (episode 61), he said that programming has always been intellectually stimulating for him. When he was 19, however, he started to feel bored, despite being a very successful programmer and working for a company that he contributed to cofounding. To ease boredom, he created *worm Samy*, the fastest-spreading virus at that time. The virus enabled him to discover some vulnerabilities in the social network *MySpace*. For his actions, Samy was sentenced to 720 hours of community service and a lifelong ban to use computers—the computer ban was then lifted after he passed probation.

We do not know all the details of Samy's real-life story but with a little imagination we can fill the gaps. We can speculate that, if boredom can ever be irrational, it was *irrational* for Samy to feel bored with programming at nineteen. After all, he was fulfilling his ambition to be a start-up founder and a brilliant programmer; and programming was still by his own admission intellectually stimulating for him. So, his feeling of boredom conveyed information ("Programming is no longer interesting for me") that may have been badly supported by the evidence available to him and have conflicted with some of his other emotions and beliefs. One interesting thing is that, although it might have been psychologically unpleasant and epistemically irrational for Samy to feel bored at that stage of his life, that state of boredom led to a significant breakthrough for himself and for the programming community at large. In the process of creating *worm Samy*, Samy learnt new skills and new facts. As a result of the spreading of the virus, valuable information was made available to others. Eventually, after his ban from using computers was lifted, Samy went back to programming and found the activity exciting again, maybe thanks to his new interest in how hacking was done and how it could be prevented. Thus, the creation of the virus not only contributed to progress in the knowledge shared by the programming community, but also suggested to Samy new ways to apply and exploit his talents, which arguably changed the course of his career for the better.

If our reading of the case is plausible, then we would have to admit that boredom as an emotion can be both *epistemically irrational* and *epistemically beneficial*. This raises a number of questions.

First, is boredom an emotion? We already saw that there are different types of boredom. Psychologists agree that one type of boredom is an emotional state that emerges when agents are exposed to specific object, such as a person, an activity, or a place, and they call it state or *situational* boredom (Van Tilburg and Igou 2012; Van Tilburg and Igou 2017). *Trait* or *habitual* of boredom, akin to the existential boredom described by Williams in his work against the desirability of immortality, is another type of boredom which does not seem to covary with the presence of one object (person, activity, or place). It spreads to most experiences in a person's life and usually has long-term negative effects on agents' mental health. Situational boredom, which is what interests us here, is usually characterized as an emotion—or at least it is acknowledged to have an important emotional component.

Second, can boredom be irrational? We will argue that emotions can be assessed for epistemic rationality if they meet some conditions, and situational boredom does seem to meet them. We cannot be certain that Samy's boredom was an irrational emotion because we do not know whether Samy had evidence conflicting with the information conveyed by his emotion at that point in his life, that is, to what extent he found programming intellectually stimulating while he started feeling bored. But it is not difficult to imagine a case in which people have evidence that a task is interesting and stimulating for them and yet feel bored with that task. The feeling of boredom can be cashed out in terms of their being unable to pay attention while performing the task or feeling that the task lacks meaning for them. In our version of Samy's case, Samy is the sort of person who finds programming interesting. One day, though, he feels bored with programming. Samy's feeling of boredom is irrational because it gives Samy information ("Programming is uninteresting for me") that conflicts with what he has evidence to believe ("Programming is interesting for me").

The situation we described is consistent with at least three scenarios.

In one scenario (*Samy1*), the feeling of boredom is misleading because the information it provides ("Programming is uninteresting for me") is incorrect: *programming is still interesting for Samy*. After gathering more evidence, Samy rejects the idea that programming is no longer interesting, overcomes the feeling of boredom, and continues to both enjoy programming and think of himself as a person who finds programming interesting.

In an alternative scenario (*Samy2*), the feeling of boredom is revealing because the information it provides ("Programming is uninteresting for me") is correct: subsequent evidence confirms that *programming is no longer interesting for Samy*. Samy stops believing that he is the sort of person who finds programming interesting or meaningful. Programming has lost its appeal for him.

Scenario three (*Samy3*) is probably the most realistic given what we know about Samy's biography: not programming as a whole, but the programming Samy used to do for his job was no longer sufficiently stimulating for him. In this case, the information boredom provided, captured by "Programming is uninteresting for me," was at best incomplete. Subsequent evidence suggests that Samy needed to change the way he thought about programming to rekindle his enthusiasm for it.

Notice that in all three scenarios above, boredom as an epistemically irrational emotion (i.e., an emotion which provides information that is not supported by evidence) has epistemic benefits. How can Samy's boredom have epistemic benefits? As boredom has a negative valence, when he is feeling bored, Samy is motivated to alleviate his boredom by directing his attention away from programming toward another activity. Boredom may lead him to try different activities that he then discovers being more interesting and stimulating than the original one or may lead him to acquire skills that he will need to perform the original activity in a more satisfying or challenging way (which is what arguably happened to real-life Samy). The motivation to engage in a different activity can be part of a process of self-revelation (*Samy2*) or self-transformation (*Samy3*) via boredom: Samy discovered what his true self had always been like (he never really enjoyed programming as a whole or the programming that was required by his job) or learned that he had changed into a person with different interests (he did enjoy programming at one point, but then he stopped).

In *Samy1* boredom is also leading to discoveries that enrich Samy's experience and skills, despite providing the incorrect information that Samy does not find programming interesting and stimulating any more. The fact that Samy stops attending to programming and ends up developing *worm Samy*, prompted by his feeling of boredom, gives rise to something novel and creative that would have been unlikely to happen if Samy had always been consistently fascinated with programming and had not looked for a diversion. The link between boredom and creative endeavors seems to be more than a coincidence, as creativity is often listed among the alleged benefits of boredom. Steve Jobs famously said that boredom allows one to indulge in curiosity (Levy 2011), and psychologists agree with him (Gasper and Middlewood 2014; Mann and Cadman 2014).

In this chapter we argue that in some situations it may be both epistemically irrational and epistemically beneficial for a person to experience situational boredom. As we anticipated, an emotion is epistemically irrational when the evidence available to the agent does not support the information the emotion conveys. Agents feel bored in situation S and come to believe that the task T they are performing in S lacks interest for them, even if they have reasons to believe that T is still interesting and stimulating for them. Boredom motivates the agents to stop engaging with T in order to escape S.

Situational boredom offers epistemic benefits independent of whether the information the agent derives from it about which tasks are interesting or stimulating is accurate. If the information is accurate, boredom contributes to self-knowledge by signaling that the agents' interests have changed. If the information is not accurate, boredom may nonetheless open new avenues and opportunities for the agents who may discover new interests as a result. It contributes to the knowledge of the agents' evolving selves and to the pursuit of their creative endeavors.

In the rest of the chapter, we start by offering an elucidation of boredom as an epistemically rationally assessable and potentially irrational emotion. Epistemic irrationality has been mostly applied to belief-like states, but we argue that it can be applied to emotions too and explain why. Next, we argue that, just like some beliefs, some emotions can contribute to an agent's epistemic functionality even when they are irrational. Finally, based on Andreas Elpidorou's account of boredom as providing the benefits of information and self-regulation, we explain how boredom's contribution to epistemic functionality is best characterized as a contribution to self-knowledge.

2. EMOTIONS AS EPISTEMICALLY RATIONALLY ASSESSABLE

Beliefs are mental states that are typically rationally assessable. From an epistemic standpoint, depending on whether the belief responds to the evidence, we consider beliefs rational or irrational. Consider the following cases.

> *Jenny the violinist.* Jenny is a talented violinist. She is involved in an explosion and as a result she loses the use of her right arm. For the clinical team at the hospital where Jenny is receiving care, it is very unlikely that she will be able to play the violin again. Jenny, however, comes to believe that it is only a question of time and her right arm will be just fine after rehabilitation. As a result, she makes plans to start playing music again. Her belief about the future does not take into account the expert opinion she has received, and it is ill-grounded—not supported by the evidence available to her. But having that belief and making plans for the future help Jenny manage the negative emotions she has been feeling after the explosion, and as a result she copes better with the pain and the stress she experiences during rehabilitation.

We may consider Jenny's belief that her arm will be just fine as epistemically irrational, because Jenny's belief does not take medical evidence into account and is not well supported by the other available evidence. As we shall see in section 4, Jenny's belief may be psychologically and epistemically adaptive by enabling her to cope at a critical time.

> *Karl the proud student.* Karl is coming to the end of medical school. He has always been thoroughly supported by his family who provided private tutoring

in the subject areas which he found particularly challenging during his studies. Partly due to the praise of his tutors, Karl starts feeling very proud about his academic achievements, although his exam results are no better than average and his lecturers are not particularly impressed by him. As a result of this, Karl puts himself forward for ambitious projects and interesting jobs with confidence, increasing his chances of being considered as a worthy candidate. He learns a lot about the job market for graduates in medicine, and gains experience in job interviews.

We may consider Karl's pride in his academic achievements as epistemically irrational, because a close examination of his university transcript reveals that he did not do any better than the average student in his cohort. Indeed, given his privileged background and the unwavering support of his family, one would have reasonably expected him to do better. That said, his pride gives him the confidence to take advantage of exciting opportunities and learn in the process.

Sunita and COVID-19. Sunita feels fear of catching COVID-19 when she reads in the newspaper that there has been a rise of coronavirus cases in the city where she lives, although she has no pre-existing health conditions that increase her risks of complications. Sunita monitors the news frequently, starts working from home, and when she is out, she strictly follows all the recommendations about avoiding crowds, wearing masks, maintaining physical distance with others, and washing her hands often.

We may consider Sunita's fear as epistemically rational. Catching COVID-19 can result into a serious illness even for people who are not at increased risk of complications and Sunita has evidence that the infection could harm herself and others to which she may pass the virus on. Moreover, her fear may also be beneficial to her, sustaining her motivation to "do the right thing" and be cautious in her everyday behavior.

In describing our cases, we treated emotions just like beliefs: we assumed that emotions can be subject to the same rationality standards as beliefs and can also be subject to something like epistemic evaluation. We saw that Karl's pride in his academic achievements is misplaced because it does not fit with an objective evaluation of his past performance relative to the cohort of students he belongs to. We saw that Sunita's fear is justified by the information available to her about the potential health risks involved in catching the virus. However, whether emotions should be subject to standards of rationality is controversial. In lay talk, it is at best ambiguous whether emotions are open to rational assessment and people often consider emotion and reason as opposites, where emotions are associated with irrationality and reason with rationality (see Bortolotti 2014, chapter 3).

In some specific contexts, emotions are labeled as rational or irrational: for instance, people talk about *rational* fears when there is a genuinely threatening situation to face, and about *irrational* fears (phobias) when the threat is exaggerated or just imagined. Sometimes, an emotional reaction is regarded as irrational when it is excessive, disproportionate to the event that caused it. Being angry after receiving an offence or a rejection is understandable, but when anger cannot be controlled and turns into an assault or another destructive or self-destructive reaction, it is usually regarded as irrational (as in *anger disorders*). To establish whether emotions can be subject to rationality standards we could identify the features that ground the epistemic rational assessability of beliefs, and see whether these features are also present in emotional states.

We consider emotions as assessable from the perspective of epistemic rationality if we can assess the relationship between the information they convey to an agent and the evidence available to that agent that is relevant to the correctness of that information. This is the case when emotions share three key characteristics of mental states that are epistemically rationally assessable, such as typical beliefs (Aliffi 2019).

To be epistemically rationally assessable, a mental state needs to satisfy at least three requirements:

(1) an *information requirement*, that is, providing agents with some information about the world or about themselves;
(2) a *motivation requirement*, that is, having an "epistemic force" that leads agents to act on the provided information;
(3) a *plasticity requirement*, that is, changing when new relevant information become available, thereby displaying informational plasticity.

Beliefs tend to display those three features. Consider Jenny the violinist. Her belief that her right arm will be just fine provides her with information about the world: it tells how her future will be like. Her belief also has epistemic force because Jenny is disposed to take the content of her belief at face value and plan accordingly. Finally, Jenny's belief displays some informational plasticity: her belief could have changed, had there been additional information to integrate that was relevant. For instance, if Jenny had been told by the rehabilitation nurse that recovery from her injury would have occurred within six months, then she would have believed that not just that her right arm would be fine, but that it would be fine *within six months*.

Emotions may also satisfy those three requirements. In Karl the proud student, pride tells Karl something about his worth, that his academic performance was better than that of his fellow students. Pride has motivational force as well. Karl is likely to believe that he is skilled and talented as a consequence of feeling proud, and also act on his pride, putting himself forward for ambitious projects and interesting jobs. Finally, Karl's pride is plastic to some extent: Karl would feel prouder of himself if he thought that his results placed him in the top 5 percent rather than the top 20 percent of the students in his cohort.

Now think of Sunita and her fear of catching COVID-19. Her fear provides information about the world, as it is describing coronavirus as a threat to her. Her fear also has motivational force, as Sunita takes the information provided by fear at face value. For instance, Sunita decides to not to go shopping at her local supermarket but to get the items she needs delivered instead. Finally, her fear exhibits plasticity: Sunita's emotional response would have been different if she believed to be already immune to the virus.

Emotions such as pride and fear seem to be the right sort of mental states to qualify as epistemically rationally assessable. Note, however, that the features that ground the epistemic rational assessability of emotions we presented apply to the emotion's *token* and not to the *type*. This leaves open the possibility that some emotional states are not epistemically rationally assessable, when they fail to fulfill one or more of the three requirements that ground the epistemic rational assessability.

We tend to think of sadness as an epistemically rationally assessable emotion. However, there can be cases of a-rational sadness. In his book *Looking for Spinoza* (Damasio 2003, chapter 2), Antonio Damasio describes one such case, an "out of the blue" emotion of sadness experienced by a woman undergoing treatment for Parkinson's disease. As Damasio narrates, the woman experienced a sudden emotion of sadness when her brain was stimulated by an electrode that was placed two millimeters below one of the contact sites that was previously observed to improve her condition. When the current started to pass through the electrode, the woman began to cry and said that she was feeling worthless and disgusted with life. This intense emotion suddenly stopped ninety seconds after the current was switched off. When she was asked why she felt so sad, the woman seemed to be unaware of the reasons for her sadness. This emotion is a good candidate for an a-rational emotion, as it does not display informational plasticity. The woman's sadness looks like a fixed response to the electrical stimulation, and it is not affected by her other emotional and belief states, as the woman is not able to articulate the reasons for her fear.

Another example of emotions that are not epistemically rationally assessable may be emotions involving fictional characters, which typically lack motivational force. Consider Helen who experiences fear of Frankenstein when reading Mary Shelley's novel. Helen knows that Frankenstein does not exist outside the book, and that his monster is not a real danger to her, so she is unlikely to take steps to avoid Frankenstein's creation or protect her loved ones from it. In the fictional world Helen inhabits while reading or thinking about the novel, her emotions may have some epistemic force, shaping her other emotional and belief states, but in her actual life that is unlikely to happen.

3. SITUATIONAL BOREDOM AS
EPISTEMICALLY IRRATIONAL

So far, we made a case for some emotions being epistemically rationally assessable. Can we include boredom among those? Boredom is often defined as the feeling that there is nothing interesting or stimulating for an agent to do. The failure to engage may be due to environmental factors when the agent is confronted with repetitive and unchallenging tasks. However, the same environmental factors can cause boredom in some individuals and not in others. Because of such individual differences, the distinction between state vs. trait boredom (or situational vs. habitual boredom) proves useful. As we anticipated, state or situational boredom is a lack of engagement that is largely determined by the environment in which agents find themselves, and thus it is often temporary and specific (i.e., agents are bored *with something*). State boredom is transitory and continuous and dependent on the situation (Gabriel 1988; Mikulas and Vodanovich 1993).

Trait or habitual boredom, instead, is a lack of engagement that is largely due to agents' states of mind—agents may lack the motivation to engage in interesting activities that are available to them due to depression or other (internal) factors. This is sometimes called *motivational* or *chronic* boredom depending on whether its most relevant feature is thought to be its source (*lack of motivation*) or its duration and pervasiveness (agents seem to be bored *with life itself*). Trait boredom is enduring, but not continuously manifested, and may be unaffected by a specific situation. In some of the boredom literature (Bargdill 2000; Fahlman et al. 2009; Vodanovich and Watt 2015), trait boredom is claimed to have lasting manifestations and effects, and a more negative impact on people's well-being and sense of purpose (see also Bortolotti and Nagasawa 2009).

It is to some extent controversial whether state boredom is an emotion (e.g., Shaver et al. 1987) as some consider it as an attitude or as a mood. However, it is not controversial that it involves affective states. Indeed, boredom is often characterized by *unpleasant feelings* and *aversion*, in terms of dissatisfaction and disengagement. Boredom also has cognitive components such as an altered perception of time and motivational components such as a disposition to change the situation. With respect to the affective components of state boredom, there is some agreement that boredom is an emotional experience with negative valence (i.e., it is unpleasant) (Goetz et al. 2014). While we do not deny that situational boredom might involve, or be accompanied by, other attitudes or that a sense of boredom may be better described as a mood, we shall focus here on boredom *as an emotion*. In particular, we shall follow some widely accepted definitions of situational boredom as the emotion agents experience when confronted with something that does not interest or stimulate them: "an unpleasant, transient affective state in which the individual feels a pervasive lack of interest in and difficulty concentrating on the current activity" (Fisher 1993, 397); "the aversive experience of wanting, but being unable, to engage in satisfying activity" (Eastwood et al. 2013).

Now that we are satisfied that it is plausible to consider situational boredom as an emotion, we can ask: is it an *epistemically rationally assessable* emotion? In all three scenarios, Samy's case fits the conditions for his boredom to be epistemically rationally assessable. Boredom (1) provides Samy with information about the world by presenting his situation as uninteresting; (2) has motivational force by leading him to do something different, that is, develop a virus targeting *MySpace*; and (3) is plastic as it is plausible that it would be intensified in the case of an especially repetitive programming task or attenuated in the light of a novel programming assignment. If boredom as an emotion is epistemically rationally assessable, it can be epistemically rational or irrational. Notice that "irrational" here does not mean "harmful." One example of "epistemically harmful boredom" could be when being bored leads a student to poor academic results—see Pekrun and colleagues (2014), for instance, for the correlation between boredom and low academic achievement. Boredom can be epistemically harmful without being epistemically irrational because it can have negative epistemic consequences even when the information it provides is supported by the evidence available to the person.

As we saw, emotions give agents evaluative information about the world. Fear alerts them to imminent danger. Anger presents things as being offensive. Disgust informs them that something is noxious. Sadness tells them about loss (Griffiths 1997). The information agents receive from their emotions is very important because it allows them to understand how and to what extent things matter to them (see, for instance, Nussbaum 2001; Helm 2001; Roberts 2003). Agents may use their emotions to form evaluative beliefs about the world.[1] They may form the belief that a certain remark is offensive drawing on their anger. They may come to believe that a fragile cliff is dangerous based on their fear. Sometimes, the information that emotions provide is correct such as when they experience fear of a fragile cliff on their way, disgust at milk that is rotten, sadness about the loss of a long-coveted job opportunity, or anger at a sexist remark. In all those cases, relative to them, the intentional object of their emotion displays the evaluative property that the emotion indicates and to the extent exhibited by the emotion. In other cases, however, agents get things wrong: they may be overly scared about spiders, disgusted about edible fried beetles, or angry about a remark that was meant to be helpful.

Samy's boredom is epistemically rationally assessable, because epistemic rationality norms apply to Samy's boredom. His emotion is epistemically rational if it conforms to norms of epistemic rationality and it is irrational if it violates them. The requirements for epistemic rationality concern evidential support and responsiveness to evidence. As we saw, for an emotion to be epistemically rationally assessable, it needs to give some information about the world to an agent; motivate the agent to take that information at face value; and be plastic, that is, sensitive to changes in the available evidence. In order for an emotion to be epistemically rational, the emotion needs to give information to an agent about the world that is well supported by the evidence available to the agent and that changes when new relevant evidence becomes available. Consider the epistemic rationality norm that dictates that an emotion is epistemically rational if the information it provides is well supported by the available evidence. We can imagine that Samy had copious evidence that programming was interesting to him: he was working for a company that he contributed to cofounding, fulfilling his ambition to be a start-up founder, and programming was something that was central to his job, something he was very talented at. Nevertheless, he felt bored. His feeling bored with programming was in conflict with the evidence he had that programming was interesting and stimulating for him. In such a situation, his feeling bored could very well be epistemically irrational, because of the mismatch between Samy's feeling of boredom and the evidence available to him about whether he found programming interesting and stimulating.

4. EPISTEMIC FUNCTIONALITY

For a mental state to match the available evidence is not the only concern when we are in the business of offering an epistemic evaluation of that mental state. We may be interested in whether a belief is well supported by evidence, but we may also want to know whether the belief is true, for instance; or whether it enables agents to fulfill their epistemic goals. In the latter case, we investigate the belief's contribution to the agent's epistemic functionality, where epistemic functionality is about the performance of an agent in relation to epistemic goals. The notion of epistemic functionality conveys the idea that, when agents pursue epistemic goals, they operate under constraints dictated by human cognitive limitations and by the environment in which their epistemic practices are embedded. Reconsider the case of Sunita and COVID-19. Sunita fears catching COVID-19 and her fear motivates her to acquire well-evidenced beliefs about the risks of infection when shopping at the supermarket. Before she goes shopping to her local supermarket, she reads about how the virus spreads in enclosed spaces and she calls the supermarket management team to ask them what changes were made to the ventilation system in the building since the start of the pandemic.

Given her goal, Sunita functions well epistemically if she acts in such a way as to acquire well-evidenced beliefs about the risks of catching COVID-19. Reading about virus transmission and investigating the relevant features of the surrounding environment might lead Sunita to attain the information she needs. These beliefs are means to the attainment of her epistemic goals and such attainment involves some interaction with the surrounding social and physical environment. Limitations to information that can be reliably acquired, due to Sunita's constraints as an agent (her physical and psychological makeup, her social status, etc.) or to the environment in which she operates, are relevant. The pursuit of her goals may be affected by time constraints, a possible language barrier between herself and others, and the unavailability of reliable information on social media, which is her primary source of information.

Beliefs and emotions can aid the agent in navigating her environment successfully and attain the desired epistemic goals (Bortolotti 2020, chapter 1). Sometimes, such states can bring considerable epistemic benefit or avert some considerable epistemic harm. A *belief* in the reliability of scientific information and a *fear* of contracting COVID-19, for instance, would help Sunita's epistemic functionality. The former state (belief) helps her discriminate among better and worse sources of information and the latter state (fear) sustains her motivation to seek information in a thorough way to avoid infection despite the difficulties.

A point that is important but often neglected is that sometimes a state that is epistemically irrational can make a positive contribution to epistemic functionality. Sunita's belief in the reliability of scientific information is an epistemically rational belief, well grounded, as there is inductive evidence about the success of science in explaining problems and predicting solutions for such problems. Her fear of catching COVID-19 is also an epistemically rational emotion, as the threats to her health from infection are genuine and not made-up or exaggerated. But there can be situations where a belief or an emotion that is not epistemically rational plays an important role in supporting agents' capacity to pursue their epistemic goals.

Recall Jenny the violinist. One might argue that the benefits of Jenny's ill-grounded belief are primarily *psychological*—the belief that she will play the violin again makes her feel better at the cost of misrepresenting reality. However, the psychological effects of the ill-grounded belief on Jenny give rise to behaviors that support her *epistemic* functionality, at least temporarily.

If, in the aftermath of the explosion, she had failed to manage her negative emotions and could not cope with the ensuing difficulties, she would be likely to suffer from depressive moods, withdraw from social interactions, and lose interest in the surrounding environment. If she believed that she could no longer play the violin, she might despair and stop engaging in rehabilitation; she may even wish to end her life. Jenny's ill-grounded belief then prevents a situation that might lead to a crisis, being conducive to a positive attitude ("I can do this!") which helps Jenny concentrate on the tasks at hand and continue interacting with her physical and social world in a way that enables her to attain, retain, and use information as opposed to disengaging. To say that Jenny's belief contributes to her epistemic functionality does not imply or suggest that it is, all things considered, epistemically *good* for Jenny to adopt that belief, or that Jenny is epistemically *praiseworthy* for adopting that belief. The belief is still undesirable due to its being epistemically irrational and may not have aided functionality in a different context, but in Jenny's case it played an important role, and a role that a more epistemically rational belief could not as easily play.

Elaborating on our example, Jenny's belief that she will play the violin again is ill-grounded and has epistemic costs—it leads to a significant distortion of reality. It might give rise to other ill-grounded beliefs and prevent Jenny from fully understanding her prospects. This in turn may cause her to make unrealistic plans for the future and may create a gap between how she sees the world and how her family and friends see the world. In such a situation, it is likely that the belief's epistemic costs override its epistemic benefits and the belief may lack justification overall. Yet, we can still regard it as having epistemic benefits if its adoption prevents an epistemic harm from occurring at a critical time and enables Jenny to continue functioning and pursuing some of her epistemic goals. Once Jenny's emotional profile has stabilized and she has started to come to terms with her life after the explosion, the ill-grounded belief that she will play the violin again might have exhausted its epistemically beneficial role and be gradually replaced by a more realistic belief. Often the epistemic benefit provided by an epistemically irrational mental state is distinctive and cannot be easily obtained otherwise. Having a different, less epistemically irrational, mental state may not be possible for the agent at that time or may not deliver the same epistemic benefit. We can imagine that in Jenny's case the better-grounded and more accurate belief that she will not be able to play the violin in the future does not have the same capacity as the original belief to keep low mood at bay.

Recall Karl the proud student. We saw that Karl's pride is misplaced but it is also a potential asset for him, because by feeling that he is an outstanding student, he puts himself forward for ambitious projects and interesting jobs with confidence, increasing his chances of being considered a worthy candidate, learning about the job market for medical graduates, and gaining experience in job interviews. For Karl, not priding himself of his academic achievements but rather feeling disappointed about his average performance would probably lead to a more realistic assessment of his prospects. This would mean that he would be less likely to feel qualified for ambitious projects and interesting jobs, fail to display confidence in his skills, and miss out on valuable opportunities. Some of these opportunities have significant epistemic advantages, among which the opportunity to learn more about the job market and gain interview experience. Different from the case of Jenny the violinist, here there is no mental state responding to a potential crisis such as serious depression, but there is still a case to be made for Karl's pride to prevent disengagement. An agent who believes to be competent and successful is more likely to engage productively with the surrounding environment and to engage in fruitful exchanges of information.

We saw that some epistemically irrational beliefs and emotions can contribute positively to an agent's epistemic functionality. The motivation for our focus on epistemically irrational and yet epistemically beneficial mental states is the need to sort epistemically irrational states into two piles: those that should be given up without hesitation, and those that should be put up with at least temporarily, because they have some positive role to play—they bring some benefit. Without them, something epistemically significant might not happen or something epistemically disastrous might happen.

The next step is to find out whether situational boredom can play the role of the belief in Jenny the violinist or the emotion in Karl the proud student, that is, whether it can contribute to epistemic functionality independent of its epistemic rationality.

5. THE EPISTEMIC BENEFITS OF SITUATIONAL BOREDOM

The case of Samy is different from that of Jenny the violinist or Karl the proud student. The epistemically irrational state does not emerge as a response to a psychological crisis or as a boost for self-esteem, and thus we cannot just extend to Samy's situational boredom the explanation we offered for the epistemic benefits of Jenny's belief and Karl's pride. More generally, an unrealistically optimistic belief about the future and an overly positive evaluation of oneself may prevent disengagement, increase socialization, and so on, and thus contribute to epistemic functionality. Agents feel better about themselves and this helps them continue to interact productively with their physical and social environment.

The case of boredom seems to be different. Emotionally, boredom is characterized by aversion. It is an unpleasant state that does not make agents feel better about themselves. However, just like Jenny's belief and Karl's pride, Samy's boredom *motivates*. Jenny's belief motivates her to collaborate with the rehabilitation team to get better, Karl's pride motivates him to apply for ambitious projects after his degree, and Samy's boredom motivates him to change his activity and do something else. It just happens that Jenny's belief and Karl's pride motivate by enhancing positive mood and Samy's boredom motivates by deflating it.

We have independent reasons to think that situational boredom may be epistemically beneficial to those who experience it, and its epistemic irrationality seems not to detract from those reasons. In the psychological literature, it is argued that boredom may give rise to enhanced productivity, creativity, goal-orientedness, self-awareness, and prosocial behavior. In the recent philosophical literature, it is argued that boredom comes with an information benefit and a self-regulation benefit. Although all these claims are to some extent relevant to our purposes here, we shall focus on the latter benefits and how they relate to agents' potential for self-knowledge.

How is boredom informative? Elpidorou explicitly links boredom with self-knowledge:

> Boredom is informative: it tells us something both about the world and about ourselves. While bored, our situation is disclosed to us as unfulfilling, uninteresting, unchallenging, or non-stimulating. On account of this disclosure, boredom also informs us of our own goals, interests, and even self-perceived wellbeing. Being bored means that we are currently engaged not only in an uninteresting or unchallenging situation, but also in a situation that fails to meet our expectations and desires. Boredom is a state that is about ourselves as much as it is about the world. (Elpidorou 2014)

There are at least two ways in which boredom enhances knowledge. First, boredom may indirectly lead the agent to acquire new knowledge about the world as the agent is likely to engage in new activities, and perhaps also try new ways of engaging in a certain activity: Samy becomes an expert hacker as a result of feeling bored with programming. From exploration and experimentation, new knowledge can be gained. Samy integrates his hacking experience in his already extensive knowledge about programming and eventually builds a career upon it.

Second, agents can gather important information about themselves by better understanding how they can successfully relieve their boredom: Samy may have discovered that he would feel disengaged as a result of completing repetitive tasks or that he would feel frustrated by the absence of challenges.

Precisely because boredom has a negative valence, agents are motivated to get rid of it. Learning the sort of things that help them decrease the intensity of their boredom can help agents avoid boredom in the future and confirm something they may already suspect about what they find stimulating or reveal to them something unexpected about themselves. Agents manage their boredom, and by doing so, they acquire knowledge about themselves and about their dispositions to experience boredom in certain contexts.

How does boredom lead to self-regulation? Elpidorou argues that boredom alerts agents that an activity is no longer stimulating for them, motivating them to make a change. Boredom "can help to promote the restoration of the perception that one's activities are meaningful and congruent with one's overall projects" (Elpidorou 2018b, 325–26). Thanks to boredom, agents change things in their lives to pursue their new interests (Elpidorou 2018a).

> Boredom, frustration, and anticipation aren't unpleasant accidents of our lives. They're neither superfluous nor necessarily burdensome psychological states that we should want to eliminate. Instead, they're the elements of a good life. Boredom, frustration, and anticipation are indications that we find ourselves stuck in unpleasant and unfulfilling situations. But they're also the incentives we need to get out of such traps. Boredom, frustration, and anticipation aren't obstacles to our goals. They're our guides. They keep us motivated. They propel us into lives that are truly our own. (Elpidorou 2020, 9)

On the epistemic side of things, self-regulation implies self-knowledge. As we saw, boredom enables agents to gain better knowledge about themselves. How we think this occurs largely depends on how we think about selves and relates to a number of debates in cognitive and social psychology concerning agency. Should we think of selves as largely static entities that we can come to know better by reflection and inquiry or as continually evolving entities that develop in response to environmental cues and other factors? Given the psychological evidence on choice at our disposal (Bortolotti and Sullivan-Bissett 2019), we are inclined to think that selves are continually evolving, almost elusive. Boredom in such a case is a helpful messenger, suggesting that something needs to change in the way agents spend their time if they want to continue enjoying themselves.

So, going back to the example we started with, what are the epistemic benefits of Samy's boredom? In *Samy1*, the feeling of boredom is misleading because the information it provides ("Programming is uninteresting for me") is incorrect: *programming is still interesting for Samy*. After gathering more evidence, Samy rejects the idea that programming is no longer interesting, overcomes the feeling of boredom, and continues to both enjoy programming and think of himself as a person who finds programming interesting.

Although boredom here is a messenger that got it wrong, the advantage of doubting how an activity is intellectually stimulating is that agents are encouraged to seek reasons to continue with the activity and may develop a more reflective stance of their likes and dislikes. Once they are confident that their activity is not the source of the disengagement, they can ask what boredom was due to, and find out something about themselves that would have otherwise remained hidden.

In *Samy2*, the feeling of boredom is revealing because the information it provides ("Programming is uninteresting for me") is correct: subsequent evidence confirms that *programming is no longer interesting for Samy*. Samy stops believing that he is the sort of person who finds programming interesting. Programming has lost its appeal for him. This is the standard case that would exemplify Elpidorou's argument for boredom as a means of self-regulation. In *Samy2*, boredom is a messenger who gets it right, and by listening to the messenger Samy may productively redirect his attention to activities that are potentially more satisfying for him than programming. This revealing boredom has benefits for knowledge of the world and knowledge of the self.

In *Samy3* it is not programming as a whole, but the programming Samy used to do for his job that was no longer sufficiently stimulating for him. The information boredom provided, captured by "Programming is uninteresting for me," was incomplete. As we suggested earlier, boredom may just signal something about the situation Samy found himself in, without offering specific information about the features or contexts of programming that lost their appeal for him.

Subsequent evidence suggests that Samy needed to change the way he thought about programming to rekindle his enthusiasm for it. Here, boredom delivers a message that needs to be unpacked and interpreted. Samy is told by his emotion that something related to his activity as a programmer is unsatisfying, but needs to embark on a process of discovery and self-discovery to realize what needs to change and what should stay the same. This third scenario shares the benefits in terms of self-regulation with the second scenario, and the benefits in terms of promoting self-reflection with the first.

6. CONCLUSIONS AND IMPLICATIONS

One may wonder about the importance of establishing whether an instance of situation boredom is epistemically irrational and yet epistemically beneficial. Being able to recognize the epistemic contribution of situational boredom may guide decisions as to how we react to the feeling of boredom. Should boredom be encouraged, tolerated, or avoided altogether? A recent debate about whether being bored is beneficial, due to its fostering independence and creativity, has been reignited in discussions about how best to approach extended periods of lockdown during the COVID-19 global pandemic (see, e.g., Shean 2020; Hunt 2020). This suggests that it is practically important to know whether some experiences that are unpleasant (at least to start with) have a positive function to play, not just psychologically but also epistemically.

So, what advantages can we gain by recognizing that boredom has epistemic benefits? When we think about aversive experiences or irrational beliefs, we tend to see their obvious disadvantages. We concentrate on how frustrated and unhappy agents may feel when they lack stimulation. We worry that a biased belief will cause agents to make unrealistic predictions. But in some contexts, as we saw, aversive experiences and irrational beliefs have a role to play without which agents may be worse off in some respects. Without the belief that one day she will be able to play the violin again, Jenny would not get out of bed in the morning. Without the pride he feels about his academic achievements, Karl would not apply for his dream job. Without feeling bored with programming, Samy would have never created *worm Samy*. What is interesting about such problematic emotions and beliefs is that they contribute to agents' epistemic functionality enabling them to continue to pursue and sometimes achieve epistemic goals that are important to them. Recognizing their positive role helps agents realize how best to react to such emotions and beliefs when they find them in others and in themselves.

Boredom has been on everybody's mind in the context of the forced isolation caused by COVID-19 containment measures in many countries around the world. Boredom has been linked to increased media use, which in the presence of a pandemic might have the effect of increasing anxiety (Chao et al. 2020). It has also been argued that boredom is a liability as it may motivate people not to adhere to the government recommendations and seek relief from their aversive experience. For instance, a person who feels bored for lack of socialization may end up failing to comply with social distancing norms (Marterelli and Wolff 2020). However, boredom also offers agents opportunities to change their situation for the better without increasing anxiety or compromising their compliance with the norms.

On an individual level, learning to recognize and use boredom in an adaptive manner might be useful. For example, making a list of realistic alternatives that are perceived as interesting and engaging, to be used when boredom arises might be promising. Next, to create optimal conditions in the environment, other possibilities to improve adhesion to containment measures are more related to internal changes, such as refocusing on the meaning of pandemic containment measures (i.e., public health) when boredom arises. This strategy should in turn also make adhering to containment measures less self-control demanding. (Martarelli and Wolff 2020)

All it takes is for agents to recognize boredom "as a messenger" and actively take steps to reduce it.

NOTE

1. For a discussion on whether emotions can justify evaluative judgments, see, for instance, Deonna and Teroni (2012).

REFERENCES

Aliffi, Matilde. 2019. *The Epistemic Rationality of Emotions: A New Defence.* PhD diss., University of Birmingham. https://etheses.bham.ac.uk//id/eprint/9424/7/Aliff i2019PhD.pdf.

Bargdill, Richard. 2000. "The Study of Life Boredom." *Journal of Phenomenological Psychology* 311, no. 2: 188–219.

Bortolotti, Lisa and Ema Sullivan-Bissett. 2019. "Is Choice Blindness a Case of Self-Ignorance?" *Synthese.* https://doi.org/10.1007/s11229-019-02414-3.

Bortolotti, Lisa, and Yujin Nagasawa. 2009. "Immortality without boredom." *Ratio* XXII, no. 3: 261–277.

Bortolotti, Lisa. 2014. *Irrationality.* Cambridge, UK: Polity.

Bortolotti, Lisa. 2020. *The Epistemic Innocence of Irrational Beliefs.* Oxford: Oxford University Press.

Chao, Miao, Xueming Chen, Tour Liu, Haibo Yang, and Brian J. Hall. 2020. "Psychological Distress and State Boredom During the COVID-19 Outbreak in China: The Role of Meaning in Life and Media Use." *European Journal of Psychotraumatology* 11, no. 1: 1769379.

Damasio, Antonio. 2003. *Looking for Spinoza: Joy, Sorrow and the Feeling Brain.* London: William Heinemann.

Deonna, Julien A., and Fabrice Teroni. 2012. "From Justified Emotions to Justified Evaluative Judgements." *Dialogue* 51, no. 1: 55–77.

Eastwood, John D., Alexandra Frischen, Mark J. Fenske, and Daniel Smilek. 2012. "The Unengaged Mind: Defining Boredom in Terms of Attention." *Perspectives on Psychological Science* 7, no. 5: 482–95.

Elpidorou, Andreas. 2014. "The Bright Side of Boredom." *Frontiers in Psychology* 5: 1245. https://doi.org/10.3389/fpsyg.2014.01245.

Elpidorou, Andreas. 2018a. "The Bored Mind is a Guiding Mind: Toward a Regulatory Theory of Boredom." *Phenomenology and the Cognitive Sciences* 17, no. 3: 455–84.

Elpidorou, Andreas. 2018b. "The good of boredom." *Philosophical Psychology* 31, no. 3: 323–51.

Elpidorou, Andreas. 2020. *Propelled: How Boredom, Frustration, and Anticipation Lead Us to the Good Life.* New York: Oxford University Press.

Fahlman, Shelley A., Kimberley B. Mercer, Peter Gaskovski, Adrienne E. Eastwood, and John D. Eastwood. 2009. "Does a Lack of Life Meaning Cause Boredom? Results from Psychometric, Longitudinal, and Experimental Analyses." *Journal of Social and Clinical Psychology* 28, no. 3: 307–40.

Gabriel, Martha A. 1988. "Boredom: Exploration of a Developmental Perspective". *Clinical Social Work Journal* 16, no. 2: 156–64.

Gasper, Karen, and Brianna L. Middlewood. 2014. "Approaching Novel Thoughts: Understanding Why Elation and Boredom Promote Associative Thought More Than Distress and Relaxation." *Journal of Experimental Social Psychology* 52: 50–7.

Goetz, Thomas, Anne C. Frenzel, Nathan C. Hall, Ulrike E. Nett, Reinhard Pekrun, and Anastasiya A. Lipnevich. 2014. "Types of Boredom: An Experience Sampling Approach." *Motivation and Emotion* 38, no. 3: 401–19.

Griffiths, Paul. E. 1997. *What Emotions Really Are: The Problem of Psychological Categories.* Chicago: University of Chicago Press.

Helm, Bennett. W. 2001. *Emotional Reason.* Cambridge: Cambridge University Press.

Hunt, Katie. 2020. "Bored of Lockdown yet? This Downtime May Have Some Benefits ... If You Do It Right." *CNN Health*, May 7, 2020. https://edition.cnn.com /2020/05/07/health/boredom-benefits-quarantine-wellness/index.html.

Levy, Steven. 2011. "Steve Jobs, 1955–2011." *Wired*, May 10, 2011. https://www.wir ed.com/2011/10/steve-jobs-1955-2011/.

Mann, Sandi. 2016. *The Upside of Downtime: Why Boredom is Good.* London: Robinson.

Mann, Sandi, and Rebekah Cadman. 2014. "Does being bored make us more creative?" *Creativity Research Journal* 26, no. 2: 165–73.

Martarelli, Corinna S., and Wanja Wolff W. 2020. "Too Bored to Bother? Boredom as a Potential Threat to the Efficacy of Pandemic Containment Measures." *Humanities and Social Sciences Communications* 7: 28. https://doi.org/10.1057/s 41599-020-0512-6.

Mikulas, William L. and Stephen J. Vodanovich. 1993. "The Essence of Boredom". *Psychological Record* 43, no. 1: 3–12.

Nussbaum, Martha. 2001. *Upheavals of Thought: The Intelligence of the Emotions.* Cambridge: Cambridge University Press.

Pekrun, Reinhard, Nathan C. Hall, Thomas Goetz, and Raymond P. Perry. 2014. "Boredom and Academic Achievement: Testing a Model of Reciprocal Causation." *Journal of Educational Psychology* 106, no. 3: 696–710.

Rhysider, Jack 2020. "Samy." *Darknet Diaries. Audio podcast,* 17th March. Ep.61 https://darknetdiaries.com/episode/61/.

Shaver, Philip, Judith Schwartz, Donald Kirson, and Cary O'Connor. 1987. "Emotion Knowledge: Further Exploration of a Prototype Approach." *Journal of Personality and Social Psychology* 52, no. 6: 1061–86.

Shean, Mandie. 2020. "Parents, You Don't Always Need to Entertain Your Kids— Boredom Is Good for Them." *The Conversation*, April 23, 2020. https://theconv

ersation.com/parents-you-dont-always-need-to-entertain-your-kids-boredom-is-go
od-for-them-136383.

Van Tilburg, Wijnand A.P. and Eric R. Igou. 2012. "On Boredom: Lack of Challenge
and Meaning as Distinct Boredom Experiences." *Motivation and Emotion* 36, no.
2: 181–94.

Van Tilburg, Wijnand A.P. and Eric R. Igou. 2017. "Boredom Begs to Differ:
Differentiation From Other Negative Emotions." *Emotion* 17, no. 2: 309–22.

Vodanovich, Stephen J. and John D. Watt. 2015. "Self-Report Measures of Boredom:
An Updated Review of the Literature." *The Journal of Psychology* 150, no. 2:
196–228.

Williams, Bernard. 1973. "The Makropulos Case: Reflections on the Tedium of
Immortality." In *Problems of the Self: Philosophical Papers 1956–1973*, 82–100.
Cambridge: Cambridge University Press.

Zomorodi, Manoush. 2018. *Bored and Brilliant*. New York: Macmillan.

Chapter 9

Boredom as Cognitive Appetite

Vida Yao

Boredom can motivate us to perform actions that are painful, imprudent, morally objectionable, or unwise in other respects. It can also give rise to forms of *akrasia:* we may be unwilling to do what we know we must, simply because we will find it boring; when we are racked with boredom—bored stiff, bored to tears—actions that might otherwise never occur to us to do can begin to appear attractive, and sometimes *remain* attractive against our better judgment. But boredom is also relevant to another set of moral or ethical concerns. Alongside questions about what we may do out of boredom, and about whether such actions are morally justifiable, conducive to our well-being, or instrumentally rational, a person's *character* can be revealed by how her dispositions of boredom express themselves. And just as our emotional dispositions can be not just criticized, but also *improved*, so we may think that our dispositions of boredom, too, may be both criticized and improved. From a virtue-theoretical approach to boredom that would encourage this shift of focus from the ethical significance of actions to include assessments of character and motive as well, three questions emerge. What *kind* of attitude is boredom, such that it can motivate (sometimes objectionable) forms of action, while also reflecting or disclosing something about the kind of character one has? What *does* it disclose or reveal about a person that she is bored by particular things, and not others, and to greater and lesser extents? And is there a virtue that could come to govern our dispositions of boredom, providing an ideal that one might aspire to?

Here, I will consider the view that boredom is an *emotion* and that the emotions are "quasi-perceptual," "*concern*-based construals."[1] In contrast to this understanding of boredom, I will highlight the respects in which it is more similar to our paradigmatic *appetites* in being less directly connected to an agent's concerns or values, as well as to her rationality, than our paradigmatic emotions are. On the proposal I will offer here, this is because the experience of boredom, like our other appetites, can arise, intensify, and be satisfied given our *bodily* condition. Given that we are embodied minds, this includes our mental condition as well. Boredom is what I will call a *cognitive appetite*.

In using this expression, I echo, but will build upon an observation of David Velleman's:

> In theoretical reasoning, the human intellect functions not as a passive recipient of information but as an active inquirer, driven by a powerful urge to understand. Anyone who has dealt at close quarters with infants or toddlers knows that the human animal is born with a voracious *cognitive appetite*, which drives it to probe and test every bit of its world, always trying to figure out how things work. (2008, 417; my emphasis)

Other philosophers have emphasized the significance of *intellectual* or *epistemic* emotions, attitudes which support the idea, as Velleman suggests, that the human intellect is not mere cold calculation, but is instead composed, among other things, by motivations and affective states, including an "urge to understand."[2] However, I will expand on this point by focusing attention on just one urge which, though *cognitive*, is less directly connected to value—including epistemic value—than our emotions are, including our love of the truth, and our desires to understand and comprehend. It is a primitive and basic need for *cognitive stimulus* which, when unfulfilled, gives rise to feelings of boredom. As I will discuss, this proposal can explain several aspects of boredom that render it similar to our more familiar appetites, and in particular, why boredom bears a different relationship to both a subject's values, and her rationality, than paradigmatic emotions such as anger and grief do.

However, one benefit of understanding boredom as a paradigmatic emotion is that ethical assessments of the emotions, understood as either *evaluative* feelings or judgments or *concern*-based construals, can easily accommodate ethical assessments of character. The emotions, such as anger, grief, and regret, reliably express an agent's *values*, and so, can be criticized in light of this connection. If boredom is an appetite, we face a prima facie difficulty in accommodating the discourse, thought, and practice of the ethical assessment of character and virtue that testify to the full ethical significance of boredom. As Robert C. Roberts writes when distinguishing the emotions from the appetites, "we might admire and praise a North American, personally unconnected with the Sudan, who feared a famine in the Sudan. But I don't suppose that anyone was ever morally praised for being hungry" (2003, 43).

To address this concern, I will draw on a conceptual resource from Aristotle's discussion of the more familiar appetites: in particular, a distinction between what he calls *common* and *peculiar* appetites, the former of which are ethically neutral, and the latter of which can come to be governed by the virtue of temperance, which incorporates, among other things, assessments of a person's values as well as her idiosyncratic tastes.[3] Thus, not only will understanding boredom as an appetite accommodate and explain aspects of boredom itself, by situating this conception of boredom against further resources that a virtue-theoretical approach may avail itself to, we will be able to vindicate the characterological significance of boredom as expressed by everyday ethical discourse, as well.

1. EMOTION AND APPETITE

Unlike mere sensations, boredom can be felt *about* objects, activities, and situations, *presenting* those intentional targets as possessing the quality, or formal object, of *being boring*. Given both these intentional and its presentational aspects of boredom, we may turn to developing the idea that there are nonsubjective anthropocentric veridicality conditions on experiences of boredom. As with our assessments of accurate color ascription, for example, which take into consideration what a normal human being with normal color vision, under certain lighting conditions, and so on, will see, our assessments of what things are boring will assume some set of "normal" human capacities, exercised under certain circumstances. Thus, we may be licensed to make assessments of *boringness* that are not purely subjective, and experience boredom in ways that can be more or less accurate (McDowell 1985). We could, without metaphysical anxiety, allow that there are objects, activities, and situations that simply *are* boring (to human beings), given those objects' possession of qualities which lend to their boringness, and given the assumption of normal capacities, of normal human beings, under certain circumstances, and so on.

But we can take a direct analogy between boredom and sense perception only so far. Among other things, we would be left unable to accommodate both the idiosyncrasies of individual dispositions toward boredom, as well as the full ethical significance of boredom. Though our sense perceptions can be assessed for their veridicality, this kind of assessment lacks any *ethical* significance. This consideration leads to another proposal: that boredom is an *emotion*.[4] The view of the emotions I will assume here emphasizes the respects in which the emotions can be more or less rational responses to one's environment or situation, can be assessed for their accuracy or veridicality, but which also bear important and ineliminable connections to a subject's *values*, or what she finds important. On this kind of view, the emotions are "*concern* based" or "*value* suffused."[5] Thus, not only are emotions assessable in the ways that other mind-to-world representational states are—for either their veridicality and/or their "fittingness," they are also assessable in terms of the *importance* attributed by the subject to the object of her emotion, where this will be a direct expression of her concerns or values (D'Arms and Jacobson 2000).[6] An episode of anger is not simply a response to a belief or construal that one has been insulted or wronged: it is also a representation of that insult or wrong as having a certain kind of importance to the subject, relative to what she finds valuable. Thus, we might criticize a person who feels no anger in response to a perceived insult in a way that is not reducible to a "pure" epistemic criticism that she either lacks the relevant belief or is inaccurately representing her circumstances. Her lack of anger may indicate, instead, that she does not take wrongs to herself to be of sufficient *importance*, itself something of ethical significance in assessing her character. She may be, as Aristotle suggests, servile, or as Kantians have suggested, lacking in self-respect, failing to adequately value her social or moral standing. That our emotions express and evince our values complements the idea that our emotional dispositions can be improved, both rationally *and* ethically—someone who comes to have better values will have that improvement manifested in improvements to her emotional dispositions.

We can now begin to contrast the appetites with the emotions. Though appetites too can be directed toward objects and present those objects in certain ways, they arise from the bodily condition of the subject, rather than from her concerns or values. While the emotions are "concern based" or "value suffused," the appetites are, in their most basic forms, value-*indifferent*. Hunger, thirst, and certain desires for sex arise given states of the body, and not in light of an object's being represented as having importance relative to what a person values or cares about. Hunger, as Plato suggests, need not be for *good* food, but just whatever food will seem to satisfy it; thirst for just whatever will seem to quench it.[7] And while the *subject* may want to eat something that is tasty, healthy, or comforting, her *hunger* will be satisfied so long as she eats anything edible.

This difference between the emotions and appetites is the central difference that I will focus on here, but there are others which accompany it. First, given that the appetites have endogenous causes, they may arise independently of a subject's thoughts and perceptions. Because of this, though episodes of hunger and thirst can, and tend to be, directed toward particular intentional objects, they *need not* be. One can experience the pangs of hunger but not be hungry *for* anything in particular. This is unlike the emotions, which *necessarily* have intentional objects, and at least *purport* to have reasons grounded in what they are about. If I am angry (and not just in an irritable mood), I am angry *about* something, seemingly for reasons; if I am grieving (and not just in a dejected and melancholy mood), I am grieving *for* something, again, seemingly for reasons.[8]

Second, the kind of intentional objects that the appetites can take are more circumscribed than those that the paradigmatic emotions can take. The emotions can take propositions as their content: I can be angry that social services have been cut, afraid that they will be, or relieved that they have not been. While one can hunger or thirst for particular objects, imagined or not, appetites neither take propositions as their objects nor do they arise given one's acceptance of propositions.

Third, a change in the way in which one is construing or representing an object can fully *prompt* or *extinguish* an emotion, in rational ways, or "for the right reasons." My anger can be prompted by my gaining a belief that something has happened: for example, that I've been wronged. And if I believe that what gave rise to my anger has been addressed (e.g., the offender has apologized or compensated for a wrong done), my anger can rationally fade in response, given this change in my beliefs, or how I now represent the situation.[9] In contrast, I cannot be *made hungry* by a change in what I am representing about the world.[10] If I am fully satiated, it will not matter how convinced I am that a dish is delicious, satisfying, or exactly as my grandmother used to make it: if I am not antecedently hungry, I will not want to eat it out of *hunger*. I may even find, in the moment, that I am averse to it, though I believe it to have qualities that would otherwise make it something that I would hunger for. And, likewise, in order for my hunger or thirst to subside, something about my *bodily state* must change. While it may eliminate my particular, hungry desire to eat a bowl of chocolate mousse if I come to believe that it is in fact a bowl of dung, this elimination of my particular desire is not an elimination of my *hunger* (as discussed by De Sousa 1990).

Fourth, appetites and emotions prompt motivations that differ in structure. Our appetitive desires are "consummatory": they aim to eliminate the unpleasant state that gives rise to them (De Sousa 1990, 216). Paradigmatic emotions are not like this. Though particular emotions, such as contempt or joy, may give rise to characteristic expressive actions (rolling my eyes in contempt or jumping for joy), they do not *aim* at *particular* actions at all (Hursthouse 1991). And even emotions such as anger, which are more closely tied to particular motivations, do not aim for their own elimination: anger may motivate someone to lash out in vengeance, seek compensation or address the wrong that has been done to them, but it does not aim for the subject to no longer be *angry*.

Again, the main difference between appetites and emotions I will focus on here is how the appetites *arise* and are *satisfied* in ways sensitive to a subject's bodily condition, rather than by being elicited by a subject's evaluative presentations, judgments, or construals of the world. Because they express a subject's values, and because they can have or are supported by propositional content, the emotions can be both rationally provoked and extinguished in ways that the appetites cannot. Should I learn that my dog in fact survived an accident that I had believed resulted in her death, my occurrent grief about my dog can be fully, and rationally, extinguished; should I learn that an unjust law has been repealed, the indignation it gave rise to can be fully, and rationally, extinguished. Again, this is not to deny that *aspects* of our appetites can be rationally intervened upon: I may, for example, lose my desire to eat any of the items in my refrigerator once I learn that it has all spoiled overnight after a blackout. But this belief will not alleviate or undermine my occurrent hunger, nor is my remaining hunger *irrational*. While a new belief might suppress or mask my occurrent hunger (perhaps by prompting an emotion such as anxiety or fear that masks or completely distracts me from *feeling* hungry), it will not *rationally* undermine it.

2. BOREDOM AS COGNITIVE APPETITE

Having contrasted the emotions with more familiar appetites such as thirst and hunger, we may already notice similarities between boredom and these appetites. Boredom, like hunger and thirst, can arise given a state of the subject and so, without being rationally responsive to her environment. After hours of attending to an otherwise interesting lecture, I may *grow* bored with it even though I simultaneously believe and would otherwise experience it as possessing qualities that, in general, engage my interests. And boredom, though able to take intentional objects, lacks the ability to take *propositions* as their objects—we are bored *by* things and people, bored *with* activities, but not bored *that* something has occurred or is taking place. And just like hunger and thirst and certain sexual desires, and unlike paradigmatic emotions, boredom is consummatory: it motivates us, principally, to alleviate itself.

But if experiences of hunger and thirst arise in response to bodily needs for nourishment, what need gives rise to the experience of boredom? I propose we understand boredom as partly constituted by a desire for cognitive stimulus, driven by the more general *need* for cognitive stimulus. We should understand cognitive stimulus broadly here: not just stimulating *thoughts*, but stimulating changes in perception, sensation, affect, and phenomenology in general. We can become bored of having the same kinds of conversations, of seeing the same color of paint on our walls, eating the same thing, listening to the same music, doing the same exercises, and so on. Just as we share our needs for food and drink with nonhuman animals, so we share with, at least some of them, a basic and primitive need for mental stimulus, and so, the disposition to feel bored.

This proposal captures many ordinary experiences of boredom, as well as certain philosophical observations about boredom: for example, the (perhaps mistaken) idea that vicious people are more *interesting* because of their seeming complexity, psychological opacity, and instability, while virtuous ones are more *boring* because of their relative psychological simplicity, transparency, or their adherence to rules that will determine their conduct;[11] the idea that means-end practical reasoning may inevitably lead to the state of boredom, perhaps partly because the content of one's ends has already been fully determined in advance.[12] And this understanding of boredom allows us to recognize the commonly observed connection between perceptions of *meaninglessness* and the experience of boredom.[13] When we experience activities, or perhaps all of human life, as just "one damned thing after another," or a cycle of repetitive activity culminating in nothing, this may give rise to a judgment that they are meaningless *and* to feelings of boredom. When we can see such activities as instead part of something that develops and progresses over time (lending them meaning through narrative restructuring) we may experience these activities now as both more meaningful, and less boring, because part of something beyond what we are currently experiencing, and so not fully predictable, or repetitive.[14]

We can, of course, experience predictability in ways other than feeling bored. For example, one may feel safe and in control given the predictability of a relationship, or a line of work, living in the suburbs, or sticking to a strict daily schedule. But such feelings are liable to turn into those of boredom once one begins to feel a growing and unsatisfied desire for *stimulating change*. Boredom can also be accompanied by other emotions that are sometimes taken to characterize the experience itself, but which, on this understanding of boredom, should be understood instead as higher-order emotional responses to our frustrated desire for stimulus. Should one think that there is some way to change the boring situation one is in (move to another country, meet new people, develop a new hobby), but believe that one should not act in this way, one may become restless, frustrated, or anxious as one's desire for mental stimulus grows while retaining some sense that there *is* a way to alleviate one's boredom that remains, frustratingly, just out of reach. One may come to feel trapped or suffocated by one's situation. Alternatively, in fully accepting that the situation *cannot* be changed or escaped one might come to feel *resigned*, and so, despondent in light of this undesirable, but unavoidable, predictability of our situation. One's boredom, in this case, may then be accompanied by weariness, detachment, melancholy, or depression.[15]

That boredom is a response to experienced predictability combined with an unsatisfied desire for mental stimulus will also make sense of why an agent's *history* with an object, activity, or situation may be sufficient to explain why it is that she is currently bored by it. First, familiarity with something over time will both render it less novel, while also increasing one's sense that it is something predictable—one has experienced it already, remembers what it is like to experience it, and can foresee what it will be like to experience it again. One's memories and future projections based on those memories will inform one's occurrent experience of boredom. But second, having engaged with something in the same way for some period of time, regardless of how interesting it may otherwise be, a person's desire for stimulus can become satiated. Her ability to take in more mental stimulus, and to notice salient changes in her experience, will be *depleted*. She may want no more of anything that she would otherwise continue to find genuinely engaging, just as she may no longer desire to eat even her favorite dish once she has eaten enough. Continued consumption of what she might otherwise find interesting may, if she is fully mentally satiated, become unpleasant.

Importantly, given that boredom can arise simply in response to a growing and unsatisfied desire for mental stimulus, episodes of boredom need not directly reflect one's values, or what it is that one finds meaningful. When one becomes bored by certain objects over time, this does not entail that such things will *no longer* be interesting to her at other times. It need not indicate that there isn't *more* about these objects would continue to engage her otherwise. And moreover, she might continue to care very deeply about these activities. But after days or weeks or years of engaging with them—writing a dissertation, perfecting one's jump shot, reading the same simple fable to her young child every bedtime—in the same sorts of ways, a person might find herself growing bored by what she cares about. This growing sense of boredom need not indicate that she is no longer concerned about what she is currently bored by. More mundanely she may just need a break, or a more varied set of activities, in order to return to them with renewed and refreshed "appetite" for them. And, likewise, one can be gripped and engaged by activities that one finds of little value or meaning at all, as long as they are able to satisfy this desire: constantly checking, for example, updates on a social media feed or news website, solving number or crossword puzzles (until, of course, these activities themselves become boring).

Consider this proposal in contrast to one offered by Roberts, who understands boredom as an emotion, understood as a concern-based construal of one's present situation or activity as "as dull, unstimulating, unfascinating, [or] unengaging" (Roberts 2003, 247). Given that emotions are, according to Roberts, responses that are relative to an agent's *concerns*, there must be some concern of hers expressed by her experiences of boredom. But Roberts, accommodating the idea that we can grow bored by things that we care about, does not treat boredom as directly expressive of one's evaluations of what one is bored by. Rather, he proposes that the defining proposition[16] for boredom is as follows:

It is very important for me to be interested, absorbed, to have my attention engaged, but everything I currently behold, and everything I currently might do, is uninteresting; may I soon be free from this state of mind. (248)

In other words, according to Roberts, boredom expresses how important it is for an agent to have certain kinds of mental states (to have her attention engaged), rather than others. But notice that a person's occurrent hunger, or thirst, involves no implicit claim that it is important to not be hungry or thirsty: one can be hungry without attributing any value to the satisfaction of this desire at all. This is what I am suggesting about boredom. We need not attribute to a bored person *either* that the situation or activity she is bored by is not of importance, nor must we attribute to her that she finds it important to have her attention engaged. And this is because what she is experiencing as boring may be motivated by her need for mental stimulus, and not given a concern she has to not be bored. Her boredom may grow, just as her hunger may grow, not because she finds it more *important* to be engaged rather than bored, or full rather than hungry. I suggest that Roberts's proposal picks out a *higher-order emotion* (such as impatience or frustration) that one feels in *response* to being bored, reflecting how much one values *not being in such a state*, rather than boredom itself.

By highlighting the similarity of boredom to our bodily appetites and contrasting them to the emotions, I am also suggesting that we see it as less rational and less connected with our values than our emotions are. But importantly, I am not claiming that experiences of boredom are entirely *insensitive* to our beliefs and judgments in the way that our bodily appetites are. Again, on the proposal I offer, when boredom is felt about an object, it is in response to an experience of its intentional object as predictable, paired with a desire for mental stimulus. But our experiences of boredom can be exacerbated by our thoughts about our situation: I might not just *find* myself bored, but, upon reflection, judge that the situation or activity I am in *is boring*. When this occurs, I am both experiencing and thinking of the activity or situation (perhaps mistakenly) as *predictable:* monotonous, repetitive, bland, and so on. Whatever will follow will just be *more of the same*, and so, unlikely to yield a novel and stimulating experience. Believing our situation to be predictable, along with experiencing it as such, we may become motivated to pay even less attention, and so become less able to notice any changes that do happen, or to register their significance—and so, as is commonly observed, boredom may beget more boredom. I may find myself bored by a movie, tell myself that the movie *is boring*, and because of this, be less inclined to attend to it in a way that may render watching it a more stimulating experience.

Likewise, to the extent that I can alleviate my experience of something as predictable through my thoughts that it is not in fact predictable, I may be able, to that extent, to alleviate my occurrent boredom. Indeed, this is how we can encourage ourselves to persist with something in the face of our feelings of boredom: we try to remind ourselves of the possible complexity that we are not yet sensitive to or aware of, we might also remind ourselves of the importance of the task at hand. If these kinds of judgment encourage us to shift our attention or draw on our imagination so that we begin to see the object in a new light or notice things about it that we did not notice before, we may to that extent alleviate our occurrent sense of boredom with it. Being a *cognitive* appetite, the relevant change needed is a cognitive one. Thus, to the extent that a person is able to occupy her mind with her own mental activity, to that extent she will be less susceptible to boredom in situations where her environment or activity fails to be sufficiently stimulating.

But importantly, the cognitive changes that can alleviate or exacerbate one's boredom are unlike changes to an emotional state given a rational transition in one's beliefs. If my judgment that a conversation is boring leads me to pay less attention to it, this may exacerbate my boredom because I will now experience it as even *less* stimulating, given my lack of attention. If, in an attempt to keep myself engaged with a boring conversation I imagine my interlocutor standing on his head, or try counting up and categorizing his verbal tics, this may alleviate my boredom not by *reasoning* with it, but by *satisfying* it.[17]

Because the desire for mental stimulus can grow and wane independently of our values, we can also find ourselves in situations where reminding ourselves of how much we value the boring activity we're engaged with does little to change our experience of boredom. Moreover, not only may our experiences of boredom be insensitive to our values or concerns, but they also may be insensitive to our judgments about what things are *boring* or *interesting*, or *worth* being bored or interested by. Again, if my desire for mental stimulus is satisfied (perhaps after a long day of gripping and challenging conversation), it may not matter how convinced I am that the newest novel by my favorite author will be gripping and fascinating. I may not be inclined to be engaged by it, because I no longer want to be engaged by anything. I may instead find myself *averse* to its complexity and novelty, preferring to watch a familiar and predictable television show, or play a simple game on my phone, instead. And certain things can capture our attention and engage our interest, without being things that we are otherwise concerned about, and independently of our reflective and more developed judgments about what activities are *worth* our interest. A person might be disappointed that all there is to watch in an airport lounge is a spectacle-laden television show that he has no deeper interest in, or concern for, and that he judges to be boring. But nonetheless, he may find that his *boredom* is alleviated by watching it, even if *he* is dissatisfied by watching it.

3. THE ETHICAL SIGNIFICANCE OF BOREDOM

In understanding boredom as an appetite, rather than emotion, I have empha-sized the respects in which it bears a less direct relationship to an agent's values and reason than the emotions do. At the same time, in everyday ethical discourse we assess and criticize one another and ourselves for finding certain things boring when we think that they should generate and captivate one's interest, instead. We may hope, for example, that we can show our children that certain people, games, intellectual inquiries, artistic creations, or aspects of the natural world are of "genuine" or "deeper" interest and think that their current boredom with such things is the result of a regrettable failure of appreciation or a form of shallowness. We might lament that the culture we live in has come to find certain traditions, bodies of knowledge, or objects too boring to attend to, learn about, let alone engage with in any serious manner, and our lamentation may not simply be because this may result in the *loss* of such things, but because of what it suggests about our culture.

Initially, it may seem that these ethical dimensions of boredom may sit uneasily with understanding it as akin to an appetite. Basic hunger and thirst, given their value indifference, are not *themselves* the kind of attitudes that we ethically assess. But though I've suggested that boredom has a less direct con-nection to our values and concerns than our paradigmatic emotions, we can nonetheless vindicate this kind of familiar ethical discourse. To show this, I will draw on resources from Aristotle: in particular, on a distinction he draws between what he calls "common" or "natural" appetites, and "peculiar" or "particular" appetites, in the context of his discussion of the virtue of temper-ance.[18] But before doing so, I will note some complexities in how it is that we assess ourselves, and one another, in light of our experiences of boredom.

First, some assessments of boredom seem to rely just on the idea of a fail-ure of accuracy in our experiences of boredom. There just *are* some things that are more stimulating than others: in general, going for a walk or reading the news is more stimulating than watching paint dry; being able to travel freely is more stimulating than being in quarantine. But importantly, the kind of accuracy here is not limited to a bare sensitivity to things that are boring, and things that are not. It is a kind of accuracy that can be honed through, among other things, the development of skills and the gaining of knowledge needed for proper *appreciation* of an object, activity, or situation. Certain objects or activities are less predictable than others, even though they do not seem so at first. They are open ended or complex. They have depths and significance that are revealed only through a more sustained and informed engagement with them, along with the development of certain capacities and competencies. And so, a person who is bored by such things may lack a particular competency, body of knowledge, or dispositions of attention, patience, and sensitivity that would make these complexities more salient to her. Perhaps she simply doesn't understand the object or activity, and though she tries to, she finds that her experience with the object does not change in any significant way. If she simply cannot understand it or engage with it more deeply or in a novel way, she may grow bored of her repeated experiences of being left in the dark and become motivated to do something she finds more easily stimulating instead.

Second, in a pluralistic and liberal society, we recognize the importance for individuals to cultivate their *own* interests and appreciate the plurality of differences in what a person finds boring or interesting. A parent may be pleased that her teenager is passionate about the intricate details of Premier League soccer, or the lives of the pharaohs, even though given differences in their tastes and sensibilities, *she* finds such things exceedingly boring. But, being a good liberal, she may think it is perfectly fine, even good, for her son to develop the competencies needed to appreciate just those things that he is interested in, while finding other interesting activities and objects boring. Certain matters of taste are simply that.

Nonetheless, there are limits to our liberalism and appreciation for plurality. Although a parent may understand and find fully intelligible that her teenager is engrossed by the gritty details of serial killings or mass murders (in a way that she may not if he were, without further explanation, fascinated for days on end reading old phonebooks), she may not only notice a difference in their interests but be disappointed or alarmed that this is the kind of thing that draws his attention and try to encourage a different kind of subject matter to turn his attention toward instead. Thus, third, we also seem to think that there are things which are—to put it in a way that must be spelled out—*worth* being interested in, and things that are *not* worth being interested in, where these judgments do not line up with our judgments of what sorts of things immediately grasp and engage us or would, upon closer inspection and with the right kind of skills and knowledge, be able to do. We do not assess a person's dispositions of boredom only for their *accuracy*, even richly understood; we also assess them in light of other *values*. Even if we can fully understand that a certain activity is interesting in this first sense, we might nonetheless think that one shouldn't *cultivate an interest* in it. This kind of assessment is sometimes expressed by the perhaps priggish-sounding claims that something is, in fact, "not worthy of one's interest," or that one "ought" to be bored by it.

To summarize, we should strive to accommodate these three dimensions of our ethical assessments of boredom and interest: (i) that we think of a person as able to *refine* or *improve* her responses of boredom and interest in order for her boredom and interest to be more *accurate*; (ii) that we recognize, and appreciate, sheer differences in taste between people that will be reflected in their dispositions of boredom and interest; and (iii) that there are some things we think of as not being *worth* a person's interest, even if they possess qualities which render them more interesting rather than boring.

Consider now Aristotle's discussion of the virtue of temperance. According to Aristotle, "common" appetites are for nourishment and repletion, in general, and will tend to vanish when they are satisfied. "Peculiar" appetites, in contrast, have more peculiar or particular content: they are not desires for nourishment and repletion in general, but are appetites for particular forms of nourishment rather than others. Such appetites are not universal in content: people differ in tastes, and so will desire different kinds of food and drink. And when a person desires a particular object that is the object of her particular appetite, she will be principally motivated by the potential appetitive *pleasure* that it will bring her, and not by its potential to satisfy her hunger, though it may also do that. This is why we often eat far beyond our needs for bodily nourishment: we come to indulge in the pleasures of dining, and not just in satisfying our general appetite for food.

When it comes to our common appetite for nourishment in general, the most we can hope for is that we are physiologically equipped in the right kinds of ways: that our hunger and thirst will operate so that we are disposed to sufficiently nourish ourselves. Importantly, a person whose common appetites are defective to the point that they fail to properly nourish themselves is not *vicious* or *akratic*, but what Aristotle calls brutish or bestial; they are *dysfunctional* rather than subject to character assessment. In contrast, the virtue of temperance can, and should in the virtuous, come to govern and shape our particular or peculiar appetites. This is because in developing our tastes we seek not just the satisfaction of our needs, but also, the *pleasures* of eating and drinking. Thus, our appetites *can* reflect our characters, by reflecting how much we value the kind of pleasures that eating particular things affords us.

According to Aristotle, a *profligate* person enjoys appetitive pleasures too much, consumes what he should not, having (mistakenly, Aristotle thinks) come to value the physical pleasures of dining too much. *Insensible* people, in contrast, enjoy too little of these physical pleasures, perhaps restricting themselves to just what it would take to replenish their appetites, and only to objects that would be consistent with their health. In Aristotle's characteristic way of acknowledging and accommodating rather than wholly rejecting our animal natures, the *temperate* person *will* properly value and so enjoy certain appetitive pleasures, to some extent, at the right time, in the right ways, regardless of whether or not they are conducive to his health. He will sometimes delight in his peculiar or particular appetites just for the sheer delight of it, as long as these pleasures do not conflict badly with other ethical concerns. For Aristotle, this will rule out peculiar appetites that are, in themselves, either ignoble nor beyond one's means. By introducing the values of health, affordability, and ignobility, we see how other values are incorporated into the virtue of temperance: one will have to, in developing the virtue of temperance, exercise one's judgments about *what kinds of peculiar appetitive pleasures* one should indulge in and learn to appreciate further, and which ones one should not.

We can now bring these resources to bear when it comes to the ethical significance of the appetite of boredom. Boredom arises given our *common appetite* for cognitive stimulus. To have this appetite at all is ethically neutral. But we also have *particular* desires for cognitive stimulus, which reflect our particular tastes and give rise to pleasures that are not identical with the pleasure of satisfying one's general need for cognitive or mental stimulus. When it comes to the particular appetites of hunger, some of us will enjoy eating cake, others pie; when it comes to the particular appetite for mental stimulus, some of us will enjoy reading, others playing sports, others playing video games. We are not motivated, in general, to develop and gratify these interests *because* we are interested in satisfying our need for mental stimulus; they provide us with a different kind of pleasure (the pleasures of learning, creation, or entertainment), and they *also* satisfy our need for mental stimulus.

In cultivating our particular appetites, we can become more refined in our sensibility as we develop our taste. We might encourage a child, or a friend, to try tasting something again, paying particular attention to certain aspects of the object they currently find unappetizing in order to discern what might be delicious about it. In just the same way, we might encourage her to focus her attention in a particular way, or to see something in a particular light, in order for her to see what is interesting about something she currently finds boring. A person must develop certain skills, competencies, understanding to be able to fully appreciate something that she initially finds boring. But for both kinds of appetite (bodily and cognitive), we recognize that even with the requisite competencies and understanding, there will remain brute differences in personal taste, as well as objects that will successfully satisfy both without being the objects of a person's *peculiar*, and more developed, appetitive desires.

And drawing this distinction between common and particular appetites will also accommodate the other dimensions of ethical assessment of a person's dispositions of boredom. For Aristotle, the values that are important for a temperate person to be sensitive to include those of appetitive pleasure, frugality, health, and an avoidance of "ignoble" pleasures. For both *our* virtues of appetitive temperance, and "cognitive temperance," we will have to take into consideration what *our* background values are and should be, and how these should inform what kind of pleasures—both gustatory *and* cognitive— we should indulge in. Some of us will shape and develop our particular tastes around considerations about what it would be healthy for us to consume, what would be more sustainable to consume, perhaps avoiding what would be cruel or shameful to consume or enjoy, and so, not want to eat just *anything* that would successfully satisfy our hunger. Though it might both satisfy our hunger *and* yield appetitive pleasure to dine on ortolan buntings or sea turtles, we may not think we should *cultivate* our enjoyment of such things. The same can be said for objects of potential interest: though it may successfully alleviate a person's boredom, *and* provide other kinds of cognitive pleasure to watch snuff films or pick fights with strangers at bars we may (again, depending on our further moral and evaluative commitments) think it best to *refrain* from developing the kind of sensibility that would be especially, or solely, mentally gratified by these kinds of activities, no matter how gripping or stimulating they are.

4. CONCLUSION

By thinking of boredom as a cognitive appetite, I have resisted thinking of it as an emotion which straightforwardly expresses a person's values or what she finds important and have provided an explanation for why experiences of boredom can be insensitive to reason in ways that differ from how our emotions may be. At the same time, I have tried to do justice to the many ways in which we may assess one another and ourselves for how our dispositions of boredom and interest express themselves.

More generally, by focusing on boredom I have hoped to bring to light how our mental lives, embodied as they are, have needs that are similar to those possessed by nonhuman animals that are physiologically similar to us. While we gain from seeing human cognition as itself emotionally and motivationally laden we should not, in doing so, conceive of those motivations as themselves always tied to our lives as rational, epistemic agents. Alongside our needs to understand, and alongside sustenance for our bodies, we also need basic forms of mental or cognitive sustenance. As Harry Frankfurt observes:

> What our preference for avoiding boredom manifests is therefore not merely a casual resistance to more or less innocuous discomfort. It expresses a quite primitive urge for psychic survival. I think it is appropriate to construe this urge as a variant of the universal and elemental instinct for self-preservation. (2004, 54)

I concur and have considered one way to understand this idea by characterizing the particular urge, or need, that gives rise to boredom. It is not merely painful or frustrating, but *damaging* to a person, should she be unable to meet this need, and stave off her boredom. We can torture or abuse a person or an animal by not providing her with something to alleviate her boredom; we can be bored stiff or bored to tears; and we can be bored, *literally*, out of our minds.[19]

NOTES

1. The view that emotions are "concern-based construals" has been prominently defended by Robert C. Roberts, among others. But given that I am concerned here with any view of the emotions which captures their direct connection with a subject's *values*, relevant views include those defended by Martha Nussbaum (2001) and Bennett Helm (2001), though on those views, emotions are constituted not by *construals* but rather, more judgment-like attitudes.

2. See, for example, Goldie (2012), Morton (2010), and Stocker (2004).

3. Also drawing on Aristotle's discussion of temperance, Heather Battaly (2010) has argued for the virtue of *epistemic temperance*, and the related vices of *epistemic self-indulgence*, and *epistemic insensibility*. Epistemic temperance, on this view, is essentially about having the right kind of relationships toward objects of knowledge. Importantly, though Battaly mentions the existence of "cognitive pleasures," her proposal restricts itself to just those emotions that are relevant to obtaining *knowledge*. Given my discussion, we will need to distinguish a kind of temperance that is different from both Aristotle's conception of temperance (which restricts itself to nonmental bodily pleasures) but is not *epistemic* temperance.

4. There is, notoriously, much disagreement about what the emotions are, and taxonomic issues may depend less on "carving nature at its joints" than on what antecedent theoretical interests one has. I will not here assume that there is *one correct theory* of the emotions that cleanly distinguishes them from the appetites. And so, I will not argue that, given the truth of this theory of the emotions, boredom is an appetite and not an emotion. One may read my conclusions here as suggesting, instead, that boredom is not a "paradigmatic" emotion, according to a standard way of characterizing what paradigmatic emotions have in common, or that that this view of the emotions is limited in ways highlighted by this discussion of boredom.

5. I take the terminology of value-suffused/value-indifferent from Nussbaum (2001), who draws on Plato's discussion of the appetites in *The Republic* in her discussion of the distinction between emotions and appetites. For a more detailed, historically focused discussion of this distinction in Plato and Aristotle, see Lorenz (2006).

6. According to D'Arms and Jacobson, the fit of an emotion is a matter of its "accuracy," where they understand accuracy here as limited to evidential considerations. For a critical response to D'Arms and Jacobson's conception of emotional accuracy, see Yao (Ms.).

7. *The Republic*, 438a; 437d–439a.

8. Thus, to realize that one in fact has no reasons for one's anger or grief puts rational pressure on one's emotions; this is not the case with the appetites, which are not dispositionally responsive to reasons at all.

9. Of course, there are familiar forms of emotional *akrasia*, in which a change in *beliefs* doesn't fully extinguish the emotion. But in these cases, either what remains

are just the *physiological* markers of the emotion (a tremble, a pain in the chest) or there is a form of *irrational* fear or anger remaining in spite of my beliefs. In contrast, my remaining hunger or thirst is not *irrational*, it is *a*rational.

10. Our appetites can be aroused and whetted by things external to us, but in many of those cases what is aroused is not *thirst* or *hunger*, but an attraction to the particular pleasure we are being enticed by; when we do experience such things as arousing the *feelings* of thirst or hunger, the hunger or thirst was *already* there, perhaps masked or not yet noticed. This is why it is best to focus on the case where one is already satisfied.

11. For a discussion of this idea, and an argument that an adequate conception of what it takes to be a good person would, in fact, reveal a level of psychological complexity and inner conflict that is interesting, see Vice (2005).

12. For the relationship between boredom and practical reasoning as instrumental reasoning, see Milgram (2004).

13. As given voice in analytic philosophy by, for example, Taylor (2018) and Williams (1973).

14. However, the connection can come apart in ways explicable by boredom's more basic responsiveness to predictability. Meaninglessness is not always boring, and meaningfulness not always interesting. There are meaningful experiences which may nonetheless be boring (think, for example, of certain rituals or ceremonies that are steeped with meaning but are nonetheless repetitive and predictable), and those that are meaningless, but which may alleviate rather than exacerbate our boredom (think, for example, of certain forms of sensationalistic entertainment, or ways in which inane websites can be designed to capture and hold attention).

15. O'Brien (2014) rightly criticizes certain discussions of boredom for overlooking the *restlessness* of boredom, while overemphasizing the feeling of *weariness*, which he thinks is closer to languor, listlessness, or torpor. My account can explain why, however, one might closely associate these emotions with boredom: it will depend on whether or not we are imagining a scenario in which the bored person has the hope that her situation can be changed. If, for example, one senses that the situation is *inescapably* boring, then one's boredom is likely to express itself in feelings of listlessness or melancholic despondency, rather than in feelings of restlessness that presume the possibility of escape from one's boring circumstance.

16. One might object that defining propositions *over-intellectualize* the emotions, but it is important that for Roberts, the proposition that distinguishes a particular emotion from another is not to be understood as manifested by thoughts possessed by the agent who feels the emotion in question. They serve as just rough ways to characterize the "construals" that constitute the emotional response.

17. Thank you to Andreas Elpidorou for encouraging me to clarify and develop this point.

18. My discussion here draws on Charles M. Young's (1988) reading of Aristotle. Aristotle draws the distinction between common and peculiar appetites in the *Nicomachean Ethics* (III.11, 1118b8-15).

19. I have benefited from discussion with panelists and audience members about a related paper on the "epistemic appetites" at the 2020 Central APA in Chicago, in a

session on the "Ethics and Aesthetics of the Self." I am also grateful for discussions with Francey Russell, George Sher, Robert Smithson, Samuel Reis-Dennis, and for comments from Andreas Elpidorou.

REFERENCES

Aristotle, W. D. Ross, and Lesley Brown. 2009. *The Nicomachean Ethics*. Oxford: Oxford University Press.

Battaly, Heather. 2010. "Epistemic Self-Indulgence." *Metaphilosophy* 41, no. 1–2: 214–34.

D'arms, Justin, and Daniel Jacobson. 2000. "The Moralistic Fallacy: On the 'Aappropriateness' of Emotions." *Philosophical and Phenomenological Research* 61, no. 1: 65–90. https://doi.org/10.2307/2653403.

De Sousa, Ronald. 1990. *The Rationality of Emotion*: Cambridge, MA: MIT Press.

Frankfurt, Harry G. 2004. *The Reasons of Love*. Princeton: Princeton University Press.

Goldie, Peter. 2012. "Loss of Affect in Intellectual Activity." *Emotion Review* 4, no. 2: 122–26.

Helm, Bennett W. 2001. *Emotional Reason: Deliberation, Motivation, and the Nature of Value*. Cambridge: Cambridge University Press.

Hursthouse, Rosalind. 1991. "Arational Actions." *The Journal of Philosophy* 88, no. 2: 57–68.

Lorenz, Hendrik. 2006. *The Brute Within: Appetitive Desire in Plato and Aristotle*. Oxford: Oxford University Press.

McDowell, John. 1985. "Values and Secondary Qualities." In *Morality and Objectivity*, edited by Ted Honderich, 110–29. London: Routledge and Kegan Paul.

Millgram, Elijah. 2004. "On Being Bored out of Your Mind." *Proceedings of the Aristotelian Society* 104, no. 1: 165–86.

Morton, Adam. "Epistemic Emotions." 2010. In *The Oxford Handbook of Philosophy of Emotion*, edited by Peter Goldie, 385–99. Oxford: Oxford University Press.

Nussbaum, Martha C. 2001. *Upheavals of Thought: The Intelligence of Emotions*. Cambridge: Cambridge University Press.

O'Brien, Wendell. 2014. "Boredom." *Analysis* 74, no. 2: 236–44.

Plato, and Allan Bloom. 1968. *The Republic*. New York: Basic Books.

Roberts, Robert C. 2003. *Emotions: An essay in Aid of Moral Psychology*. Cambridge: Cambridge University Press.

Stocker, Michael. 2004. "Some Considerations about Intellectual Desire and Emotions." In *Thinking About Feeling: Contemporary Philosophers on Emotions,* edited by Robert C. Solomon, 135–48. New York: Oxford University Press.

Taylor, Richard. 2018. "The Meaning of Life." In *Exploring Philosophy: An Introductory Anthology* (6th Edition), edited by Steven M. Cahn, 679–87. New York: Oxford University Press.

Velleman, J. David. 2008. "A Theory of Value." *Ethics* 118, no. 3: 410–36.

Vice, Samantha. 2005. "On the Tedium of the Good." *Ethical Theory and Moral Practice* 8, no. 4: 459–76.

Williams, Bernard. 1973. "The Makropulos Case: Reflections on the Tedium of Immortality." In *Problems of the Self: Philosophical Papers 1956–1973*, 82–100. Cambridge: Cambridge University Press.

Yao, Vida. (Ms.) "Virtue and Emotional Accuracy." (Unpublished manuscript.)

Young, Charles M. 1988. "Aristotle on Temperance." *The Philosophical Review* 97, no. 4: 521–42.

Chapter 10

Boredom, Interest, and Meaning in Life

Wendell O'Brien

Boredom and meaning in life, or, rather, meaninglessness in life, are intimately linked. Although this link has been mentioned by many philosophers who write about meaning in life, the precise character of this link has not been articulated in detail. The link, however, seems to me to be significant and in need of further exploration. It may reveal something important about boredom, or at least reinforce the importance of something already noticed about it, but perhaps underappreciated. It may also reveal something central to meaning (or meaningfulness) in life which is usually absent from philosophical analyses. As the present chapter argues, an investigation into the relationship between boredom and meaning in life reveals that interest is a crucial element relevant both to boredom and to meaning.

This chapter is tentative. It raises questions, problems, and possibilities more than it provides answers and solutions. My hope is that others will be prompted to address the questions it raises and show what is wrong with the answers I do give, if I give any.

1. BOREDOM

Six years ago, I analyzed boredom as an unpleasant mental state characterized by a lack of interest in something to which one is subjected. This lack, I argued, is accompanied by (or involves) weariness and restlessness, which it either causes or is caused by (O'Brien 2014a, 237–38). I now believe that this analysis and other things I said in the article in which it appeared require revision. I am not going to present a new analysis in this chapter, but I will indicate what I am unhappy with in the old analysis and the article in which it appeared.

I claimed that boredom was just one sort of thing, that my analysis covered *all* cases of it, and that anything it didn't capture wasn't really boredom at all but something else. Further reflection and the works of several philosophers and novelists have convinced me that I was wrong.

I now think that there are two significantly different kinds of boredom (and possibly two distinct senses of the *word* "boredom"—two different concepts). These are "situative" boredom and "profound" boredom. Analytic philosophers usually focus on the former and continental philosophers (Heidegger 1983; Svendsen 2005) and novelists (Bernanos 1982; Moravia 1999; Pessoa 2003) seem to be concerned primarily with the latter.

Situative boredom is really what I analyzed in my chapter. It is boredom that arises from the situation one is in or one's attitude toward that situation. One is being subjected to something in which one has no interest. But one does *have* interests; it's just that she can't pursue them at the moment because she is trapped in some situation, say, a departmental meeting, which is as dry as dust. In extreme cases of situative boredom, one *usually* feels trapped in such a situation. To have this condition is to have a chronic disposition to be bored in the situative way almost all the time and by just about everything—to be bored with *existence*. Generally, though, those plagued by this malady *want* to have interests. They tend to seek things that will not just interest them, but excite and thrill them; the things they find normally don't do the trick. This existential condition is extreme and is often called "boredom proneness" (Elpidorou 2020, 45–46).

So situative boredom itself may usefully be divided into two kinds, on the basis of its frequency (and maybe severity). One of these is the sort of basic common boredom that most of us experience from time to time, relatively briefly. The other kind of situative boredom is extreme boredom proneness.

What I failed to bring to the forefront in my earlier chapter was the motivational or propelling character of situative boredom. The work of Andreas Elpidorou has convinced me of this. I did say, in the chapter, that when I am bored in the basic, common (situative) way "I lack energy, interest, and patience to attend to what is at hand; *but I do have energy to burn, and I long for something else to burn it on*" (O'Brien 2014a, 239, emphasis added). I should have included something like that in the basic analysis of boredom. At the time, I was thinking that the restlessness and unpleasantness of boredom imply it, but maybe they don't, since they may be present in profound boredom, in which there is no tendency to be propelled to do or seek anything.

In profound boredom one lacks interest in everything and does not feel propelled to find interest in anything. One is, in a way, unpleasantly "becalmed," has no interest in anything, and despairs of finding anything that will capture one's interest and attention in any way. Restlessness and unpleasantness may be there, but they provide no motivation or propulsion to move into a better state. Profound boredom is, or is like, malaise, world-weariness, *tedium vitae*, hopelessness, and deep dark depression.

I'm inclined to think that profound boredom also comes in two varieties which, like the two kinds of situative boredom, are distinguished by their frequency and severity. One of these would be the kind one undergoes when one has a relatively brief experience of it. The other would be a chronic, continual condition in which one is profoundly bored just about all the time.

As I've indicated, everyone, or nearly everyone (even the normal person— if such a creature exists), experiences brief situative boredom occasionally. It seems to be unavoidable in the kind of human life we must live. But I also think that there are occasions when the typical person—even if she is English or American—experiences profound boredom, or something like it. These occasions occur when you are in the depths of depression (for which you may take medication that sometimes doesn't work too well) or when you are in a state of withdrawal from intemperate use of drugs and alcohol. On these occasions, you might lack interest in everything and feel that there are no interests worth pursuing or seeking. It's all despair and hopelessness.

I want to stress that *lack of interest* is a necessary condition of both kinds of boredom. In situative boredom you lack interest in what is at hand (whatever it might be if you suffer from extreme boredom proneness). In profound boredom, as in extreme boredom proneness, you lack interest in nearly everything. In fact, lack of interest is the hallmark of boredom. Patricia Meyer Spacks puts it succinctly: "Interesting means not boring; the boring is the not interesting" (Spacks 1995, 116).

One kind of case that is noteworthy is that of a person who must, day after day, do uninteresting, mindless, monotonous, or repetitive work in the factory or the accounting department. She has interests, but she is never given the opportunity to pursue them. She gets no vacation time. She's always stuck doing boring work she has to do in order to bring home the bacon. What's interesting to me about her is that, although she is bored all the time, she might not be boredom prone at all, and she may never fall into profound boredom. She just has to endure continually the sort of situative boredom that most of us have to deal with only from time to time, and usually only relatively briefly.

2. MEANING IN LIFE

In the dictionaries, as well as in philosophical analyses of "the meaning of life" and "meaning in life," the idea of "meaning" is almost always treated as a notion having something to do with (a) significance, importance, what matters (objectively, or to somebody) or (b) purpose, point, or goal (and maybe a plan to achieve it). Sometimes, too, the idea of love or care or attachment appears.

Here are the relevant *OED* definitions of "meaning," "meaningful," and "meaningfulness."

"Meaning" (n) is:

1a. the significance, purpose, underlying truth, etc., of something; 1b. significance, import; implication; . . . 1d. something which gives one a sense of purpose, value, etc., esp. of a metaphysical or spiritual kind; the (perceived) purpose of existence or of a person's life. Frequently in *the meaning of life*.

"Meaningful" (adj.) is:

a. full of meaning or expression, significant; communicating something that is not explicitly or directly expressed; b. having a serious, important, or recognizable quality or purpose.

"Meaningless" (adj.) is "without meaning or signification; devoid of expression; without purpose."

Recent philosophers—I can speak of only a few of them, but those I don't mention usually say things in the same vein as those I do speak of—who have ventured an analysis of the concepts of "meaning," "meaningful," "meaningless," and so on, or who have provided (or said things that suggest) conceptions or theories of meaning, have given us the following. Robert Nozick distinguishes several modes, senses, and kinds of meaning. All the relevant ones have to do with importance, significance, and mattering (Nozick 1981, 574–75). He goes on to characterize meaning as a matter of connecting with things beyond oneself and transcending limits, since that's the way to make one's life matter (Nozick 1981, 594–95). Thomas Nagel usually conceives of meaning as really mattering; something is (really) meaningful if and only if it really matters—maybe cosmically, or (at least) in a way that requires no further reasons or justification (Nagel 1979, 11–23; Nagel 1987, 95–101). According to Harry Frankfurt, as I understand him, to live a meaningful life is to have final ends, purposes one cares deeply about, and to engage in activities that are means to the achievement of those ends and purposes (Frankfurt 1999, 84–85). Julian Young takes a meaningful life to be one that possesses a life project (Young 2014, xiv), and therefore, I take it, has some point or purpose, and a plan of some kind for realizing it. Thaddeus Metz offers a pluralist, family resemblance, account of the concept of meaning in life. Meaning has to do with ends most worth pursuing for their own sake, with transcending one's animal nature, and with esteem and admiration of things in life that merit them—or with some or all the above (Metz 2013, 34). Still, Metz too regards "important," "significant," "matters" and "has a point" as *synonyms* of "meaningful" (Metz 2013, 18). I myself have characterized the notion of meaning as ambiguous and possibly vague. "In asking about the meaning of life, one may be asking about the essence of life, about life's purpose, about whether and how anything matters, or a host of other things" (O'Brien 2014b). Mine, I guess, is (or was) a kind of "hodgepodge" view of meaning.

In philosophy there is an ongoing debate about whether meaning has an objective component. Some, perhaps the majority, argue that it does. Others argue that meaningfulness is an entirely subjective thing.

I do not want to get involved in that debate here. No doubt it is important, but (in this chapter) I am not concerned with the question of whether meaning has an "objective" element. I neither affirm nor deny that it does. And— though I do not view them as unimportant—I am not interested here in vexing questions about whether God or something supernatural, cosmic, or infinite has anything to do with meaningfulness.

What I *am* concerned with is the *subjective* aspect of meaning—in a "sense" of meaningfulness, a "feeling" of meaningfulness, or a life (or part of it) that "seems" meaningful. My concern is something like what Thomas Nagel has in mind when he speaks of a "feeling of significance" your life might have (even if it really isn't significant at all) (Nagel 1987, 97). My question about meaning is: What is required for, or what is involved in, the subjective component of meaning? Or, stated otherwise, what is needed in order for one's life (or some portion of it) to *feel* or *seem* meaningful?

Whether or not it has an objective component, I'm inclined to think that meaningfulness, in most cases, has *some* subjective aspect, that there is *something it is like* to live a meaningful life, or to go through a meaningful period, to be engaged in something that has meaning for you. The idea that a life could be meaningful even though its subject feels that her life is meaningless, empty, pointless, dull, and so forth seems implausible to me. If it *is* possible for a life or part of it to be meaningful for entirely objective reasons, without any subjective sense of meaning, then that sort of meaningful life is not my concern in this chapter.

Although I have been speaking of it as a feeling of *meaningfulness*, I don't think the subjective element must involve *explicitly* any thought about meaning or meaningfulness. It may well be the case, however, that one living a life with this element in it would usually, on reflection, answer the question "Are you living a meaningful life?" by saying (sincerely) "Yes." Mental or emotional states of, for example, interest, engagement, absorption, attraction, fulfillment, love, and such may well be enough for subjective meaning. Wolf makes this point clearly, and I think she is right (Wolf 2010, 111–12). Which particular subjective states are involved in meaning is something I will explore below. Right now, I don't want to rule any of them out.

A (subjectively) meaningful *life*, I take it, is one in which there are many slices of it that seem meaningful (or absorbing, fulfilling, etc.). I don't know whether *most* slices have to seem like that, but on the whole, the life must feel meaningful, or feel some way which would give reason to the one living the life to say, on reflection, that it feels meaningful.

Finally, here, I should add that I am concerned with (a sense of) meaning in an *individual*'s life, not with the meaning in (or the meaning of) life in general.

3. DISMISSAL OF CONCEPTIONS OF MEANING IN LIFE ON GROUNDS OF BOREDOM

One rarely finds a definition or an analysis of "meaning," "meaningful," or "meaningfulness" that mentions anything like "interest," "absence of boredom," "interesting," or "not boring." But, as Metz observes (Metz 2013, 134–35), in actual recent philosophical discussion of what the meaning of (or in) life might be, accounts of meaning are often rejected if they recommend a life that is *boring*, or devoid of much that is in any way of *interest*, to the subject of its life.

Bernard Williams in effect dismisses certain views of meaning by appealing to the idea that a boring life cannot be meaningful (Williams 1973, 82–83, 89). Susan Wolf does the same kind of thing, contrasting a meaningful life with one that is boring (Wolf, 2010, 9, 17, 111–12). Other philosophers have followed suit. Julian Young, for instance, rejects certain conceptions of a meaningful life by observing that a life lived in accordance with those conceptions would be intolerably boring. The main problem with the life of Camus's absurd hero, he says, is that it is "a life of deadly tedium, a life of *boredom*" (Young 2014, 197). And Young states: "A life the overall character of which is boredom cannot be one that is worth living" (Young 2014, xiv).

4. MEANING IN LIFE AS INTEREST OR ABSENCE OF BOREDOM

What is going on here? Is it possible that "meaningful" has taken on a sense that amounts to something like "interesting" or "not boring"?

I am entertaining this idea. Perhaps, on its subjective side, meaning in life, in one sense at least, should be conceived, not in terms of importance or significance, nor in terms of point, purpose, or plan, but in terms of *interest*. A meaningful life, or part of life, is an *interesting* life, one *not boring* to the one living it. If one were brave enough to offer an analytic-style account of meaning, one might suggest that a life is subjectively meaningful if and only if it is interesting to the one living it. There are some reasons—admittedly not at all conclusive—for such an analysis.

First, there are objections on grounds of boredom to conceptions of meaning in life presented above. These objections suggest that—whatever account they may give of the concept of meaning—those who raise the objections really have, maybe unconsciously, the idea that the meaningful is the interesting.

Second, there is what my own ear tells me about boredom, interest, and meaning in the common talk of laypeople—where I live in the United States, at least. In standard, daily, ordinary talk, people frequently contrast meaning and boredom, and say things that suggest they think of the meaningful as the interesting. I find this in flea markets, peddlers' malls, meetings, and conversations with people on my street who want to talk about nothing but rocks.

Third, for what it's worth, there is my own experience. Normally, I am deeply interested in one thing or another, and then my life seems quite meaningful, or I would sincerely say it seems so if I were asked about it. There are, however, periods—brief and rare, thank goodness—when I am unable to find anything interesting, and in those periods life feels meaningless and not worth living.

Fourth, some writers worthy of being taken seriously have suggested something like the suggestion I have offered. Schopenhauer, for example, says that "Boredom is nothing other than the sensation of the emptiness of existence" (Schopenhauer 1970, 53). Emptiness, I think, is equivalent to meaninglessness, or very near it, anyway. So maybe we can construe what Schopenhauer says as the claim that boredom is the feeling of meaninglessness. William James points out that mere instinctive curiosity about, for example, what the next day's newspaper will contain can be a preventative to suicide and make life worth living from day to day (James 1956, 46–47, 51). Curiosity is, or is close to, interest, and a life worth living is, or is close to, a meaningful life (in the thinking not only of James but of many others). Spacks observes that interest and meaning are linked. She says that, for a character in a novel she is analyzing, the meaning of things "essentially inheres in their interest" (Spacks 1995, 178).

Fifth, there are a few recent exceptions to the standard philosophical accounts of meaning (meaningfulness) in life I spoke of earlier. I will mention only the most prominent one. Susan Wolf conceives of meaning in life as a thing that is distinct from both happiness and morality, and at the core of a meaningful life, she claims, is a propensity to be guided by "reasons of love" (Wolf 2010, 3, 8). Wolf then says famously that "meaning arises when subjective attraction meets objective attractiveness" (Wolf 2010, 9). She proceeds to give what can, perhaps, be taken as (part of) her analysis of the concept of meaning in life: "A person's life can be meaningful only if she cares . . . about some . . . things, *only if she is gripped, excited, interested, engaged . . . as opposed to being bored by* or alienated from *most or all that she does*" (Wolf 2010, 9; emphasis added).

If the idea that a (subjectively) meaningful life is an interesting one is right, then it could be the case that interest has replaced and superseded importance, significance, point, purpose, and so forth in the concept of meaning. (This might relate to a contemporary loss of conviction in our culture that anything really is important and that life can have any point or purpose.) Or it could be the case that, while the older concepts of meaning, the ones defined in dictionaries and analyzed in most philosophical accounts, still exist, a new sense of meaning has joined them. And maybe, in a family resemblance account of meaning such as Metz provides, "interest" or "absence of boredom" should be included in the list of meaning bestowing things. What I am inclined to think is that "meaning" has indeed taken on a new sense, but that the other more established senses of meaning remain and are well entrenched.

5. INTEREST

If my claims so far are correct, *lack of interest* is essential to boredom, and *interest* is essential to (subjective) meaning in life.

I don't have to offer, in any strict sense, an analysis of the concept of interest. I can say that what I have in mind is not *self-interest* or advantage, and it has nothing to do with money.

According to the *OED*, "interest" and its relatives in the sense(s) I have in mind are defined as follows.

"Interest" (n) is:

7a. The feeling of one who is concerned or has a personal concern in any thing; hence, the state of feeling proper to such a relation, or a particular form or instance of it; *a feeling of* concern for or *curiosity about a person or thing*. (My emphasis)

Synonyms, in the *OED* thesaurus, include close attention and judgment, inquisitiveness, curiosity, wonder.

"Interest" (v) is "to excite the curiosity or attention of."
"Interesting" (adj.) is "2. Adapted to excite interest; having the qualities which rouse curiosity, engage attention, or appeal to the emotions."

Synonyms, near-synonyms, and definitions in the OED thesaurus include fascinating; engaging the mind or attention in a pleasing way; engrossing, absorbing; striking, producing a vivid impression on the mind; adapted to excite interest; having the qualities which rouse curiosity, engage attention, or appeal to the emotions; arresting, that takes hold of the attention; riveting, that holds one's attention; compelling, enthralling, fascinating; engrossing, that fully occupies or absorbs the attention, faculties, etc.

Not just any interest suffices to provide meaning. It must be a deep interest, one that engages, absorbs, captivates, and lasts for a considerable time. A passing, superficial, casual interest will not do. Any interest that bestows meaning must be gripping, absorbing, captivating, engrossing, and hard to shed. Deep curiosity, wonder, and close attention are part of the interest in question. One in the grip of such attention is most certainly *not bored*.

Moreover, the interest that brings meaning with it must be a kind of *positive* interest in a way that is hard to define. Threatening things—COVID-19, the eminent collapse of the economy, the prospect of losing your job, the nagging worry that the lingering sore on your toe is gangrene—may interest and captivate you to a high degree, but these negative interests are not the kind of interest that gives your life its meaning.

There must be millions of potentially gripping positive interests. Some are things to learn, others are things to do. They can be *consuming* interests, and I believe they can give meaning to life.

To live a meaningful life, you do not have to *seek out* these interests. You might never *try* to become interested in any of them. The interests can just grab you, and it seems to you that you cannot resist them. Sometimes I wonder whether an interest that brings with it meaning must be of this nature. And I wonder whether you are fortunate in being subject to this captivation. It means you are rarely, almost never, bored. And if the bold analysis suggested in the previous section is on target, it means that your life almost always seems meaningful (except, maybe, when you are trapped in circumstances that bring on situative boredom, or when you are suffering from a bout of something like profound boredom).

6. MORE ON MEANINGFULNESS AS INTEREST

In what kind of interest must (subjective) meaning lie? Must one feel that one's work or one's life is important or matters? Must one feel that there is some kind of point or purpose to what one is or does? Must one love, care about, or be attached to something?

My own inclination is to reject outright the suggestion that subjective meaning necessarily has anything to do with a feeling of the importance of one's life or belief in it. You can feel that your life is meaningful (or good in some other way) without having the delusion that you are important whatsoever, except to other beings (people and animals) close to you. You can think that, in the grand scheme of things, you are nothing, that it won't be long until it will be as though you never existed, and that the same is true of those to whom you matter. And you can be reconciled to that, even relieved by it to some degree. On the subjective side, then, I do not believe that you must feel that your life is important, or that what you do matters, in order to experience meaning in life.

I get some support for the rejection of the link between interest and importance from Spacks. In her erudite exploration of the history of boredom, Spacks argues (by scrutiny of novels and the etymology of words) that "interest" and "importance" were closely related in the *old* and now for the most part obsolete sense of interest. In this old sense, alive until the early nineteenth century, genuine interest lay in attraction to what is really (objectively) important. If you are interested in something, it must be something important. This sense of interest, however, was replaced by a newer sense, now dominant, which first appeared in the eighteenth century. In this new sense, interest has nothing to do with objective importance. The interesting is whatever you take an interest in, whatever you are attracted to, regardless of its alleged objective importance (Spacks 1995, 114).

I'm also averse to the idea that a meaningful (or otherwise good) life must have any kind of point, purpose, or goal, or any plan for attaining it—any "life project" in Young's sense—or even that it must *seem* to have such a thing. My aversion here lies partly in the affinity I feel for certain strains of Buddhism (exemplified in Ayya Khema's *Being Nobody, Going Nowhere*; Khema 2016), ancient philosophical Daoism, especially the strain presented in *Zhuangzi* (Zhuangzi 2013), Stoicism, and (perhaps surprisingly) an essay by the logical-positivist philosopher Moritz Schlick (Schlick 2008). Zhuangzi commends a life of "free and easy wandering." His wise man has no plans, schemes, or purposes. He just lives in the moment and goes with the flow. His area of expertise is "doing nothing" (Zhuangzi 2013, 1, 25, 28, 40–43, 50, 56, 59, 67, 75, 80, 83, 92, 93, 99, 114, 120, 129, 152, 154). Schlick speaks against having goals and working toward them. He argues that meaning is found in *play*. He contrasts play with work. Unless you can turn it into play, work does not provide meaning. Ordinary work (work not turned into play) is doing things not for their own sake but for the sake of further ends. Play is something like doing things for no further purpose, just because you enjoy them; and that's where meaning lies (Schlick 2008, 63, 64, 69).

I turn now to the question of whether the sort of interest in which meaning lies essentially involves caring about things, feeing love for them, and being attached to them. I hope not, and I don't think it does.

I like it that Susan Wolf speaks of the subjective element in meaning as *attraction*, and for the most part I agree when she says, in the passage I quoted above, "A person's life can be meaningful only if she cares . . . about some . . . things, *only if she is gripped, excited, interested, engaged . . . as opposed to being bored by* or alienated from *most or all that she does*" (Wolf 2010, 9; emphasis added). What I like in this are the parts to which I have added emphases. But I have reservations about the inclusion of the words "cares . . . about some . . . things." Wolf, here and there, speaks of the subjective element of meaning, not only as care but also as love, attachment, and so forth. But these things, in my opinion, are not necessary for interest, nor, I believe, for meaning.

There is such a thing as a *detached interest*. I have had it. Thomas Nagel recognizes it when he says:

> Humans have the special capacity to step back and survey themselves, and the lives to which they are committed, with that *detached amazement* which comes from watching an ant struggle up a heap of sand. (Nagel 1979, 15, my emphasis)

Iris Murdoch recognizes it too, in several places. One of these is in a novel in which she writes, "The child looked at Ludens with calmness, with understanding, without surprise or hostility or fear, but with *a cool, interested detachment*" (Murdoch 1989, 78, my emphasis).

It is entirely possible to be deeply interested in things one does not love, does not care about (in a way), and is not attached to. I know a (truthful) man in my neighborhood who has been deeply interested in—completely engrossed in—such things throughout his life. His current obsession is rocks, especially varieties of quartz and chalcedony. He goes looking for these rocks. He collects them. He works on them with saw and hammer. He turns them into gemstones in his rock tumbler. He sits, gazes, and studies them for hours. He reads everything he can about them. Right now, he can hardly think or talk of anything else (which can be irritating). I asked him whether he thought rocks were important. He answered that he was not inane enough to think that rocks and his particular current interest in them were of any importance whatsoever. I pressed on and asked him whether he would care if he broke his leg and couldn't look for rocks anymore, or if some inconsiderate home intruder broke into his house and ran off with all his rocks before he could shoot him. He said he might care about his leg, but not really about his inability to go rockhounding, and if his rocks were stolen, although he might be briefly disappointed, he really wouldn't care all that much. He would simply begin rebuilding his collection, or else turn to some other thing of the sort that can grip him—something like native local trees or different kinds of knots. This is anecdotal evidence for the point I'm making.

Two points need to be made here to clarify what I am claiming: (1) The claim about the (dis)connection between meaning and a sense, feeling, or thought of importance, purpose, or care is only that neither of the latter three (importance, purpose, or care) is *necessary* for meaning. No doubt a sense of one or two or even all three is often, perhaps *usually*, accompanied by subjective meaningfulness. (2) When such a sense *is* present, I propose, it supplies subjective meaningfulness because it brings with it what *is* required for meaning, namely, some kind of strong positive *interest*.

7. BOREDOM, INTEREST, MEANINGLESSNESS, AND MEANING

The sense that everything is meaningless may result in loss of interest in anything and thereby land one in a state of severe boredom. One who is severely bored may, because of her state of mind, find everything meaningless. So, interestingly, there seems to be, if not a conceptual, a causal connection that tends to run both ways: boredom can produce lack of meaning, and lack of meaning can produce boredom.

Chronic severe boredom need not, but can, lead to a sense of the meaninglessness of life, which has a tendency, not only to induce deep depression but also to produce horrific things like war, mass murder, suicide, and alcoholism. That is why boredom is more important or serious than some have thought (Russell 1930, 48, 51).

But not *all* boredom is bad. Elpidorou has argued persuasively that brief periods of situative boredom are a *good* thing, propelling one to a *more* meaningful (or otherwise better) life, and I agree with him. What seems to be bad in an unqualified sense is profound boredom of both sorts and, perhaps, extreme situative boredom proneness. I don't know what to say about the noteworthy case of the woman I described above, the one who suffers neither from profound boredom nor situative boredom proneness, but who must spend her life in a boring state, doing boring things. Her life is bad, I guess.

8. LIFE WITH INTEREST BUT NO MEANING?

Suppose my suggestion that a meaningful life is, or can be, one in which there is deep interest (and little boredom) but little or no point, purpose, plan, life project, importance, care, concern, love, or attachment is rejected as a thoroughly implausible account of a meaningful life—even a category mistake. Suppose my suggestion that there is a new sense of "meaningfulness" is rejected outright. Suppose I accepted all this. Suppose I conceded (as I do not) that meaningfulness lies only in importance or attachment or whatever. What then?

I think the answer might be that the best life is a meaningless one. Meaning (in the received, traditional sense) isn't always a good thing. It might even be a bad thing.

A life in which one has "got over" purpose, plan, desire, passion, care, and attachment is, in many Eastern and in some ancient Western traditions, the kind of life that is most fulfilling, rewarding, and best to live. The traditions here include, but are not limited to, those of certain strains of Daoism, Buddhism, and Stoicism, as well as the works of certain Western philosophers influenced by those traditions.

One of those Western philosophers is Arthur Schopenhauer. For Schopenhauer, "salvation" (if not meaning) lies in the total denial of the will. Knowledge of will and world should function as a quieter of the will, leading it to cessation of willing and extinction of itself (Schopenhauer 1969, 285). Thinking in this vein, a Schopenhauerian might say that (true) meaning in life lies in the denial, quieting, and eventually abolition of willing. On the other hand, a Schopenhauerian might say that the best life is one without meaning.

Camus said precisely that "life . . . will be lived all the better if it has no meaning" (Camus 1991, 53).

You can be attracted to such views, for you may be one who has always cared *too much*. Care, love, and attachment make you vulnerable to loss, and they can make you miserable. They can produce anxiety and depression, a sense of gloom and doom. They may make you want to drink. When figures like Nagel speak as though the problem of life's meaning is that of whether anything matters, your gut response can be that you hope not. Life would be much more tolerable and enjoyable for you, you might think, if it were incredibly interesting, but not important. You do, but perhaps you don't want to, care about things. Deep concern brings with it unbearable misery.

Metz says that he takes for granted that meaning is desirable, and that by definition meaning is valuable. He writes:

> I stipulate here that by "meaning" I am . . . conveying something that is worthy for its own sake, something that provides a person with at least some . . . reason to prize it. (Metz 2013, 4)

I too once asserted, without argument, that to consider something meaningful is to evaluate it positively (O'Brien 1996, 354). But now I'm not so sure, if meaning is taken in the traditional sense. The evaluative nature of judgments of meaningfulness (in the old sense) *has* in fact been denied, and in prominent places. Paul Edwards, for instance, denies it in his entry, "The Meaning and

Value of Life," in *The Encyclopedia of Philosophy* (Edwards 1972, volume 4, 472).

I really don't know whether meaning in this old sense is good or not. Perhaps it is good up to a certain point, but a massive amount of it is too much to bear. If meaning does not lie in interest, perhaps it is better to give it up and just live a life that is, on the whole, not boring. But I want to insist that, in current predominate usage, the meaningful is the not boring.

REFERENCES

Bernanos, Georges. 1982. *The Diary of a Country Priest*. Translated by Pamela Morris. Cambridge, MA: Da Capo Press.

Camus, Albert. 1991. *The Myth of Sisyphus and Other Essays*. Translated by Justin O'Brien. New York: Vintage Books.

Edwards, Paul. 1972. *The Encyclopedia of Philosophy*. New York: Macmillan/ Collier.

Elpidorou, Andreas. 2020. *Propelled: How Boredom, Frustration, and Anticipation Lead Us to the Good Life*. New York: Oxford University Press.

Frankfurt, Harry G. 1999. *Necessity, Volition, and Love*. Cambridge: Cambridge University Press.

Heidegger, Martin. 1983. *Die Grundbegriffe der Metaphysik*. Frankfurt: Vittorio Klostermann.

James, William. 1956. "Is Life Worth Living?" In *The Will to Believe and Other Essays in Popular Philosophy*, 32–62. New York: Dover.

Khema, Ayya. 2016. *Being Nobody, Going Nowhere*. Somerville, MA: Wisdom Publications.

Klemke, Elmer Daniel, and Steven Cahn. 2008. *The Meaning of Life* (Third Edition). New York: Oxford University Press.

Metz, Thaddeus. 2013. *Meaning in Life*. Oxford: Oxford University Press.

Moravia, Alberto. 1999. *Boredom*. Translated by Angus Davidson. New York: New York Review Books.

Murdoch, Iris. 1989. *The Message to the Planet*. New York: Viking Penguin.

Nagel, Thomas. 1979. *Mortal Questions*. New York: Oxford University Press.

Nagel, Thomas. 1987. *What Does It All Mean? A Very Short Introduction to Philosophy*. New York: Oxford University Press.

Nozick, Robert. 1981. *Philosophical Explanations*. Cambridge: Harvard University Press.

O'Brien, Wendell. 1996. "Meaning and Mattering." *The Southern Journal of Philosophy* XXXIV: 339–57.

O'Brien, Wendell. 2014a. "Boredom." *Analysis* 74, no. 2: 236–43.

O'Brien, Wendell. 2014b. "The Meaning of Life: Early Continental and Analytic Perspectives." In *Internet Encyclopedia of Philosophy*, edited by James Fieser. https://iep.utm.edu/mean-ear/.

Oxford English Dictionary. Oxford: Oxford University Press.

Pessoa, Fernando. 2003. *The Book of Disquiet*. Translated by Richard Zenith. New York: Penguin Books.

Russell, Bertrand. 1930. *The Conquest of Happiness*. London: Liveright.

Schlick, Moritz. 2008. "On the Meaning of Life." In Klemke & Cahn 2008, 62–71.

Schopenhauer, Arthur. 1969. *The World as Will and Representation,* Volume I. Translated by E. F. J. Payne. New York: Dover Publications.

Schopenhauer, Arthur. 1970. *Essays and Aphorisms*. Translated by R. J. Hollingdale. London: Penguin Books.

Spacks, Patricia Meyer. 1995. *Boredom: The Literary history of a State of Mind*. Chicago: The University of Chicago Press.

Svendsen, Lars. 2005. *A Philosophy of Boredom*. Translated by John Irons. London: Reaktion Books.

Williams, Bernard. 1973. "The Makropulos Case: Reflections on the Tedium of Immortality." In *Problems of the Self*, 82–100. Cambridge: Cambridge University Press.

Wolf, Susan. 2010. *Meaning in Life and Why It Matters*. Princeton: Princeton University Press.

Young, Julian. 2014. *The Death of God and the Meaning of Life*, Second Edition. London: Routledge.

Zhuangzi. 2013. *The Complete Works of Zhuangzi*. Translated by Burton Watson. New York: Columbia University Press.

Chapter 11

Parallels to Boredom in Nonhuman Animals

Rebecca K. Meagher and Jesse Robbins

Anyone reading this chapter is likely aware that boredom is a state we typically wish to avoid. While many of us expect that nonhuman animals feel similarly, this is difficult to determine. Aside from the problem of "Other Minds" which prevents us from stating with absolute certainty that other animals have an inner experience comparable to our own (Nagel 1974), there is the additional complication of determining which of the millions of species of animals experience similar states. Here we will focus on those species that can be assumed to be conscious based on current evidence (vertebrates and certain invertebrates such as cephalopods [Low et al. 2012], with emphasis on mammals and birds). The word "animals" will thus be used throughout this chapter to refer to these species, with the exception of humans. Within this group, there is likely to be variation in the experience and certainly in triggers of boredom, as will be discussed below.

As this volume attests, boredom is a growing topic of scientific interest. Cross-species comparisons have a rich history in the study of anatomy, physiology, cognition, and even emotion. However, boredom has received little attention in animal research, especially relative to other common and negatively valenced emotions like pain or fear. This lack of attention stems in part from general skepticism regarding our ability to understand emotions scientifically in beings who lack the ability to verbally self-report on their mental states (Tinbergen 1951; LeDoux 2014). Such concerns have a long tradition in the study of comparative cognition where, for decades, anthropomorphism has been considered a cardinal sin. The limited attention to boredom in animals may also reflect the view that boredom is relatively less important than other emotions such as pain and fear. Evidence of this can be seen in our everyday lives, where claims about being bored are not viewed with the same degree of urgency and importance as, for example, pain and fear. Among humans, the experience of boredom is often seen as a weakness of will—someone who is bored is simply not trying hard enough to find things to do (Darden 1999).

We begin this chapter by discussing different definitions and frameworks used in the study of human boredom and compare the definitions and empirical evidence available from animals to those frameworks. We then argue for a comparative approach to the study of boredom and discuss how bringing the human and animal research into alignment could benefit research in both areas. Given recent interest in boredom's status as a moral emotion, we conclude with a brief discussion of the practical moral implications of animal boredom as they pertain to animal welfare and ethics.

1. ANIMAL VS. HUMAN LITERATURE

How Boredom Has Been Defined and Categorized

One of the major challenges for establishing whether animals experience states analogous to human boredom is the lack of consensus in the human literature about what boredom actually is. How does one assess the validity of an analogy when there is no single coherent definition and set of symptoms against which to compare? While boredom can be discussed as a state or a dispositional trait (e.g., Fahlman et al. 2013; Farmer and Sundberg 1986), this chapter will focus on state boredom—boredom as an emotion, which is a precondition for trait boredom. However, even when focusing only on state boredom, there are disparate ways of conceptualizing it.

Among the theoretical frameworks for categorizing emotions, two-dimensional categorization based on valence and arousal (also called "activation"; Russell and Barrett 1999) is popular in the animal literature. The dimensional categorization clearly describes features of emotions that are relevant to welfare and its assessment. Valence and to some extent arousal (when combined with valence to identify the type of state, or used to assess intensity of similarly valenced states) are linked to motivation (see Mendl, Burman, and Paul 2010), and whether animals are able to fulfill their motivations is considered a key determinant of welfare (see Fraser and Nicol 2018). However, boredom has proved difficult to place in this framework. This is in part because there are conflicting views and evidence regarding its place on the arousal continuum (reviewed by Eastwood et al. 2012; Fahlman et al. 2013). Another issue is that a two-dimensional framework may not be sufficient to distinguish boredom from other emotions that are subjectively experienced quite differently in humans (Burn 2017); Russell and Barrett (1999) argue this is true for all discrete emotions. For example, depression and boredom are both negatively valenced and might involve low arousal. Mendl and colleagues (2010) propose a combination of perspectives, wherein core affect or mood (longer-lasting affective states not related to any specific event) can be categorized based on the two dimensions of arousal or valence, and this core affect is known to interact with, but not fully characterize, discrete, felt emotions. This suits our current understanding of boredom, as a discrete, negatively valenced emotion with a unique constellation of symptoms and causes (e.g., Eastwood et al. 2012; Van Tilburg and Igou 2017) that is both affected by and likely affecting arousal but not clearly linked to a fixed arousal level (Elpidorou, 2020).

What, then, should be considered the defining features of boredom? Varied definitions have been proposed. After reviewing existing definitions, Eastwood and colleagues (Eastwood et al. 2012) propose a common definition of "the aversive experience of wanting, but being unable, to engage in satisfying activity" (482). The human literature generally seems to agree that, like most emotions, boredom has both affective (aversion or dissatisfaction; Elpidorou 2014) or more broadly, experiential components (e.g., altered arousal, awareness of altered mental function and agency) and cognitive/ motivational components (reduced attentional focus, increased motivation for new activity, altered perception of time; Eastwood et al. 2012). Based on this conception, more comprehensive ways of measuring boredom in humans that take into account the most consistent features have been proposed. For example, Fahlman and colleagues (2013) propose a scale with arousal, attention, time perception, and "disengagement." This accounts for a broad range of the experiential components of boredom, although it does not directly measure degree of aversion. Comparison of these scores between groups of people (or between species) might therefore not fully reflect the degree of boredom felt. For example, young children typically seem to perceive time as moving somewhat more slowly than it does for adults (Wittmann and Lehnhoff 2005), may show quite variable arousal, and have less developed attentional capacities (Atkinson and Braddick 2012). Does this mean that they experience more boredom? Some authors also argue that lack of meaning (Van Tilburg and Igou 2017) or of agency (Eastwood et al. 2012) might be defining features of boredom. The capacity for intentional action or agency has been shown to inversely correlate with boredom (Martin et al. 2006; Mercer-Lynn et al. 2014; Steinberger et al. 2016). This link with lack of agency may be best reflected by the model of boredom types resulting from low perceived meaning and/or reduced attentional engagement as opposed to boredom caused only by mismatched attentional demands (Westgate 2020; Westgate and Wilson 2018).

Boredom in animals has been discussed predominantly as an emotional state defined by the situation (i.e., the lack of relevant stimulation) and the aversion to it. Specifically, motivation to seek stimulation, particularly novel stimulation, has been considered the central feature (Kirkden 2000; Meagher and Mason 2012). The first author's empirical work on the subject thus operationalized boredom using behavioral indicators of elevated motivation to explore (Meagher and Mason 2012; Meagher, Campbell, and Mason 2017). This was based primarily on Berlyne's seminal work (1960), which conceptualized boredom as a drive to obtain stimulation, induced by low or monotonous stimulation. Berlyne's definition covers both the perceived cause and the core motivational feature, thus combining environmental or arousal-based theories of boredom with psychodynamic or functional theories (as described by Westgate and Wilson 2018). This definition does not cover boredom that arises out of internal causes such as those postulated by Eastwood and colleagues (2012), nor does it consider the other experiential components identified by some of the subsequent human literature. Burn (2017) has thus suggested extending the animal work to provide a more comprehensive picture of boredom as it is currently conceptualized.

Empirical Evidence in Animals

The first empirical work on boredom using this operational definition of elevated exploratory motivation was conducted using farmed mink. This series of studies (Meagher and Mason 2012; Meagher, Campbell, and Mason 2017; Polanco et al. 2021) has demonstrated that, compared to mink housed in enriched (preferred, stimulating) environments, mink housed in relatively monotonous environments with fewer behavioral opportunities (e.g., no water in which to perform natural behaviors such as wading or head dipping, and no objects added that they could manipulate) are more interested in exploring a range of stimuli. This was particularly true for stimuli that would normally be aversive (e.g., predator-related sights or smells) or that had no expected biological relevance to the species (e.g., plastic water bottles). Mink's interest was inferred from the time they spent oriented to and in contact with (sniffing or touching) these stimuli. The enriched treatment used in these studies had previously been shown to reduce a number of signs of poor welfare including fecal cortisol metabolites and locomotor stereotypic behavior (e.g., Meagher et al. 2013). The differences in response to stimuli were not replicated in the most recent mink study (Decker 2019), but housing treatments in that case were less extreme and the measure may not have been sensitive enough to detect more subtle differences in boredom. The same boredom measure was recently used for a study in laboratory ferrets, where a within-subject design found that exploration of aversive and ambiguous stimuli was reduced after an opportunity to play (Burn et al. 2020). This supports Burghardt's (2014) hypothesis that play may relieve boredom.

Of the defining features listed in the more recent human frameworks discussed above, these studies reflect not only the motivational component (motivation for new activity) but also the related affective component of aversion or dissatisfaction. This assumption is based on their choice to engage, and prior evidence that mink were motivated to access more complex, variable, and less monotonous environments. Although direct assessment of boredom per se has not yet been conducted in most species, there is evidence of a range of mammals being averse to environments that are monotonous or low in stimulation, and/or having poor welfare when confined in such environments for extended periods of time (reviewed in Meagher 2019). Birds similarly exhibit signs of improved welfare when appropriate stimuli are added to such environments and may be more motivated for stimulation when housed in barren cages (e.g., Meehan and Mench 2002).

A number of papers have explicitly suggested that behavioral differences seen in these non-preferred environments might be the result of boredom, although they did not assess defining features of the state directly. In cattle, these behaviors include restlessness during periods when they were not allowed access to the outdoors (Crump et al. 2019), and are proposed to include certain lying postures, although these have not yet been linked to a specific emotion (e.g., lying with head up and ears backward, more common in indoor, unenriched housing; Hintze et al. 2020). In dogs, waking inactivity was proposed to indicate boredom, and correlated with expert ratings of the dogs as bored but also depressed (Harvey et al. 2019). Behavioral responses to being removed from a confined, non-preferred environment can also be considered as evidence, as in the case of meat chickens showing higher levels of play when given free space than those that came from more stimulating, "enriched" environments did (Liu 2019); this possible "rebound" effect could occur because of accumulated motivation for play and exploration in their previous environment.

Ryan (2017) directly compared one hypothesized symptom, stereotypic behavior, in humans and nonhuman primates (rhesus macaques) exposed to a situation that humans find boring, being forced to wait through a five-minute delay. This behavior correlated with self-reported boredom in nonclinical human subjects during waiting. Macaques also performed stereotypic behavior in this situation (one of the two situations used to induce boredom in humans), albeit less than the humans did, suggesting that they might also have experienced boredom.

To What Extent Does This Support Inferring Boredom in Animals?

There are actually multiple questions to answer here. First, is the evidence of boredom in animals analogous with at least one model of boredom in humans? Insofar as monotonous environments which are known to reduce welfare seem to increase motivation for stimuli in the species studied, and that both restlessness and inactivity have been reported but do not seem to be reliably linked to boredom-like states, the results from the studies described here are largely congruent with the human literature. More formally, the answer to this question depends on considering several types of validity. Second, can we distinguish different subtypes of boredom in animals and if so, which ones apply? Finally, *which* animals experience boredom?

As reviewed by Anisman and Matheson (2005), the established methods for determining whether an animal model of a psychological condition (typically, a mental disorder rather than a simple emotion) is valid depend on demonstrating (1) face validity based on the symptom profile; (2) etiological validity or similarity of cause; (3) predictive validity, typically demonstrated by selective response to treatments that work on humans; and (4) construct validity, which the authors equate with underlying neurobiology. The above work on mustelids (mink and ferrets) exhibits both face validity and etiological validity for the model of boredom that was being tested. That is to say, the symptom tested for was present, and the cause matched that which situational models of boredom in humans typically describe: confinement in a situation that lacked satisfying stimuli to engage their attention. This etiology has also been the basis for inferring boredom in the other animal studies mentioned. Establishing predictive validity and similarity of neurobiological underpinnings is more complicated because boredom is not a mental disorder for which we have well-validated treatments, nor is there extensive literature on the neurochemistry of the state in humans. Given that the primary aim of the animal work has not been to use the animals as a model for screening of pharmacological treatments for humans but to understand them for their own sake, pharmacological validation is perhaps less necessary although it could still be useful when possible. It is, however, important to determine more generally whether boredom can be alleviated by the things that would alleviate it in humans. So far, the studies show this predictive validity: hyper-responsiveness to stimuli was rapidly reduced when mink were moved from an aversive, monotonous environment to the enriched one (Polanco et al. 2021), and when ferrets were given an opportunity to play (Burn et al. 2020). More work remains to be done on the variety of possible causes and thus treatments of boredom that may exist for humans, and to ensure that interventions which are not effective at alleviating boredom in humans are similarly unsuccessful in other species. Finally, although construct validity cannot yet be firmly established based on neurobiology due to the limited relevant human data, this form of validity can be established in other ways. Typically, this is done through testing for correlations with other putative measures of the same construct (in this case, the same emotional state), particularly if those measures are already validated (convergent validity or criterion validity when using a gold standard measure; Cronbach and Meehl 1955). More direct evidence of negative affect that covaries with the motivation for stimuli, for example, using cognitive bias techniques to assess the cognitive component of the emotion, would help to validate this measure. Conversely, the measure should not covary tightly with measures to which it is not theoretically related (divergent validity).

The answer to the first question is thus a tentative "yes," in that evidence to date supports the inference that at least some animals likely experience a state analogous to human boredom. However, as is clear from the discussion of current human frameworks, this may not fully reflect the range of human boredom causes and experiences. Measuring additional signs and symptoms will be helpful in determining the degree to which these states are actually analogous.

Other proposed defining features of boredom based on the human literature discussed above (e.g., Van Tilburg and Igou 2017; Fahlman et al. 2013; Westgate and Wilson 2018) include nonoptimal arousal, low attention to tasks or stimuli and/or low perceived meaning in a situation, and perception of time slowing. Arousal is one component of many conceptions of boredom that can be measured with relative ease in animals. This could be done, for example, using salivary cortisol or even behaviors such as rate of blinking, as suggested by Burn (2017). This would support the interpretation of boredom as far as the two-dimensional model of emotion can capture it, but again would not necessarily distinguish it from other emotions. Animals' time perception can be inferred from tasks such as fixed interval responding or time discrimination, or even from "clock watching" (Burn 2017), as will be discussed below. Measures of attention and attentional failure are likewise possible in animals, albeit often impractical in some settings where we might want to assess boredom because they require time-consuming video analysis, extended training of the animals, or special technology (e.g., sustained attention: five-choice serial reaction time task; Robbins 2002). Drawing inferences about what is "meaningful" to another species is more difficult and likely to attract criticism on the grounds of anthropomorphism. Lack of meaning might seem like a human-specific or at least ape-specific problem depending on the interpretation of what gives meaning to life. Lack of meaning on a grand scale is what comes to mind with the term "existential boredom," associated with a more depressive-type state and distinct from the typical lay understanding of boredom or the related scientific concept of boredom states reflected in the research (Toohey 2011; Elpidorou and Freeman 2019). Empirical work on lack of perceived meaning in boredom has included demonstrating that people make changes that might give them a deeper sense of purpose, such as strengthening political views and in-group affiliation or wanting to express more prosocial behavior (reviewed by Van Tilburg and Igou 2017), while self-report measures have used the general term "meaning" (Van Tilburg and Igou 2012). If we assume life meaning requires the capacity for metacognitive reflection on the value of various states of affairs, a sense of self existing over time, and/or abstract concepts such as "life" and "purpose," many people would doubt whether this applies to animals. However, Purves and Delon (2016) have put forth a less demanding notion of meaning which consists of the capacity for intentional action (or agency) toward the pursuit of valuable states, such that things can contribute meaning to one's life despite one not being aware of or motivated by the reason-generating value of those actions. Similarly, Svendsen (2019) argues agency and caring about various objects and activities are sufficient for meaning and thus apply to animals. The lack of meaning that would thus be conferred by progress toward currently valued outcomes is what Westgate and Wilson (2018) describe in their model of "meaningless" boredom. Since this does not necessarily require the kind of metacognition or abstract thought underlying existential angst, this understanding of meaning makes it possible to test whether this might play a role in animal boredom.

Other possible indicators that have been suggested in animals which are not defining features of the state but relate to symptoms sometimes reported in humans and could prove useful for practical assessment of boredom if validated include sleep disruption (Burn 2017), stereotypic behavior, restlessness, and waking inactivity as described above. To return to the mink studies, it was found that among enriched mink in the first study (Meagher and Mason 2012), waking inactivity was positively correlated with the core boredom indicator, exploration of diverse stimuli. However, such a result did not hold: Analysis with the three experiments pooled together found no correlation between this indicator and either stereotypic behavior or waking inactivity (Polanco et al. 2021). However, ferrets showed more of this waking inactivity during the control treatment than after play opportunities (Burn et al. 2020), suggesting this may still be worth investigation as a sign of boredom in some contexts.

In answer to the second question of *which subtypes* of boredom can be identified in animals, there are again multiple typologies of boredom to consider. Although some authors have tried to divide boredom into subtypes based on symptoms (e.g., Malkovsky et al. 2012; Goetz et al. 2014), evidence to date does not clearly support this division of state boredom (Elpidorou 2020). Individual humans also often show a mix of symptoms within a bout of boredom (Berlyne 1960; Eastwood et al. 2012), which may explain why there was no clear correlation with inactivity or stereotypic behavior in the mink. These proposed subtypes are thus unlikely to be helpful in trying to understand potential symptoms of the state in animals.

Proposed distinctions between types of boredom based on cause may be more relevant. This includes the model proposed by Westgate and Wilson (2018), which divides boredom into "attentional" and "meaningless," and further divides attentional boredom depending on whether the cause is understimulation or overstimulation. In the case of overstimulation, this model proposes that demand(s) for attention exceed the cognitive resources available, leading to inability to focus on the required or available task or activity (Westgate and Wilson 2018). In support of the contention that this can result in boredom, the authors offer the example of students reporting most boredom in classes they find too difficult (e.g., association with "over-challenge": Daschmann et al. 2011). Animal research has largely considered whether environments provide stimuli to occupy animals' attention rather than whether those resources are "meaningful," as noted above. However, the two major forms may be interrelated, as stimuli without biological meaning may not hold animals' attention (see, e.g., Newberry 1995 who suggested enrichment must be biologically relevant to be effective and that stimuli to which animals have never been exposed may have little meaning to them). The overstimulation prediction is currently untested in animals, to our knowledge. One could experimentally induce overstimulation, but it would be hard to judge in advance what will be overly challenging cognitively. In practice, captive animals might sometimes deal with overstimulation, for example, from excess noise and crowds of people in zoos or public places where one might take a dog, but being cognitively overchallenged is probably rare, with a possible exception being working animals. Potential detection or service dogs may be rejected due to insufficient cognitive ability (e.g., MacLean and Hare 2018). This model does suggest, however, that in some situations, removing stimuli rather than adding them would alleviate boredom.

Finally, while the evidence above indicates that at least some animals experience some forms of boredom, more work is needed to strengthen this conclusion. The question of how generally this applies to "animals" still remains. To date, boredom has been studied or inferred from specific data in a very restricted range of species. The extent to which humans believe animals can experience emotions depends on the specific animal in question and one's relationship or experience with that animal (Demoulin et al. 2004). It may well be true that species differ in the types of emotion they experience or even in the specifics of that experience. Whatever capacities they have, species may also differ in the likelihood of experiencing boredom regularly due to differences in their management when in captivity.

2. A CROSS-SPECIES APPROACH TO
THE STUDY OF BOREDOM

Why Would We Study Boredom from
a Comparative Approach?

In order to gain a more comprehensive understanding of boredom, future research should include a comparative perspective. Comparative psychology is a term encompassing all fields that explore the psychological mechanisms underlying human and animal behavior. The core premises of comparative psychology are (a) psychological processes, like physical processes, are biological adaptations with evolutionary histories, and (b) an underlying continuity exists between human and animal psychology (Haun et al. 2010). Historically, comparative psychology has been focused on understanding animals as means of understanding the evolution of human traits. Today, however, the field has pivoted from this anthropocentric approach to one that focuses on understanding psychological phenomena more generally (Watanabe and Yamazaki 2009). If adopted, this would entail shifting from studying human and animal boredom to simply studying boredom. This deeper, shared understanding will have implications for future research and interventions.

There are many challenges with this approach, none of which are new. The most formidable challenge is characterizing the subjective experience component of boredom, which many view as central to emotions (but see Berridge 2018). A major limitation in the study of animal models is that self-report data is not an option. Researchers studying emotions in animals must rely on behavioral and physiological indicators believed to correlate with underlying emotional states. Based on the assumption of psychological continuity, we typically infer subjective experiences in animals on the basis of their behavioral expressions and introspection about our own subjective experience (Watanabe 2000). This does however raise important questions about the validity of such extrapolations to organisms with aforementioned major differences in evolutionary histories. Our intuitions about the capacity to experience boredom are likely to be less accurate when it comes to animals with histories very different from our own, and those with which we have less contact and have not formed close bonds. This means that while people frequently describe their dogs and cats as being bored, when it comes to other animal species such as cattle, snakes, birds, fish, or insects we may be less certain of the likelihood of the presence of boredom, and inferences regarding their emotional experiences may be increasingly difficult.

Even if animals could linguistically self-report their subjective experience of boredom, we as humans would necessarily need to interpret those data using our own "humanized expressions of their subjective world" (Watanabe and Yamazaki 2009). We do not have a ready solution to this problem other than to recognize it and to call for greater attention to the context in which emotional expression occurs (i.e., what happens right before and after the expression), and where possible, assessing commonalities in components of emotion such as physiology and cognition. If these components are affected in animals presumed to be in boredom-inducing situations in the same way as they are in humans, we believe the researcher can be justified in assuming that the animal's affective experience is likely similar as well (Mehta and Gosling 2011).

It has been contended by human boredom researchers that self-report is likely necessary for this state in particular due to the lack of a single consistent pattern of symptoms defining the state, and the constructionist view that boredom and other emotions depend on people's analysis of their own symptoms and situation, which cannot be directly observed (Westgate and Wilson 2018). Despite these concerns, however, there is considerable evidence that self-report is also an imperfect measure of emotion and motivation (Nisbett and Wilson, 1978; Greenwald and Banaji, 2017). Human researchers too are thus interested in identifying valid behavioral signs that can be measured objectively (Eastwood et al. 2012). In addition, advances in animal research have included clever methods of assessing animals' appraisals of situation, bringing us closer to comprehensive assessments of their emotional states (Mendl et al. 2009). Meanwhile, there are a number of important questions that a comparative approach using well-matched methods and consistent definitions across species could help to answer, some of which will be outlined below.

How to Study Boredom across Species

How should we approach this valuable research? It could include direct parallel experiments, such as the Ryan's (2017) work on humans and non-human primates described above. The measure of responsiveness to stimuli developed for animals could likewise be applied in humans; orientation to rewards, one component of this measure, has already been suggested as a measure of boredom in humans (Milyavskaya et al. 2019). However, given the aforementioned major differences in evolutionary histories, it is crucial that a cross-species investigation of boredom considers the natural ecology of the species (Hare 2001), to make sure any findings reflect true species differences (or similarities), and not simply methodological differences or inappropriate methodologies for the species (Andrews 2011). There may be a balance between ecological relevance and generalizability when designing tasks to assess phenomena across species (Sarter 2004). Using formal comparative methods to test evolutionary hypotheses also requires controls for phylogenetic relatedness (see Mason 2010).

As an example of the challenges that will be faced in cross-species research, we can consider time perception as a feature of boredom. Several studies in humans have found boredom to be associated with the perception of time dragging (Fahlman et al. 2013; Mercer-Lynn et al. 2014). We are not aware of any animal studies examining how boredom might affect their perception of time (Droit-Volet 2013; Burn 2017). Novel experimental paradigms such as that employed by Spinka et al. (1998) have demonstrated the ability of pigs to reliably differentiate between different time scales and could be adapted to explore the relationship between boredom and time perception in a wider array of species. In particular, the rate at which time is perceived varies across animal species, with smaller-sized animals with faster metabolic rates (e.g., some birds) perceiving more information per unit of time, likely leading them to experience time more slowly than larger-sized animals with slower metabolic rates do (Healy et al. 2013). Such factors will have to be considered on a species-by-species basis if we are to arrive at an accurate picture of susceptibility to boredom in all of its possible manifestations.

Similarly, while core features of boredom such as motivations are expected to be consistent across species, other potential behavioral signs to be used as rapid indicators of boredom are likely to differ between species. For example, Hintze and colleagues (2020) point out that lying awake may sometimes be a symptom of boredom in ferrets, as discussed above, but would not be a logical indicator in cattle, who have evolved to spend many hours per day lying awake to ruminate. Thus, these indicators need validation for each species.

What Could Comparative Research Teach Us about Boredom and Those Who Are Likely to Experience It?

Categorization and Scope

Emotions can be categorized as primary (also called basic) or secondary. Primary emotions are suggested to be universal among humans (Damasio 1999). In Panksepp's categorization, the term "primary" specifically refers to emotions tied to neurobiological circuits that have been highly conserved in the evolution of mammals, which he argues indicates that they served a function in dealing with challenging situations that were common in evolutionary history (Panksepp 2004). Secondary emotions are more complex to define. They may be combinations of primary ones (e.g., remorse as a mixture of disgust and sadness; Plutchik 2001), and in the case of some emotions (e.g., envy or guilt), may also require the ability to evaluate behavior against an abstract standard or rule (Morris et al. 2005). Consequently, they tend to appear later in development (Damasio 1999) and are influenced by social mores (i.e., they involve some degree of social construction); they are therefore also sometimes referred to by the overlapping term "social emotions" (as in Panksepp 2004). Secondary emotions are believed by some to be limited to primates based on the intellectual capacities many of them require (e.g., Morris et al. 2008). If boredom evolved as a social emotion, it might occur in some nonhuman animals with complex social structures including certain primates, but would certainly be less likely to occur in predominantly solitary animals. Nonetheless, the evidence above suggests that mink, a naturally solitary animal, may experience boredom; given that most of their phylogenetically closest relatives are similarly solitary, social systems are thus unlikely to explain the existence of boredom in all cases.

Boredom is not typically included on lists of basic emotions (most authors include at least joy, sorrow, fear, anger, and surprise; Plutchik 2001); however, there is no complete consensus, and some authors have hinted the list should be expanded to include several other emotions including boredom (Keltner and Cordaro 2017). Boredom may in a sense be more basic than many of those already categorized as such. Unlike basic emotions initiated by the perception and subsequent evaluation (consciously or subconsciously) of particular stimuli, boredom may be initiated by a fundamental perception of a general lack of stimuli. By this account, boredom bears a close association with curiosity (Silvia 2008)—a key construct in Panksepp's SEEKING system which he argues is the most basic system. The alleviation of boredom occurs once the organism's attention has been reengaged, which typically takes the form of exploration, proposed to be motivated by curiosity (Lilley et al. 2017). Remaining in a confined situation carries an "opportunity cost"—using up time and potentially other resources that could be put toward pursuing goals likely to provide more benefits (Kurzban et al. 2013; Westgate and Wilson 2018). However, since exploration to acquire information is costly, organisms cannot be in perpetual state of curiosity. Boredom may thus function as an adaptive signal for managing the unavoidable trade-off between exploration and exploitation of the environment (Geana et al. 2016), or in more traditionally human terms, to look for more satisfying activities, which might provide opportunities to attain social, cognitive, and emotional stimulation that could have otherwise been missed (Bench and Lench 2013).

The potential adaptive value of boredom makes it plausible to suspect this state extends to many species. The comparative approach in this way may shed light on boredom's place in the taxonomy of emotions or call into question whether secondary emotions are truly human specific. Knowing whether boredom is a primary or secondary emotion, and whether it evolved as a social emotion, is also clearly relevant to which animals we might expect to experience it.

Evolutionary Function

A full accounting of an emotion requires an analysis of its evolutionary function, since evolution is a core organizing principle of biology. Studying boredom across taxa has great potential for answering questions about the function of boredom, which would be relevant to the subsequent discussion of how and when we should try to alleviate it in humans and animals alike. At the moment, this potential is largely unexplored. For example, neophilic or generalist species have been proposed to be more likely to suffer from boredom (Burn 2017). Experimental work directly assessing distinct features of boredom has been limited to a few, relatively neophilic species. We can therefore only suggest possible approaches to answering these functional questions.

More broadly, most theoretical and empirical research into animal emotions has focused on mammals. Fundamental homologies in brain structure and molecular neurophysiology have been used as the basis of arguments that animals in these taxonomic groups share our emotions because they share the same underlying physiological mechanisms and behaviors that typify many human emotions. Despite the undeniable utility of this approach for generating testable predictions, it is necessarily limited when applied to animals less closely related to humans such as invertebrates. Because vertebrates split off from the rest of the animal phyla early in the evolution of life, the physiological systems and behaviors associated with emotions could be very different in these animals, and thus difficult to identify (Allen and Trestman 2017). This presents a formidable challenge for establishing the extent to which emotions are shared across more distantly related species.

Those Affected

Comparative research clearly aims to tell us about who is affected at the species level. It may demonstrate that most cases of boredom are in fact in nonhumans, given the billions of farm and companion animals, hundreds of millions of laboratory animals, and hundreds of thousands of zoo animals kept worldwide. If we are interested in boredom and not simply human boredom, the generalizability of our current theories needs to be tested in a much wider array of species. This line of animal research can also tell us about which individuals of a species are likely to be affected (Meagher 2019), and about the genetic, neurobiological, and developmental factors in boredom and boredom proneness (see Burn 2017 for a more extensive summary).

Expanding the study of boredom to animals can also help to answer questions about the psychology and behavioral needs of those at risk of boredom and the possible consequences of chronic boredom. For example, if it is determined that lack of agency or the ability to seek information is a major cause of boredom, that may suggest that animals who suffer from boredom have a higher level of self-awareness than is required for some simple goal-oriented behavior (Špinka 2019). By contrast, if boredom is simply caused by unfilled time (Webster 2008) or lack of stimulation, it would not require much cognitive complexity. Agency has previously been proposed to be important to welfare (Bassett and Buchanan-Smith 2007; Špinka 2019), but current legal and other protections for animal welfare largely do not consider such concepts, focusing instead on preventing suffering due to obvious physical needs not being met (Mellor 2016). Evidence of a psychological need for agency would thus affect animal care because it would indicate that to improve welfare, we need to allow animals some control over their environments rather than simply adding more stimuli.

Thus, the answer to the question "Why would we take a comparative approach?" is that it can teach us both about the nature of boredom itself, and the experiences and needs of animals. This research can help us to understand who might be affected, both at the individual level (including in humans) and at the species level. It can also inform decision-making about how best to intervene to prevent or alleviate boredom based on the likely causes, but also help inform us about the emotional lives of animals, which is of significant ethical importance. The moral implications of this will be discussed below.

3. ANIMAL BOREDOM AND MORALITY

The comparative study of boredom in humans and animals may also yield important conceptual and moral insights. For example, some authors have argued boredom should be classified as a moral emotion ("emotions that either help or hinder our attempts to live a moral life"; Elpidorou 2017, 31). However, such a classification would seem to require the capacity for moral agency. Despite a brief but fascinating period in Western history (Evans 1906; Girgen 2003), animals have not generally been considered moral agents (Clement 2013; Johannsen 2019 but see Pierce and Beckoff 2012). The reason for this, as expressed by Korsgaard (2004), is that animals are seen as lacking the capacity for "normative self-government" or autonomy. She elaborates on this idea by noting that

> humans do not merely *have* intentions, good or bad. We assess and adopt them. . . . It is at this level that morality emerges. The morality of your action is not a function of the content of your intentions. It is a function of the exercise of normative self-government. (112)

We argue the classification of boredom as a moral emotion requires refinement to specifically address whether moral emotions are restricted to moral agents. There is good reason to question the classification of boredom as a moral emotion on the grounds that certain categories of beings (e.g., small children and nonhuman animals) are believed to experience boredom, and we are gathering evidence that this is the case, yet they lack moral agency. Thus, much like the debate regarding boredom as a secondary emotion, either moral emotions like boredom can be experienced by beings lacking moral agency or boredom is not a moral emotion (or at least is not always so; Elpidorou 2017). Regardless of whether one classifies boredom as a moral emotion or not, animal boredom has obvious ethical implications for how we interact with animals.

Greater attention to boredom in animals has practical moral implications as well. In the past 100 years, ethical concern about the treatment of animals has been increasing. Like most large-scale sociocultural changes, the causes of this shift are difficult to pinpoint. Commonly cited causes include increases in standard of living, inclusion of pets as in-group members, and decreases in the proportion of the population directly involved in animal use (e.g., farming), scientific findings challenging human exceptionalism, and moral arguments (Pinker 2012). Results of multiple large-scale, representative polls show that substantial majorities of people are concerned about the care and welfare of animals (e.g., Riffkin 2015), although by and large, people do not appear to be categorically opposed to the use of animals. This has spawned a variety of legislative, regulatory, and private quality assurance programs aimed at addressing public concerns.

While ethical concerns regarding the treatment of animals are not restricted to welfare (Sandøe and Christiansen 2013, 22), animal welfare plays a central role in our ethical deliberations. As a result, growing societal concern has spawned the development of a relatively novel academic discipline known as animal welfare science. Animal welfare science is a highly interdisciplinary field comprised of scientists who draw on methods of ethology, epidemiology, physiology, animal science, and psychology to make inferences about animal welfare. This morally motivated field has grown rapidly, with the number of animal welfare publications increasing 10–15 percent each year (Walker et al. 2014).

Although there is no unified theory of animal welfare, many scientists working in the field hold a mental state conception whereby welfare is ultimately reducible to changes in affective experience (Robbins et al. 2017). Not unlike human psychology, the field has had a largely pathocentric bias, focusing mostly on negatively valenced affective states such as pain, stress, and fear (Perrson and Shaw 2015). Despite this, boredom has received relatively little scholarly attention. The prevailing hedonic conception of welfare among animal welfare scientists makes the impact of boredom on animal welfare clear—as a negatively valenced mental state, boredom directly harms animals (reduces their welfare) by virtue of its negative hedonic tone. Objective List Theories of welfare also allow for the possibility of boredom to diminish welfare due to its hedonic tone, yet unlike hedonism, these theories also leave open the possibility of construing boredom's impact on welfare instrumentally, as a symptom of a failure to live a meaningful life. According to the meaning-based models discussed above, regardless of boredom's hedonic tone, its presence likely signifies a lack of agency (a failure to engage with one's environment) and therefore meaning. This relationship between the experience of boredom in animals, on the one hand, and agency and meaning, on the other hand, deserves much greater consideration. Currently, meaning does not typically enter discussions of what constitutes a good life for animals, but it may perhaps underlie, even if unconsciously, some ethical concerns about treatment of animals that focus on "naturalness," that is, it may explain why many people seem to value animals living what they perceive as natural lives (Yeates 2018) even when science and/or logic suggest that some natural experiences would negatively influence welfare (e.g., exposure to predation threat; Browning 2020).

Despite the immense power of science to further our understanding of boredom in humans and animals, we must acknowledge that it is necessarily limited when it comes to understanding the ethical implications, as is true with other aspects of welfare. It is often contended that the experience of boredom is necessary for proper functioning and only when boredom becomes prolonged or chronic should we be concerned (e.g., Elpidorou 2018). Nonetheless, specifying the point at which boredom becomes "prolonged" or "chronic" entails a subjective judgment. Recognizing this does not imply such judgments are meaningless or mere matters of opinion. Just as it is not possible to objectively demarcate the point at which night turns to day or hot turns to cold, such is the case for the point at which boredom negatively affects animal welfare, leaving room for reasonable people to disagree on this threshold. However, there will be many more cases at the extremes where the experience of boredom is so enduring that few will doubt its impact on animal welfare.

4. CONCLUSIONS

While boredom has long been acknowledged as a common emotional state in humans, and suspected in a number of other species, its importance is now being better recognized. It is believed to be functional, motivating us to seek out valuable opportunities and focusing our attention. Boredom in animals is hypothesized to be caused by housing animals in austere environments that do not match those they evolved to inhabit and the motivations that flow from that history; this is analogous to the constrained, monotonous situations that elicit the state in humans. It has been demonstrated that such situations result in a core feature of boredom, elevated general motivation for stimuli, in mink and ferrets, suggesting they do experience boredom-like states. Other mammals and birds are likely to have similar motivations for novel or otherwise engaging stimuli. However, much is still not understood about boredom and the ways it might manifest or be experienced across species. Broadening the research through inclusion of a comparative perspective can have benefits for understanding boredom as a whole, and its practical and moral implications for humans and for other animals.

REFERENCES

Allen, Colin, and Michael Trestman. 2017. "Animal Consciousness." In *The Blackwell Companion to Consciousness* (Second Edition), edited by Susan Schneider and Max Velmans, 63–76. Malden, MA: Wiley Blackwell.

Andrews, Kristin. 2011. "Beyond Anthropomorphism: Attributing Psychological Properties to Animals." In *The Oxford Handbook of Animal Ethics*, edited by Tom L. Beauchamp and R. G. Frey, 469–94. New York: Oxford University Press.

Anisman, Hymie, and Kim Matheson. 2005. "Stress, Depression, and Anhedonia: Caveats Concerning Animal Models." *Neuroscience and Biobehavioral Reviews* 29, no. 4–5: 525–46.

Atkinson, Janette, and Oliver Braddick. 2012. "Visual Attention in the First Years: Typical Development and Developmental Disorders." *Developmental Medicine & Child Neurology* 54, no. 7: 589–95.

Bassett, Lois, and Hannah M. Buchanan-Smith. 2007. "Effects of Predictability on the Welfare of Captive Animals." *Applied Animal Behaviour Science* 102, no. 3–4: 223–45.

Berlyne, Daniel E. 1960. *Conflict, Arousal, and Curiosity*. New York: McGraw-Hill.

Browning, Heather. 2020. "The Natural Behavior Debate: Two Conceptions of Animal Welfare." *Journal of Applied Animal Welfare Science* 23, no. 3: 325–37.

Burghardt, Gordon M. 2014. "A Brief Glimpse at the Long Evolutionary History of Play." *Animal Behavior and Cognition* 1, no. 2: 90–98.

Burn, Charlotte C. 2017. "Bestial Boredom: A Biological Perspective on Animal Boredom and Suggestions for Its Scientific Investigation." *Animal Behaviour* 130: 141–51.

Clement, Grace. 2013. "Animals and Moral Agency: The Recent Debate and Its Implications." *Journal of Animal Ethics* 3, no. 1: 1–14.

Cronbach, Lee J., and Paul E. Meehl. 1955. "Construct Validity in Psychological Tests" *Psychological Bulletin* 52, no. 4: 281–302.

Damasio, Antonio R. 1999. *The Feeling of What Happens: Body and Emotion in the Making of Consciousness*. San Diego: Houghton Mifflin Harcourt.

Darden, Donna K. 1999. "Boredom: A Socially Disvalued Emotion." *Sociological Spectrum*, *19*, no. 1: 13–37.

Daschmann, Elena C., Thomas Goetz, and Robert H. Stupnisky. 2011. "Testing the Predictors of Boredom at School: Development and Validation of the Precursors to Boredom Scales." *British Journal of Educational Psychology* 81, no. 3: 421–40. https://doi.org/10.1348/000709910X526038.

Dawkins, Marian S. 2004. Using Behaviour to Assess Animal Welfare. *Animal Welfare* 13, no. 1: 3–7.

Decker, Samuel. 2019. "Welfare Benefit from Enrichment Provision Schemes in American Mink (*Neovison vison*)." PhD diss., University of Guelph.

Demoulin, Stéphanie., Jacques-Philippe Leyens, Maria-Paola Paladino, Ramón Rodriguez-Torres, Armando Rodriguez-Perez and John Dovidio. 2004. "Dimensions of 'Uniquely' and 'Non-Uniquely' Human Emotions." *Cognition and Emotion* 18, no. 1: 71–96.

Droit-Volet, Sylvie. 2013. "Time Perception, Emotions and Mood Disorders." *Journal of Physiology-Paris* 107, no. 4: 255–64.

Eastwood, John D., Alexandra Frischen, Mark J. Fenske, and Daniel Smilek. 2012. "The Unengaged Mind." *Perspectives on Psychological Science* 7, no. 5: 482–95.

Elpidorou, Andreas. 2014. "The Bright Side of Boredom." *Frontiers in Psychology* 5: 1245.

Elpidorou, Andreas. 2017. "The Moral Dimensions of Boredom: A Call for Research. *Review of General Psychology* 21, no. 1: 30–48.

Elpidorou, Andreas. 2018. "The Good of Boredom." *Philosophical Psychology* 31, no. 3: 323–51.

Elpidorou, Andreas. 2020. "Is Boredom One or Many? A Functional Solution to the Problem of Heterogeneity." *Mind & Language*. Advance online publication. https://doi.org/10.1111/mila.12282.

Elpidorou, Andreas, and Lauren Freeman. 2019. "Is Profound Boredom Boredom?" In *Heidegger on Affect*, edited by Christos Hadjioannou, 177–203. Cham: Springer International Publishing.

Evans, Edward Payson. 1906. *The Criminal Prosecution and Capital Punishment of Animals*. London: William Heinemann.

Fahlman, Shelley A., Kimberley B. Mercer-Lynn, David B. Flora, and John D. Eastwood. 2013. "Development and Validation of the Multidimensional State Boredom Scale." *Assessment* 20, no. 1: 68–85.

Fahlman, Shelley A., Kimberley B. Mercer, Peter Gaskovski, Adrienne E. Eastwood, and John D. Eastwood. 2009. "Does a Lack of Life Meaning Cause Boredom? Results from Psychometric, Longitudinal, and Experimental Analyses." *Journal of Social and Clinical Psychology* 28, no. 3: 307–40.

Farmer, Richard, and Norman D. Sundberg. 1986. "Boredom Proneness—The Development and Correlates of a New Scale." *Journal of Personality Assessment* 50, no. 1: 4–17.

Fraser, David, and Christine J. Nicol. 2011. "Preference and Motivation Research." In *Animal Welfare* (Third Edition), edited by Michael C. Appleby, I. Anna Olsson, and Francisco Galindo, 213–31. Wallingford: CABI.

Girgen, Jen. 2003. "The Historical and Contemporary Prosecution and Punishment of Animals." *Animal Law 9*: 97.

Goldberg, Yael K., John D. Eastwood, Jennifer LaGuardia, and James Danckert. 2011. "Boredom: An Emotional Experience Distinct from Apathy, Anhedonia, or Depression." *Journal of Social and Clinical Psychology* 30, no. 6: 647–66.

Goetz, Thomas, Anne C. Frenzel, Nathan C. Hall, Ulrike E. Nett, Reinhard Pekrun, and Anastasiya A. Lipnevich. 2014. "Types of Boredom: An Experience Sampling Approach." *Motivation and Emotion* 38, no. 3: 401–19.

Greenwald, Anthony G., and Mahzarin R. Banaji. 2017. "The Implicit Revolution: Reconceiving the Relation Between Conscious and Unconscious." *American Psychologist* 72, no. 9: 861–71.

Healy, Kevin, Luke McNally, Graeme D. Ruxton, Natalie Cooper, and Andrew L. Jackson. 2013. "Metabolic Rate and Body Size are Linked With Perception of Temporal Information." *Animal Behaviour* 86, no. 4: 685–96.

Hintze, Sara, Freija Maulbetsch, Lucy Asher, and Christoph Winckler. 2020. "Doing Nothing and What It Looks Like: Inactivity in Fattening Cattle." *Peer J* 8: e9395.

Insel, Thomas R. 2007. "From Animal Models to Model Animals." *Biological Psychiatry* 62, no. 12: 1337–39.

Johannsen, Kyle. 2019. "Are Some Animals Also Moral Agents?" *Animal Sentience* 23, *no.* 27. DOI: 10.51291/2377-7478.1404.

Keltner, Dacher, and Daniel T. Cordaro. 2017. "Understanding Multimodal Emotional Expressions: Recent Advances in Basic Emotion Theory." In *The Science of Facial Expression*, edited by José-Miguel Fernández-Dols and James A. Russell, 57–75. New York: Oxford University Press.

Kirkden, Richard David. 2020. "Assessing motivational strength and studies of boredom andenrichment in pigs." PhD diss., University of Cambridge.

Korsgaard, Christine. 2004. "Fellow Creatures: Kantian Ethics and Our Duties to Animals." In *The Tanner Lectures on Human Values*, edited by Grethe B. Peterson, 79–110. Salt Lake City: University of Utah Press.

LeDoux, Joseph E. 2014. "Coming to Terms With Fear." *Proceedings of the National Academy of Sciences* 111, no. 8: 2871–78.

Lilley, Malin K., Stan A. Kuczaj, and Deirdre B. Yeater. 2017. "Individual Differences in Nonhuman Animals: Examining Boredom, Curiosity, and Creativity." In *Personality in Nonhuman Animals*, edited by Jennifer Vonk, Alexander Weiss, and Stan A. Kuczaj, 257–75. Cham: Springer.

Liu, Zhenzhen. 2019. "The Effects of Environmental Enrichment on the Health, Behaviour, and Welfare of Fast-Growing Broilers." PhD diss. University of Guelph.

Lockard, Robert B. 1971. "Reflections on the Fall of Comparative Psychology: Is There a Message for U All?." *American Psychologist* 26, no. 2: 168–79.

Low, Philip, Jaak Panksepp, Diana Reiss, David Edelman, Bruno Van Swinderen, and Christof Koch. 2012. "The Cambridge Declaration on Consciousness." Presented at the Francis Crick Memorial Conference on Consciousness in Human and Non-Human Animals at Churchill College, University of Cambridge, UK, July 7, 2012.

MacLean, Evan L., and Brian Hare. 2018. "Enhanced Selection of Assistance and Explosive Detection Dogs Using Cognitive Measures." *Frontiers in Veterinary Science* 5: 236. https://doi.org/10.3389/fvets.2018.00236.

Malkovsky, Ela, Colleen Merrifield, Yael Goldberg, and James Danckert. 2012. "Exploring the Relationship between Boredom and Sustained Attention." *Experimental Brain Research* 221, no. 1: 59–67.

Mason, Georgia J. 2010. "Species Differences in Responses to Captivity: Stress, Welfare and the Comparative Method." *Trends in Ecology & Evolution* 25, no. 12: 713–21.

Meagher, Rebecca K., Dana L. M. Campbell, and Georgia J. Mason. 2017. "Boredom-like States in Mink and Their Behavioural Correlates: A Replicate Study." *Applied Animal Behaviour Science* 197 (Supplement C): 112–19. https://doi.org/10.1016/j.applanim.2017.08.001.

Meagher, Rebecca K., and Georgia J. Mason. 2012. "Environmental Enrichment Reduces Signs of Boredom in Caged Mink." *PLoS One* 7, no. 11: e49180. https://doi.org/10.1371/journal.pone.0049180.

Meehan, Cheryl and Joy Mench. 2002. "Environmental Enrichment Affects the Fear and Exploratory Responses to Novelty of Young Amazon Parrots." *Applied Animal Behaviour Science* 79, no. 1: 75–88.

Mehta, Pranjal H., and Samuel D. Gosling. 2008. "Bridging Human and Animal Research: A Comparative Approach to Studies of Personality and Health." *Brain, Behavior, and Immunity* 22, no. 5: 651–61.

Mellor, David. 2016. "Updating Animal Welfare Thinking: Moving beyond the Five Freedoms towards A Life Worth Living." *Animals* 6, no. 3: 21. https://doi.org/10.3390/ani6030021.

Mendl, Michael, Oliver HP Burman, Richard MA Parker, and Elizabeth S. Paul. 2009. "Cognitive Bias as an Indicator of Animal Emotion and Welfare: Emerging Evidence and Underlying Mechanisms." *Applied Animal Behaviour Science* 118, nos. 3–4: 161–81.

Mendl, Michael, Oliver HP Burman, and Elizabeth S. Paul. 2010. "An Integrative and Functional Framework for the Study of Animal Emotion and Mood." *Proceedings of the Royal Society B-Biological Sciences* 277, no. 1696: 2895–904.

Morris, Paul H., Christine Doe, and Emma Godsell. 2008. "Secondary Emotions in Non-Primate Species? Behavioural Reports and Subjective Claims by Animal Owners." *Cognition and Emotion* 22, no. 1: 3–20.

Morris, Paul, Sarah Knight, and Sarah Lesley. 2012. "Belief in Animal Mind: Does Familiarity With Animals Influence Beliefs About Animal Emotions?." *Society & Animals* 20, no. 3: 211–24.

Nagel, Thomas. 1974. What Is It Like to Be a Bat? *The Philosophical Review* 83, no. 4: 435–50.

Newberry, Ruth C. 1995. Environmental Enrichment: Increasing the Biological Relevance of Captive Environments. *Applied Animal Behaviour Science* 44, no. 2–4: 229–43.

Nisbett, Richard E., and Timothy D. Wilson. 1977. "Telling More Than We Can Know: Verbal Reports on Mental Processes." *Psychological Review* 84, no. 3: 231–59.

Panksepp, Jaak. 2004. *Affective Neuroscience: The Foundations of Human and Animal Emotions*. Oxford: Oxford University Press.

Persson, Kirsten, and David Shaw. 2015. "Empirical Methods in Animal Ethics." *Journal of Agricultural and Environmental Ethics* 28, no. 5: 853–66.

Pinker, Steven. 2012. *The Better Angels of Our Nature: Why Violence Has Declined*. New York: Penguin Group USA.

Polanco, Andrea, Rebecca K. Meagher, and Georgia Mason. 2021. "Boredom-like exploratory responses in farmed mink reflect states that are rapidly reduced by environmental enrichment, but unrelated to stereotypic behaviour or 'lying awake.'" *Applied Animal Behaviour Science* 238: 105323.

Purves, Duncan, and Nicholas Delon. 2018. "Meaning in the Lives of Humans and Other Animals." *Philosophical Studies* 175, no. 2: 317–38.

Riffkin, Rebecca. 2015. "In U.S., More Say Animals Should Have Same Rights as People." May 18, 2015. *Gallup Social Series: Values and Beliefs*. https://news.gallup.com/poll/183275/say-animals-rights-people.aspx.

Robbins, Trevor. 2002. "The 5-Choice Serial Reaction Time Task: Behavioural Pharmacology and Functional Neurochemistry." *Psychopharmacology* 163, no. 3–4: 362–80.

Robbins, Jesse, Becca Franks, and Marina von Keyserlingk. 2018. "'More Than a Feeling': An Empirical Investigation of Hedonistic Accounts of Animal Welfare." *PLoS One* 13, no. 3: e0193864.

Rowlands, Mark. 2013. "Animals and Moral Motivation: A Response to Clement." *Journal of Animal Ethics* 3, no. 1: 15–24.

Russell, James A., and Lisa Feldman Barrett. 1999. "Core Affect, Prototypical Emotional Episodes, and Other Things Called Emotion: Dissecting the Elephant." *Journal of Personality and Social Psychology* 76, no. 5: 805–19.

Ryan, Amy. 2017. "The Effects of Predictability on Stereotypic Behavior in Nonclinical Adult Humans (*Homo sapiens*) and Rhesus Macaques (*Macaca mulatta*)." PhD diss. University of Massachusetts-Amherst.

Sandøe, Peter, and Stine Christiansen. 2013. The *Ethics of Animal Use*. Oxford: John Wiley & Sons.

Sarter, Martin. 2004. "Animal Cognition: Defining the Issues." *Neuroscience & Biobehavioral Reviews* 28, no. 7: 645–50.

Shapiro, Paul. 2006. "Moral Agency in Other Animals." *Theoretical Medicine and Bioethics* 27, no. 4: 357–73.

Špinka, Marek. 2019. "Animal Agency, Animal Awareness and Animal Welfare." *Animal Welfare* 28, no. 1: 11–20.

Špinka, Marek, Ian Duncan, and Tina Widowski. 1998. "Do Domestic Pigs Prefer Short-Term to Medium-Term Confinement? *Applied Animal Behaviour Science* 58, no. 3–4: 221–32.

Stevens, Jeffrey. 2010. "The Challenges of Understanding Animal Minds." *Frontiers in Psychology* 1: 203.

Svendsen, Lars. 2019. "Animal Boredom." In *Boredom Is in Your Mind*, edited by Josefa Ros Velasco, 135–47. Cham: Springer.

Svendsen, Lars. 2005. *A Philosophy of Boredom*. London: Reaktion Books.

Tinbergen Nico. 1951. *The Study of Instincts*. Oxford: Clarendon Press.

Toohey, Peter. 2011. *Boredom: A Lively History*. London: Yale University Press.

Van Tilburg, Wijnand A.P., and Eric R. Igou. 2012. "On Boredom: Lack of Challenge and Meaning as Distinct Boredom Experiences." *Motivation and Emotion* 36, no. 2: 181–94.

Van Tilburg, Wijnand A.P., and Eric R. Igou. 2017. "Boredom Begs to Differ: Differentiation From Other Negative Emotions." *Emotion* 17, no. 2: 309–22. https://doi.org/10.1037/emo0000233

Walker, Michael, Maria Diez-Leon, and Georgia Mason. 2014. "Animal Welfare Science: Recent Publication Trends and Future Research Priorities." *International Journal of Consumer Studies* 27, no. 1: 80–100.

Watanabe, Shigeru. 2007. "How Animal Psychology Contributes to Animal Welfare." *Applied Animal Behaviour Science* 106, no. 4: 193–202.

Watanabe, Shigeru, and Yumiko Yamazaki. 2009. "Editorial: New Waves and Purpose of Comparative Cognition Study." *Japanese Psychological Research* 51, no. 3: 111–14.

Webster, John. 2008. *Animal Welfare: Limping Towards Eden*. Oxford: Blackwell Publishing.

Westgate, Erin C. 2020. "Why Boredom Is Interesting." *Current Directions in Psychological Science* 29, no. 1: 33–40.

Westgate, Erin C., and Timothy D. Wilson. 2018. "Boring Thoughts and Bored Minds: The MAC Model of Boredom and Cognitive Engagement." *Psychological Review* 125, no. 5: 689–713.

Wittmann, Marc, and Sandra Lehnhoff. 2005. "Age Effects in Perception of Time." *Psychological Reports* 97, no. 3: 921–35.

Wong, Albert H.C., and Sheena A. Josselyn. 2016. "Caution When Diagnosing Your Mouse With Schizophrenia: The Use and Misuse of Model Animals for Understanding Psychiatric Disorders." *Biological Psychiatry* 79, no. 1: 32–8.

Yeates, James. 2018. "Naturalness and Animal Welfare." *Animals* 8, no. 4: 53. https://doi.org/10.3390/ani8040053.

Chapter 12

The Long Hard Road Out of Boredom

Josefa Ros Velasco

The phenomenon of boredom is of utmost importance today for researchers in a wide variety of disciplines, including those in mental health sciences, social and political sciences, and pedagogy. In the preceding centuries, however, boredom also captured the attention of philosophers, critical theorists, theologians, and writers from a moral perspective. Boredom was considered a shameful phenomenon in ancient Greece, a cardinal sin in the Middle Ages, and a product of alienation in modernity. Today, though, boredom is defined not so much in terms of its moral nature or its—social and cultural—environmental causes, but in terms of its underlying psychological conditions and its relationship to the deviant behaviors and transgressive thoughts at the individual and social level that result from efforts to cope with it. The aim of this chapter is to present briefly the history of boredom from a moral perspective from ancient times to today, and to explore the evolution of our understanding of boredom according to different ethical-social paradigms.

The long hard road out of boredom[1] probably started much earlier than scholars dare to admit. In his posthumous work *Description of Man* (2006), the German philosopher Hans Blumenberg stated that boredom might have been the metaphysical beginning of the world, echoing the Kierkegaardian fiction in *Either/Or*. There, Kierkegaard writes:

> The gods were bored; therefore they created human beings. Adam was bored because he was alone; therefore Eve was created. Since that moment, boredom entered the world and grew in quantity in exact proportion to the growth of population. Adam was bored alone; then Adam and Eve were bored en famille. After that, the population of the world increased and the nations were bored en masse. To amuse themselves, they hit upon the notion of building a tower so high that it would reach the sky. This notion is just as boring as the tower was high and is

a terrible demonstration of how boredom had gained the upper hand. Then they were dispersed around the world, just as people now travel abroad, but they continued to be bored. And what consequences this boredom had: humankind stood tall and fell far, first through Eve, then from the Babylonian tower. (1987, 286)

The passage suggests that the world itself might be the creation of all-powerful beings bored with their own eternity, whose response to such boredom (creation) would in turn become the problem of boredom for the rest of us. In addition to Kierkegaard and Blumenberg, Nietzsche also stated in *The Antichrist* (2005, 46) that from a bored God only a bored man could have resulted since he was created in his own image and likeness:

The old God, wholly "spirit," wholly high-priest, wholly perfection, takes a stroll in his garden: but he is bored. Even gods cannot escape boredom. What does he do? He invents human beings,—the human is entertaining. . . . But look, even the human is bored.

And so perhaps it is because of boredom that "the world [went] backwards," for boredom was "the root of all evil," as Kierkegaard writes (1987, 286). Or quoting Blumenberg this time, "the end of the world might have the same motivation: the boredom with it" (UNF 2461).[2]

Putting aside myths of what boredom might have caused or will cause, Blumenberg is certain that boredom was an essential part of the life of our most remote ancestors (Ros Velasco 2017b). He considers boredom to be one of "the strongest driving passions of man" ([card without title]) that, at the beginning, acts as a paralyzing force, but then triggers a "violent repulsion" ([card without title]) against the boring environment, thus avoiding the over-adaptation to which all beings naturally tend and preventing stagnation. In this sense, Blumenberg understands boredom as one of those negative emotions that act as an alerting system to protect life and facilitate self-preservation. Boredom, he writes, "is a unitary form of anticipatory behavior adjusted to anthropogenic situations" (2006, 699). The ability to experience boredom, seen as an adaptive emotion in Blumenbergian terms, was acquired at some point in our evolutionary race, probably by the last pre-sapiens.[3] For Blumenberg, it was precisely the need to cope with boredom through a wide variety of inventions—storytelling, mythology, dances, music, art or decoration, among others—that caused our ancestors to acquire higher levels of intelligence (1968–1988, 021851). Again, before Blumenberg, Nietzsche (1997, 229) also claimed that "mythology, its song, its dance, its linguistic inventiveness [. . .] [were] a lascivious antidote to the exhaustion and boredom of its existence." Nevertheless, at that time, the archaic societies were not sophisticated enough to make boredom a moral experience.

The first conjectures about boredom as a moral phenomenon can be traced back to ancient Greece. However, boredom was barely mentioned in the great literary and philosophical works of the time (Leslie 2009). Indeed, after Peter Toohey (1987, 1988, 1990, 1997) and Reinhard Kuhn's (1976) efforts for tracking the signals of boredom in ancient Greek works were met with only partial success,[4] scholars asked themselves whether Greeks experienced boredom. According to Toohey (1988, 153), "It would be incredible to maintain that Greeks did not feel such an emotion." Moreover, Martin, Sadlo, and Stew (2006, 194) supported the idea that "boredom was a subject which concerned the ancient Greeks." So, why is it so difficult to find references to boredom in their writings? Following Isis Leslie (2009), in ancient Greece, political responsibilities and self-cultivation through discipline were more important than personal preferences and desires. Being bored evidenced free time availability and a lack of interest in and dedication to the *polis*. From a moral perspective, the experience of boredom would have been considered to be a vice: to have time to be bored, as a result of not being committed to public life, was tantamount to giving up an aspect of human existence. And so: Did the ancient Greeks get bored? Quite probably. Yet, they did not write about their boredom very often, for they did not want to be remembered as the subjects of such a morally problematic emotion.

The situation was different for the Epicureans, for whom acquiring virtue required the liberation from political affairs, and being idle and bored was a natural consequence of the acquisition of leisure time. The spreading of Epicurus's ethics and the loss of popularity of the *homo politicus* were inherited from Roman Greece to the time of the Roman Empire. During the latter period, the norm was to obey laws and government, which left time for private issues and boredom. Here, we can find complaints about boredom and means to cope with it in several literary and philosophical works, including, to name a few, Lucretius's *On the Nature of Things*, Horace's *Epistles* and *Satires*, Seneca's *Letters from a Stoic* and *On the Tranquility of Mind*, Aelianus's *Various History*, and Diogenes of Oenoanda's *Fragments*. According to these and other authors' claims, boredom was a very common experience of wealthy people who did not know how to meaningfully spend their time. Although they did not have to get involved in public affairs, such wealthy individuals still needed to feel they were living life to the fullest. The works of Roman authors are replete with examples that denote the *horror loci* and its relationship to boredom, as well as with hints as to how to escape boredom through philosophical and contemplative reflection.

An excess of contemplation was the main reason that medieval monks suffered from boredom. When Christianity became the absolute value system in the Middle Ages, men of faith, who were fully dedicated to love God in monasteries, experienced what it has been called "acedia" in the literature. This is, we can say, a kind of boredom resulting from the satiety of having to spend all of one's time doing the same religious task over and over. Boredom of this sort—if we can still speak of boredom—was understood to be a cardinal sin and condemned by Christian morality for representing a deviation from devoting one's time to the contemplation of divinity. Many examples of this condemnation can be found in the works of the philosophers and theologians of the time.[5]

The pressure of Christian morals affected not only the clergy but the whole society. Following Ángel Aguirre Baztán's analysis (1994, 94), "until the 10th century, monastic acedia was considered as a temptation [. . .]. In the 11th century, leisure and drowsiness are highlighted, in the 12th century, the protagonist is lack of fervor, and, in the 13th century, acedia is understood as internalized or depressive sadness." To Baztán's claim, I would add that, during the first ten centuries, boredom was considered to be primarily a sin and a vice, and that after that period, depression and sadness turned boredom into melancholy. At this point, acedia had gone through the three phases Wenzel speaks (2017) of: the monastic, the scholastic, and the popular one.

Moving forward in time, the Renaissance is one of the most challenging periods to talk about boredom and its moral character. During this time, two events were relevant to understanding the role of boredom: on the one hand, the discovery and valorization of scientific knowledge and, on the other hand, the rejection of the medieval monastic and religious life. As announced earlier, acedia was replaced with melancholy in an attempt "to legitimize the monastic notion scientifically and subtract it from the religious domain" (Peretó Rivas 2011, 13), that is to say, to secularize boredom. This happened toward the end of the Middle Ages, when the trend was to consider boredom in light of its relationship to psychopathological states such as depression and sadness. While acedia was an emotion linked to the moral domain, its union with these psychological states moved boredom toward the natural level. In other words, acedia affected the soul whereas melancholy the body. The couple of acedia-melancholy continued to belong to this intermediate state between spirituality and medicine for centuries, as the works of many writers demonstrate, including, among many others, Dante's *Hell* and *Purgatory*, Petrarch's *My Secret*, Ignatius of Loyola's *Spiritual Exercises*, John of the Cross's *Dark Night of the Soul*, and even the famous *Anatomy of Melancholy* by Robert Burton.

Boredom, then, in part a physiological phenomenon, was curiously revalorized. For a time, the condemnation of boredom stopped. There was a "lasting eclipse" of the blaming of and disdain for boredom (Forthomme 2005, 29). Its presence and link to melancholy and depression were thought to account for intriguing personalities, both reflexive and talented and which were reminiscent of the geniuses that Aristotle talked in his *Problems* (2011) for the first time. "Renaissance glamorized it [boredom]" (Solomon 2014, 295): the painful experience of boredom was considered part of the painful process of self-affirmation of intellectuals during Reformation.

At the same time, the birth of the Protestant ethic and the spirit of capitalism promoted another kind of intellectual individual: one fixated on producing large amounts of work (Ros Velasco and Larrión Randez 2017). In its Calvinist side, Protestant ethic focused on efficient performance and self-promotion in God's eyes. Since salvation or condemnation was predestined by God, the only way to know what the future held was success in labor. The work of people in a state of grace should be perfect, whereas inefficiency and imperfection would demonstrate that one was fated to be condemned (Weber 2002). Thus, Calvinists worked tirelessly to demonstrate to themselves that they were in a state of grace. Such a mentality gave birth to self-confident, active, and persevering individuals suitable for the spirit of capitalism whose moral duty was to increase capital. Weeks and days were divided into hours of work; natural time was replaced with repetitive clock cycles. In such a context, as expected, the fact of having time to get bored was seen as immoral— the best illustration of this conception of boredom is Richard Baxter's *The Saints' Everlasting Rest*.

Over time, the wealth generated by Protestant ethic ended up drying the religious roots and swapping the divine spirit for technical, bureaucratic, and rational aspects. Western socioeconomic structures had their own resources to contain the individual identity. The regular order managed by the administration was able to control society through risk elimination. The accelerated pace of modern life, with the pressures of the schedules and punctuality, and the performance of jobs that did not demand too much mental effort (Simmel 2002), resulted in the complete absence of values and the lack of significant commitments necessary to reach an authentic existence—a full life. Its primary disadvantage was the "lack of tension, the poverty of excitement, the exclusion of Darwinian situations that, for good archaic reasons, remain the most interesting and reliable in terms of intention" (Blumenberg 2006, 715). In the paradigm in which obedient citizens left the responsibility of self-management to the state (Habermas 1992), what remained was a boredom born out of the new ascetic and its ideal of progress, on the one hand, and the new ethics and its morality, on the other hand (Blumenberg 2006). Again, the exceedingly high demands placed on social agents and the lack of time for boredom resulted in exhaustion and fatigue. Redundancy throughout Enlightenment planted the seeds for a sense of deep weariness. This modern boredom anticipated the bourgeoisie's common mood of those unable to enjoy their feelings, unpredictable adventure, and beauty (Weber 2002).

Throughout the nineteenth century, the interest in boredom increased to the point of being considered, by French writers and philosophers, the *disease* of the time.[6] The malaise of ennui was labeled as the mal du siècle. There were multiple conceptions of boredom that intermingle the praises of the melancholic intellectual, the rejection of leisure time by wealthy people, and the weariness of the social impositions and cultural structures and cannons—the latter two were a consequence of Protestant ethics. The modern individual felt bad when they had time for leisure because they felt that they were not taking advantage of their time to make money and obtain social fame. On the contrary, they were doing nothing or nothing meaningful or always the same. The modern individual also felt bad while working for they got bored with routine and rationalized time, with institutions and lifestyle. This demonstrates the moral polarity of boredom at this point—first noted by Paul Valéry's distinction between *l'ennui passager* (*"passing weariness"*) and *l'ennui de vivre* (*"the weariness of living"*) (1989, 51), and, after him, by Siegfried Kracauer's distinction between *vulgäre Langeweile* ("vulgar boredom") and *radikale Langeweile* ("radical boredom") (1995, 331).

This multimoral approach to boredom, which, as we can see, continues to this day, was taken seriously by scholars from two distinct disciplinary sides at the beginning of the twentieth century: sociology and critical theory, on the one hand, and psychology and psychiatry, on the other hand.[7] Thinkers belonging to the first group considered boredom to be the consequence of economic and cultural institutions and structures that forced poor people to work without a break, and wealthy people to follow social cannons and protocols. The second group understood boredom as a result of physiological and psychological malfunctions. Let's develop both perspectives and their implications in moral terms.

When, at the turn of the century, the working class started demanding the reduction of the working day, the concept of *leisure time* spread to the whole society and the experience of boredom became democratized. Not only people from different social strata bore the brunt of structural and institutional weariness, but they also got bored in their spare time. Institutions responsible for social numbness were destined to disappear in the short or long term. However, in the meantime, it was necessary to keep "people employed until the installation of the new forces knocking at the door" (Deleuze 1992, 4). Thus, the same industrial machinery that created habitual boredom scenarios devised a corrective and counterweight solution to the problem through the promotion of the cultural industry of mediated entertainment and moderated emotions. Theaters, theme parks, stadiums, museums, and galleries proliferated to save society, in general, and its members, in particular, from boredom and its resemblance to the nonsense of life. It was a matter of putting an end to the experienced malaise through the "intensification of emotional life" and "the swift and continuous shift of external and internal stimuli" (Simmel 2002, 11).

What was at the very beginning an exciting metropolitan life that made people be continuously in a state of alert became the source of boredom again (Simmel 2002). The arousing life in the metropolis hid long periods of solitude, repetition, predictability, and boredom (Lefebvre 2012). In this sense, the solution to boredom through mediated consumption of mass entertainment was a failure since boredom increased, as promises of massively produced excitation did too. This attempt to create a cultural institution to generate novelty to avoid boredom regularly resulted in a greater experience of boredom.

Boredom resulting from the products of mass culture turned into anguish, anxiety, and existential unease throughout the first half of the twentieth century: the Sartrean *nausée*, in the literal sense. A nasty weariness was a recognizable part of everyday life (Blanchot 1987) and offered two contradicting options at the same time: to desire something and not to desire anything. To fight against boredom, people had no choice other than "giving one's own personality a certain status within the framework of metropolitan life" and adopting "the strangest eccentricities [. . .] extravagances of self-differentiation, of caprice, of fastidiousness [. . .] [as] a form of 'being different'—of making oneself noticeable" (Simmel 2002, 8). Boredom began leading individuals to a regression to the most primitive psychological states—bestiality, fear, childishness—which resulted in transgressive behavior and thinking.

It has been said that, during this period, boredom gave rise to terrible atrocities. We cannot say what was more annoying and distressing. Was it getting bored with doing nothing? Or was it getting bored with something that was meant to alleviate one's boredom? Still, there was no doubt that for the Western societies of that time the cure was worse than the disease. Boredom was condemned as a symptom of an ailing society by sociologists, philosophers, and critical theorists, as the most exceptional desires of madness were deemed to arose from its suffering. Boredom promoted the taste for the deviant and the dangerous (Blumenberg 2006) and stimulated compulsive action as a means to compensate through amplification. Many testimonials show that boredom woke up the "most intimate wishes of death" (Blumenberg 2006, 719). For example, Paul Valéry said he was "longing for a great monstrous war" (quoted in Blumenberg 2006, 718) to wipe out boredom; Théophile Gautier stated he preferred "barbarism rather than boredom" (Steiner 1971, 11); and Agnes Heller talked about "the outbreak of World War I as an exciting experience and potential for the Great Adventure" as a consequence of "the monotony of everyday life with its repetitive activities" (2009, 37). The first one even admitted, in a letter to André Gide, to be envious of the soldiers who took part in an 1891 massacre in which ten demonstrators were assassinated. Such was "the aesthetic nature of revolts against boredom" (Blumenberg 2006, 717).

People asked themselves why they should not kill somebody just to kill boredom. Soldiers' testimonies like that of the decorated World War I combatant Berthold Feuchtwanger reveal that boredom was a reason for killing others as a pastime (Blumenberg UNF 2348). According to Blumenberg, "people [even] become terrorists because they get bored with the established order, but they also cease to be terrorists because this is boring" (2006, 707). Doctors even diagnosed figures of extreme historical importance (e.g., Adolf Hitler) as patients who suffered from profound and severe boredom (Blumenberg UNF 2935–2939). And so boredom, it has been said, "had claimed more victims than hatred" (Blumenberg UNF 2348).

However, boredom not only woke up a morbid taste for war, barbarism, and the death of others, but also promoted expectations for self-death and self-destruction. Regarding the latter, drug consumption beyond medicinal use became a trend among the most elitist circles. Thinkers like Freud and Hammond agreed that cocaine was a valuable substance not only for strictly therapeutic purposes but for recreative uses (Eschotado 1999). Regarding suicide, its close relationship to boredom was posited in the literature of the previous century and continued to be a literary resource at the beginning of the twentieth century—see, for instead, Gustav Flaubert's *Madame Bovary* (2004) or Samuel Beckett's *Malone Dies* (1991). Indeed, some sociologists took seriously the relationship between boredom and suicide, as Émile Durkheim did in his *Suicide: A Study in Sociology* (2002).

Apart from the taste for transgressive and morbid thinking and behavior through war admiration, drug consumption, and suicidal ideation, other risky and pathological behaviors were linked to boredom, such as those of people suffering from hysteria and hypochondria (Blumenberg 2006; Ros Velasco 2014, 2016). Boredom was elevated to the status of an infestation as if it were "cholera and plague, leprosy and variola" (Blumenberg UNF 166–167). Authors like Kuhn (1976) pointed out that this pathological characterization of boredom was not one topic among others in the twentieth century, but the predominant theme. That is the reason why thinkers like Benjamin (1999) stated that boredom began being considered an epidemic in the 1940s.

Sociologists and critical theorists claimed that the only way to stop the epidemic was to cease waiting for a new paradigm to come naturally, and to start criticizing and undoing the social structures that were promoting boredom and its deviant responses. It was necessary to overcome mass media, commodification, and mass entertainment. Siegfried Kracauer (1995), Theodor Adorno, and Max Horkheimer (2002), among many others, were examples of thinkers whose works attempted to demonstrate the problems of the mass culture and the boredom it produced through a kind of entertainment for the masses. Mass culture was no other thing than an extension of work under late capitalism. Consequently, it was urgent to end the vicious circle of production.

Nevertheless, beyond critical theorists' initiatives to wake up society through social and cultural criticism, other kinds of specialists became interested in the deviant consequences of boredom: these were the specialists in mental health and consciousness disorders. They took the metaphor of *boredom as a disease* at face value. Although the first signs of interest in boredom on the part of mental health professionals took place in the nineteenth century, as evidenced by Brière de Boismont's work, for example, it was not until the first half of the twentieth century that boredom became a matter of concern for psychologists and psychiatrists. At the very beginning, they were in communication with sociologists and philosophers who pointed out that boredom was a constructed emotion caused by the alienating conditions of capitalism—see, for example, one of the first studies on boredom in the workplace by psychologist Hugo Münsterberg (1913). However, when boredom started to become a threat for those who aimed to "compensate for their lack of moral value by seeking intense, but fleeting, experiences" (Leslie 2009, 38), attention moved from social structures to the affective and cognitive particularities of the individuals experiencing boredom.

Although it began with Theodor Lipps's *Guide to Psychology* (1909) and Otto Fenichel's "On the Psychology of Boredom" (1934), the idea that boredom might be a problem of the individual who experiences a mismatch between their capability of being mentally engaged and the inner need for mental activity eventually spread among many scholars. Boredom was no longer a matter of a cultural or social circumstance, but an individual and bodily problem. It was considered a phenomenon rooted inside the subject affecting their individual and social development, but always caused by a conflict between the subject's need for excitement and their own inability to self-stimulate or engage with the environment itself, even when external conditions change.

Boredom understood as a pathological personality trait elicited many reactions. Some psychiatrists decided on experimenting with the bored person by impairing their cognitive and perceptual capacities. For instead, psychiatrist Joseph Barmack experimented with the environmental conditions of a room to see how this affected the bored individual (1939a) and, also, he started supplying benzedrine sulfate and ephedrine hydrochloride to *patients* (1938, 1939b, 1939c). In the most extreme cases, specialists such as Edmund Bergler (1945) contended that boredom was a psychotic disorder with several neurotic implications that must be intervened at the neurological level. Throughout the twentieth century, especially during the second half, works on boredom focused on its physiological nature, its neural aspects, and its measurability, as well as its consequences and therapeutic and pharmaceutical treatments. Boredom was recognized as a pathological personality trait since 1996 by Campbell's *Psychiatric Dictionary* and was included in several encyclopedias of psychology, applied psychology textbooks, and even pharmacological manuals (Bennet and Brown 2007; Hancock and McKim 2013). The study of endogenous/chronic boredom entered the twenty-first century even while denying the historical and social roots of boredom (Ros Velasco 2017a, 2018, 2022).

When considering boredom from a physiological perspective, there seems to be little or nothing to say concerning its morality. Sociology, in the last century, was purely critical of capitalist and consumerist ethics: boredom was the consequence of the time period, and the bored person the victim of its symptoms. Now, we are talking of something else, something resembling a mental illness, especially when boredom is chronic. The bored person is also a victim, but in this case they are a victim of themselves, not of society. However, nowadays, the moral point concerning boredom lies precisely in the need for setting limits to the psychology and psychiatry of boredom through criticizing medical institutions and their trend for turning daily annoyances into mental diseases and for medicalizing them. It has been acknowledged that there is a lack of agreement by specialists on what is boredom, its cognitive implications, and neurological base (Danckert and Allman 2005; Eastwood et al. 2012; Merrifield 2014), despite the growing literature on this complex issue (Ros Velasco 2017a, 2022). Many scholars claim that the study of boredom is in its infancy and has not been paid the attention deserved—an entirely false statement, as I have previously demonstrated (Ros Velasco 2017a), even if we are only paying attention to mental health disciplines (Ros Velasco 2022; Elpidorou 2020). The lack of assessment and measuring instruments remains however a fact, making it impossible for researchers to reach a real understanding of the matter (Vogel-Walcutt et al. 2012; Ros Velasco 2019a).

In short, there are substantial limitations to diagnosing boredom-related issues and to treating them. That is the reason why it is crucial to be cautious and maintain a critical attitude toward the elevation of boredom and other daily annoyances to the status of mental pathology. We have to bear in mind, according to De Chenne and Moddy (1987), that mental health professionals are not merely phenomenologists, but involved participants—theoreticians, therapists, and administrators of drugs. Foucault (2004) was one of the first thinkers in the previous century to highlight how medicine was extending beyond the patients' needs and was in fact an act of authority over patients' lives. More recently, even the editor of the fourth edition of the *Diagnostic and Statistical Manual of Mental Disorders (DSM)*, Allen Frances (2014), pointed out that many psychologists and psychiatrists are promoting life medicalization. They are expanding the number of pathologies and causing normal behaviors to become diseases. They pathologize human suffering and support medicalization to avoid it to the extent that, in the United States, 20 percent of people take psychiatric drugs daily, and a fourth of the population has been diagnosed with a mental disease. Frances (2014) warns that if specialists follow the recommendations of the *DSM-V*, 81 percent of people between eleven and twenty-one years old may be diagnosed with some mental disease. According to Frances (2014), mental health specialists are selfish and unable to look beyond their own perspectives. They have turned daily annoyances into diseases by making wrong decisions and overstating the importance of their fieldwork. The situation is further complicated if we talk about children and adolescents. Campolongo et al. (2015, 141) sounded the alarm in this regard: "in our clinical practice with children, we see how the different problems of daily life have started being medicalized: motivation, academic failure, hyperactivity, lack of attention, boredom, sadness, etcetera."

Turning now specifically to boredom, Blumenberg was perhaps the first to highlight, in the past century, that the understanding of boredom as a mental illness was the result of the imposed definition of *health* as "the complete physical, emotional, and social well-being" by the WHO, which entails that "everything becomes illness and [. . .] the need for treatment is continuous" (2006, 690). This is something professionals have taken advantage, for they found a way to transform their "therapeutic pretensions" into a way to earn a living (2006, 694). According to Blumenberg, making boredom—a widely spread phenomenon today—a mental pathology is a "diagnosis with a great future" for mental health professionals (2006, 713).

The moral problem is not just that of mental health specialists going beyond their *patients'* needs and their own diagnostic capabilities. Nor is it one concerning the economic interests underlying this trend—everybody knows the real beneficiary of the situation is the pharmaceutical industry (Frances 2014; Foucault 2004). The moral problem is the one that Frances points out: In a culture in which people take pills to alleviate their problems, people's ability to cope with stress and also self-security is drastically reduced. Indeed, if this behavior becomes widespread, society as a whole will be weakened (Frances 2014). The moral urgency of carrying out this criticism of mental health authority and the role of medical institutions are of self-preservative nature. Thus, this new step in the road out of boredom brings us back to its evolutionary origins.

As mentioned earlier in this chapter, authors like Blumenberg (Ros Velasco 2019b) understood boredom as an adaptive emotion that was acquired at some point in our evolutionary race for its capacity to make us react against what is not going as desired or expected and for its ability to help us avoid over-adaptation. Like all living beings, human beings tend by nature to seek comfort and an optimal level of adaptation. However, over-adaptation is not desirable since too much comfort is also unbearable (Gehlen 1961). As Kuhn claims (1976, 17):

> Absolute harmony is inseparable from monotony, becomes an ideal to strive for. However, there is something inhuman about such an ideal. Is it even possible for a man to support such sameness in perfection? The likelihood of finding this sought-after condition of perfection intolerable seems evident because the human is incompatible with absolute perfection.

Even most important, such "perfection" reduces our ability to react to future challenges (Blumenberg 2006). Notably, following Blumenberg, boredom helps us to cope with excessive stillness and over-adaptation. It moves us out of an environment in which there is no longer a challenge. It is, thus, responsible for breaking our natural inertia and preventing evolutive stagnation.

How—or *why*—do emotions like boredom do this? They make us react for the simple reason that they are painful and lead us instinctively to fight to escape from them. The experience of boredom is one we cannot ignore. When we are bored, a feeling of disgust and scarcity invades us. We notice an irritation we wish to escape. Boredom even promotes the rejection of existence when it appears as a stillness similar to death. It evokes a great malaise: time stops and life empties of sensations. During the experience of boredom, we feel the annoying impression that time passes more slowly, and when we remember the moment in which we were bored, we face the memory of a hollow experience of impressions that brings to our mind the shortness of life and the guilt of wasted time. That is why it forces us to react: it makes us aware of the circumstances that gave rise to it and motivates us to change those circumstances. It is the combined experience of "stimulus poverty and prohibition of the consequence of falling asleep [which] [. . .] generates internal compensation as an invisible movement" (Blumenberg 2011, 708).

Since boredom causes displeasure, it makes us react in two stages. First of all, it forces us to examine what is wrong with our environment and ourselves. If "primary emotions," according to Toohey (2011, 32), "have their adaptive and Darwinian role in that they help creatures to survive and flourish [. . .] more complex social emotions [. . .] do take some of their impetus from self-consciousness." Boredom is an "adaptation of this primary emotion of disgust" (Toohey 2011, 17) that

> acts as an early warning system designed to protect against situations which may be dangerous for psychological well-being, situations which might encourage agitation and anger and depression. [. . .] [B]oredom increases during a

repetitive and predictable experience [. . .] that it would be in our best interests to escape. [. . .] Boredom [. . .] seems to be a beneficial emotion, warning us away from potentially much more damaging situations. [. . .] [B]oredom should be viewed [. . .] as a sign of worse things to follow unless there's a change in lifestyle. (Toohey 2011, 32)

Second, once we are aware of what needs to be changed, boredom encourages us to do something to promote such a change.

To sum up, boredom drives the movement from self-consciousness to action. Moreover, this not only happens at an individual level. When society as a whole is not satisfied with the context—its structures, institutions, cannons, and so on—it also gets bored, and its boredom pushes it to change by rebelling or reacting to the causes of its dissatisfaction. Boredom acts as a robust social counterweight. That is why history can be considered, following Cioran, in *History and Utopia* (1998), as a result of fear of boredom.

Given that boredom is, according to Blumenberg and others such as Toohey,[8] an essential and necessary, functional and positive life leveler, despite being emotionally painful, we need to learn to tolerate it. It seems to them that we have lost the ability to bear boredom. This is, perhaps, because we understand boredom as a disease itself, not as a symptom. Alternatively, if we are taking it as a symptom, physically and socially speaking, we are focusing our efforts on reducing—or even avoiding all together—the consequence instead of facing the cause. Furthermore, we are paying attention mainly to harmful reactions to boredom, which might be the result of environmental or personal circumstances that resist change and not the outcome of a personality trait or of chronic boredom. However, as a counterpart, many scholars are writing about the creative power of boredom and why it is good to be bored. Following Toohey (2019), I will not state whether boredom is a good or a bad thing—we shouldn't define boredom in terms of our good or bad, constructive or destructive, responses to it, which depend on both ourselves and our context. On the contrary, I want to focus on its functionality and on the knowledge we can achieve from its experience to move our society and ourselves forward. My aim is not to promote or condemn boredom, but to let it be and, ultimately, not to anesthetize it in order to allow evolution and progress for good or bad.

The moral approach to boredom currently requires that we make an effort to understand boredom in history and in our society as a failure that allows some other adjustments in order for the species to survive and improve. It is impossible to eliminate boredom—to do so, it would be to put an end to humanity. Thus, we need to learn to live with boredom and become interested observers of this symptom. The uncomfortable pastime of discommodity is preferable both to risky diagnoses based on insufficient scientific basis and to evolutionary stagnation. This is how I understand the moral issue of boredom.

Table 12.1 The Moral History of Boredom

Historical Period		Moral Paradigm	Name	Classification	Boredom/Leisure Valorization
Prehistory					—
Ancient Times	Classical Greece	Socratic Ethics	ἅλυς	—	Negative (Vice)
	Roman Greece	Epicureanism	ἅλυς / Taedium		Positive (Virtue)
	Roman Empire	Stoicism	Taedium		Negative (Horror Loci/ Depression)
Middle Ages	I–X	Christianity	Acedia		Negative (Capital Sin)
	X				Negative (Vice)
	XI				Negative (Temptation)
	XII				Negative (Drowsiness)
	XIII				Negative (Apathy)
					Negative (Depression)
	XIV–XV		Acedia/melancholy		Negative (Depression)
Renaissance					Positive (Genius)
Modernity	Reformation	Protestant Ethics			Negative (Not in grace state)
	XVII				Negative (Not in grace state)
	XVIII	Capitalist Ethics	Boredom/ Langeweile/Ennui/ Spleen . . .		Negative (No productivity)
	XIX			Passing boredom Boredom of Living	Negative (Meaningless) Negative (Weariness) Positive (Genius)
	XX			Passing boredom Boredom of Living	Negative (Meaningless) Negative (Weariness)
	XXI			Passing boredom Boredom of Living Boredom Proneness	Negative (Meaningless) Negative (Weariness)
Postmodernity		Mental Health		State-boredom	Negative (Disorder) Positive (Functional emotion)
		Anthropology		—	Neutral (Adaptative)

This chapter traced a brief moral history of boredom, its contemporary understanding, and some alternative approaches to build upon the moral psychology of boredom. I aimed to highlight the ethical problems of mental health disciplines concerning their diagnoses regarding boredom at present. Moreover, I aspired to introduce a neglected and useful approach in boredom studies that understands boredom to be an adaptive emotion, instead of a moral one. A survey of the rich and long history of boredom shows that it is a force that drives human behavior (see table 12.1).[9]

NOTES

1. The title of my chapter is a nod to Brian Hugh Warner's (Marilyn Manson) autobiography *The Long Hard Road Out of Hell* (1998). With this choice of words, I want to highlight the importance of the historical path through which human beings have tried to escape boredom and how challenging it was to meet this goal, especially as a result of its moral implications associated in each period, as this chapter aims to demonstrate.

2. This kind of in-text citation corresponds to the unpublished text of Hans Blumenberg, available for consultation at the Deutsches Literaturarchiv Marbach (DLA) in Germany. Henceforth, I will cite them by its identifier UNF or card number (*Karteikarte*). In the list of references, they will appear following the complete location route according to their classification at the DLA, including case (*Schuber*) and folder (*Mappe*), as well as the year of writing and other information when available.

3. Such a claim is not too farfetched given that many scholars are now advocating for the existence of animal boredom. In particular, research on the living conditions of animals in captivity has been able to show that animals can experience moments of boredom. See, for example, Wemelsfelder (1985), Charlton (2000), Meagher and Mason (2012), Ros Velasco (2017b, 2019b), and Svendsen (2019).

4. Vague mentions of boredom can be found in Homer's *Iliad* and *Odyssey*; Pindar's *Odes*; Aristophanes's comedy *The Acharnians*; Euripid's tragedies *Iphigenia in Aulis* and *Medea*; Plato's dialogues *Gorgias*, *The Laws*, and *The Symposium*; and, finally, in Aristotle's *Problems*.

5. Including the *Septuagint* and the Holy Scriptures, as well as Augustine of Hippo's *Confessions* and *The First Catechetical Instruction*; Evagrius of Pontus's *The Praktikos* and *Antirrhetikus*; John Cassian's *Institutes*; Gregory the Great's *Moral Reflections on the Book of Job*; and Thomas Aquinas's *Summa Theologica*, among others.

6. The list of authors is almost endless, but some I have worked on include, from the French side, key representatives such as Sainte-Beuve, Senancour, Châteaubriand, Madame de Staël, Stendhal, George Sanz, Baudelaire, Verlaine, Mallarmé, Flaubert, and Helvétius. Their works inspired the first medical treatises on boredom like that of Brière de Boismont *On Boredom, Tired of Life* in 1850. Also, such works were an important influence on the voluminous writings on boredom by German thinkers. For

example, as representatives of German Romanticism, we might mention Schlegel, Novalis, Hölderlin, Heine, Schiller, Kleist, Büchner, Hoffmann, Tieck, and Goethe; of German Idealism, Kant, Fichte, Schelling, and Hegel, and its critics, Hamann, Schopenhauer, Nietzsche, and Marx; and of German psychology, Freud, and Lipps—not to mention others such as Jacobi, Reinhold, Schubert, Schulze, Feuerbach, Dilthey, and Cassirer. Moreover, we should not forget, of course, Kierkegaard's existentialism, in the same period. See Ros Velasco (2017b).

7. Here we should not forget Heideggerian phenomenology, which will not, however, discuss on this occasion.

8. Likely, Blumenberg was one of the first philosophers to talk about boredom in terms of its functionality, even though there are hints in the works of other thinkers prior to him such as Nietzsche and Schopenhauer. Toohey is really close to Blumenberg in this sense, but he was never familiarized with the German philosopher (basically because his writings on boredom were not published until 2006 and most of them remained unpublished until I compiled them in my PhD Dissertation [2017b]). Toohey's background on the functionality of negative emotions comes from Robert Plutchik and Henry Kellerman (1980) and Antonio Damasio's (1999, 2003) works. At present, a strong core of research is being devoted to explicating the purpose of boredom. Representatives of the functional theories of boredom emphasize "the role that emotions play in conveying information relevant to one's current circumstances. These approaches theorize that boredom acts as a distress signal that motivates behavioral or cognitive change" (Westgate and Wilson 2018, 691; see Elpidorou 2014, 2017). Simply said, boredom signals whether an activity is useful (Bench and Lench 2013), meaningful (Van Tilburg and Igou 2017a, 2017b), and invokes opportunity costs (Kurzban, Duckworth and Myers 2013).

9. This work has benefited from the project FFI2016-78285-R, financed by the Spanish Ministry of Science and Innovation. Some essential ideas are collected in my monograph, *La enfermedad del aburrimiento*, that discusses the history of boredom as a pathology, to be published in 2022 by Alianza Editorial. I want to thank Andreas Elpidorou for including this chapter in his book project.

REFERENCES

Adorno, Theodor, and Max Horkheimer. 2002. *Dialectic of Enlightenment*. Palo Alto: Stanford University Press.

Aguirre Baztán, Ángel. 1994. *Estudios de etnopsicología y etnopsiquiatría*. Barcelona: Marcombo.

Aristotle. 2011. *Problems*. Cambridge: Harvard University Press.

Barmack, Joseph. 1938. "The Effect of Benzedrine Sulfate (*Benzyl Methyl Carbinamine*) Upon the Report of Boredom and other Factors." *Journal of Psychology* 5: 125–33. https://doi.org/10.1080/00223980.1938.9917557.

Barmack, Joseph. 1939a. "A Definition of Boredom: A Reply to Mr. Berman." *American Journal of Psychology* 52, no. 3: 467–71.

Barmack, Joseph. 1939b. "Studies on the Psychophysiology of Boredom: Part I. The Effects of 15mgs of Benzedrine Sulphate and 5mgs of Ephedrine Hydrochloride on Blood Pressure, Report on Boredom, and Other Factors." *Journal of Experimental Psychology* 25, no. 5: 494–505. https://doi.org/10.1037/h0054402.

Barmack, Joseph. 1939c. "Studies on the Psychophysiology of Boredom: Part II. The Effect of Lowered Room Temperature and an Added Incentive on Blood Pressure, Report of Boredom, and Other Factors." *Journal of Experimental Psychology* 25, no. 6: 634–42. https://doi.org/10.1037/h0060574.

Beckett, Samuel. 1991. *Malone Dies*. New York: Grove Press.

Bench, Shane W., and Healther C. Lench. 2013. "On the Function of Boredom." *Behavioral Sciences* 3, no. 3: 459–72. https://doi.org/10.3390/bs3030459.

Benjamin, Walter. 1999. *The Arcades Project*. Cambridge: Harvard University Press.

Bennett, Peter N., and Morris J. Brown. 2007. "Drug Abuse." In *Clinical Pharmacology*, edited by Peter N. Bennet, and Morris J. Brown, 142–74. Oxford: Elsevier Health Sciences.

Bergler, Edmund. 1945. "On the Disease-entity Boredom ("alyosis") and its Psychopathology." *Psychiatric Quarterly* 19, no. 1: 38–51.

Blanchot, Maurice. 1987. "Everyday Speech." *Yale French Studies* 73: 12–20. https://doi.org/10.2307/2930194.

Blumenberg, Hans. 1968–1988. "021851." In *Zettelkasten 01: Anthropologie*. Marbach am Neckar: DLA.

Blumenberg, Hans. 2006. *Beschreibung des Menschen*. Stuttgart: Suhrkamp.

Blumenberg, Hans. n.d. [*Card without Title*]. In *Zettelkasten 26 U-Welt*. Marbach am Neckar: DLA.

Blumenberg, Hans. n.d. UNF 166-167 Diesseits der Langeweile. In S1, M2. Marbach am Neckar: DLA.

Blumenberg, Hans. n.d. UNF 2348 Die Indifferenzen der Langeweile. In S5, M7. Marbach am Neckar: DLA.

Blumenberg, Hans. n.d. UNF 2461 Umkehrung eines Mythos. In S6, M3. Marbach am Neckar: DLA.

Blumenberg, Hans. n.d. UNF 2935-2939: Hitlers Bakterien. In S7, M4. Marbach am Neckar: DLA.

Campbell, Robert. 1996. *Psychiatric Dictionary*. New York: Oxford University Press.

Campolongo, Diana, Andrea Martin, María Soledad Tammaro, and Mora Torregiani. 2015. "Niños medicalizados. VII Congreso Internacional de Investigación y Práctica Profesional en Psicología—XXII Jornadas de Investigación—Décimo Encuentro de Investigadores en Psicología del MERCOSUR. University of Buenos Aires." Acta Académica. Accessed December 4, 2019. https://www.aacademica.org/000-015/714.

Charlton, Bruce G. 2000. "Evolution and the Cognitive Neuroscience of Awareness, Consciousness and Language." *Cognition* 50: 7–15.

Damasio, Antonio R. 1999. *The Feeling of What Happens: Body and Emotion in the Making of Consciousness*. New York: Harcourt Brace & Co.

Damasio, Antonio R. 2003. *Looking for Spinoza: Joy, Sorrow, and the Feeling Brain.* North Eugene: Harvest.

Cioran, Emil. 1998. *History and Utopia.* Chicago: University of Chicago Press.

Danckert, James, and Ava-Ann A. Allman. 2005. "Time Flies When You're Having Fun: Temporal Estimation and the Experience of Boredom." *Brain and Cognition* 59, no. 3: 236–45. https://doi.org/10.1016/j.bandc.2005.07.002.

De Chenne, Timothy K., and Andrea J. Moddy. 1988. "Boredom: Theory and Therapy." *The Psychotherapy Patient* 3, no. 3–4: 17–29. https://doi.org/10.1300/J358v03n03_03.

Deleuze, Gilles. 1992. "Postscript on the Societies of Control." *October* 59 (Winter): 3–7.

Durkheim, Émile. 2002. *Suicide: A Study in Sociology.* London: Taylor & Francis.

Eastwood, John D., Alexandra Frischen, Mark J. Fenske, and Daniel Smilek. 2012. "The Unengaged Mind: Defining Boredom in Terms of Attention." *Perspectives on Psychological Science* 7, no. 5: 482–95. https://doi.org/10.1177/1745691612456044.

Elpidorou, Andreas. 2014. "The Bright Side of Boredom." *Frontiers in Psychology* 5: 1245. https://doi.org/10.3389/fpsyg.2014.01245.

Elpidorou, Andreas. 2017. "The Good of Boredom." *Philosophical Psychology* 31, no. 3: 323–51. https://doi.org/10.1080/09515089.2017.1346240.

Elpidorou, Andreas. 2020. "Neglected Emotions." *The Monist* 103, no. 2: 135–46. https://doi.org/10.1093/monist/onz031.

Eschotado, Antonio. 1999. *A Brief History of Drugs: From the Stone Age to the Stoned Age.* South Paris: Park Street Press.

Fenichel, Otto. 1951. "On the Psychology of Boredom." In *Organization and Pathology of Thought: Selected Sources*, edited by David Rapaport, 349–61. New York: Columbia University Press.

Flaubert, Gustav. 2004. *Madame Bovary.* New York: Oxford University Press.

Forthomme, Bernard. 2005. "Émergence et résurgence de l'acédie." In *Tristesse, acédie et médecine des âmes*, edited by Nathalie Nabert, 15–35. Paris: Beauchesne.

Foucault, Michel. 2004. "The Crisis of Medicine or the Crisis of Antimedicine." *Foucault Studies* 1: 5–19. https://doi.org/10.22439/fs.v0i1.562.

Frances, Allen. 2014. *Saving Normal: An Insider's Revolt Against Out-of-control Psychiatric Diagnosis, DSM-5, Big Pharma, and the Medicalization of Ordinary Life.* New York: William Morrow Paperbacks.

Gehlen, Arnold. 1961. *Anthropologische Forschung.* Hamburg: Rowohlt.

Habermas, Jürgen. 1992. "Further Reflections on the Public Sphere." In *Habermas and the Public Sphere*, edited by Craig Calhoun, 421–61. Cambridge: The MIT Press.

Hancock, Stephanie, and William A. McKim. 2013. *Drugs & Behavior.* New York: Pearson.

Heller, Agnes. 2009. *A Theory of Feelings.* Plymouth: Lexington Books.

Kierkegaard, Søren. 1987. *Either/Or Part I: Kierkegaard's Writings III.* New Jersey: Princeton University Press.

Kracauer, Siegfried. 1995. *The Mass Ornament.* Cambridge: Harvard University Press.

Kuhn, Reinhard C. 1976. *The Demon of Noontide: Ennui in Western Literature.* New Jersey: Princeton University Press.

Kurzban, Robert, Angela Duckworth, Joseph W. Kable, and Justus Myers. 2013. "An Opportunity Cost Model of Subjective Effort and Task Performance." *Behavioral and Brain Sciences* 36, no. 6: 661–79. http://doi.org/10.1017/S0140525X12003196.

Lefebvre, Henri. 2012. *Introduction to Modernity.* New York: Penguin Random House.

Leslie, Isis I. 2009. "From Idleness to Boredom: On the Historical Development of Modern Boredom." In *Essays on Boredom and Modernity,* edited by Barbara Dalle Pezze, and Carlo Salzini, 35–59. New York: Brill.

Lipps, Theodor. 1909. *Leitfaden der Psychologie.* Leipzig: Wilhelm Engelmann.

Martin, Marion, Gaynor Sadlo, and Graham Stew. 2006. "The Phenomenon of Boredom." *Qualitative Research in Psychology* 3, no. 3: 193–211. https://doi.org/10.1191/1478088706qrp066oa.

Meagher, Rebecca K., and Georgia J. Mason. 2012. "Environmental Enrichment Reduces Signs of Boredom in Caged Mink." *PLoS One* 7, no. 11: 1–10. https://doi.org/10.1371/journal.pone.0049180.

Merrifield, Colleen. 2014. "Toward a Model of Boredom: Investigating the Psychophysiological, Cognitive and Neural Correlates of Boredom." PhD diss., University of Waterloo.

Münsterberg, Hugo. 1913. *Psychology and Industrial Efficiency.* Boston: Houghton-Mifflin.

Nietzsche, Friedrich. 1997. *Untimely Meditations.* New York: Cambridge University Press.

Nietzsche, Friedrich. 2005. *The Anti-Christ, Ecce Homo, Twilight of the Idols, and Other Writings.* New York: Cambridge University Press, 2005.

Peretó Rivas, Rubén. 2011. "Acedia y depresión. Aportes para una reconstrucción histórica." *Eä Journal* 3, no. 1: 1–20.

Plutchik, Robert, and Henry Kellerman. 1980. *Emotion: Theory, Research, and Experience,* vol. 1. New York: Academic Press.

Ros Velasco, Josefa. 2014. "Perspectivas filosóficas sobre la hipocondría." In *Blumenberg: La apuesta por una Ilustración tardía,* edited by José Luis Villacañas Berlanga, 85–106. Barcelona: Anthropos.

Ros Velasco, Josefa. 2016. "El diagnóstico kantiano sobre la pareja 'Aburrimiento e hipocondría' y su recepción blumenberguiana." In *Nuevas perspectivas sobre la filosofía de Kant,* edited by Juan Manuel Navarro Cordón, Rafael Orden Jiménez, and Rogelio Rovira Madrid, 315–22. Madrid: Escolar y Mayo: Madrid.

Ros Velasco, Josefa. 2017a. "Boredom: A Comprehensive Study of the State of Affairs." *Thémata* 56: 171–98. https://doi.org/10.12795/themata.2017.i56.08.

Ros Velasco, Josefa. 2017b. *El aburrimiento como presión selectiva en Hans Blumenberg.* PhD diss., Complutense University of Madrid.

Ros Velasco, Josefa. 2018. "Boredom: Humanising or Dehumanising Treatment." In *The Neurobiology-Psychotherapy-Pharmacology Intervention Triangle: The Need for Common Sense in 21st-Century Mental Health*, edited by João G. Pereira, Jorge Gonçalves, and Valeria Bizzari, 251–66. Wilmington: Vernon Press, Cognitive Science and Psychology Series.

Ros Velasco, Josefa. 2019a. "The Helix Center Roundtable on Boredom (New York, April 2018)." In *Boredom Is in Your Mind. A Shared Psychological-Philosophical Approach*, edited by Josefa Ros Velasco, 149–67. Cham: Springer.

Ros Velasco, Josefa. 2019b. "Hans Blumenberg's Philosophical Anthropology of Boredom." In *Metaphorologie, Anthropologie, Phänomenologie. Neue Forschungen zum Nachlass Hans Blumenbergs*, edited by Josefa Ros Velasco, Alberto Fragio Gistau, and Martina Philippi, 91–107. Freiburg: Karl Alber Verlag.

Ros Velasco, Josefa. 2022. *La enfermedad del aburrimiento*. Madrid: Alianza Editorial.

Ros Velasco, Josefa, and Benjamin Larrión Randez. 2017. "The Melancholic and the Choleric: Two Kind of Emotional Intellectuality." *Azafea: Revista de Filosofía* 19, no. 1: 221–49.

Simmel, Georg. 2002. "The Metropolis and Mental Life." In *The Blackwell City Reader*, edited by Gary Bridge, and Sophie Watson, 11–19. Oxford/Malden: Wiley-Blackwell.

Solomon, Andrew. 2014. *The Noonday Demon: An Atlas of Depression*. New York: Simon & Schuster.

Steiner, George. 1971. *In Bluebeard's Castle. Some Notes Towards the Redefinition of Culture*. New Haven: Yale University Press.

Svendsen, Lars. 2019. "Animal Boredom." In *Boredom Is in Your Mind*, edited by Josefa Ros Velasco, 135–48. Cham: Springer.

Toohey, Peter. 1987. "Plutarch, Pyrrh. 13: ἅλυς ναυτιώδης." *Glotta* 64, no. 3–4: 199–202.

Toohey, Peter. 1988. "Some Ancient Notions of Boredom." *Illinois Classical Studies* 13, no. 1: 151–64.

Toohey, Peter. 1990. "Acedia in Late Classical Antiquity." *Illinois Classical Studies* 15, no. 2: 339–52.

Toohey, Peter. 1997. "Trimalchio's Constipation." In *Inventing Ancient Culture: Historicism, Periodization and the Ancient World*, edited by Peter Toohey, and Mark Golden, 50–65. New York: Routledge.

Toohey, Peter. 2011. *Boredom. A Lively History*. New Haven: Yale University Press.

Toohey, Peter. 2019. "Is It a Good Thing to Be Bored?" In *Boredom Is in Your Mind. A Shared Psychological-Philosophical Approach*, edited by Josefa Ros Velasco, 1–10. Berlin: Springer.

Valéry, Paul. 1989. *Collected Works of Paul Valéry. Volume IV: Dialogues*. New Jersey: Princeton University Press.

Van Tilburg, Wijnand A., and Eric R. Igou. 2017a. "Boredom Begs to Differ: Differentiation from Other Negative Emotions." *Emotion* 17, no. 2: 309–22. https://doi.org/10.1037/emo0000233.

Van Tilburg, Wijnand A., and Eric R. Igou. 2017b. "Can Boredom Help? Increased Prosocial Intentions in Response to Boredom." *Self and Identity* 16, no. 1: 82–96. https://doi.org/10.1080/15298868.2016.1218925.

Vogel-Walcutt, Jennifer J., Logan Fiorella, Teresa Carper, and Sae Schatz. 2012. "The Definition, Assessment, and Mitigation of State Boredom Within Educational Settings: A Comprehensive Review." *Educational Psychology Review* 24, no. 1: 89–111. https://doi.org/10.1007/s10648-011-9182-7.

Warner, Brian H. 1998. *The Long Hard Road Out of Hell*. New York: Harper Collins.

Weber, Max. 2002. *Protestant Ethic and the Spirit of Capitalism*. New York: Penguin Random House.

Wemelsfelder, Francoise. 1985. "Animal Boredom: Is a Scientific Study of the Subjective Experiences of Animals Possible?" In *Advances in Animal Welfare Science 1984*, edited by Michael W. Fox, and Linda Mickley, 115–54. Boston/Dordrecht/Lancaster: Martinus Nijhoff.

Wenzel, Siegfried. 2017. *The Sin of Sloth: Acedia in Medieval Thought and Literature*. Chapel Hill: University of North Carolina Press.

Westgate, Erin C., and Timothy D. Wilson. 2018. "Boring Thoughts and Bored Minds: The MAC Model of Boredom and Cognitive Engagement." *Psychological Review* 125, no. 5: 689–713. https://doi.org/10.1037/rev0000097.

Index

About the Contributors

Matilde Aliffi is currently a software engineer at *The Economist*. She received her PhD in Philosophy from the University of Birmingham, with a thesis on the epistemic rationality of emotions. She is interested in emotions, epistemology, rationality, affective computing, and artificial intelligence.

Shane W. Bench is a social psychologist and assistant professor in the Department of Psychology at Utah State University. His research interests include emotions, perceptions of risk, the self, and substance use disorder. He earned his BS from Weber State University and PhD from Texas A&M University.

Lisa Bortolotti is professor of Philosophy at the University of Birmingham and works in the philosophy of psychology and psychiatry with a special focus on belief and rationality. She is also interested in what makes people's lives happy and meaningful. Recent books include *Philosophy of Psychology: An Introduction* (Polity 2021), coauthored with Kengo Miyazono; *The Epistemic Innocence of Irrational Beliefs* (OUP 2020); and *Delusions in Context* (Palgrave 2018).

James Danckert is a professor in the Department of Psychology and the cognitive neuroscience area head at the University of Waterloo. An expert on the psychology of boredom, he also studies the neuroscience of attention and the consequences of strokes.

John D. Eastwood is an associate professor of Clinical Psychology at York University. He investigates the intersection of cognition and emotion with a focus on boredom and mental effort. He is coauthor of *Out of My Skull: The Psychology of Boredom.*

Andreas Elpidorou is a Professor in the Department of Philosophy at the University of Louisville. He specializes in the philosophical study of the human mind and has published on the nature of emotions. He is the author of *Propelled: How Boredom, Frustration, and Anticipation Can Lead Us to the Good Life* (OUP 2020) and of other works.

Dana Gorelik is a third-year PhD student in the adult Clinical Psychology program at York University. Her research focuses on understanding and improving the measurement of boredom proneness. She is also interested in understanding the personality factors and in-the-moment feelings that contribute to the dislike of delay (i.e., delay aversion). As part of her clinical training, she completed two internal practicums at the York University Psychology Clinic, and an external practicum at the inpatient unit at Sunnybrook's Thompson Anxiety Disorders Centre. She is currently completing an external practicum at the North York General Hospital Assessment and Wellness Centre.

Eric R. Igou received his PhD from the University of Heidelberg in 2000 under the supervision of Herbert Bless. Since then, he worked at the University of Mannheim, the New School University, and New York University during his postdoc fellowship (2002–2004), Tilburg University (tenured; 2004–2008), and the University of Limerick (since 2008). He developed two master programs, served as their course director, and has operated for several years as head of Department. His research centers on existential experience (e.g., boredom, disillusionment), person perception, and human biases in judgment and decision-making.

Kaitlyn Kaiser is a research assistant in the Department of Psychological and Brain Sciences at Texas A&M University. Her research interests include satisfaction in interpersonal relationships, decision-making, and goal pursuit. She earned her Bachelor of Arts degrees in Psychology and Anthropology from Southern Methodist University.

Heather C. Lench is an affective scientist and professor and head in the Department of Psychological and Brain Sciences at Texas A&M University. Her research focuses on emotions as the foundation of cognitive and social processes, from affective responses to specific emotions like boredom. Her work has been covered in multiple outlets such as Wired and Business Insider, awarded by the American Psychological Association, and supported by the National Science Foundation and the John Templeton Foundation working group on Virtue, Happiness, and Meaning in Life.

Rebecca K. Meagher is an assistant professor in the Department of Animal Science and Aquaculture at Dalhousie University. She holds a BSc in Zoology from the University of Toronto and a PhD in Animal Science from the University of Guelph, and did her postdoctoral training at the University of British Columbia (UBC). Her research is on farm animal behavior and welfare, with a focus on the effects of housing and management on their welfare and behavioral development, and the assessment of relevant emotional states. Her main study species have been mink and cattle.

Wendell O'Brien received his BA from Malone University, an MTS from Harvard University, and an MA and PhD in Philosophy from the Johns Hopkins University. Now retired from active teaching, he is professor Emeritus of Philosophy at Morehead State University, Kentucky, USA. His publications include, among other pieces, articles in *Analysis*, the *History of Philosophy Quarterly*, and *The Southern Journal of Philosophy*, as well as entries in the *Internet Encyclopedia of Philosophy*. He lives in Morehead, Kentucky, with his wife and dog.

Kenneth A. Perez is an Assistant Professor-in-Residence in the Department of Psychological Sciences at the University of Connecticut, Avery Point. His research examines the emotion of awe and its effects on psychological well-being. He earned his Ph.D. in Psychology from Texas A&M University.

Jesse Robbins is a postdoctoral research associate at the Iowa State University College of Veterinary Medicine. He earned his PhD from the UBC Animal Welfare Program. His research explores conceptual and empirical questions in both the natural and social sciences. He has published on a diversity of topics including the folk concept of welfare, the relationship between farm size and animal welfare, animal-assisted therapy, factors affecting public trust in modern food production, the effect of nontherapeutic surgeries (i.e., tail docking and ear cropping) on perceptions of both dogs and their owners, and factors affecting public attitudes toward the creation of genetically modified animals.

Josefa Ros Velasco is a postdoctoral researcher in the Department of Philosophy and Society at the Complutense University of Madrid. Previously, she was assistant professor and postdoctoral fellow in the Department of Romance Languages and Literatures at Harvard University (2017–2019). Ros Velasco is a specialist in boredom studies and investigates the evolution of the concept of boredom as psychopathology in Western philosophical, literary, and theological narratives. Currently, her research is focused on the experience of boredom in older adults. She is the founder and president of the International Society of Boredom Studies. Her list of publications includes titles such as *Boredom Is in Your Mind* (Springer, 2019), *The Culture of Boredom* (Brill, 2020), *The Faces of Depression in Literature* (Peter Lang, 2020), and *The Disease of Boredom* (Alianza, 2022).

McWelling Todman, a clinical psychologist by training, is a professor of psychology at the New School for Social Research (NSSR), in New York City, and the founding director of the Concentration in Mental Health and Substance Abuse at that university. Dr. Todman is the current co-chair of the Psychology Department at the NSSR and the former director of Undergraduate Studies in Psychology at Eugene Lang College. Dr. Todman's research focuses on the intersection of behavioral/chemical addictions and psychopathology, with particular emphasis on the impact of boredom and self-monitoring deficits on the course and severity of various psychiatric disorders, including the psychoses and substance misuse. Dr. Todman received his BA degree from Swarthmore College, and his PhD in clinical psychology from the Graduate Faculty at NSSR.

Dr. Wijnand A. P. van Tilburg is an experimental social psychologist in the Department of Psychology at the University of Essex. His research interests include emotion, decision-making, meaning, and motivation. He received his bachelor's and master's degrees in psychology at Tilburg University in 2006 and 2008, respectively. In 2011, he completed a PhD degree at the University of Limerick. He then became lecturer (assistant professor) at the University of Limerick. In April 2013, he joined the School of Psychology of the University of Southampton as research fellow and was lecturer in the Psychology Department of King's College London from September 2015 to November 2019.

Yidou Wan is a PhD student in the Department of Psychological and Brain Sciences at Texas A&M University. His research interests include specific emotions and their effects on people, decision-making, impulsivity, and culture. He earned his Bachelor of Science from the University of North Carolina at Chapel Hill.

Erin C. Westgate is a social psychologist and assistant professor of Psychology at the University of Florida, where she studies boredom, interest, and why some thoughts are more engaging than others. She received her PhD in social psychology from the University of Virginia in 2018, and her BA in psychology from Reed College in 2010. Much of her research has been on the conditions under which people enjoy or do not enjoy their own thoughts. She has extended that work to the larger question of why people become bored, developing a new model of boredom that explains what boredom is, why we experience it, and what happens when we do.

Vida Yao is currently assistant professor of Philosophy at Rice University, working at the intersection of ethics and moral psychology. She has published on the relationship between boredom and *akrasia*, and more generally, on weakness of will and other forms of "disharmonious" agency.

Meltem Yucel is a postdoctoral associate at Duke University. She received her MA and PhD in psychology from the University of Virginia, and her BA in psychology from Özyeğin University in 2015. Her primary interest lies in the development of social cognition and morality, specifically focusing on how and when children become moral beings. Using behavioral, eye-tracking, pupillometry, and social network methods, her research investigates how children and adults understand and enforce norms, and the role of affect in moral decision-making.

www.ingramcontent.com/pod-product-compliance
Lightning Source LLC
Chambersburg PA
CBHW021809270326
41932CB00007B/109